PLASTIC COMPOUNDING, MASTERBATCHES, PET AND OTHER PLASTIC PROCESSING INDUSTRIES

PLASTIC COMPOUNDING, MASTERBATCHES, PET AND OTHER PLASTIC PROCESSING INDUSTRIES

Written By

EIRI BOARD OF CONSULTANTS & ENGINEERS

ENGINEERS INDIA RESEARCH INSTITUTE

4449, Nai Sarak, Main Road, Delhi - 110 006 (India)

Ph:. 91-11-23918117, 23916431, 23920361, 23960797

Fax: 91-11-2391 6431, 2391 8117

* E-Mail : eirisidi@bol.net.in

*Website: www.startindustry.com

Sole Distributor :

INDIAN INSTITUTE OF CONSULTANTS, 4/27 ROOP NAGAR, DELHI - 110007

PRINTED & PUBLISHED BY

ENGINEERS INDIA RESEARCH INSTITUTE

4449, Nai Sarak, Main Road, Delhi - 110 006 (India)
Ph:. 91-11-23918117, 23916431, 23920361, 23960797
* Fax: 91-11-23916431, 23918117
* E-Mail : eirisidi@bol.net.in
* Website: www.startindustry.com

DISTRIBUTED BY

SMALL INDUSTRY RESEARCH INSTITUTE
INDIAN INSTITUTE OF CONSULTANTS

ISBN : 81- 86732-49-7
Printed in New Delhi (INDIA)

Rs. 750

Printed & Published by Sudhir Gupta for "Engineers India Research Institute" 4449 Nai Sarak, Main Road, New Delhi - 110 006

Preface

The book ***PLASTIC COMPOUNDING, MASTERBATCHES, PET AND OTHER PLASTIC PROCESSING INDUSTRIES*** *covers almost all the basic and advanced details to setup own Plastic Processing Industry. The new edition of the book is covering latest technology including Polyethylene, Extrusion, Injection Moulding, Blowmoulding, Polyester Terephthalate (PET), Rotational Moulding, Post Extrusion Process, Vacuum Metallizing, Identification of Plastic Materials, Thermosetting Plastics, Recycling, Additives for Polymers, Virgin Quality from Reprocessed, Specialty Additives and Masterbatches, PVC Compounding with Formulations, Automobile Injection Moulded Plastic Components, Colour Master Batch for various Plastics, Compact Disks, Co-Extruded Multilayer Film and Laminated Multilayer Film, Egg Trays from Plastics, Ethylene Vinyl Acetate Sheet and Sole, Polypropylene Multifilament Spinning Yarn, Plastic Films and Sheets with Printing, Plastic Granules from Fresh Resin, Plastic Injection Moulding Products, Plastic Mats, PET Bottles from Pre-form, PET Pre-form from PET Resin, PVC Pipes and Fittings, PVC Extrusion Profiles, Computer Ribbon Cartridges, HDPE/PP Woven Sacks (Bags), Semi-Conductive Compounds and Masterbatches, Plastic Sutli, Disposable Plastic Syringes, Plastic Water Storage Tanks, Thermocole Based Disposable Glass, Cups and Plates, Plastic GranulesCross Linked Polyethylene (XLPE) Compound for XLPE Cables, Manufacturers/Suppliers of Plant, Equipments & Machineries, Manufacturers/Suppliers of Raw Materials etc.*

Frankly speaking- the book is also quite indispensable for those who have also setup their industry.

The book has been written for the benefit and to prove an asset and a handy reference guide in the hands of new entrepreneurs & well established industrialists.

Director

ENGINEERS INDIA RESEARCH INSTITUTE

Nai Sarak, New Delhi (INDIA)

E-Mail : eirisidi@bol.net.in

1

Polyethylene

The simple definition of polyethylene as a thermoplastic material formed through the polymerization of ethylene gas falls far shot of describing this versatile many faceted polyolefin which, since 1958 has been the largest member of the plastics family in both production of the plastics family in both production and sales.

Polyethylene varies from type to type according to the particular molecular structure of each type (i.e. its crystallinity molecular weight and molecular weight distribution) The molecular structure in turn is dependent upon the temperatures, pressures, catalyst types, modifiers and reactor design used in manufacture of the polyethylene raw material It varies in physical properties from hard to soft, rigid to flexible and tough to weak. It ranges in optical properties from clear to opaque and from glossy to dull. Its flow rates during processing range from extremely high to extremely low.

Basically PE is produced by polymerizing ethylene gas (C_2H_4) with a catalyst in a reactor at some combination of temperature and pressure. The result is a joining together of the ethylene molecules into long polymer chains.

Polyethylene was discovered in the early 1930s. The discovery led to the development of a high pressure process which accounts for all but a very small portion of the low and medium density PE produced today.

In the 1950s, a low pressure process was developed for the production of high density PE.

Melt index and density

ASTM defines LDPE as 0.910 to o.925 g./cu. cm., medium density as 0.926 to 0.940, and high density as 0.941 to 0.965.

Density in unmodified PE is an indicator of the crystallinity of a resin Density and melt index (an indicator of average molecular weight) are the two most commonly used criteria for categorizing PE. Being related to basic molecular structure, they are indicators of the end-product properties and processing characteristics. Molecular weight distribution is likewise important in determining PE properties; but it is much more diffcult to measure and to relate to other properties, Table I summarizes the typical effects of changes in melt index and density on some of the key properties and processing characteristics.

Additives

While a substantial amount of PE is produced without additives the majority is not. In many cases where additives are desired, they are supplied as additive concentrates and mixed with the PE during the extrusion step. This approach allows processors a considerable amount of flexibility in their operation due to the fact that they can inventory fewer resin types. The most common additives are heat and light stabilizers, slip, antiblock and antistatic agents, flame retardants and pigments.

Stabilizers maintain the chemical and physical properties of the resin at or near their original values throughout storage, processing and service life of the finished item.

The influence of environmentalists has caused a considerable amount of activity for the use of photodegradable and biodegradable additives. There are many who feel that the ability of PE to withstand attack of micro-organisms is an advangate in a landfill operation due to the fact that it does provide stability. Obviously, a biodegradable PE in a land fill operation would not provide this long term stability, This point of contention is yet to be resolved.

Slip agents, commonly some types of amide, improve slip and may prevent blocking to a degree. They do this by blooming to the surface of the film after extrusion and forming a very thin, invisible layer of additive that lowers the film's coefficient of friction.

Antistatic agents show up most often in molding grade PE Their purpose is to reduce static buildup in molded parts and thereby reduce or eliminate dust pick-up during the shelf life of the molded item.

Compounds and concentrates are available that can make PE flame retardant. However this is always at an increase in price and some sacrifice in physical properties of processability.

Polyethylene is easily colored with dry pigments or concentrates. While dry pigments are initially the least expensive in most cases, they are messy; thus, concentrates are more commonly purchased from custom compounders.

Polyethylene can be made crosslinkable by the addition of chemical crosslinking agents, usually peroxides.

Most crosslinkable PE to date is used in wire and cable coating applications; however, crosslinkable PE compounds are available for rotational moulding, injection moulding and film extrusion.

Several blowing agents are available to produce a foamed material. These are usually organic compounds that liberate gases when heated.

The shortage of PE has also focused even greater attention to the reduction as well as the utilization of scrap. Many machinery systems are available for the reclamation of PE scrap from most of the processing techniques.

Printing, decorating, gluing

Polyethylene is an inert material in its virgin from and does not accept most printing inks and glues. The surface of a product must be altered to make if receptive. This can be done by a relatively simple treatment of the PE surface to oxidize an extremely thin layer. In the case of films or coatings, this treatment us usually done electronically, while flame is used on most molded items. Chemical treatment is possible, but is seldom used because of the economics involved and the difficulty in handling the treating chemicals.

Processing techniques

Most processing techniques common to plastics in general are utilized with PE Extrusion is the principal technique used in the production of blown and cast film, sheeting, profiles and coatings on flat wire and cable. Blow molding and injection molding (usually by extrusion, although occasionally by ram) are common. Polyethylene powders are rotationally molded or coated on substrates by spray, dip or sintering line techniques. Very small amounts of PE are calendered, compression molded, machined and forged.

Table - 1

How two basic molecular properties affect essential polyethylene or end-product properties

	Basic molecular properties	
Physical properties	*If density (crystallinity) is increased within the range of **0.915 to 0.965***	*If melt index is increased, or the average molecular weight is lowered*
Melt viscosity	Higher	Lower
Vicat softening temperature	Much higher	Lower
Surface hardness (abrasion resistance)	Higher	Slightly lower
Resistance to blocking and mold sticking	Higher	Slightly lower
Slip	Higher	No effect
Minimum heat-seal temperature	Higher	Slightly lower
Heat-seal range	Narrower	Narrower
Tensile Strength yield	Much higher	Slightly lower
Tensile strength: Break	Slightly lower	Lower
Tensile strength: Elongation	Lower	Lower
Resistance to creep	Higher	Slightly lower
Flexural stiffness	Much higher	Slightly lower
Flexibility	Lower	--
Film impact strength (toughness)	Lower	Lower
Resistance to film brittleness	Lower	Slightly lower
Resistance to low-temperature brittleness	Lower	Lower
Resistance to environmental stress cracking	Lower	Lower
Optical properties:Clarity	Higher*	Higher
Optical properties : Freedom from haze	Higher*	Higher
Optical properties:Gloss	Higher*	Higher
Draw-down rate	Slightly higher	Much higher
Barrier properties:WVT rate	Lower	--
Barrier properties: Gas and liquid transmission	Much lower	--
Barrier properties: Greaseproofness	Much higher	Slightly lower
Neck-in and beading	Higher	Much higher

Contd....

Adhession to substrates (especially physical adherence to porous substrates)	Slightly lower	Slightly lower
Shrinkage	Higher	Lower
Warpage	Slightly higher	Lower
Electrical properties	Slightly higher	No effect

*Not true in the high density range.

Low and medium density PE

The first commercial PE was low density resin used for under-water cable coating and later for coatings on radar cable and line wire.

Originally, all commercial low and medium density PE was sold in cube or pellet from. since this was the most suitable from for extrusion and molding But during the 1950s, PE powders were ground from the cubes and pellets, and a significant marked developed in the powder molding and coating fields.

Some medium density resins are made by blending low and high density resins together. Blown film extrusion is the most common technique for making PE film. It produces a film with balanced orientation for better toughness, Chill roll cast films are still produced for some soft goods packaging and cling wrap. Tougher films can be made at higher output rates using a water quenched blown film, but there is little demand for such a product.

Injection molding is the second largest market. Domestic usage is in housewares, closures, toys and containers.

Rotational molding, powder coating and pipe extrusion are the other significant markets. None of these areas has seen any unusual change over the past few years.

High density (linear) PE

Most HDPE is made by the Philips process, developed by Philips Petroleum Co. In the past few years new low pressure processes have been developed and commercialized, The primary differences between these processes are their catalyst systems.

Most HDPEs are classified as homopolymers (0.96 densities) and copolymers (0.95 densities) The latter materials are usually butene of hexene copolymers. The homopolymers are stiffer and more suited for thin wall containers, where stress cracking is not likely, such as bleach bottle. The copolymers are more stress-crack resistant, and thus more suitable for applications such as the detergent bottle.

The primary processing techniques are blow and injection molding. Just slightly over half the HDPE is converted into containers, toys and other hollow objects by the blow molding technique. Another 25% of more is screw injection molded. While ram-type blow molding are still in use, most HDPE blow and injection molding involves extrusion.

LINEAR-LDPE (LLDPE)

Certain generalization can be made concerning the properties in which Liner LDPE differs from conventional LDPE. Qualitatively most of the functional advantages and disadvantages apply to the Linear-LDPE regardless whether it is produced by any process, although there are minor differances process,

Compared to conventional LDPE. Linear - LDPEexhibits

* Improved Puncture Resistance
* Improved Tear Strength
* Higher Melting point at the same density.
* Higher Stiffness at the same density.
* Sharper Melting point.
* Greater Resistance to Warping
* Better Low Temperature Brittleness Property
* Better Resistance to Environmental Stress-cracking
* Better Flex Life
* Remarkable Draw-down Property

Fig 1 : Tensile strength of LLDPE/ LDPE Blends

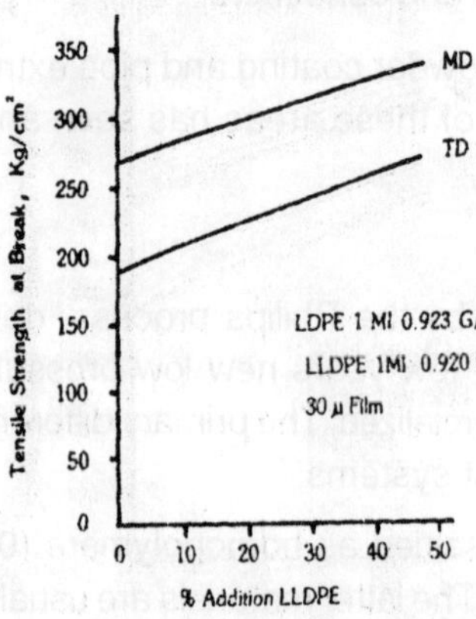

PROPERTIES OF LLDPE BLEND FILMS

LLDPE/ LDPE

Conventional blown film lines employed for processing of LDPE. Can't handle 100% LLDPE resin However, it is possible to enjoy the benefits of both LLDPE and LDPE by extruding LLDPE as a minor component in blends with LDPE using blown film lines meant for conventional LDPE

The following technical benefits are expected to be achieved by dry blending LLDPE with LDPE.

Addition of LLDPE offers substantial improvement in tensile strength and percentage elongation. The increase imparted to tensile strength at break for a 1.0 melt index LDPE resin is shown in figure no . 1 This level of improvement in tensile properties could support 20% downgauging of film without significant loss of tensile strength for most LDPE grades.

LLDPE/LDPE blend films show mixed results for properties like tear strength in M/D and dart impact strength. The dart impact of 100% 1.0 melt index LLDPE film is superior to that of 1.0 and 2.0 melt index LDPE film but is slightly lower than 0.3 melt index LDPE film

Figure 2 shows the increase in puncture resistance of 0.3. , 1.0 and 2.0 melt index LDPE by addition of LLDPE from figure it can be seen that resistance to puncture of LLDPE and LDPE blend film appears to be proportionally in creasing with contents of LLDPE in the blend This can show synergism at higher gauges of the films made using such blends.

Fig 2 : Puncture Resistance of LLDPE/LDPE Blends

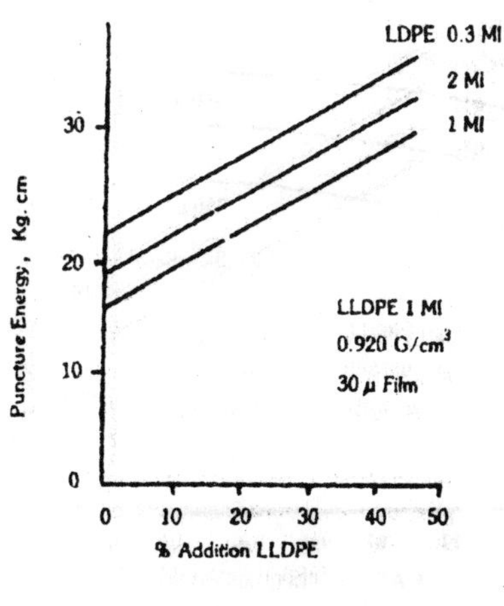

Figure 3 shows that addition of LLDPE reduced the impact strength of 0.3 melt index LDPE film at low thickness of 30 µm (However reverse phenomenon is observed at higher guages say around 200 mm see Fig. 5 and 6) However blends with1 and 2 MI of LDPE have shown increasse in impact strength. Tear strength in transverse direction (T/ D) increases with addition of LLDPE

Fig 3 : Impact Strength of LLDPE/LDPE Blends

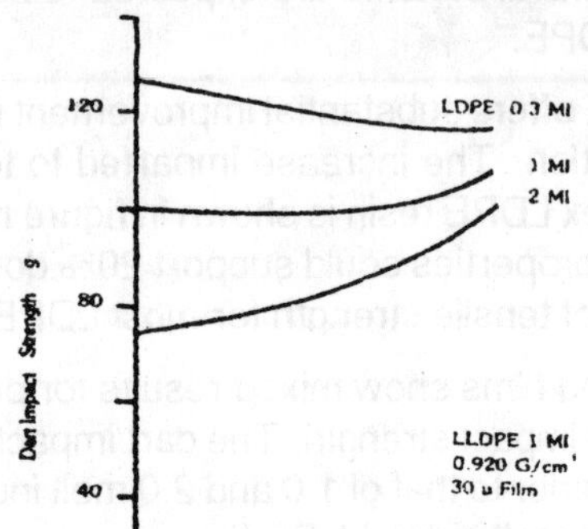

Fig 4 : Impact Strength of LLDPE/LDPE Blends for Heavy Duty Sacks

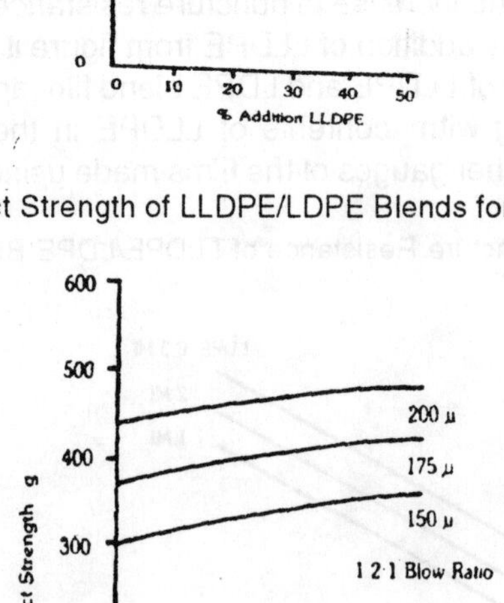

Figure 5 shows the increase in film rigidity of stiffness of a LDPE resin of 0.920 gm/cm density when blended with LDPE However the effect is proportional to film thickness and is relatively small at lower addition levels.

Fig 5 : Film Rigidity of LLDPE/LDPE Blends.

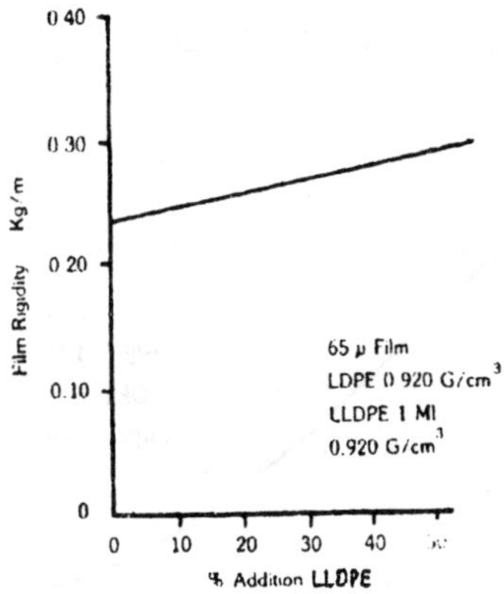

The addition of LLDPE in LDPE gives film with improved heat-sealing characteristics, i.e. better hot tack and cold seal strength. The seal strength at sealing temperature. close to hot-tack strength Figure 6 shows increase in hot-tack strength of LLDPE/LDPE blend films with increasing contents of LLDPE

Figure 7 illustrates the improvement in draw-down capability of a 0.3

Fig 6 : Hot Tack Strength of LLDPE/LDPE Blends

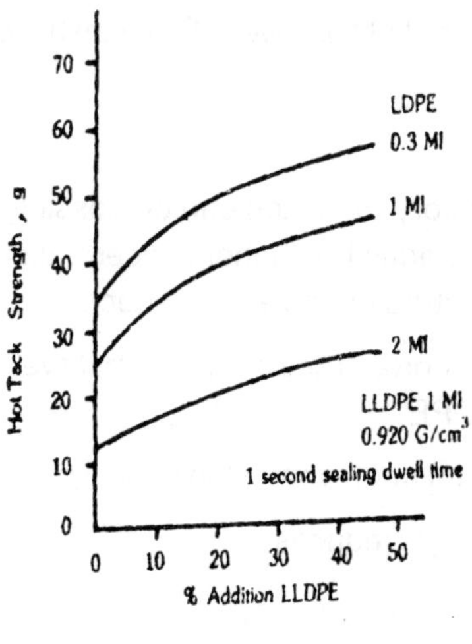

melt index LDPE with addition of LLDPE However for all purposes the excellent drawdown capability should not be utilised for down gauging of blend film. The scope of down gauging a film depends solely on designing a film for a particular end-use application and keeping in view the required properties.

Fig 7 : Film Drawdown of LLDPE/ LDPE Blends

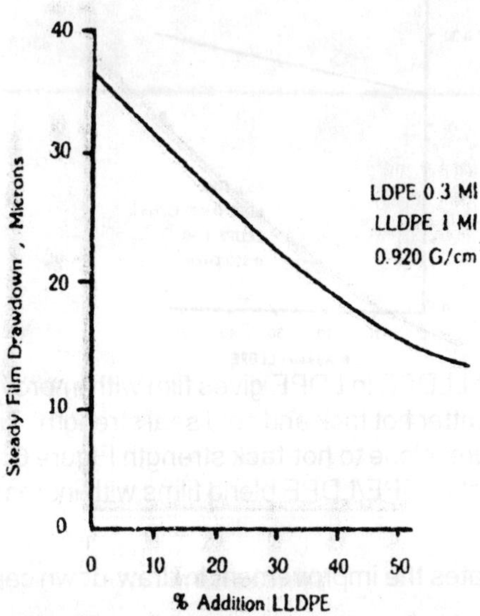

Environmental stress crack resistance (ESCR) of LLDPE is 4 times better than LDPE Blends of LLDPE with LDPE can be formulated to enhance ESCR property

LLDPE/HDPE

Although satisfactory extrusion can be possible by blending LLDPE into HDPE blown film grades but higher concentration of LLDPE in HDPE may result into kelt fracture or shark-skin effect.

The following film properties may be observed with blending 10 to 30% cf LLDPE into HDPE

* No Significant improvement in optical properties.
* Impact strength reduces.

* Slight increase in tear strength in machine direction (M/D) and considerable increase in transverse direction (T/D)
* Puncture resistance energy is generally greater.
* No significant improvement in tensile strength but film ridigity reduces.

LLDPE/HM-HDPE

Unlike conventional LDPE, Linear LDPE contains no long chain branches. Its linear structure and narrow MWD makes ir more compatible to HDPE than LDPE However positives of negative effect of blending LLDPE with HD-HDPE depends more on manufacturing process adopted for production of HM-HDPE resin.

Following changes may be expected while 10 to 20% of LLDPE is blended with HM-HDPE

* Percentage elongation increases whereas ultimate rensile strength increases upto 10% additon At 20% addition, ultimate tensile strength of film is lower than film from HM-HDPE
* The puncture resistance energy is not affected by blending LLDPE with HM-HDPE.
* Tensile yield strength decreases in almost proportional manner.
* Tear strength not greately affected due to presence of LLDPE

APPLICATIONS

In view of its exvellent properties like tensile strength rigidity environmental stress crack resistance puncture resistance heat-seal strength, draw down capability etc., LLDPE is used in number of film and non-films application. For films, large number of markets still employ LDPE rich blends with LLDPE. However 100% LLDPE film applications like stretch wrap heat-seal layer in multi-layer films are emerging. In addition 100% LLDPE is also used for rotational and injection moulded products due to excellent combination of properties as mentioned above. Wire and Cable is another market where suitable LLDPE/LDPE blends can be formulated to enhance ESCR properties. For applications, such as pipes, conduits & blow moulded products 100% LLDPE is used for its superior properties. The tables given highlight the main applications for LLDPE in various sector and its advantages over conventional LDPE.

ADVANTAGES OF LLDPE BLOWN CAST AND FILM

Merit of LLDPE	*Applications*
Superior Mechanical Strength and Puncture Resistant	* Heavy duty Bags * Industrial Liners * Agricultrural Film * Carrier Bags * Stretch Wrapping Film
Superior Chemical Resistance and Environmental Stress Crack Resistance	* Detergent Packaging Bags * Food over Wrap
Superior Heat Resistance and Low Temperature Brittleness	* Sterilized Film for Food Packaging * Frozen Food Packaging
Superior Draw Down Ability	* Grocery Bags * Bakery and confectionery packaging * Miscellaneous Packaging
Superior Hot Tack Strength	* Heat Sealing Layer of Co-extruded Structure * Heat Sealable Film to be Laminated withother Film.

ADVANTAGES OF LINEAR-LDPE AND LINEAR-MDPE FOR WIRES AND CABLES

Merit of LLDPE	*Applications*
Superior Low Temperature Brittleness and Environmental Stress Crack Resistance	* Telecommunication Exchange Cable Sheathing
Resistant to Petroleum Jelly	* Telecommunication Jelly/Filled Cable * Insulation

LINEAR LOW AND MEDIUM DENSITY POLYETHYLENE APPLICATION

EXTRUSION

BLOWN FILM
* Carrier Bags
  - Cut out hand grip
  - With handel
  - T-Shirt type
  - Bick-up bags
* Grocery bags
* Milk pouches
* Miscellanous Packaging uses
* Bakery and Confectionery packaging
* Heavy duty bags and industrial liners
* Agricultural
  - Greenhouse
  - Fumigation
  - Nursery bags
* Detergent Packaging bags
* Frozen food packing
* Stretch Film
* Shrink Film

CAST FILM
* Food over Wrap
* Pallet over Wrap
* Stretch/cling film
* Diaper liners
* Sealing layer of Co-extruded films
* Sealing layer of multilayer laminates

WIRE & CABLE
* Teleco-mmunication cable sheathing
* Petroleum jelly filled Jacketing

PIPE & CONDUIT
* Drip irriga-tion pipe
* Potable Water pipe
* Low Pressure gas distribution pipe Conduits

MOULDING

INJECTION MOULDING
* Snapon lids
* Caps and Closures
* Refrigerator parts
* Shopping baskets

ROTATIONAL MOULDING
* Industrial containers
* Drum liners
* Agricultural tanks
* Water tanks
* Toys
* Carbouys for Chemical Transportation

BLOW MOULDING
* Small squeeze bottles
* Hot fill food container

2

Extrusion

The extrusion process converts raw thermoplastics in powdered or granular form into a continuous melt stream which is formed by a die into a variety of shapes. End products include pellets packaging fibers; sheet; pipe; tubing; profile for the construction, automotive and applicance industries; fibers; insulation covering; extrusion coated webs; parisons for extrusion-blow molding; and foam for cups, insulating sheet, packing material, and other uses

Single-screw extruder

By far the most common and most versatile extruder in use today is the single –screw extruder. A schematic of a typical single screw extruder is shown in Fig1. Single screw extruders are characterized by two dimensions, the bore diameter (D) and the length of the barrel in bore diameter of L/D ration. For example a 2 1/2 in 20;1 L/D extruder has a barrel bore of 2 1/2 in ID and a barrel length of 50 in. (2 1/2 × 20 diameters in length).

Common commercial sizes of extruders range from 2 to 8 in. Machines are available as small as 3/4 in for laboratory or specialized use and as large as 24 in or more on special order. Common L/Ds range from about 5:1 minimum through 34:1 and o 40+:1 for some multiple venting application. Generally the shorter machines (through 20:1) are applied to elastomer processing; the longer one (20:1 L/D and above) are applied to thermoplastic processing.

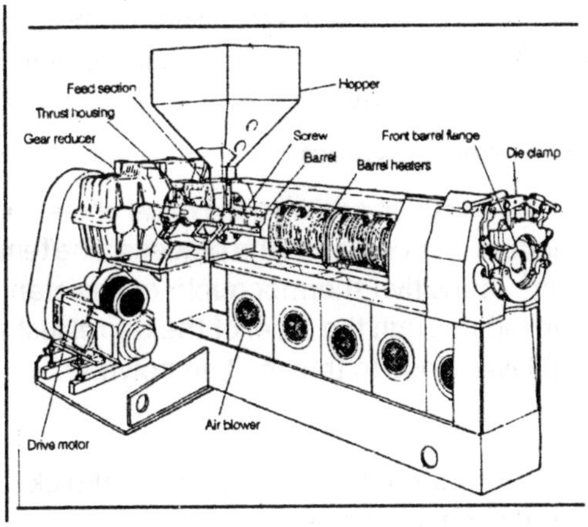

Extruder barrel and feed section

The section barrel or single –screw extruder usually is a long thick–walled tube of alloy steel into which a hard, highly crystalline wearresistant alloy has been centrifugally cast After the casting the bimetallic tube is straightened and honed, usually to a tolerance of ± 0.001 in. on the ID The barrel must tolerate an internal pressure of 10,000 p.s.i. without elastic deformation above the 0.15% strain at which the internal alloy will cack in tension.

Attached to the feed end of the barrel (often as a separate casting) is an opening into the barrel bore for raw material feeding. It usually is jacketed for room temperature water cooling to prevent premature melting of polymer.

Barrel heat input and extraction mechanisms

The barrel must be provided with means to both add and extract heat. Though heaters vary in design, the most common ones are cast aluminum. The heater halves are clamped to the barrel to provide intimate contact between the steel of the barrel and the aluminum of the heater. The heat sink is either air of a liquid coolant.

The heaters are arranged in zones, often 4 to 5 on a 24:1 L/D extruder. Auxiliary systems provide heat sinks for heat absorption probably the simplest is a blower mounted under each zone heater to blow air over the surface of the heater. extracting heat from it and depositing it into the planct ambient air. The blowers are switched on and off either by automatic controllers or manually.

Where greater heat extraction is needed, a liquid cooled system is used. The preferred liquid is distilled water which may or may not be boiled into steam depending upon design and operating conditions. Alternately, oraganic heat transter fluids may be used.

Barrel temperature control system

Each zone of the extruder, and also the head or die, must be controlled to a specific temperature, depending on the process, The temperature usually is sensed with a tip –sensitive thermocouple or resistance thermometer mounted in hole drilled through the steel of the barrel just to the outside of the wear–resistant layer close to the melting polymer.

Screw

Inside the barrel is a rotating feed screw that picks up polymer and advances it into and along the barrel.

Gearbox and thrust bearing

Common operating speed of medium-size extruders range between 50 and 150 r.p.m. The speeds of medium-hp drive motors i.e. 40 to 200 hp., are usually 1750 r.p.m. Motor speed is reduced to the screw speed usually with a gear reducer which simultaneously increases the available torque as it reduces the speed.

The gearboxes supplied by extruder manufacturers may be horizontal or vertical, cast iron of welded. They may have helical, herringbone or worm gears, 2 1/2 in. and larger extruders use helical or herringbone gearboxes.

Drives

The most common extruder drives are statically rectified d.c. drives operating on 460v three-phase power. As the armature voltage is reduced from nameplate rating to zero, the speed reduces linearly to zero, while maintaining full load torque capability.

D .C. drives usually are equipped with tachometers and drive regulators which hold speed within 1% regulation and 2% long-term drift. The signals from these tachometers can be fed into coordinate modules and master references to drive the extruder speed up and down with process line speeds, tandem extruders, coextrusion extruders, etc.

Though the power factor drops off materially. d.c., drives tend to be relatively efficient in energy use. Other types of drives that are used include eddy current a.c. motors, and hydraulic drives.

Venting

Some polymers contain small amounts of volatile monomer moisture or entrapped gases which adversely affect the extruded product. These may be removed through vents in the barrel.

TYPE OF DIES FOR FILM EXTRUSION

1. *SIDE-FED DIE FOR BLOWN FILM :* In such die, polymer melt is fed to die from side and melt is divided in two streams. This has disadvantage of Joint/weld line, where film can be weak in strength.

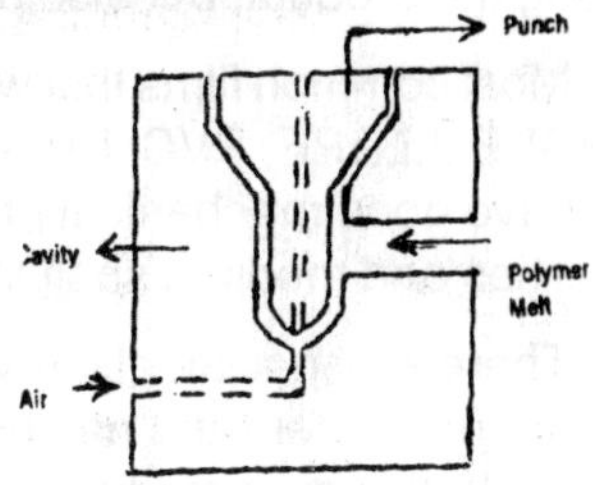

2. *BOTTOM-FED DIE FOR BLOWN FILM* : In such die, polymer melt is fed to die from bottom of punch and hence does not involve any weld line problem. This is most common type of die

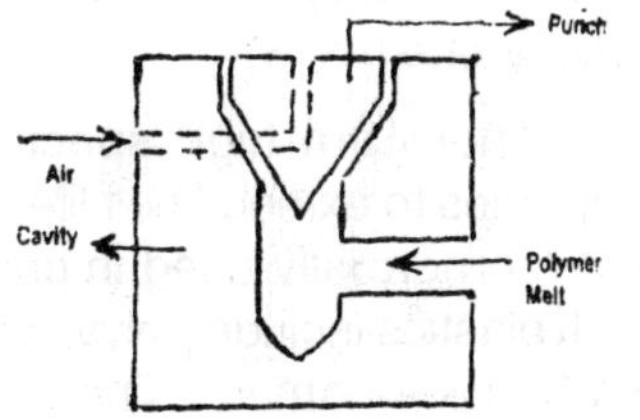

3. *SPIRAL FLOW DIE* : There are different varieties such as 2 start, 4 start, 8 start, spiral flow dies. This spiral flow die gives distinct advantage of better homogenity of melt, even distibution of melt pressure & better melt stability.

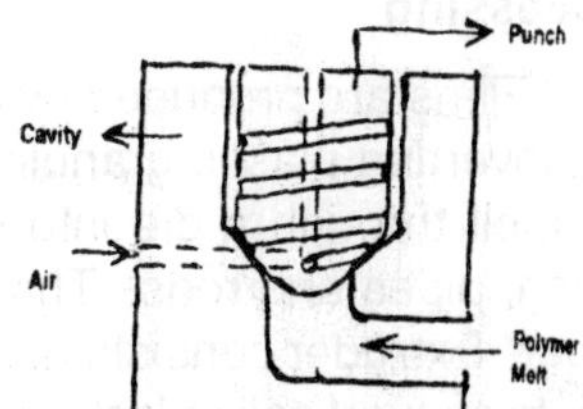

4. *T-DIE (COAT HANGER DIE) :* This type of die is generally used for:

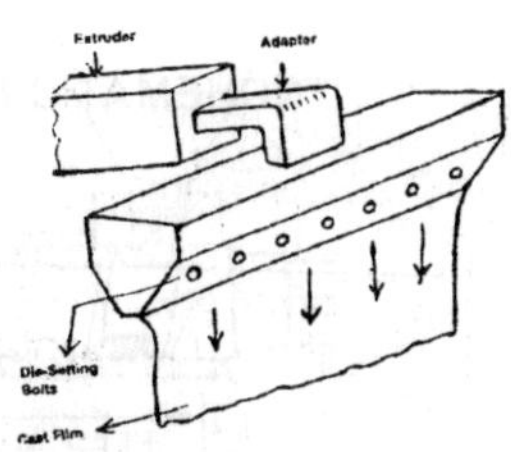

- Cast film extrusion
- Slit tape extrusion for woven sacks.
- Extrusion coating.
- BOPP film co-extrusion

EXTRUSION OF PLASTIC FILMS

Introduction

The use of Plastic Films in India has shown phenomenal growth during past decades especially in Packaging. Films play a major role in not only packing the product, but also protecting and displaying the products.

Most common films that we come across are made from LDPE. HDPE, HMHDPE, LLDPE, PVC, PP, etc. which form the commodity films. These films have good mechanical properties and reasonably good water barrier properties and medium shelf life of product packed.

There are speciality films which are higher priced and high performance i.e. superior water and gas barrier properties giving longer shelf life and also aesthetic appearance of printed films. These are made from Bi-axially oriented polyester (BOPET), Bi-axially oriented polypropylene (BOPP), Mono-axially oriented polypropylene, Cellophane, Oriented Nylon (OPA), Oriented polystyrene (OPS).

There are high speciality plastics which impart excellent barrier properties to extend shelf life of production packed. They are very expensive and are normally used in combination with other commodity plastic films such plastics include polyvinylidene chloride (PVDC), Ethylene Vinyl Alcohol (EVOH) & Ionomers. These plastics are used with commodity plastics by way of Blown film co-extrusion 3,5 and 7 layers.

Processing

Films are produced by a process called Extrusion, which comprises of converting plastic granules into a continuous uniform melt and forcing the melt through a die into various desired shapes such as film, sheet, tubing, pipes and rods. The process of extrusion is carried out in an extruder. Extruder consists of cylindrical barrel in which a screw rotates and help to convert solid plastic granules into homogenous molten plastic mass and to convey the same to the die continuously. The size of extruder is defined by diameter of its screw.

SCHEMATIC DIAGRAM – EXTRUSION PROCESS

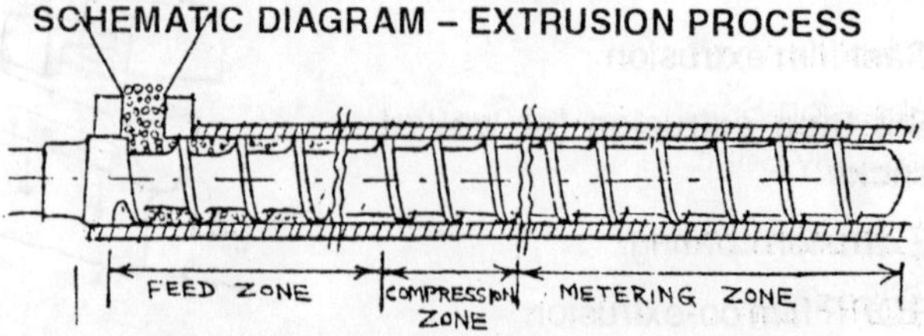

HOPPER COOLING HELPS TO AVOID BRIDGING

TEMPERATURE PROFILE : (CAMEL BACK)

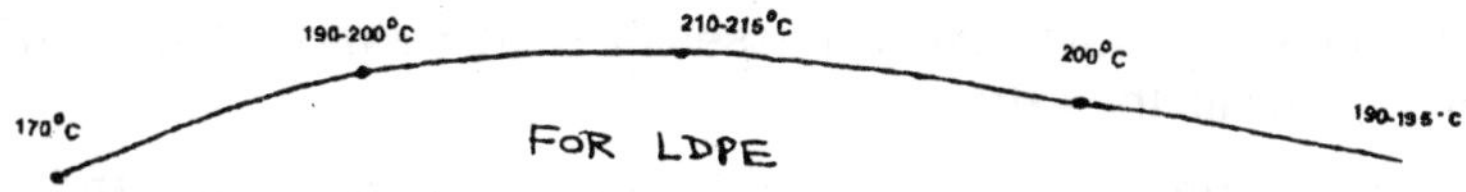

FOR MDPE - 180°C to 220°C

For pp - 190°C to 240°C

For HDPE - 190°C to 230°C

For LLDPE - 190°C to 240°C

POLYMERS	SCREW DETAILS		
	L/D RATIO	COMPRESSION RATIO	
LDPE	24 : 1 TO 30 : 1	3. 40 : 1	
LLDPE	24 : 1 TO 26 : 1	2.5 : 1 TO 3 : 1	PITCH =
MDPE	24 : 1 TO 26 : 1	3.4 : 1	DIAMETER
HDPE	24 : 1 TO 26 : 1	3 : 1 TO 3 .4 : 1	HELIX ANGLE =
PP	24 : 1 TO 26 : 1	3.5 : 1 TO 3.8 : 1	16.5° TO 17°

Mixing Sections – Maddock Type

For Better Melt – Mixing Pins / Rings

Homogenisation – Grooved Barrels.

MATERIAL OF CONSTRUCTION :

Screw : Nitrided Steel or Carbide Metal

Barrel : Nitrided Steel

New Superior Materials : (A) Titanium Carbide Composites (FERROTIC)

For Hard Facing (Trade Name "FERRO-TIC")

Cobalt - Nickel alloys are gaining accepance for wear resistance.

No Abrasion Screw -Xaloy, Pulasky, USA, have Deposition Process for Metalurgically Bonding Tungsten carbide to surface of screw.

Xaloy- 800 Barrel with Tungsen carbide bonding has superior resistance to wear & corrosion.

Components of extruder are described below :

Hopper : It is mounted at the opening end of the barrel for the entry of raw material. The raw material passes through the vertical opening in the feed section into the extruder barrel.

Barrel : Barrel is a cylindrical housing, which is heated and cooled externally and in which the screw rotates.

Screw : Screw is a helical flighted shaft which when rotated mechanically homogenizes and conveys the material being processed.

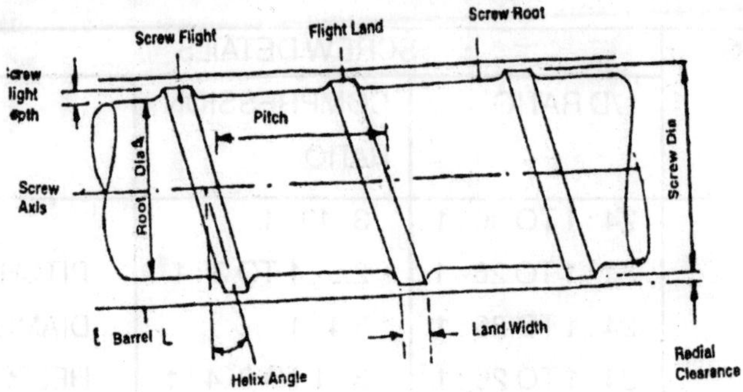

Screw Flight : The helical metal thread of the screw.

Flight Land : The surface at the radial extremity of the flight constituting the periphery or outside diameter of the screw.

Screw Diameter : The diameter developed by rotation of flight land about the screw axis.

Root Diameter : Diameter at the root of the screw flight.

Helix Angle : The angle of the flight at the periphery relative to a plane perpendicular to the screw axis.

Pitch : Distance in axial direction between two consecutive flights.

Flight Depth : Distance in the radial direction from the periphery of the flight to the root.

Diameteral Screw Clearance : The difference in diameter between screw and barrel bore.

Radial Screw Clearance : Half the diameteral screw clearance,

Screw Zones

A typical screw is divided into three zones :

Feed Zone : The function of this zone is to receive material coming from hopper and feed it to compression zone. The root diameter in feed zone is minimum and is generally constant over the entire zone length.

Compression Zone : This zone has a gradual decreasing depth or decreasing pitch of screw, because of which material is gradually compressed and compacted. Transition of material from solid form to molten form takes place in this zone, because of heat and shearing action.

Metering Zone : This portion of screw acts as a pump and it delivers molten material to the die at a constant rate. Flight depth in this zone is generally less than that in feed zone and is contant throughout.

Important terms associated with the Screw Design

Compression Ratio (CR) : It can be expressed as a ratio of volume of the screw channel at feed opening to volume in the metering zone. In case of screws with constant pitch, CR is the ratio of depths at feed end metering end.

L/D Ratio : It is the ratio of length of the screw, which is the distance from the forward edge of feed opening to the screw tip, to the barrel bore diameter.

These two design parameters are specific to the type of polymer. The recommended values of L/D and CR for PE are 24 to 28 : 1 and 2.5 to 3.0 : 1 respectively. Many a times mixing sections in the screw are recommended for processing LLDPE.

Heating and Cooling Systems

Controlled heating is provided using external electrical resistance or in duction heaters arranged in several groups or zones along the barrel. Thermocouples are fitted at regular intervals on barrel for temperature measurement and control. Cooling is done using blowers of cooling water jackets to remove excess heat from the polymer melt.

Breaker Plate and Screens

Breaker plate is to break spiral motion of melt and support screen pack. Screen pack, which is a combination of screens with different mesh sizes, is used as a filter.

The screen pack combinations, which generally used are 40/60/40, 60/80/60 or 40/60/60/40 mesh.

Downstream Equipments

Blowers, quench tank, guides, winders, cutter slitter etc. constitute the downstream equipments for an extruder, which change according to the type of extruder and also the product being processed.

Now film extruders with either oscillating platform, rotating die or oscillating haul – off (Take up) assembly are developed, which enable to obtain better quality hump free film Rolls.

Different types of Film Processing Techniques

Blown Film Process : It is a process in which a plastic tube after extruding through an annular die is inflated by air to desired diameter, cooled collaped and wound in the form of rolls.

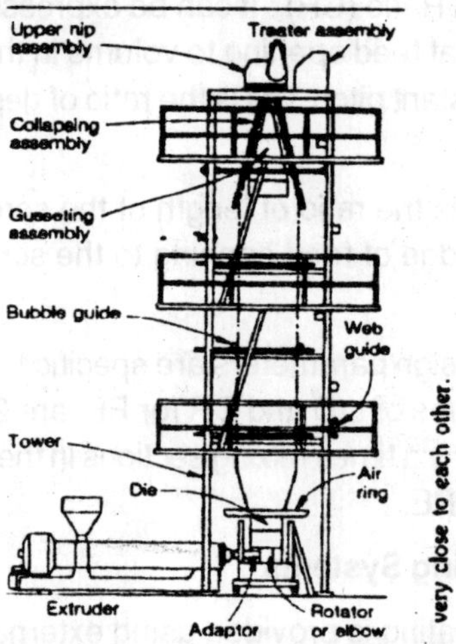

BLOWN FILM EXTRUDER

In India, Blown film extrusion process is found economical and is used by most of the processing units. In this process, there are two types:–

(1) Single layer blown film extrusion and

(2) Multi-layer (2 to 5 layers) blwon film co-extrusion.

The film properties achieved in this process are dependant on various processing conditions, such as Blow Ratio, Processing Temperature Profile, Draw Ratio, Relation of screw speed and haul - off speed, film thickness uniformity. Frost line height (FLH) and adjustment of cooling air through air ring, etc.

1) BLOW-UP RATIO (BUR)

This is the ratio of diameter of film bubble to diameter of Die. This is calculated by simple formula :–

$$BUR = \frac{\text{Perimeter of bubble}}{\text{Perimeter of Die}} = \frac{\pi D}{\pi d}$$

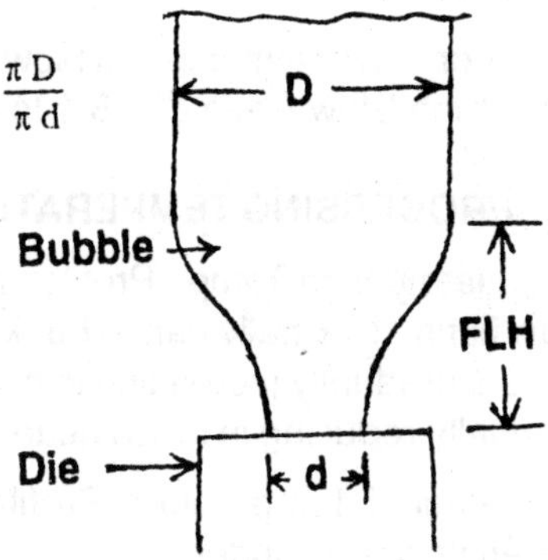

where,

D = Diameter of Bubble

d = Diameter of Die

$\pi = \frac{22}{7} = 3.14$

Simplified approx formula is

$$d \sim \frac{LFW}{1.5 \times BUR}$$

Higher the Blow ratio, better are mechanical properties (Tensile, Impact etc.) due to better orientation of molecules in cross direction (Transverse direction) For LDPE and LLDPE Films, Ideal BUR is 2.1 to 2.5 :1 which results in good balanced mechanical strength of film in both machine & cross directions.

Following Table give ready values of Blow Ratio in relation to size of diameter of die and lay flat width (LFW) Blown film. LFW of film is half of cut open width of Blown film.

Die Diameter	Blow Ratio				
Inch (mm)	1:1	1.5:1	2:1	2.5:1	3:1
	Values of Lay Flat Width, inch (mm)				
2 (50)	3.14 (80)	4.71 (120)	6.29 (160)	7.86 (200)	9.43 (240)
3 (75)	4.72 (120)	7.07 (180)	9.43 (240)	11.80 (300)	14.15 (360)
4 (100)	6. 29 (160)	9.43 (240)	12.58 (320)	15.72 (400)	18.86 (480)
6 (150)	9.43 (240)	14.15 (360)	18.87 (480)	23.58 (600)	28.30 (720)
8 (200)	12.60 (320)	18.87 (480)	25.16 (640)	31.45 (800)	37.73 (960)

for LDPE, LLDPE and HDPE films, processing at Low Blow Ratio, (Some-times Less than 1:1) is not advisable, since orientation of molecules is insufficient & unblanced, which results in inferior mechanical strength of the resultant films.

For TQPP film, normal blow ratio used is 1.2:1 to 1.5:1 For HMHDPE films, high Blow Ratio of 4.5:1 to 5.5:1 is used.

2. PROCESSING TEMPERATURE PROFILES

Adequately high Temp. Profiles results in good mechanical properties of blow films. Normally camel back profile is found useful. i.e. Lower in feed zone & gradually increasing in compression and metering zones and then gradually reducing in cross head & Die zones.

Typical Temperature Profiles for film extrusion for popular plastic materials are as under :

LDPE FILM Grades	*Barrel Zones*	*Cross Head*	*Die Zones*
Heavy Duty (0.2MI)	170/195/205	200/190	185/180°C
Milk Pkg. (0.5MI)	160/185/195	190/85	180/170°C
General Purpose			
Pkg. (2MI)	160/180/185	185/180	170/160°C
(4MI)	150/170/170	160/155	150/145°C
LLDPE FILM Grades.	*Barrel Zones*	*Cross Head*	*Die Zones*
Heavy Duty (1.0MI)	160/185/195	195/185	180/170°
General Purpose			
(2MI)	160/180/185	180/175	175/170°
HMHDPE Film			
Grade,	170/220/230	210/220	200/190°C
TQPP Film	170/195 to	200/190	190/180°C
Grade (10MI)	200/205		

3. FROST LINE HEIGHT (FLH)

This is the distance between the die and the zone where the bubble solidifies and assumes it's final diameter. This FLH is dependent on the rate of cooling by air from cooling ring. Higher the rate of cooling. Lower is FLG & Vice-Versa.

Normally recommended FLH for various plastic blown film materials are as under :-

1. For LDPE and LLDPE blown film extrusion, one foot to two feet, depending on diameter of the bubble.
2. For PP blown extrusion, 6 inches to 10 inches.
3. For HDPE blown film extrusion, 6 inches to 15 inches.
4. For HMHDPE blown film extrusion, FLH is as high as two feet to four feet, depending on diameter of bubble.

4. FILM THICHKNESS CONTROL

Film thickness is controlled by adjusting screw speed and Nip Roll speed.

5 THICKNESS VARIATION CONTROL

It is very essential to control film thickness in narrow range, preferably within ± 5% This variation is controlled by -

(a) Setting the die gap uniform all along the periphery, with help of the die setting bolts. It is ideal to have 8 to 10 Nos. die setting bolts.

(b) Adjusting air flow of air cooling ring.

The film with low variation in thickness has superior & reliable mechanical properties and is free from thick bands or humps on the roll, which enhances the printing quality of the film.

Cast Film Process : Polymer melt is extruded through a flat die either onto a rotating chilled roll or into a water quench tank, where the melt is rapidly cooled and frozen to form a film called the cast film.

Advantages of this process over blown film Extrusion are :-

1. Superior transparency & clarity of film
2. 4 t0 5 times higher output, since no limitations on cooling of film.

The only limitation of cast film process is relatively lower orientation & strength of film in transverse direction.

Coextrusion Film Process :- It is a process in which two or more polymers processed on separate extruders are passed together through a common die to form a film. It can be either a blown or cast film process. This process is widely used for, producing barrier films, stretch films etc. Coextrusion film process leads to a co -extruded film or multilayer film.

Such films offer specific advantages such as higher shelf-life superior mechanical properties of the film & pouches (Tensile strength, pucture resistance, Impact strength), better heat seal strength, better hot tack strength etc. due to the combination of different plastic materials used in the multi-layer structures.

Some of the multilayer structures based on polyethylene and their applications

Material combination	*Important fields of application*
1. LDPE + LLDPE in 2 or 3 layers	milk film, carrier bags, general packaging
2. LDPE/ EVA LLDPE/EVA LLDPE/LEPE	heavy-duty bags, stretch packaging, medical articles.
3. HDPE/ EVA foodstuffs	blood plasma, bakery goods,
4. HDPE/ LDPE or LLDPE LDPE /HDPE/LDPE LLDPE /HDPE /LLDPE	bakery goods, foodstuffs, tomato concentrate, pet food, cornflakes.
5. LDPE/TL/Nylon-6/TL/LDPE or LLDPE /TL/Nylon-6/TL/LDPE	Packing of meat, sausage, Cheese, ham, fish, ready made meal.
6 LDPE/HDPE	Vansaspati Ghee pouches
7. LLDPE /LDPE/HDPE	Edible oil pouches-short shelf life
8. LLDPE/TL/Nylon-6/TL/ IONOMER	Edible oil pouches-longer shelf life.

STRETCH - EXTRUSION PROCESS

In this process, after primary extrusion. the product is again re-heated and stretched/oriented in one or two directions (machine and transverse directions) in order to impart superior mechanical properties to final products.

Examples of such stretch extruded products are :

1. Biaxially oriented PP films and Polyester films, having superior mechanical properties and barrier properties.
2. Flat Tapes for HDPE & PP woven sacks also known as 'Raffia'.
3. PP & HDPE monofilaments, twines and sutli.
4. PP, Nylon-6 Box strappings.

In above process, the extruded product is re -heated and then stretched in machine director and Transverse direction. The stretch ratio depends on type of Plastic, for example for PP it is 1:7 to 1:8 and for HDPE it is lower 1:5 to 1:6 After stretching the product is agian heated (PP to about 130 to 135°C & HDPE to 100° to 120°C) for purpose of stress-Relaxation in the product. After this, the product is ready for final winding.

In secondary operations, Flat tapes are taken on looms for weaving,. monofilaments on Rope making machine, etc.

In the following schematic Diagram, Flat tape stretch extrusion line for PP Raffia is shown. This is versatile line, since with only the change of die other products monofilaments or Box strappings can also be produced.

Popular applications of BOPP Film are :-

* Wrapping of cigarette cartons and tobacco packing.
* Packing of potato chips, noodles, sevia, etc,
* Packing of Bakery products.
* Paper print Laminations.
* Pressure sensitive adhesive tapes.
* Printed synthetic paper applications.

  Visiting cards, invitation cards, calenders, Technical Brochures etc.

Popular applications of HDPE Woven Sacks and Cloth are :-

* Packing of Fertilizers & chemical powders.
* Tarpaulin (Black or Blue) covers for protection on Trucks.

Polypropylene woven sacks are preferably used for packing of Cement, since same are more suitable to withstand hot-filling of cement powder. PP woven cloth is also preferred for Bulk Bags (250 kg., 500kg. Bags) since the same is stronger than HDPE woven cloth.

3

Injection Moulding

Injection Moulding is a process of forming an article by forcing the molten plastic material under pressure into a closed metal structure known as mould where it is cooled and solidified into the contours of the mould.

Injection Moulding is used for the formation of intricate plastic parts with excelloent dimensional accuracy. A large number of items assocaited with our daily life are produced by way of injection moulding. Typical product categories include housewares, toys automotive parts, building supplies and household furnishings.

ADVANTAGES OF INJECTION MOULDING

1. Accuracy in weight of moulded articles.
2. Choice of desired surface finish and colours.
3. Choice of ultimate strength of moulded articles.
4. Faster production and lower rejection rates.
5. Faster start-up and shut-down procedures.
6. Minimum wastage.
7. Stability of processing parameters.
8. Versatility in processing different raw materials.
9. Option in article sizes by changing the mould.
10. Minimum post-moulding operations.

INJECTION MOULDING MACHINES

Injection moulding machines can be classified by the type of injection unit and clamping unit used.

CLAMPING UNIT (Locking Unit)

Many types of locing unit have been divised, most of which can be classified into two types namely:

1. Direct Hydraulic Locking Systems.
2. Toggle Systems.

1. Direct Hydraulic Locking Systems :

The basic hydraulic locking system is shown in Fig. 1. This system uses a large diameter hydraulic cylinder mounted in the rear platen. The moving platen of mould is attached to the cylinder ram which both opens and closes the mould and provides clamping force.

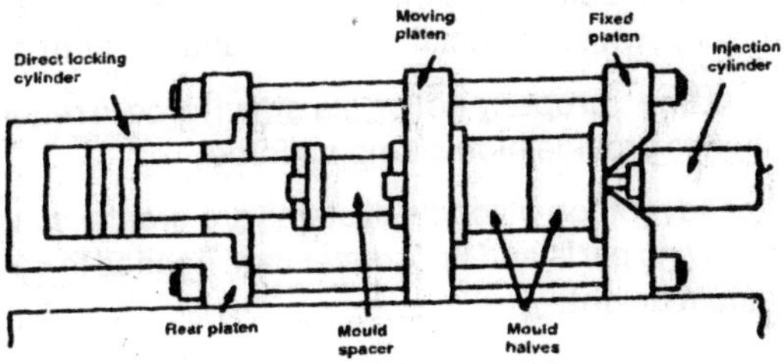

Fig .1 SIMPLE DIRECT HYDRAULIC LOCKING SYSTEM

(The design illustrated incorporates a mould spacer which is useful in reducing the length of stroke of the ram, which is limited to the mould opening necessary to eject the moulding)

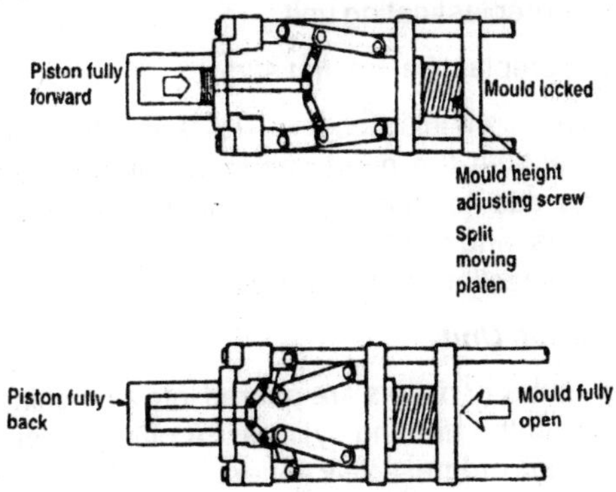

Fig . 2 SIMPLE DOUBLE-TOGGLE MOULD LOCKING SYSTEM

- The advantages of the system are:
- The cylinder is self -lubricating and the system has few moving parts.
- Variation in mould heights are easily accommodated.
- The ram speed is controlled by varying the oil flow rate.

Main disadvantage of this system is that it is frequently necessary to move around large quantities of pressurized oil which is wasteful both in terms of power consumption and time.

2 **Toggle Systems :**

A simple form of toggle mechanism is shown in Fig. 2. By means of the toggle, rapid mould closing may be effected by a small locking cylinder. However, as the toggle bars come into line, the rate of movement of the mould platen slows down to protect the mould surfaces from damage.

If the unit has been properly set only a small force in required to keep the bars in position to provide high clamping force.

The main disadvantage of toggle systems are greater susceptibility to wear and tear of moving parts and the greater care needed to set the system for the correct mould height.

INJECTION UNIT

There are four basic types of injection units used for commercial injection moulding. The four types are :

1. conventional injection unit
2. piston type preplasticating unit
3. screw type preplasticating unit and
4. reciprocating screw injection unit. The reciprocating screw injection unit has become the most common unit for modern plastics processing due to faster cycles, lower melting temperature requirements, and bettter mixing. A brief description of each of the heating/injection systems follows.

Conventional Injection Unit

The plastic granules or pellets are poured into a machine hopper and fed into the chamber of the heating cylinder. A plunger compresses the material forcing it through progressively hotter zones of the heating cylinder. The material flows from the heating cylinder through a nozzle into the mould. This type of moulding machine will produce mottled coloured moulded parts since colourants are not thoroughly mixed wtth the plastic material in the heating cylinder unless pre-coloured polymers are used as feed.

Piston Type Preplasticating

This injection moulding machine uses a heater to preplasticate the plastic granules. The fluid plastic is then held in a holding chamber until it is molten enough to be forced into the die. A piston then rams the plastic through the nozzle into the mould. This machine produces pieces faster than a conventional machine because the holding chamber can be filled to shot capacity while a part is cooling in the mould. This process is used to produce large moulded parts although it is not in wide commercial use.

Screw Type Preplasticating

In this system, an extruder is used to plasticize the plastic material. The rotating screw feeds the pellets forward to the heated interior surface of the extruder barrel. The molten plastic moves from the extruder into a holding chamber and is forced into the die by an injection plunger. The use of a screw provides :

★ better mixing and shear action of the plastic melt

★ better colour blending

Reciprocating Screw Injection Unit

This type of injection moulding utilities a horizontal extruder in place of the heating chamber A rotating screw moves the plastic material forward through a heated extruder barrel. As the molten plastic material moves forward, the screw backs up to a limit switch that determines the volume of material collecting in the front of the barrel. The screw then acts as a ram and injects the plastic material into the die. The screw rotates backwards to begin the next cycle. The advantages of this system over the other three are :

★ it more effeciently plasticizes heat sensitive materials.

★ blends colours more rapidly, and

★ heat requirements are lower.

MACHINE SPECIFICATIONS

To determine suitability of moulding machine for an injection moulded product, the following machine specifications need to be checked :

★ Maximum shot weight capacity of the machine should be more than total weight of article/articles (in case of multicavity mould) plus the runner system.

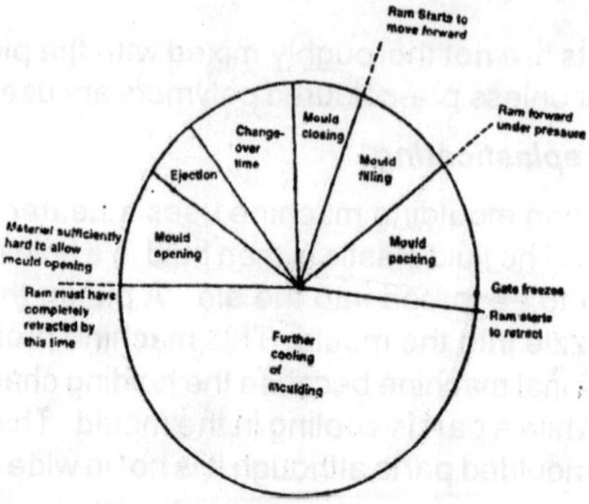

Fig . 3 THE INJECTION MOULDING CYCLE

- ★ Injection pressure should be sufficient to fill the cavities without any short shots.
- ★ Clamping Tonnage required to hold the mould in locked condition should be adequate (otherwise there will be flashes).
- ★ Daylight opening of the machine should be higher than sum total of mould height, plus article height, plus space required for removal of articles.
- ★ Minimum mould height specified for the machine should be less than actual mould height to be mounted.
- ★ Distance between tie-rods should be greater than mould size
- ★ Type of screw barrel (L/D ratio and Tip design) should be suitable for material to be processed.

Injection Moulding Cycle

A typical injection moulding cycle is illustrated in Fig. 3.

The first stage, mould closing should be as fast as possible consistent with the final part of the closing operation not being so fast as to cause damage to the mould.

As soon as the mould is closed, the screw starts to move forward and the mould filling stage commences. When the ram is fully forward and the mould cavity is filled, the pressure on the melt increases and this helps to consolidate the material in the cavity. This is known as mould packing stage. During this stage, the gate freezes.

Once the gate has frozen, the screw is retracted, thereby keeping the material ready for the next cycle. In the meantime cooling of moulding occurs, which is often known as mould cooling stage.

When the moulding is sufficiently solidified, mould opening takes place and the moulding is ejected.

There may be some change over time before commencing the next cycle, for mould cleaning of placing inserts etc.

Cycle Time

Cycle time can be defined as time elapsed from meshing of two mould halves till the part gets ejected after opening, and mould starts closing for next cycle and two mould halves mesh again. This is generally expressed in seconds.

CONVENTIONAL TWO-PLATE MOULD

1. The Locating Ring
2. The Sprue Bushing
3. The Clamp Plate
4. The Cavity
5. The Cavity Retainer plate
6. The Leader Pins
7. The Runner System
8. The Gate
9. The Core
10. The Sprue Puller Pin
11. The Ejector Ping
12. The Ejector Pin Retainer Plate
13. The Ejector Plate
14. The Ejector plate Return pins
15. The Core Retainer Plate
16. The Support Plate
17. The Support Pillars
18. The Ejector Housing

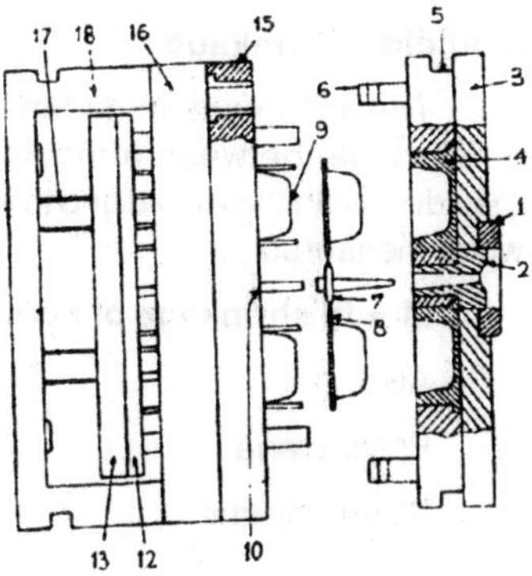

SECTIONAL VIEW OF VERTICAL INJECTION MOULD

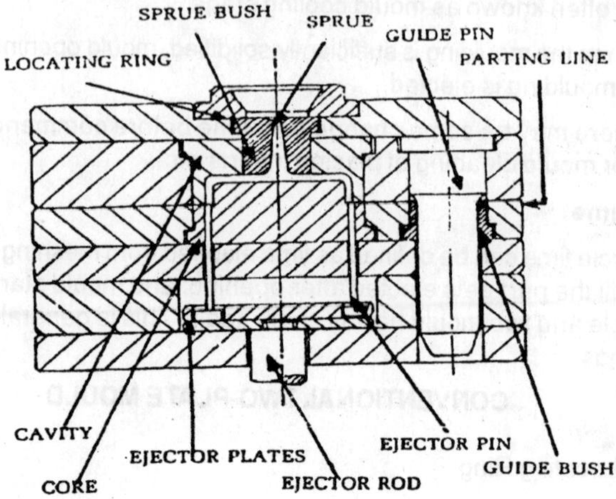

Moulding Shrinkage :

The difference in dimensions, expressed in inches per inch or as percentage, between a moulding and the mould cavity in which it was moulded, both the mould and the moulding being at normal room temperature when measured.

Mould shrinkage of some thermoplastics

ABS	-	0.5
Polystyrene	-	0.5
Polypropylene	-	1-2
HDPE	-	1.5-2.5
LDPE	-	1.5-2.5
SAN	-	0.5
PVC rigid	-	0.2-0.4
Nylon-6	-	0.7-1.5
Acetal	-	2-3.5
Polycarbonate	-	0.6

Spiral Flow Test

The spiral flow is another way of expressing the flow of a particular grade inside the mould and is determined on a standard mould having a spiral cavity marked in centimetres.

Following are the results obtained from a spiral flow test, using different polypropylene moulding grades :

MELT INDEX OF PP GRADE	Spiral flow (cms) At 260°C cylinder temperature 700 kg/cm² injection pressure
1.70	25.0
3.00	32.0
5.60	36.5
10.00	46.25

Spiral had a semi circular cross section of 5 mm diameter.

METHOD OF CALCULATING THE SHOT CAPACITY AND LOCKING FORCE REQUIREMENT

Example :

Take the following example of a rectangular box to be moulded in polypropylene.

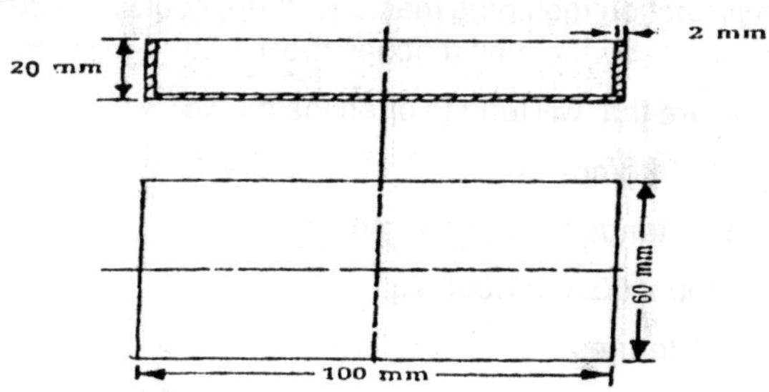

Shot capacity requirement

The first step is to calculate the weight of the moulding.

Approx. volume of moulding in mm^3

$= (100 \times 20 \times 2) \times 2 + (60 \times 20 \times 2) \times 2$

$+ 100 \times 60 \times 2$

$= 8{,}000 + 4{,}800 + 12{,}000$

$= 24{,}800\ mm^3$

$= 24.8\ Cm^3$

Density of polypropylene = $0.91\ gm/cm^3$

Weight of the moulding

$= 24.8 \times 0.91 = 22.5$ gms

Say. 30 gms, including the weight of the sprue.

Normally, the shot capacity of an injection moulding machine is defined in terms of polystyrene and only 70% of that value can be taken for polypropylene.

Therefore, the shot capacity of the machine should be

at last $\frac{30}{0.7} = 43$ gms

Locking force requirement

The box is to be moulded as shown in the following figure.

The projected area of the moulding will be

$100 \times 60 = 6{,}000$ sq mm

$= 60$ sq cm

Assuming that the injection pressure required is 800 kg/cm^2 on a screw pre-plasticising injection moulding machine, there could be a 50% drop in the injection pressure as the melt reaches the mould.

$\therefore$ the pressure that will tend to open the mould

$= 400\ kg/cm^2$

The force that tends to open the mould

$= 400 \times 60 = 24{,}000$ kg

$= 24$ tonnes

Therefore to mould this componet, the injection moulding machine should have a minimum shot capacity of 43 grammes and a locking force of 24 tonnes.

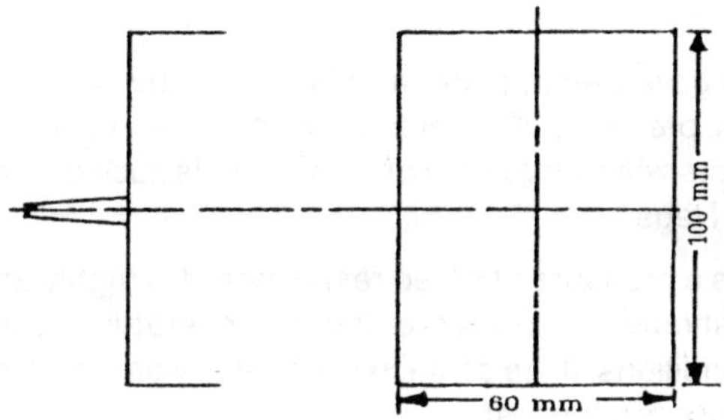

TESTING OF INJECTION MOULDED PRODUCTS

Tests on injection moulded product are usually custom designed for a particular product and are not formalized and described in industry standards (Few Indian Standards are used for ready reference). However, some of the common testing procedures are :

1. IMPACT TESTING

(A) PART DROP TESTING

Injection moulded containers which can be provided with lids are usually tested by filling them with liquid and dropping them from various heights onto a rigid base. (Refer Fig. 5). Products are preconditioned at zero degree, temperature which can be achieved using glycol mixtures. The point of impact can be changed to test various parts of the container. Parts which cannot be provided with lids can be filled with weights before drop testing. Part drop testing is multiaxial impact test which accurately stimulates real life service requirements. Failure will generally be in one location, identifying the weakest section of the part.

(B) DART DROP TESTING

Specific areas of parts, or parts which are not suitable for whole part drop tests, can be impact tested using a dart drop test. (Refer Fig. 6). This test is most useful for testing the weakest area of parts, frequently the gate area.

(C) TOP LOAD STRENGTH

The ability of a part to withstand a top load is frequently an important factor in determining the serviceability of the part. Many containers are filled with various products and stacked on pallets for storage and shipment. A container which fails under these top loading conditions could result not only in loss of product, but an unstable stack which could present a safety hazard.

Top loadability is governed by material stiffness and by design factors such as wall thickness, presence of stiffening ribs and stress concentrating elements, and by factors which introduce off centre loads such as side wall taper of offset support legs.

Top loadability is a measure of creep resistance. It is highly affected by temperature and should be measured under temperature conditions simulating end use conditions. If the container is normally provided with lid, then is should be included in the test.

The equipment for this test is shown

(D) STRESS CRACK TESTING

Injection moulded parts can be tested for stress crack resistance by immersing the whole part in a heated bath containing a surfactant solution. Cracks which develop in the part will assist in solving moulding problems by identifying highly stressed areas, as well as identifying the resin inadequacies.

IS Specifications for some injection moulded products are listed below:

IS 3730 - 1988	:	Specification for high density polyethylene bucket.
IS 5322 - 1988	:	Specification for high density polyethylene wash bowls.
IS 9848 - 1987	:	Specification for briefcases, plastic body.
IS 11584 - 1986	:	Specification for high density polyethylene (HDPE) crates for milk sachets.
IS 9907 - 1981	:	Specification for high density polyethylene (HDPE) crates for 500 ml, glass milk bottles.

MATERIALS

High Density Polyethylene (HDPE)

It is easy to process this material and use it for injection moulded household wares and other containers, HDPE is successfully used for making moulded articles like buckets, bread containers, luggage, some automobile interior parts, bottle closures in snapfit designs in the pharmaceutical and cosmetic industry.

PROPERTY REQUIREMENTS OF INJECTION MOULDING POLYETHYLENE RESINS

For injection moulding, resin should have good glow properties and these must be balanced against the need for toughness and stress crack resistance. Other properties such as part stiffness, resistance to warpage and surface gloss are also important considerations.

Generally, the injection moulding resins are made with narrow MWD, which inherits low warpage characteristics high surface gloss and high toughness values. Flow properties can be varied over a wide range by varying melt index. Stiffness and stress crack resistance can be easily varied by changing density.

In specific instances, grades have been developed with intermediate and broad MWD. Although these grades have lower melt indices they improve stress crack resistance, while maintaining high shear properties.

Injection Moulding Polyethylene grades should possess the following properties :

1. Material should have good flow
2. It should have reasonably good rigidity to maintain the shape.
3. It should have fair impact strength.
4. Material should have narrow MWD which will help in achieving good warp-free articles at shorter cycle times (as heat-input will be less due to even chain lengths).
5. It should have very high gloss.

Applications

1. Crates. Moulded Luggage. Moulded Furniture, Industrial Containers etc.

The properties required for this application are :-

1. Material should have high dendity and rigidity
2. It should have low warping tendency.
3. It should possess good impact strength.
4. Environmental Strees Crack Resistance should be fairly good.

5. It should have reasonably good gloss.
6. Flow properties should be sufficiently good to fill the item without overpacking.
7. Antioxidant level in the resin should be relatively high to protect resin against high processing temperatures encountered in some applications, and to ensure long service life.
8. Material should be adequately stabilized with UV stabilizer for the applications requiring outdoor exposure.

Table 1 lists the grades available in the Indian market for this application.

2. Housewares, buckets, pails, planters etc,

The grades available in the Indian market for these applications is listed in Table 2.

HDPE Grades Available in Indian Market for Housewares, Pails, Buckets, etc.

Manufacturer	*Grade*	*Density*	*MFI*
NOCIL	PIL GA 7260	0.957	16.0
IPCL	Indothene HD 50 MA 180	0.950	18.0
RELIANCE	Relene M 60200	0.958	21.0
SABIC	Ladene M 200056	0.956	20 .0
MOBIL	Mobil HMA 016	0.957	20.0
PHILIPS	Marlex HMN 55180	0.955	18.0
	Hiden M 691	0.963	20.0
EXXON	Escorene 6801	0.956	20.0

HDPE Grades Available in Indian Market for Crates, Moulded Luggage and Moulded Furniture Applications

Manufacturer	*Grade*	*Density*	*MFI*
NOCIL	PIL GC7260	0.957	8.0
IPCL	Indothene HD 58 MA 075	0.958	7.5
RELIANCE	Relene M 60075	0.960	8.2
	Relene L 60075 UV stabilized	0.960	8.2
SABIC	Ladene M 80064	0.964	8.0
MOBIL	MOBIL HMA 035	0.964	8.0
PHILIPS	Marlex HMN6060	0.963	7.5

Talc or $CaCO_3$ Filled PPHP & CP	*Polystyrene-Plain & High Impact*
★ Radiator cooling fan	★ Cabinets of radio, tape recorders speakers (both front & back)
★ TV back covers	★ Audio & video cassete body & cover
★ Regulator covers	★ Casting of wall and table clocks
★ Monoblock chairs	★ Air conditioner parts
★ Garden benches	★ Refrigerator parts
★ Dash board assly parts	★ TV components ★ Stencils
★ Parts of air cooler	★ Toys ★ Cosmetic containers

ABS	*Polyacetal Homopolymers*
★ Telephone parts	★ Gears, levers, cams, bushes
★ Mixer & food processor parts	★ Window handles & knobs
★ Parts of appliances- Vacuum cleaners, washing m/cs, hair dryers, etc	★ Valve & valve parts « Pipe fittings
	★ Couplings « Luggage clips
	★ Threaded fastner clips
	Poly Acetal Copolymers
★ Camera components	
★ Parts of tape recorder & tape deck	
★ Automobile parts-Radiator grill, instrument panel	★ Body trim clips ★ Shower heads
★ TV components ★ Fan parts	★ Cistern ball valves
★ Business machines housings	★ Furniture castors ★ Aerosol valves
★ Helmet ★ Type writer parts	★ Seat belt buckets
★ Cooling fans for a/c	★ Conveyor belt slots

Injection Moulding Problems & Remedies

Defect	*Possible Cause*	*Suggested Solution*
Streaking or specks	Poor pigment of master batch dispersion	★ Improve mixing procedure ★ Increse screw back pressure ★ Decrease screw speed.
	Degraded material or contamination	★ Lower material temperature. ★ Use less re-ground material.

Contd....

		★ Check for contamination and see that cylinder and nozzle are clean.
Shrinkage varying from estimated value	Shrinkage is too high	★ Lower material temperature if gate is unrestricted. ★ Lower mould temperatue. ★ Increase injection pressure ★ Increase hold-on time ★ Increase material feed ★ Use high MFI grades. ★ Increase gate size
	Excessive difference between in-line and transverse shrinkage	★ Increase material temperature ★ Decrease injection pressure ★ Increase injection speed. ★ Increase number of gates.
Poor impact strength	Crack propagation from notches and sharp corners	★ Provide radii to all sharp corners and intersections
	Moulded-in stresses	★ Reduce injection pressure by increasing material and mould temperature. ★ Increase injection speed.
	Incorrect choice of grade	★ Change grade, if necessary and where suitable in other respects.
	Degraded material or contamination	★ Reduce material temperature ★ Use less re-ground material. ★ Check for contamination
Ejection difficult	Insufficint cooling	★ Increase cooling time. ★ Lower mould temperature ★ Lower material temperature
	Excess pressure in cavity	★ Decrease injection pressure ★ Decrease pressure hold-on time
	Insufficient taper	★ Increase taper, as required

Defect	*Possible Cause*	*Suggested solution*
	Poor sufrace finish of core or cavity	★ Polish in line of draw
	Area or positions of ejectors unsatisfactory	★ Add larger or additional ejectors.
	Sprue not in alignment with nozzle	★ Re-align nozzle and sprue
Dripping from nozzle when mould opens	Degradation due to over heating	★ Lower the cylinder temperature and carefully purge the material
	polymer has become too fluid and is giving off gas	★ Purge the material and re-start the machine with proper cylinder temperatures.
Sinking and / or voiding	Moulding conditions causing excessive localised shrinkage	★ Increase material feed. ★ Increase pressure hold-on time. ★ Increase injection pressure ★ Lower mould temperature ★ Check that machine capacity is adequate.
	Incorrect cooling of the mould	★ Increase cooling time. ★ Lower mould temperature (sinking) ★ Raise mould temperature (voiding)
	Incorrect choice of grade	★ Use higher MFI grades.
	Faulty design of mould	★ Ensure that the gating leads to the of product thickest section of the moulding ★ Increase gate size ★ Eliminate thick sections.
Warping and bowing	Differential shrinkage caused by (a) high residual stresses due to improper moulding conditions	★ Decrease injection pressure. ★ Increase injection speed. ★ Raise material temperature. ★ Raise mould temperature. ★ Use higher MFI grades. ★ Re-locate gates.

		★ Increase number of gates.
	(b) High residual stresses from unbalanced cooling	★ Arrange cooling circuit to give opposing temperature gradient to that of material, e.g. connect water

Defect	*Possible Cause*	*Suggested Solution*
		inlet to gate area and arrange outlet from edges.
	(c) Wall thickness variation	★ Re-design product. Give even wall thickness throughout
	(d) Inadequate cooling	★ Increase cooling time. ★ Lower mould temperature ★ Lower material temperature
Dull Patches	Poor flow behaviour of melt	★ Raise material temperature. ★ Increase injection speed. ★ Increase injection pressure ★ Raise mould temperature ★ Use higher MFi grades. ★ Eliminate section variations.
	Material temperature variation Entrapped air	★ Improve nozzle heating or insulation ★ Improve venting ★ Ensure that material or Pigments do not contain moisture.
De-lamination	Skin of material freezing off permanently Incompatible material	★ Raise material temperature. ★ Raise mould temperature. ★ Check for contamination for other plastics in hopper or cylinder.
Scabbing (Jetting)	Material jetting into thick sections of cavity	★ Position gate to feed the material against a wall or break up flow by other means, like tab gate
Surface defects	Mould too hot	★ Lower material temperature. ★ Lower moould temperature,

Contd....

around gates		if possible. ★ Provide water inlet near the feed if possible Otherwise, consider providing extra cooling.
Poor weld strength	Converging streams of material not welding properly at interface	★ Raise material temperature. ★ Raise mould temperature ★ Increase injection speed. Improve venting.

Defect	*Possible Cause*	*Suggested Solution*
		★ Re-arrange gatting to avoid converging flows, particulary over long distances, or move weld lines to more acceptable areas ★ Use higher MFI grades, where possible.
	Foreign material at the interface of converging streams	★ Use less mould lubricants. ★ Check for contamination.
Short moulding	Insufficient pressure	★ Increase injection pressure.
	Insufficient heating	★ Increase barrel temperature gradually
	Material freezing off before mould filling	★ Increase injection speed. ★ Increase mould temperature ★ Consider increasing number of gates and size of runners.
	Inadequate shot capacity	★ Increase feed setting or transfer the mould to a larger machine.
	Inadequate ait vents	★ Provide adequate air vents.
Flashing	Melt viscosity too low	★ Reduce material temperature.
	Mould opening under	★ Check that projected area of the mould is within the limits of machine locking capacity increase clamp pressure if possible.

Contd....

	★ Decrease injection pressure. ★ Enlarge gates to reduce filling pressure. ★ Balance gates & runners where applicable. ★ Reduce material feed.
Parting surfaces of the mould not matching	★ Re-face and re-align where necessary. Ensure that no foreign material is present on the mould faces. ★ Check for tool deformation.

PVC COMPOUNDS- BASIC FORMULATIONS

Pipe, Profiles and Tubing :

Rigid PVC Pipe

PVC resin (K-65 to K-67)	100
Stabilizer TBLS	1.4-1.6
Stabilizer DBLS	0.6-0.8
Stabilizer LS	0.3-0.4
Calcium Streate	0.3-0.4
Stearic acid	0.2-0.4
HCW	0.2-0.3
GMS	0.1-0.2
TiO2	0.4-0.5
Carbon black	0.01
Calcium carbonate (Treated)	6-8

Injection Moulding :

Rigid Pipe Fittings

PVC resin (K-57)	100
Stabilizer (tin mercaptide)	1.0-2.0
Impact modifier (ABS type)	8.0-10.0
Processing aid (acrylic type)	1.0-3.0
External lubricant (paraffin wax)	0.05.1.0
Internal / External lubricant (calcium stearate)	0.8-1.0
Filler (Calcium carbonate)	0.10.0

Properties of Plastics

Polymer	*Clarity (Opacity)*	*Density Specific Gravity*	*melting Point°C*	*Deflection temp at 66 PSI under stress*	*Mould Shrinkage %*	*Injection Moulding Temp°C*
THERMOPLASTICS						
ABS	Opaque	1.03 to 1.06	105 to 115	102 to 108	0.4 to 0.9	200-270
Acetal	Opaque	1.42	181	170	2	194-245
Acrylic	Clear	1.17 to 1.2	90-105	80-170	0.1-0.8	160-260
Cellulose Acetate	Clear	1.2 to 1.34	230	49-98	0.3-1	168-355
Nylon-6 (Plain)	Translucent	1.1-1.14	225	185	0.6-1.5	230-285
Nylon-6 (30 to 35% Glass)	Opaque	1.35-1.42	225	220	0.4	250-290
Nylon 6/6 UF	Translucent	1.13-1.15	265	190	0.8-1.5	270-330
Nylon 6/6 (33% GF)	Opaque	1.38	265	260	0.5	270-300
Polycarbonate (Plain)	Clear	1.2	150	132-143	0.5-0.7	252-345
Polycarbonate (15 = 40% Glass)	Translucent	1.24-1.52	150	150-155	0.1-0.4	300-345
Polyester (Plain)	Translucent	1.3-1.38	111-131	116-190	1.5-2	225-275
Polyester	Opaque					

contd......

(33% Glass)	Opaque	1.73	111-131	250	0.1-0.3	260-290
Polythylene-LD	Translucent	0.91-0.925	110-130	38-50	1.5-5.0	149-315
Polythylene-HD	Translucent	0.941-0.965	120-140	60.88	2-5	149-315
Polypropylene						
(Copolymer)	Translucent	0.89-0.905	160-175	85-113	1-2.5	205-285
Polypropylene	Translucent	1.05-1.25	176	152-155	0.2-0.8	205-290
ABS						
Polystyrene (GP)	Clear	1.04-1.09	100	82-110	0.1-0.6	163-260
Polystyrene (HI)	Opaque	1.04-1.1	100	82-105	0.2-0.6	177-315
SAN	Clear	1.075-1.1	115	—	0.2-0.7	190-300
PVC	Clear	1.3-1.6			1-5	160-196
THERMOSETTING MATERIAL						
Phenol Formal		1.3	—	116-133	1.1-2	130-160
dehyde (UF)	Opaque					
Urea Formal	Opaque	1.5	—	127-143	6.1-4	135-177
dehyde						
Malamine	Opaque	1.48	—	148	1.1-1.2	149-167
(UF)						
Polyesters	Opaque	1.9	—	150	0.3	—

4

Blow Moulding

Blow Moulding as known and the name exemplifies is a process of manufacturing Hollow Articles.

Types : The process is mainly divided in 4 major categories.

1. *Extrusion Blow Moulding*

This is one of the simple and well known process amongs blow moulding.

In this process the parsion or Hollow tube of melt if formed by Extruder. Most of the heat required to the Raw material to melt is passed on by the frictional heat. This gets generated in the shearing action of Raw material graunles with screw and Barrel of Extruder and Contributes to almost 75-80% of heat required. The remaining 15-20% of heat is generated by the Barrel heat's placed on the Barrel of Extruder by convectional heating.

The Extruder goes on giving through an annular orfice a continuous parison of melt into an acculmalator. The accumulator's presence depends on the size of Article and the amount of material the article is going to need in one shot generally accumulator is required for large sized articles. (35 litres and above) In small sized, articles the presence of accumulator is not required. In such circumstances the parison when of sufficient length is directly engulfed into a split cavity mould. The mould halves close around the parison and pinches of cuts the lower or one end of the parison. The compressed air is passed into it, which Blows the parison towards the Hollow Mould walls surfaces and contacts it, the air cools the parison by that stage to form the shape of the Hollow Mould. The mould opens to throw out or eject the Blown Article & closes again to repeat the previous cycle again for a new shot of article this is known as continuous Type & Extrusion Blow Moulding.

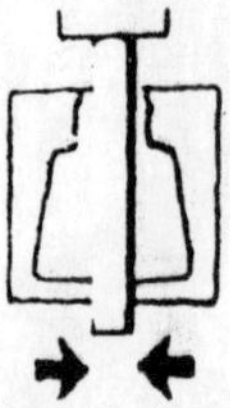

1) **Mould Grips Parsion**

2) **Blowing by Compressed Air**

In the case large articles accumalar stores the material. Once sufficient material is collected as per required shot weight, The Material is pushed out of it in a parison form and other procedure as previously is repeated. This is known as intermittent type of Extrusion Blow Moulding.

3) **Cooling**

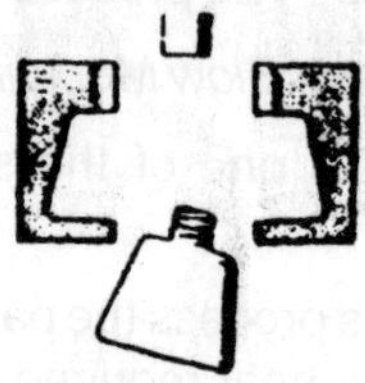

4) **Ejection**

2. *Injection Blow Moulding*

This is the second type of Blow Moulding and involves 3 stages in it, they are as follows :

STAGE : (1) : *Injection Moulding of a parison on a steel core pin.*

The polymer melt is first moulded on the steel core pin in an injecton mould. The steel core pin is movable one The melt moulded on this pin is known as perform.

STAGE : (2) : *Transfer of Core pin with preform in a Blow Mould.*

The Transferable core pin with its preform is moved from the injection mould and placed in Blow Mould placed next to it. As a regular Blow Moulding cycle the compressed air is Blown through a cavity of core pin out in the Preform. As a result the preform Blows and touches the walls of Blow mould and cools down. It takes the shape of the contours of Blow mould.

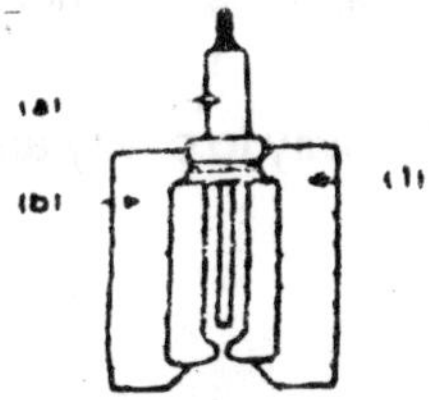

5) Transfer pin in position

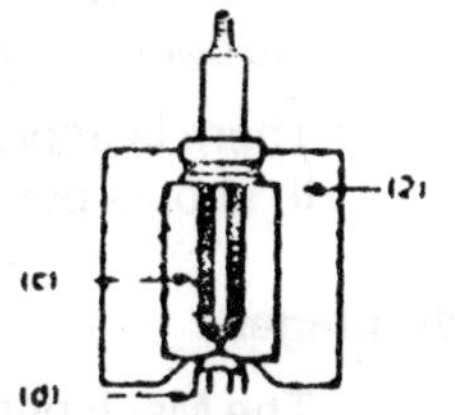

6) Material injection

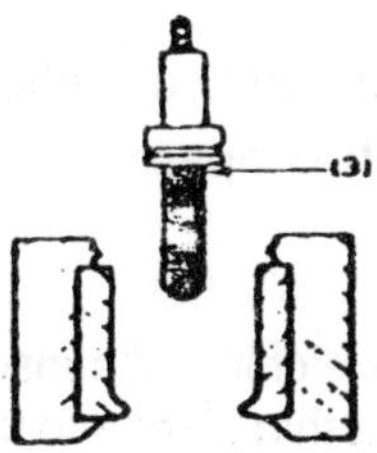

7) Hot Perform Ejected

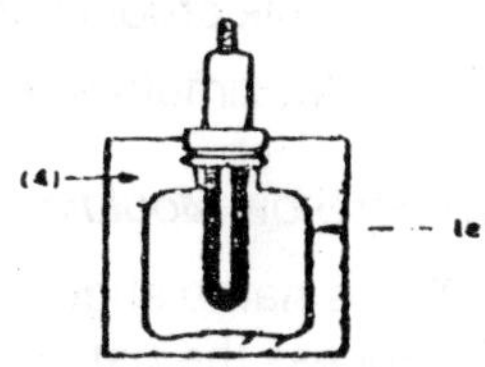

8) Transfer to Blow Mould

STAGE (3) : ***Ejection of Article from Blow Mould.***

The 2 movable halves of Mould seperate out.

The Blown Article is ejected out of it

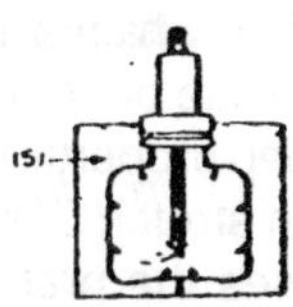

9) Blowing

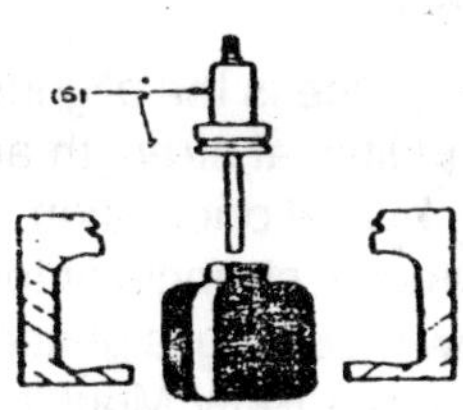

10) Ejection

Advantages

1. As the parison is injection moulded one. The Containers have a high gloss surface finish and high dimensional accuracy on (the sizes containers weight)

2. As the welding seams doesn't appear it does't have any weak points. As flashis don't form no ancillary equipment to reprocess these flashes are required.

3. As orientation is done the mechanical properties are improved in the containers made from this process.
4. There is improved weight control both cavity to cavity and shot to shot is possible.

Disadvantages

1. The Machinery and the moulds are costly.
2. The processs produces only centre neck containers or articles. So odd shaped and odd necked containers can't be manufactured with it.
3. Bulk production is essential for production run's cost efficiency.
4. Maximum size manufactured is up to 1 litre Capacity.

3. *Stretch Blow Moulding*

As the name suggests this process involves stretching of parison. In this process the parison is stretched Bi-axially and than blown to take shape of the mould. The Blowing is done by chilled air, so as to cool the parison as early as possible.

In the Bi-axial orientation the parison are stretched lenghwise by the External gripper or by an internal Rod. The Radial stretching is done by Blown air to form the finished product.

The Process

In this process the alignment of molecules along two planes is done, providing additional strength and better barrier properties, which are only possible by biaxial orientation. The other advantages include better clarity, increased impact strength or toughness and reduced creep properties. The stretch blow moulding is generally divided into Extrusion stretch Blow and Injection stretch Blow Moulding. In both these processes the preform is formed in a preform mould, in extrusion by extrusion process and in Injection by an internal rod. Then it is transfered to different stretch moulds. This preform formed in both the processes are heated till its orientation temperature. Once it reaches the orientation temperature. it is axially stretched by the internal Rod (in Injection stretch Blow) and by external gripping in (Extrusion stretch Blow Moulding.) In a simultaneous process it is Radially blown by chilled air to complete Bi-axial orientation.

This process can be In-line or 2 stage One. The Inline machine involves only, one machine on which in-line processing is done. While the 2 stages process involves 2 extrusion or Injection line to form the preforms while a Re-heat Blow moulding machine to make the finished product.

(I) EXTRUSION STRETCH BLOW MOULDING

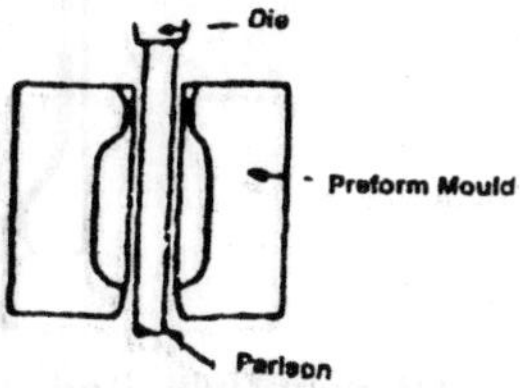

1) Preform Moulding

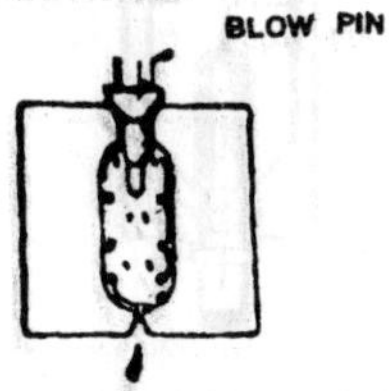

2) Parison Blown to Preform

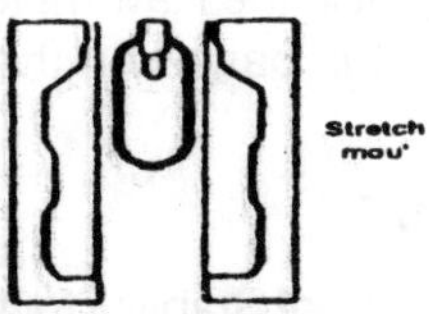

3) Preform Transferred to Strecth Blow Mould

4) Stretched to shape by Extension Rod.

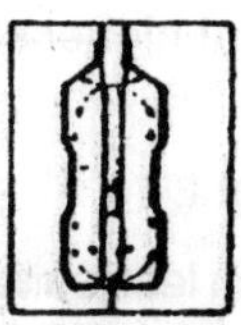

5) Blowing

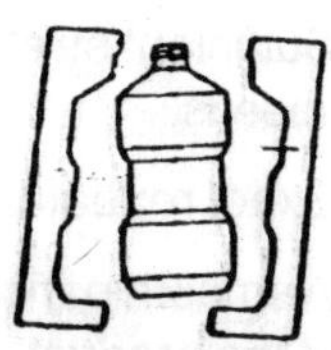

6) Ejection

(III) DIAGRAM-INJECTION STRETCH BLOW MOULDING

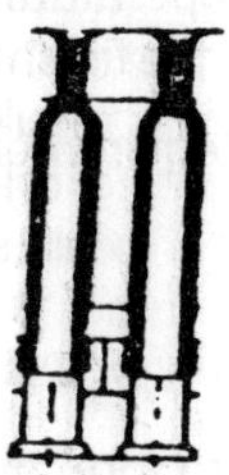

1) Injection Moulding of Preform

2) Re-heating & Orienting of Parison.

3) Axial Orientation with Internal Rod

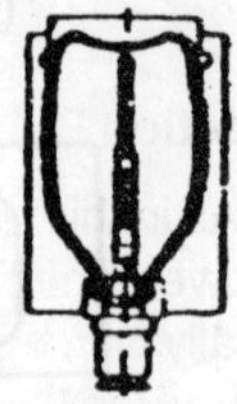

4) Blowing with Radial Orientation

MATERIALS USED IN BLOW MOULDING

There are specific requirement to be present in the Raw material to be used for Blow Moulding process successfully. It is based on the process used to Blow mould an article.

(a) *PROCESS SPECIFIC REQUIREMENT*

* The material should have sufficient Thermal Stability for the range processing Temperature for repeated processing.
* The material should have sufficient flow (MFI) with a Homogeneous and plasticised melt.
* Sufficient stretchability (Swell) of the parison at higher stretching speeds.
* Exact repeatability of parison length and weight.
* A smooth parison surface for better and scratch less surface finish of the product.
* The material should have sufficient compatibility with master batches, any other Additive pigments, to be added into it.
* A Sufficiently vide range of processing Temperature should be there which will finally impart the properties to the finished product.

As the process changes some of the special Requirement also are listed for *Extrusion and Injection Blow M'ing.*

1. Extrusion Blow Moulding

The plasticised Melt strems should re-uniform to form a consistent parison, to resist the sagging Phenomenon The extruded parison should have sufficient melt strength. Good welding should be doned especially at the area of *Pinch-off* to avoid leaking unsturdiness problem.

2. **Injection Blow Moulding/Stretch Blow Moulding**

As in this process the parison is supported on a core Rod, the material with lower melt strengths can be utilised over here. The multicavity moulds generally with hot runner system require easy melt flow and low adhesion to the core Rod.

(b) *Depending on end* use requirement of raw material criteria :

* The Raw material must have chemical resistance, permeability.
* Good environmental strees crack resistance.
* Good Mechanical properties like Impact Resistance. Creep and Weather resistance.
* Physiological properties like Food contact applications, Optical properties.

(c) *For the material to be packed into it*

* Depending on the material to be packed inside the requirements.

1. Stiffness under load and Dimensional stability at higher and lower Temperature.
2. Good surface finish, which is important for printing to be made on it.
3. Good Drop Impact even at lower Temperatures.

(d) *Parts used in specifically technical industries*

For such parts, High Dimensional properties like Mechanical properties are important, some time high gloss, surface painting is also required. So for the same, excellent surface quality should be there in the material.

RAW MATERIAL SELECTION

(A) The Thermoplastics used in *BLOW MOULDING* can be placed basically into the type of Polymerisation

a) Addition Polymerisation

b) Condensation polymerisation.

(B) Depending on the size of container of product the Raw material is decided accordingly also it is according to the practical application point of view.

a) *Small parts, under 5 litres :*

1) Polyolefins (HDPE/LDPE/PP/PPCP)

2) Polyvinyl Chloride (PVC)
3) Polyacrylonitrile (PAN)
4) Polystyrene (PS)
5) Styrene Acrylonitrile (SAN)
6) Polyvinylidene Fluoride (PVDF)
7) Polyester Terpethalate (PET)

b) *For Larger parts over 5 Litres & Technical Industrial Parts:*

1) Polyolefins (HDPE/HMHDPE)
2) Polycarbonate (PC)
3) Polyacetal (POA)
4) Polyamide (PA)
5) Polyvinylidene Fluoride (PVDF)

MOST COMMONLY USED BLOW MOULDING RAW MATERIALS ARE DISCUSSED HERE

1. **Polyethylenes**

The Polyethylenes are basically sub-divided based on Density, as low medium and high densities. The density decided by the ASTM standards are as below :

1.	LOW Density	-	0.910	to	0.925 gms/cc
2.	Medium Density	-	0.926	to	0.940 gms/cc
3.	High Density	-	0.941	to	0.959 gms/cc

Along with the Density it will have specific relation with melt flow index. The low density polyethylenes used for Blow Moulding will have their MFIS in the range of 0.1 to 4 gm/s 10 min (90°c with 2.16 kg. load ASTM method)

The generally manufactured products are cosmetic squezzable bottles, and meducal devices. The medium or linear Low density polyethylene are used where intermediate stiffness with very high E.S.C.R is required.

High density polyethylenes available have MFI in the range of 0.1 to 1.00 gm melt flow Index and is in the range of 0.941 to o.960 Density. This is used mainly in the application of shipping drums up to capacities of 50 litres carboys, Cans, Mouse shaped containers.

The molecular weight distribution also has its effect on the properties like Impact and diamensional stability. The high molecular weight High density grades are also available and are used for container of about 75 to 100 litres capacity of Articles like Gasoline tanks, shipping drums. Some special grades HMHDPE have also been developed for manufacturing 200 litre big blow moulded Barrels which have been getting popular for Bulk chemical packaging system, by replacing the MS or SS based Barrels.

Processing of Polythylene

Polyethylenes are suitable for processing on both extrusion and injection blow moulding machine, but commonly the Extrusion Blow Moulding is used as a cost advantage reason.

The single screw Extruders are used most often. For high molecular wt. material a grooved Barrel extruder is preferred so as to get better out puts at lowest possible Temperatures :

The Melt Temperatures of Polyethylene are in the Range as Follows

Low Density PE	-	160°	-	170°c.
Linear Low Density PE	-	160°	-	185°c.
High Desnsity PE	-	160°	-	210°c

The general mould temperatures are kept in bet 10°c to 40°c and are sandblasted for good venting properties.

Special characteristic of swelling in High Devisity swelling is an special cnaracteristic often seen in MD or HDPE while processing them.

The HDPE has small to medium chains of moleules, which have intermolecualr force of attraction with each other in molten stage they coil themselves with each other. When they are forced out of a Die the uncoiling takes place and a stress in direction of blow once they come out they tend to relax. As a resutl of this a Building gets formed which is known as swelling properties.

The HDPE manufactured by different process have different swell characteristics. The swell can be in the diametre of parison or in the in thickness of the parison. The swell is adjusted by shaping the tooing design. The divergent tooling gives thickness swell while the convergent tooling gives diametre swell of parison, as per requirement the swell is adjusted by tooling.

Polypropylene

Polypropylene has some desirable properties because of which it is used for Blow Moulding, that are :

1. Very low density with High stiffnes and surface hardness.
2. Very good Chemical and High Temperature Resistance.
3. Good clarity gloss with low water absorbtion and Transmission.
4. Good toughness when alloyed with Elastomers at low Temperatures.

The Polypropylene Homopolymers as well as co-polymers of ethylene can be Blow Moulded.

The PPHP have melt flow index, ranging from 0.5 to 3.00 gm/10 min which are used in Blow Moulding Applications.

The P.P.C.P. have got better clarity as well as Impact Resistance than the P.P.H.P. They have M.F.I. Ranging from 1 to 3 gms/10 min.

The get better melt and colour stability moderate quantity of antioxidants have to be added in it at the raw material manufacturing stage. To impact special properties additives can also be added to P.P. at the processing stage.

In Injection Blow moulding grade to release the core in pin very small amount of calcium stearate is added. The Glass filled or Talc filling can impart the Hardness, stiffness, heat stability and flexibility, even at lower temperature, while Elastomer adding increases toughness and flexibility.

Application

P.P. Blow Moulded products find applications in Medical products such as bottles for cough syrup, sterile fluid. Antacids, cold stored medicines and mouth washes. Cosmetic applications include containers for cream, lotions, jellys, eyeliners.

In Technical Industrial parts due to its impeccable properties their use have been started and is getting popular Day-By-Day.

Processing of P.P.

The machine screw used for P.P. should have Compression Ratio of about 3-3.5:1, while the L/D Ratio should be atleast 20:1 with longer length of screw.

The Barrel Temp. Range of Processing is from 170°c-190°c-210°c while the melt temp is approx in between 180°c-240°c

POLYPROPYLENE has about 70% of swell as compared with HDPE. By using polished moulds Glossy Appearance on the surface could be generated, while the mould Temp are kept in the Range of 10°c-40°c

5

Polyvinyl Chloride

It is used widely in packaging due to its special characters like Gloss, Clarity with Smooth Surface Finish, low Gas and Aroma permeation with low thickness and high stiffness also.

In P.V.C "K" value is a significant value denoting the flow properties of material. The P.V.C used for Blow Moulding generally have its k value in the range of 57 and 65.

Because of its properties mentioned above it has captured the matket of plastic bottles virtually of cosmetics. Toiletories, Pharmaceutical, Chemicals, oil, mineral water bottles etc.

P.V.C. can be generally Extrusion Blow moulded as well as STRETCH BLOW MOULDED.

Processing of P.V.C.

P.V.C. is one of the those raw materials which cannot be used in its own virgin form, but has to be compounded with different additives, to make it workable, they are :

1. Heat stabiliser
2. Internal & External Lubricants.
3. Processing Aids &
4. Impact modifiers.

So, a Compound as per requirements is processed on the specialised P.V.C. screw, single or two stage machines as per the process suggests, while the additives added, are based on the end use product requirement.

P.V.C. being highly corrosive in nature the Extruder barrel and screw are made with corrosion resistant material like NITRIDED STEEL. Generally

Tapered screw with compression ratio of 1.8 /2.3. : 1 are used The Barrel cooling system is one of the important parts of machine. and important for the process also.

The processing temperature ranges from 140°C to 150°C while the melt temperature ranges in between 190°C to 215°C . Polished Moulds are used for P.V.C. for getting high gloss properties.

For Mineral water	100
PVC resin (k-57)	
Stabilizers	
Zinc Octoate	0.15-0.20
Calcium Stearate	0.05-0.10
Co-stabilizers	
Distearyl pentaerythritol diphosphite	0.4-0.5
Epoxidized soyabean oil	3.0
Impact modifier (MBS type)	10.0
Processing aid (acrylic type)	0.5-1.0

6

Polyesterterephthalate (Pet)

This is a Thermoplastic Polyester Raw material having properties like.

1. Excellent Gloss and Clarity.
2. Good dimensional stability alongwith very high toughness at even lower Temperature below 0°c
3. Good chemical resistance alongwith low permeability to Carbon Dioxide

P.E.T is generally used to manufacture stretch Blow moulded Bottles due to the in comparative properties mentioned above. It is been exclusively used in Carbonated Beverage Industry in Foreign Countries, and is getting popular in India with multinational brand pouring in the country.

For packaging food products like Pickles, Honey, Edible oil, Juices, it is being used due to its safe food contact properties.

Processing

P.E.T which is generally available in chipform and is processed on a INJECTION STRETCH BLOW MOULDING MACHINE on either one stage or two stage machines.

The key part in processing of P.E.T. is to cool the parison below its (Tg) i.e. Glass Transion Temperatrue when it is on core pin and then reheated to stretch blow it. The preblown form of pet is known as preform which is then stretched to form required shape

The Preform is made in the Injection Mould once the preforms are made they are transfered to second i.e. Blow mould where it is blown to form the final product. In this process unifomity in Temperature of preform is essential part of it.

Blow Moulding Trouble Shooting

Defect	*Possible Cause*	*Suggested Solution*
Excess parison Stretch	High melt temperature	* Reduce stock temperature * Lower die temperature
	Slow extrusion rate	* Increase extrusion rate
Rough surface (Parison)	Low melt temperature	* Increase the parison bushing temperature : * use high flow resin
	Melt fractures	* Lower extrusion rate : Streamline the die design
Non-uniform wall thickness (Circumferential)	Eccentric pin setting in die bushing	* Set the pin correctly
	Improper die design	* Improve upon the die design
	Non uniform melt temperature	* Check for melt temperature uniformity
	High extrusion rate	* Lower extrusion rate
	Lack of symmetry in the product	* Increase Parison thickness then use larger Parison
	Sagging Parison	* Reduce melt temperature and increase rare of extrusion
Non-uniform wall thickness (Longitudinal)	Product shape irregularity	* Use parison control
Bubble (in parison)	Material contains moisture	* Dry material
	Trapped air in the melt	* Increase back pressure, increase screw speed
Streaks (in parison)	Degraded material in the equipment and die from previous run	* Clean the die
	Degraded material from over-heating of melt	* Check for hot spot
Black particles	Contaminated resin	* Check for resin contamination
	Degraded material in die	* Clean the die and flow

Contd....

Roll formation of the parison	Too high temperature difference between hot pin and cooler bushing	* Reduce the temperature differences
Low gloss	Poor flow of melt	* Use high flow material * Increase temperature
Parison has ripples, product is having grooves or lines	Not very sound die design	* Check the die design and improve upon it
	Contaminated die lip	* Clean the die lip

Contd....

	High extrusion rate	* Reduce extrusion rate
	Damage die lip	* Check for nicks and other defects on the die and repair
Parison is smooth but fishscales, pits etc. appear on product surface	Air trapped in the mould	* Arrange proper venting in mould, sand blast the mould surface for polyethylene polish it for pvc
	Water condenses on mould surface	* Increase mould temperature to reduce moisture condensation. * Check for water leakage
	Low blow pressure	* Increase blow pressure
Weak weld line	Poor welding due to low melt temperature	* Increase melt temperature
Product sticking to mould surface	High mould temperature	* Reduce mould temperature
	Inefficient cooling	* Increase cooling and cooling time
Parison pinch off to product	Long parison tail	* Reduce parison length arrange additional cooling * improve tail cooling
Blow out	Rapid blow up	* Slow down blow up
	High blow pressure	* Reduce pressure
	Very high blow up ratio	* Use larger diameter parison
	Sharp and hot pinch-off	* Check the pinch -off, lower melt temperature
	Thin section in the Parison due to contamination	* Check for contamination

Contd....

Excessive Shrinkage	High melt temperature Inefficient cooling	* Lower melt temperature * Improve cooling and increase cooling cycle raise blow pressure for better cooling contact with the mould surface
Thin wall at pinch-off	Too sharp pinch-off	* Increase pinch-off land * reduce relief area to hold and cool pinched-off material
	Inadequate venting	* Improve venting in the mould
	Inadequate blow	* Increase blow pressure

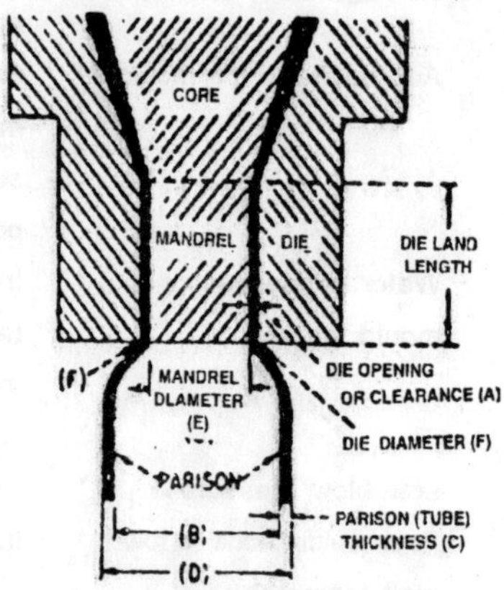

Fig. PARISON SWELL

$$\text{WEIGHT SWELL (\%)} = \frac{C - A}{A} \times 100$$

$$\text{DIAMETER SWELL (\%)} = \frac{D - F}{F} \times 100$$

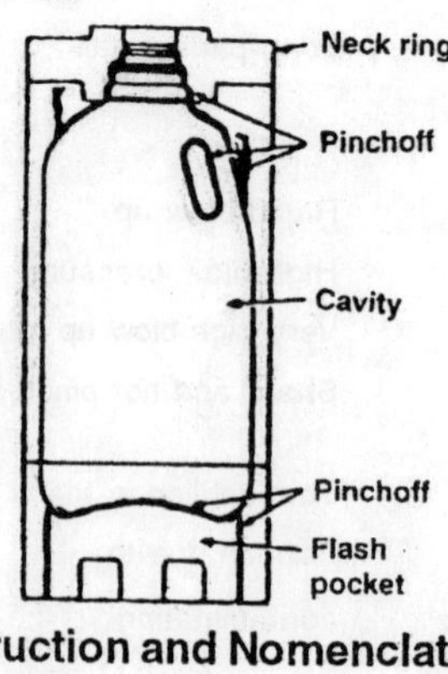

Blow Mould Construction and Nomenclature

7

Rotational Moulding

This is also known as Rotomoulding or Rotational Casting. This is a process which is known since early 1940. But due to various Technological Reasons it was less popular. with development of knowledge about polymer science and process control accuracies there has been a significant increase in the use of this process. Certain advantages have given it an edge over the well known and common processes of Injection and Blow moulding like Economic production of complex, designed, large sized and stress free hollow articels. It is a unique process involving heating shaping and cooling of plastic powder inside a mould without application of pressure.

In this process the pre-weight, pulverised plastic raw material powder is charged or poured inside and the mould is heated from outside. At this time the mould Rotates about two axes perpendicular to each other, which helps the material powder to get equally distributed all over the inner surfaces of the mould. By heating mould the material gers fused and a hollow article gets made inside. This mould is then cooled slowly so that release of article becomes easy after opening separating of mould. With increase of awareness about Rotational Moulding process It has led to several processors choosing it to conventional mouldings to make more complex, asymmetrical shaped articles.

The process can produce product from a small earning to Giant storage tank in wide variety of shapes.

The Process

Generally most of the polymer material used for Rotomoulding are available in granule form. These granules or Pallets are pulverised to a fine powder form of around 500 uM (35 mesh). This insures the fusion or homogenity in it as most of the polymer raw materials are conducters of heat. Whenever any additives are to be added generally for colour or impact etc, first the granules are melt compounded and then pulverised. The moulds are given a layer of release agents from inside for easy demoulding of the articles.

At the Loading point the preweighed pulverised powder is charged or poured into the mould. The weight of powder charged determines the wall thickness of articles. The mould is closed and then Rotated about 2 axes to each other, in an oven or in presence of External convectional heating systems like Burners.

Due to the Biaxial Rotation of mould the powder distributes itself evenly all over the corner and inside surface of the mould. Due to the External heat applied either through oven or by any other heating media, the material reaches its fusion temperature of Tg and starts geting fused evenly all along the inner surface of the mould. Once it is fully fused it emerges into taking shape of the mould. The mould is then taken to cooling point, where it is cooled by air and by a chilled water at a very slow rate as a reason the fused powder solidifies After the mould is properly cooled it is opened and the moulded article is removed out.

Rotomoulding also offers a rather easy process to produce multilayer products. The multilayer system offer distinct advantage like increased stiffness, improved barrier properties impact properties and cost savings.

While producing such multilayered article the 1st process is the same. While the 2nd layer powder is charged once the 2nd layer is completely fused. As before, the External heating also fused the newly charged powder into the inner layer, once such desired no. of layers are formed, cooling system is applied as discussed above and multilayered product is made at a relativley easy way.

While making multilayered products following points hold a key to success.

1. Bonding and fusing compatibility of charged powder of raw material.
2. Shrinkage of the raw materials.
3. Viscosity. Thickness of raw material melt which may clog at certain points when Rotation of mould is stopped for charging of next powder of any additives into it.
4. The process parametres like mould Rotation. Temperature Heating time and the pulverised particle size of raw material powder.

The wall thickness of each layer is determined by Rotation Ratio of major and miner axis revolutions per min i.e.R.P.M. for most of the new design this ratio is decided by trials.

Generally most of the Rotomolding articles are produced in natural colours of raw material powder. For coloured articles either a precoloured raw material of Dry additive pigments are used to colour the articles at the stage of pouring of pulverised powder. The dispersion of these pigments is a critical part and can have effect on the performance properties of the final product.

ADVANTAGES OF ROTATIONAL MOULDING

1. Moulds-simple, comparatively inexpensive.
2. On the same machine (provided with diff Arms) Different sized and shaped mould can run simultaneously.
3. The article gets uniform and good wall thickness compared to blow or thermoformed article.
4. Large articles which generally involve undercuts and intricasies can be modified into simple articles which are stress free.
5. The product designer has got tremendous scope and design flexilbility.
6. Generally this process of rotomoulding is suitable for short production cycles.
7. This process generates very low scrap or qualitative product.

Disadvantages

1. As the raw materials available are in granule or pellet form and then have to be pulverised to fine powder and melt compounded. The material cost becomes relatively high.
2. This process involves very long cycle time so is not suited for large production of small articles.
3. As loading and unloading is to be done manually this process is labour intensive.
4. Solid Ribs or Bosses are difficult to mould.
5. Raw material choice is limited (the polyethylenes are nearly 90% of materials used).

Machines

As the basic concept of Rotomoulding involves Rotating the mould about two axis to each other. At the same time its heated and cooled. This gives rise to different kind and variety of machine configurations and variety ways of supplying heat and cooling systems.

They are as follows :-

1. *Rock and Roll*

These are one of the earliest type of machines and still very popular in the field. In this machine a mould is mounted on a spindle which is rotated in 360°The spindle is made to rock back and forward by mechanical means or Hydraulic means. The mould is generally heated by series of Gas, Diesel of kerosene Burners placed under the mould. The cooling of mould is done at the same place after putting off of the burners, generally by Air cooling from outside. This type of machines can produce simple shaped articles but has got limitation in producing intricate articles. As in this method complete Bi-axial Rotation, can't be achieved.

2. *Carousal Type*

The limitation in Rock & Roll machine gave rise to these type of machines. These are Bi-axial machine. They consists of a enclosed heating station system (oven) and a cooling station chamber with loading and unloading stations. In the machines it has 3 or 4 arms on which the moulds are mounted. The arms are classified as straight & offset arms. The offset arm accomodates large size moulds. All these arms are individually motorised by variable motor drive (The advanced microprocessor based system allows each arm to operate independently with diff heating and cooling cycle systems) The ovens are normally heated with Gas oil or diesel and are equipped with blowers to distribute this heat. While the cooling system consists Air cooling fans and water mist sprayers enclosed inside the cooling chamber.

3. *Shuttle Type Machines*

There are the machines utilised for large shaped articles In these Machine the arm is mounted on a bed which is in turn mounted on tracks. This bed is then moved between heating and cooling stations.

4. *Clam Shell*

This is a new variety which is the latest amongs the Rotomoulding Machine. It has only one arm and uses an enclosed oven as both heating and cooling place or station. So the arm with the mould doesnot have to be moved out of the enclosed oven. As whole process gets completed inside the chamber.

Moulds

The moulds used for Rotational moulding are easiest and least expensive to fabricate and maintain as compaired to the moulds of other process. Generally they are 2 piece moulds. But sometime for larger and intricate articles 3 piece moulds. are used to have easy demoulding. While designing mould, you have to consider the factors like heat transfer of mould metal, mounting parting (Jointing line) Location, clamping mechanism, venting and raw material stability. The commonly used metals are cast aluminium, SS, MS, electroformed or vapour formed nickel.

As these moulds are designed with no draft angles, they are coated with release agent to prevent adhesion of article to mould. This happens due to the surface oxidation and formation of Bond between mould and molten raw material.

The commonly used agents are silicones, siloxanes and flurocarbons. They form a heat stable permanent layer on the inner mould surface and helps in releasing of article. This coat generally gets baked in the oven to form a stable (coat which lasts for a number of cycles. While applying this coat proper care should be taken of cleaning the mould surface completely.

Trouble Shooting Guidelines

Defects	*Probable Causes*	*Suggested Remedy*
Poor release from mould	Lack of release agent. Improper release agent. Degradation, Improper design. Insufficient cooling.	Apply more release agent. Reduce temperature and/or heating time. Modify design Increase cooling time.
Warped moulding	Sagging of hot plastic, collapse due to vaccum formation excessive shrinkage.	Reduce oven temperature, mould Shorten cycle time. Select proper resin grade.
Discoloured moulding	Polymer degraded	Decrease oven temperature and/ or time
Bridging of powder in mould poor flow	Poor design. Improper rotation	Modify the mould design Select proper grade. Modify rotation ratio and/ or speed.
Pin holes, bubbles, rough inner surface	Maximum temperature attained by polymer too low.	Increase cycle time, oven temperature, use proper grade, Reduce wall thickness. Provide venting.

Contd....

Poor impact	Cooling too slow.	Check venting. Increase cooling rate.
Excessive flash	Poor parting line.	Remake parting line Check venting.
Long oven cycles	Oven temperature too low. Oven capacity insufficient Mouids shielded.	Increase oven temperature Increase air circulation. Avoid any shielding of mould. Use Proper grade.

MATERIALS USED IN ROTOMOULDING

Materials

Generally polyethylenes, PVC Nylons, polycarbonates can be Rotomoulded to form different variety of products.

Most common amongs them are polyethylenes which are widely used and account for over 90% of total Tonnage of plastics used in Rotomoulding. They can be subdivided into :

1. Low Density Polyethylene (LDPE) :
2. Linear Low Density Polyethylene (LLDPE)
3. Medium Density Polyethylene (MDPE)
4. High Density Polyethylene (HDPE)

Generally as the density increases from LDPE to HDPE the properties like :

1. Stiffness
2. Shrinkage
3. Chemical Resistance
4. Hardness increase while the properties like Impact strength and stress crack resistance decrease with density increase. The basic diff. between LDPE & HDPE is linearity of molecules, LDPE has branched structure, while HDPE has linear chains of molecules with short branched structure.

With the new development of LMDPE (Linear Medium density PE) which have medium density side branches, but linear than LDPE The mechanical properties go on increasing with Linearity. The L.M.D.P.E. has struck a balance between LDPE & HDPE having medium densities and high MFI This helps in achieving better processability as well as mechanical properties. While broad molecular weight distribution helps in improving ESCR.

Polyethylenes

S.No.	Resing	Advantages	Disadvantage
1)	LDPE	Flexibility warp resistance uniform shrinkage	Low shrinkage Low ESCR
2)	LMDPE	Excellent ESCR} good warp resistance sufficient mechanicals.	Low heat deflection temperature
3)	HDPE	Excellent stiffness, high heat deflection temperature.	Low ESCR inconsistant warpage shrinkage.

8

Post Extrusion Process

PAINTING

Painting plastics items to improve appearace or performance is an established part of plastics industry. Industrial coatings are now available with relatively high volumes solids levels to meet increasingly stringent EPA solvent emission standards.

Plural-component coatings combine low cure temperatures and lowsolvent contents, delivering both energy efficiency and low emission characteristics. Water-borne coatings formulated with low solvent content provide increased user safety. They are now available with curing temperature range & similar to solventbased coatings.

Powder coatings, although offering good emission characteristics and superior properties, are largely limited in application to those materials, such as phenolics, which can tolerate the higher cure temperatures required. Surface contaminants such as oil, grease, and release compounds must be removed before parts are coated. The cleaning process depends on the contaminants and plastic type.

Pretreatment

Plastics with low surface adhesion characteristics must be treated prior to coating Common treatment methods include flame oxidation, acid etching, and exposure to chemicals or UV light.

Electrostatic coating requires the surface of the plastic to be electrically conductive. Pretreatment solutions to increase conductivity can be sprayed on, or the part can be dipped. Spraying is preferred; dipping is more expensive, less efficient, and more sensitive to labor costs. The use of conductive compounds in the plastic formulation can eliminate the need for pretreatment.

Application methods

Dipping flow coating roller coating, curtain coating, and spraying are the more conventional application methods.

Conventional air spray painting is by far the most widespread coating method in use. It is fast, versatile, and properly controlled, can produce a finish of unmatchable quality. Equipment can range from a single air atomizing spray gun used to manually apply a coating to large multiple-gun systems or painting robots.

Some types of spray equipment can be relatively inefficient for certain tasks, such as coating very small or open parts like grilles, louvers, etc. Overspray results in considerable waste of coating materials and potential violations of proposed Environment standards. This is particularly true of conventional air-atomized spray equipment Airless spraying equipment is generally more efficient in this regard and is usually employed when the process requires high delivery rate.

The current economic and environmental concerns are causing a shift to electrostatic application and it is already the method of choice in such high-volume industries as automotive, office machinery, computer and athletic and recreation equipment. Applying the electrostatic principle greatly increase the coating transfer efficiency. Over-spray is reduced, resulting in lower material costs, fewer rejects, and easier compliance with Environment regulations.

The very high transfer efficiency of the electrostatic system derives from the fact that opposite charges attract. a.d.c. voltage of 60 or 120 kv. is applied to the atomizer with the part to be coated at ground. When the coating is atomized, it is charged, and the particles are drawn to the grounded part. The attraction of the coating particles to the part is so strong that it creates a wrap-around effect: the charged, atomized particles can turn corners to deposit on the sides and rear of the object being coated. Over-spray is subsequently reduced to a minimum.

The latest generation of electrostatic equipment uses a disk of bell-shaped metal atomizer rotating at very high speed to atomize the coating. The centrifugal force of a bell rotating at 10,000 to 60,000 r.p.m spins the coating outward in a cone-shaped pattern that can be as much as 48 in. wide. Atomization is much finer than either air or airless processes, and transfer efficiency is even higher than conventional air atomizing electrostatic equipment. Fluid delivery rates can be very high resulting in increased production capability.

Automated finishing

High production rates and consistent quality are difficult to achieve using purely manual coating methods. Even plants producing relatively small quantities of identical or similar parts can be at least partially automated and the payback on a properly designed system can be fast.

In the past, automated finishing has consisted primarily of transverse and reciprocating rype machines equipped either with conventional of electrostatic spray equipment. Many finishing lines have never been fully automated as manual reintorcement has been required in recess areas. This is typically true of the plastics industry, as today's molding processes produce not only parts, but whole units, with a wide variety of shapes and sizes and many recess areas.

The answer to today's plastic finishing needs is robotics. Robots (of the painting variety) have been in existence in the U.S. for approximately ten years and in the last several years have gained considerable popularity. The robots can be equipped either with conventional of electrostatic spray equipment, with the latter capable of being used as both. This capability is important because the electrostatic charge can be controlled by the robot, alternately charging and uncharging the paint, so that high transfer efficiency can be achieved on large sufcace areas while recess areas can be coated duting the same sequence.

Robots are being used in the plastics industry to coat such items as shutters, computer components, bumper fascias, etc. Applications such as texture coating of computer terminals also have seen a recent surge of interest. The advantage of using a robot for these types of applications is quality and repeatability along with high transfer efficiency.

PRINTING

In the plastics industry, various printing methods are used for applying functional information and/or decorations to products. For lay-flat film products such as bags, packaging materials, wrapping papers, etc., gravure and flexographic printing presses are most commonly used. For three-dimensional objects. Silk screening and jet printing are used or traditional printing is first done on labels, decals, or hear-transfer webs and then applied to the product.

Most of the processes for printing on paper also apply to printing methods for plastics are flexography and gravure Other methods like screen printing, jet printing or modifications of gravure also are used but account for a small market share.

Letterpress is by far the oldest method of printing flat plastic substrates. However, its use is rapidly giving way to such process as gravure and flexography which contribute higher quality reproduction and faster line speeds.

Gravure (also called rotogravure) transfers ink from cells etched or engraved on a copper and chrome-plated cylinder to the material being printed. The cylinder rotates in an ink fountain and the cells pick up the liquid ink. A doctor blade then wipes excess ink from the roller, leaving ink only in the cells.

As the plastic substrate moves between the cylinder and the impression roll, ink is transferred from the cells onto the substrate in the form of the etching of image. The number and volume of the cell controls the amount of ink applied to the plastic substrate.

For colours which appear to be solid to the eye, cells of a uniform size are used various shades are created by cotrolling the size and volume of the cells. The gravure process is capable of reproducing fine tone and process-colour graphics.

The low viscosity liquid inks used in the process contain volatile solvents for rapid drying. A series of printing units with driers in tandem are used to apply a layer of color and dry it before the next color is applied.

Gravure is used when designs require good continuity of sharp pattern details and rich color effects. It is a high-speed process often used for printing quality packaging films, plastic-based wall coverings and other products run in high volumes. However it can be expensive for shorter runs because of the high cost of the gravure cylinders.

Flexography is a widely used method for printing short to medium runs but also adaptable to long runs. Flexography prints by transforming images from a flexible raised printing plate directly to the material.

A uniform film of ink is applied to the raised portion of the printing plate by bringing it in contact with the anilox cylinder (form roller) The plate continues to rotate until it contacts the substrate and transfers the image to the plastic substrate. Individual colors applied by a series of separate decks (printing stations)

Fast-drying liquid inks and general reliability of this method make it a prime choice for printing on packaging films cartons labels, and plastic-based wall coverings.

Improvements in photopolymer printing plates and inks along with the upgrading of the press themselves have given flexography high-quality capabilities. Although not yet able to match the color effects possible with gravures, flexographic presses are narrowing the gap.

Printing press manufacturers in recent years have combined gravure and flexography systems in single presses. These hybrids can create patterns and images that blend the best of gravure and flexography in a single run. Quick automatic changes can be made on some models from one process to the other to give better production flexibility.

The combination presses also avoid the difficulties that can be encountered in transferring partially printed rolls of film from one press to another.

Screen Printing was originally known as silk screen printing, but in recent years other supporting materials for the stencil image have replaced silk. Most commercial screen printing is now accomplished with stainless steel mesh with openings much finer than those possible with silk or other textiles, and stencils are now made by photographic processes.

In screen printing ink is forced through the stencil screen onto the plastic surface by a squeegee made of a flexible material such vinyl. Printing from flat bed or rotary systems makes is possible to decorate large or complex parts. However despite the richness of color attained as a result of the thick film of ink that is applied only one color can be applied per pass through the system. Another factor is that image sharpness is of lower quality than with other processes.

The major uses for screen printing have been for short-run applications on molded products with complex contours on flat substrates, or in order or achieve special color effects.

Jet printing needs no printing plates; ink in droplet form in impinged onto the substrate at high speeds. The electrically charged ink droplets pass from a series of nozzles through an area that is flanked with plates of the opposite charge. The intensity of charge on the ink determines its deflection which controls the nature of the character printed. Electronic circuitry provides the information from which the image is formed.

Pad transfer printing is a gravure-like process offering versatility for printing on a variety of shapes and surfaces. Unlike gravure, the image is not transferred to an etched plate directly to a substrate but to a special silicone pad instead. The pad is very soft and flexible and conforms itself to almost any shape to be printed. The transfer properties of the pad are such that all of the ink is released to the surface to be printed, and the pad is clean and ready for the next printing cycle. Multiple colors are applied one at a time, drying is not usually required.

Besides high speed, this new method offers extremely accurate control to images. The equipment is highly specialized but promises much for the future.

Web printing In web printing which is the largest volume process, the choice between gravure and flexography may be decided by specific features of the printing equipment. For example the choice may be one of having printing done on presses in stacked, in-line of common impression arrangement.

Each of these designs has features that affect printing capability. The stacked arrangement has printing decks arranged one on top of the other with space between it is less flexible than in-line systems that allow quick changes from flexography to gravure back again. The in-line presses have printing decks arranged in a horizontal sequence that gives better access to modular printing sections. Common impression systems have printing decks arranged around a large single cylinder that supports the web and is expecially suited for thin plastics.

Selection factors

The primary considerations for the converter or product manufacturer are the substrate (material) quantity or volume. Graphics product form and cost. Plastics normally require a pretreatment for ink adhesion and special inks are used. Some plastics are sensitive to drying temperatures, so there may be restriction on which inks may be a applied.

The number of parts or web footage will have a direct effect. On the method of printing and the printing press chosen. It is sometimes necessary for economic reasons to switch from one process to another as volume increase. Thus screen printing may be practical at first, but with increasing volume flexography, or even gravure may show an advantage.

The cost of a particular graphic treatement depends on a variety of factors including the color effects desired, volume of the run, and size of the surface to be printed. Halftones will only be possible with cerain methods, and methods that do not yield sharp register of the tiny dot patterns will detract from the overall effect.

Flexographic printing quality is improving in its ability to reproduce halftones, or often it can be teamed up with gravure providing the sharp background colors, with gravure providing the sharp pattern detail screen printing, especially where low volumes are involved can impart heavy opaque color over solid colors to produce rich, bright effects.

Printing of molded shapes requires radically different equipment than printing on web stock. Screen printing normally is applied to injection molded and bloe molded shapes; gravure and flexography are the choices for web stock, however, there are also rotary screen techniques for web printing.

Quality may be the prime factor along with volume, lead time, and special production costs related to the printing method employed. It is sometimes possible to bring cost in line with market requirements by compromising high graphic standards to achieve a lower-cost final product. For example flexography sometimes is a more attractive method than the higher quality gravure system because of the lower costs, especially in low- to medium volume runs.

POST MOULDING PROCESSES

Hot Stamping

In hot stamping, decoration from a hot brass die is generally transferred to the package surface by heat and pressure through a coated hot-stamp foil made of 12 to 25 micron thick polyester film. Hot stamping is a dry process and no wet ink or prestreatment is required. The most commonly used colour is gold for attractive appearance, such as for lipstick and cosmetic containers.

In-mould Decoration

The system utilizes a paper or a reverse printed plastics film lable with a heat activated coating on the reverse side. The label is placed in the mould and the plasticized material on the parison, in case of blow moulding, is introduced into the mould cavity. The label is held in position by vacuum suction. The label thus gets attached to the moulded surface.

Ultrasonic welding

The sealing of two plastic parts or metal inserts to plastic parts by the application of vibratory mechanical pressure at ultrasonic frequencies.

Electroplating

The disposition of metal on the plastic for finish purposes.

9

Vacuum Metallizing

Vacuum metallizing is the application of a metal onto a substrate in a vacuum. Traditionally, this has meant the large-scale decorative application of thermally evaporated aluminum onto a plastic substrate. The pastic is usually, but not always, ABS and the metallized layer is supported by two organic coating layers-a basecoat and a topcoat. The primary function of the basecoat is to produce a smooth surface on molded plastic parts so that the metallizing layer will have a maximum luster. The basecoat, constituting a clean new surface, maximizes the adhesion of the metal to the plastic workpiece. The primary function of the topcoat is to protect the metal layer from physical of chemical deterioration.

Equipment and processing for batch systems.

For decorative metallizing three pieces of equipment are required : (1) a vacuum metallizing system, (2) a coatings application system and (3) a drying system.

The vacuum metallizing system most used in large-capacity industrial applications cylindrical in shape, horizontally positioned and operated in the batch mode. Commercially available vacuum chambers range in size from small laboratory models (e.g, 24 in. diameter by 24 in. long) to very large (84 in. diameter by 110 in. long) production models. Large horizontal chambers are also used for semicontinuous operation. The chamber is pumped down to firing pressure by a series of vacuum pumps. The firing pressure for aluminium usually is 0.5 micron or 5 x10 Torr.

Batch metallizing is usually limited to the use of a bank of tungsten filaments that are sourced with aluminum "stables" or "canes" The actual time of firing is approximately 15 to 30 sec., after which the chamber is repressurized and the metallized product removed. The door- to door cycle time of batch metallizing is on the order of 12 to 15 min.

The coating applications system can be as simple as a hand sprayer with spray booth to an elaborate automated flow coater. Although dipping, spraying, and flow coating are all viable coating techniques the majority of installations use the flow coater. A flow coater has an array of nozzles that eject a continuous stream of coating onto a rotating reel. The reel continuously rotates after the spray period thereby flowing the resulting material in an even distibution about the fixtured workpieces. The same flow coater may be used for both basecoats and topcoats in many applications.

The third system is the drying installation. Typically the coatings are dried in a bank of convection ovens at approximately 150° F However because of the continuing increase in energy costs many firms ave gone to IR or UV drying. The present market trend is to UV drying where applicable because the associated coatings are 100% solids. The utilization of these types of coatings not only elimimates the solvent emission problem but also reduces the drying time from the order of 1 hr. to approximately 1 min. Throughput is then only limited by the evaporation cycle.

Applications

Decorative metriallizing adds beauty to components of the automotive, appliance toy and packaging industries. Increasingly, the trend is from decorative to functional use. Some of the latest developments have been in the following areas.

Electronics : Evaporated conductive and barrier metal layers are being applied in computer and microwave circuit technology/

EMI : An electronics market has developed because of FCC regulations for shielding plastic computer and radio housings The two major evaporated materials that have been used thus far have been aluminum and copper.

Video disks : Aluminum is being metallized on plastic recording disks for both the video and audio markets.

Solar technology : Metal layers are being applied in the manufacture of large-area solar cells.

Semicontinuous processing

The two major characteristics that differentiate semicontinuous metallizing from batch processing are : 1) the length of processing and 2)the form of the substrate The semicontinuous process time is normally between 1/2 and 2 hr. and the substrate is usually a roll of plastic film. Present equipment is capable of coating roll widths from 40 to 84 in. Roll width and length are determined primarily by economic considerations. The dominant coating metal is aluminum The vacuum level and metal thickness are on the order of 0.5 micron and 2 micro in, respectively Because the vacuum level is the same as in batch metallizing, both technologies require similar types of vacuum pumping equipment. From atmospheric to about 100 microns pressure a mechanical booster is used. After this rough pumping cycle is concluded, the pumping manifold is switched to the fine pumping assembly that includes a diffusion pump together with its associated hold pump.

The semicontinuous process (Fig1) has the following structures that differentiate It from the more common batch process.

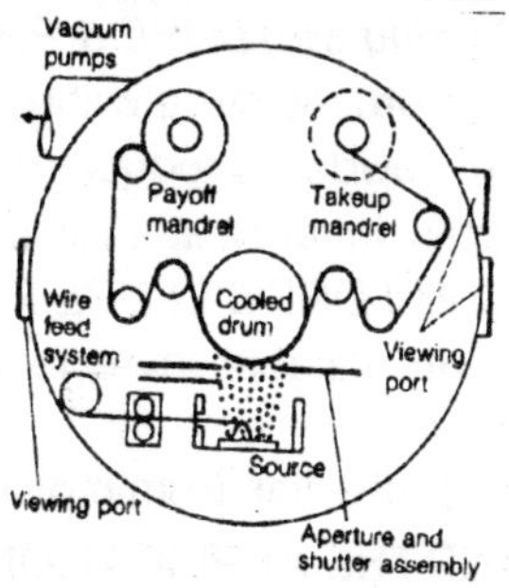

Fig. 1 : Semicontinuous metallizing arrangement.

1. Feed/takeup reel assembly for the film substrate.
2. Sooled plating drum, required because of the radiant hear produced by the source holder during the extended plating time.
3. Wire feed assembly for continuous source replenishment.
4. Source holder configuration and material type Normal configuration is a shallow boat made of boron nitride alone or with titanium diboride.
5. Shutter assembly for exact startup and termination of deposition, as well as a film shield while roll is not in motion.

Semicontinuous operating cycle

A typical metallizing cycle includes the following steps :

1. Load substrate roll onto feed shaft and interlace about feed, coating and takeup rolls. Test-wind a small section.
2. Clean and load evaporation feed assembly.
3. Evacuate chamber and heat source holders to temperature.
4. Start feed roll and remove shutter to begin evaporation.
5. Close shutter and decelerate feed roll to terminate evaporation.
6. Coll sources, vent chamber, and remove coated roll.

Applications

Metallized plastic and paper film products are used in a wide variety of industries for decorative and functional applications. The majority of uses for semicontinuous. The majority of uses for semicontinuous products are functional, with the packaging industry being the major end user Many types of food products (particularly processed foods) are packaged in metallized films. Other functional uses include capacitors reflective insulation. Tobacco products, and solar control products. Some of the typical decorative products. Being metallized include wrapping papers and commercial and residential laminations for housewares.

Purpose of Extrusion Coating with LDPE & PP :

1. T0 provide protection from moisture water and dust.
2. To prevent leakage of powdery products from woven sacks.
3. To provide woven sacks, inner heat-sealable layer.

Purpose of Lamination with LDPE & LLDPE Films :

1. To provide inner heat-sealable layer to substrates which are otherwise not sealable
2. To provide additional protection from moisture, water and dust.

IMPORTANT LAMINATES AND THE APPLICATIONS

STRUCTURE	**END-USE APPLICATIONS**
(I) *EXTRUSION COATING :*	
* HDPE Woven Fabric/LDPE	Packing of fertilisers, pharmaceutical & Chemicals.
* HDPE Wovenfabric/LDPE kraft paper	Packing of polymers, pharmaceuticals etc.
* While Poster Paper/LDPE HDPE Woven	Packing of white cement.
* Jute fabric/LDPE	Packing of foodgrains.
* Glassing Paper/LDPE	Pharmaceutical tablets packing.
* Poster Paper/LDPE	Packing of detergent cakes and powder.
* Paper/LDPE/Al. Foil/LDPE	Packing of Biscuits, Confectionary,Coffee, Electral, Powder etc.
(II) *HEAT-PRESSURE LAMINATION :*	
* Aluminium Foil/LDPE	Packing of pharmaceutical tablets and capsules.
(III) *ADHESIVE LAMINATION :-*	
* Polyester (pet)/Adhesive/LDPE and PET/Adh./LLDPE	Packing of Biscuits, Tea, Spices Powders, Instant food powder, Potato chips,
PET/Adh./LDPE/LLDPE	Pan masala, Hybrid seeds,
PET/Adh./LDPE/HDPE	Shampoo, Lubricating oil etc.
* BOPP /Adhesive/LDPE/ Al Foil/LDPE and PET/Adhesive/LDPE	Packing of Coffee, confectionary, Shampoo, etc.

Al Foil/LDPE

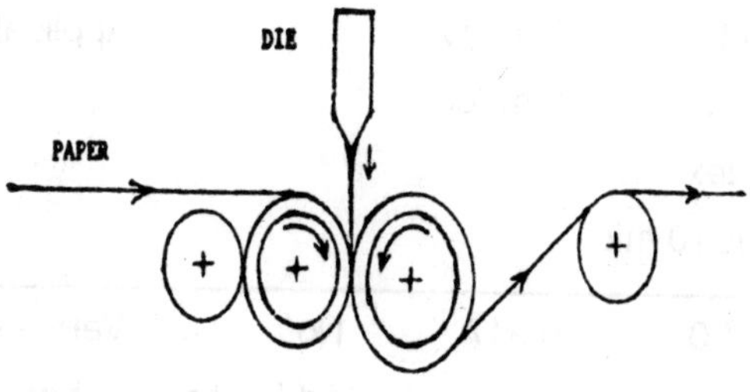

SANDWICH EXTRUSION COATING PROCESS

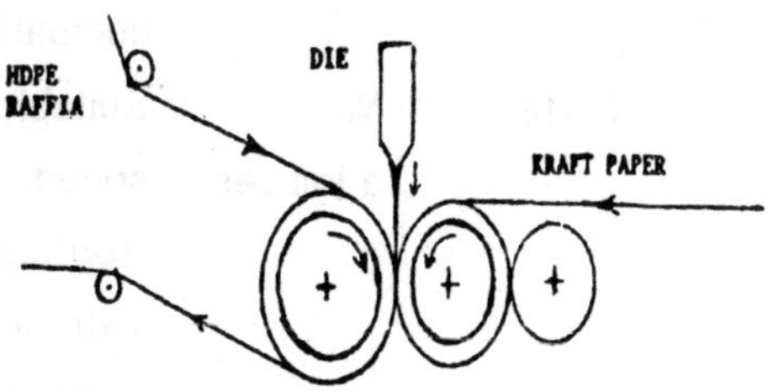

HEAT PRESSURE LAMINATION PROCESS

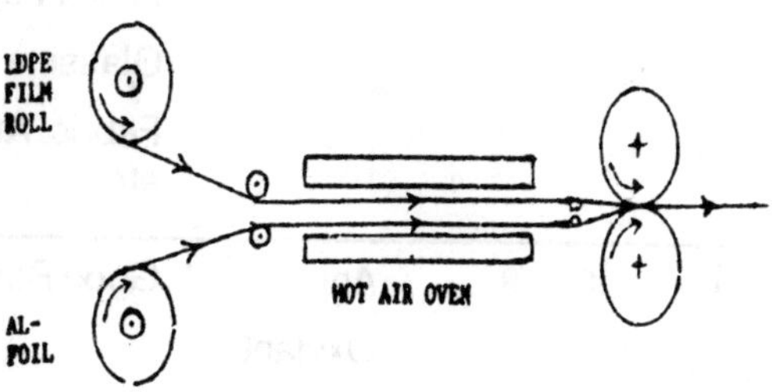

ADHESIVE LAMINATION PROCESS

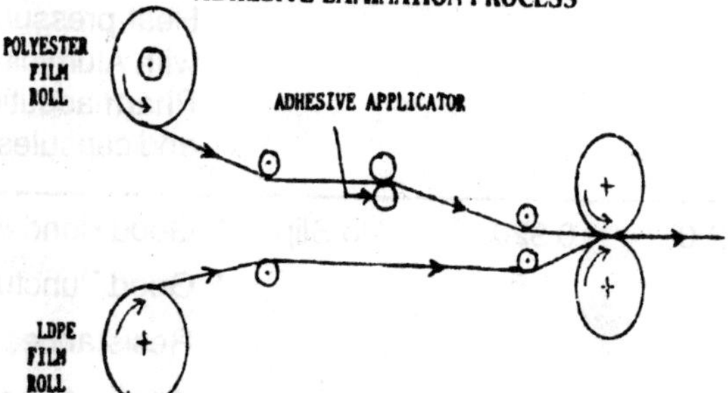

SIMPLE EXTRUSION COATING PROCESS

Polymer and Grade	Average Melt Flow Index gm/10 min	Average Density Gm /cc	Additives	Characteristics and Applications
LDPE INDOTHENE 1070LA17 and	7.0	0.917	No additives	* Very good bond strength adhesion to substrates. * Low Neck-in & fluctuations of Neck-in.
INDOTHENE 2OFA060	7.0	0.918	No additives	* Suitable for high line speeds. *Applications :* Extrusion coating on various substrates such as HDPE Woven Fabric, Poster Paper, Kraft paper, Glassine Papers, Jute Fabric, Aluminium Foil, etc.
LDPE INDOTHENE 18LA060	7.0	0.918	Anti-Oxidant	* Good Bond Strength. *Applications :* Heat-pressure lamination with Aluminium Foil for Pharmaceutical tablets and capsules packaging.
LDPE INDOTHENE 1020FA 20 and	2.0	0.920	No Slip	* Good Bond Strength. * Good Puncture Resistance. *Applications :*

FNS 2000	2.0	0.920	No Slip	Adhesive Lamination with Polyester films.
LLDPE	1.0	0.920	No Slip	* Good Bond Strength.
INDOTHENE-LL				* Good Puncture Resistance
LL20FA010 and				* Very good heat sealability
LL20FA020	2.0	0.920	NO Slip	*
				Applications:
				Adhesive Lamination with polyester film.

TESTING & IDENTIFICATION

TESTING OF FILMS

A part from resin properties, operating variables involved during the manufacturing process highly influence the film properties. In making comparison between film resins, respective processing conditions will frequently differ making direct comparison difficult. Evaluation of film resins should therefore be conducted over a range of processing conditions and film thicknesses, simulating actual commercial conditions to get meaningful results.

Important properties to be evaluated for films are :-

* Impact strength
* Tensile properties
* Tear strength
* Coefficient of friction
* Hot tack strength
* Heat seal strength
* Haze

Impact Strength (ASTM D 1709)

Impact strength of film is determined by measuring the loss in kinetic energy of a free falling dart as is penetrates film specimen. Impact strength of film is not a simple function of thickness and therefore results should not be normalized for comparison purposes.

Tensile Strength and Elongation (ASTM D 882)

Tensile strength and elongation of film are measured using a tensile testing machine. Film samples must be tested in the machine direction and in the cross direction. Tensile properties give indication of mechanical strength of the film.

Tear Propagation Resistance (ASTM D 1922)

Tear Propagation resistance is one indicator of the toughness of film. It is measured using a calibrated pendulum apparatus commonly known as the Elmendorf tear tester. Polyethylene film is anisotropic due to the orientation effect introduced in it during manufacture. Tear resistance will therefore vary, depending upon whether it is measured in the direction of maximum orientation, or across it. The ratio of tear resistance in two directions is a measure of "balance " in mechanical strength of the film. Tear resistance is not a simple function of film thickness and therefore values obtained from specimens of different thicknesses cannot be normalized for comparison purposes.

Hot Tack Strength

"Hot tack strength " is an excellent measure of ability of a film to form a strong heat seal and to withstand mechanical stress which might be applied to the still molten seal during packaging operations. Hot tack strength is measured by applying a predetermined stress to a sealed specimen immediately after the sealing operation. The test procedure is started at a relatively low stress level and repeated at higher levels until the level of separation of the seal is greater than I mm. Hot tack strength is usually determined at various sealing temperatures and the results described in graphical form.

Heat Seal Strength

A test specimen of film is heat sealed under standard sealing conditions, and the force required to peel the cold seal apart is measured on a tensile testing machine

Haze (ASTM D 1003)

It is the scattering of light within or at the surface of a nearly clear specimen responsible for cloudy appearance seen by transmission. In other words, haze is the ratio between diffuse light transmittance and total light transmittance. 0% haze indicates a perfectly clear transparent material and 100% haze indicates an opaque material. The equipment is calibrated in transition mode using a standard white tile and black card. Then the sample whose haze is to be measured is placed in the transmission mode and the value is displayed on the screen.

Gloss (ASTM D 523)

Gloss is the amount of light reflected at the specular angle, the angle equal and opposite to the angle of light hitting the sample. For most gloss measurements, light is directed on to a sample at 60° from the perpendicular The percent of light that is reflected at the specular angle (60°) is reported as the gloss 60° is the most commonly used gloss angle. However angle of 85° is used for low gloss samples and 20° is used for high gloss samples.

PRODUCT SPECIFICATIONS

Requirements for the packaging film used in certain specific applications are :-

* **Liquid Milk Packaging**
  - Superior hot tack/heat seal strength
  - Ability to seal through contamination
  - Good mechanical strength
  - Low co-efficient of friction
  - Superior pin hole resistance
  - Barrier to oxygen
* **Edible oil /Vanaspati**

  Apart from all the above properties, additional requirements are :
  - Odour & flavour retention
  - Barrier to moisture & oxygen
* **Polyethylene Bags**

  Polyethylene Bags (LDPE, LLDPE, HDPE,& HMHDPE) Bags are widely used for packing of food products, grocery items, industrial products, textile products, nursery plants, etc.

BIS Specifications

Every product has to conform itself to certain terms and conditions in order to align itself with the latest technology, test methods and trade practices. Certain specifications have been formulated by Bureau of Indian standards (BIS) for various applications.

PE Pouches for Packaging Liquid Milk (IS 11805-1989)

Material	:	LDPE, LLDPE. Food grade
Film Structure	:	monolayer or co-extruded, from any of the blend of LDPE & L LDPE.
Thickness (micron)	:	Tolerance on specified thickness $\pm$ 7.5% 75 Mic. for 1 litre pouches 60 Mic. for 1/2 litre pouches
Width	:	+ 2, - O mm of the specified value
Tensile Strength (kgf/cm²)	:	Lengthwise $\geq$ 160 Crosswise $\geq$ 140
Elongation At Break (%)	:	Lengthwise Crosswise < 75 μ : 200 400 $\geq$75 μ : 300 500
Dart Impact Strength (F_{50}, gf)	:	60 μ : 150
(66 cm height)	:	75 μ : 185
Coefficient of friction (kinetic)	:	$\leq$ 0.25
Leak Test	:	Pouches kept flat with side seal on top and loaded for 10 minutes will not show leakage. 1/2 lt pouch : 2.5 kgf load 1 lt pouch : 5.0 kgf load
Drop Test	:	16 pouches dropped from 1.2 mtrs height in different orders will not show more than 4 failures.

Flexible Packaging Materials For Packing Refined Edible Oils
(IS 12724 : 1989)

Material	:	Food grade flexible packaging material
Thickness	:	Tolerance on thickness ± 10% of specified value
Vibration Test	:	Filled pouches (total nos. to carry 10 Lt. oil) are subjected to vibration test for 30 minutes. Minimum failure not more than one pouch.
Storage Test	:	Samples after vibration test are checked for any form of leakage, delamination or oil rancidity, during storage for 30 and 90 days.
Stack Load Test	:	Four filled pouches are subjected to uniformly distributed stack load for 72 hours under ambient conditions. Pouches leaded according to their capacities should not show any leakages at the seams or bursting of the pouch.
Drop Test	:	Five filled pouches are dropped vertically twice, at ambient conditions from the height of 1.2 mtr. Not more than one pouch should fail.
Dart Impact Resistance	:	Impact failure load obtained from height of 152.4 cm, should be ≥ 2N (200 gf)
Tensile Strength Elongation Water Vapour Transmission Rate (WVTR) & Oxygen Transmission Rate (OTR)	:	Values obtained by these tests are used as controlling specifications for acceptance tests.
Overall Migration	:	Max extractables ≤ 10 mg/dm^2 and ≤ 50 ppm

Flexible Packaging Material For Packing of Vanaspati

(Upto 5 kg packs- Is 11352 : 1994)

& (For 10 & 15 kg packs -Is 14129 :1994)

Material	:	Food grade flexible packaging material
Thickness	:	Tolerance in thickness ± 10% of specified value
Vibration Tests	:	16 Nos. filled pouches subjected to vibration test for 30 minutes. Not more than one pouch should show leakage (4 samples for 10 & 15 kg packs)
Storage Test	:	Samples undergoing storage test should not show any form of leakage, delamination oil rancidity, increase in values of moisture content, free fatty acid and peroxide.
Overall Migration	:	Max. extractables ≤ 10mg/dm² and ≤ 60 ppm
Stack Load Test	:	Four packs subjected to uniformly distributed load (depending on capacity) shall not show any leakage or bursting for 24 hrs.
Drop Test	:	Five filled pouches are dropped vertically twice, at ambient temperature from the height (depending on capacity) will not show failure of more than 1 No .

Pack Capacity	Drop Height
< 1 kg	1.2 m
1 kg, 2 kg, 5 kg	0.75 m
10 kg & 15 kg	0.50 m

WVTR, OTR Tensile Strength & Elongation	:	Values obtained by these tests are used as controlling specifications for acceptance tests

Indian Standards (IS : 2508) For Polyethylene bags

For reference of our members we are here with giving the Tolerances for various specification of Polythene bags.

		Tolerance
1) Thickness :-	a) Upto & including 40 microns	± 25 %
	b) Above 40 microns	± 20%

2) Width :-	a) Upto 500 mm		± 5 mm
	b) Between 500 & 1250 mm		± 8 mm
	c) Between 1250 & 2500 mm		± 20 mm
3) Yield :-	a) Lots of 250 kg		± 10%
	b) Lots between 250 kg &1250 kg		± 5%
	c) Lots over 1250 kg		± 3%

4) Dimension :- Bag dimension shall be exclusive of seals if not mentioned

5) Recommended film thickness for polyethylene bags.

Net mess to	Suggested film thickness in micron		
be packed (gm)	HM HDPE	LDPE(HV.Duty)	LDPE(G.P.)
Upto			
100	15	25	25
200	25	25	40
500	30	30	50
1000	45	45	60
2000	60	60	100
5000	90	90	150

INDIAN STANDARDS ON PLASTIC MATERIAL TESTING METHODS AND PRODUCT

MATERIALS :

1.	PE Material	IS : 2530
2.	HDPE Material	IS : 7328
3.	LDPE Material	IS : 3395
4.	PP Material	IS : 10951
5.	PS Material	IS : 2267
6.	Nylon 6 Material	IS : 13463
7.	Nylon 66 Material	IS : 13464

8.	Celulose Acetate	IS : 2543,IS: 7166,IS:7188
9.	PVC Resin	IS : 4669,IS:12235
10.	PVC Compound	IS : 9766
11.	PET & PBT Material	IS : 13193
12.	PF Material	IS : 1300, IS:867
13.	UF Material	IS : 3389, IS:2221
14.	MF Material	IS : 3669, IS:2221
15.	Polyester Resin for FRP	IS : 6746
16.	Glass Fibre for FRP Products	IS : 11551,IS :11320,IS :11273
17.	Thermosetting Material	IS : 2213
18.	SMC Material	IS : 13410.IS:1998
19.	DMC Material	IS : 13411,IS:1998
20.	Terms used in Plastics Industry	IS : 2828
21.	Terms used in Plastics packaging	IS : 7019

TESTING METHODS

1.	Methods of Testing	IS : 13360(P1 to 11)
		IS : 8543(P1 to 13)
2.	Migration Test	IS : 9845

TESTING METHODS

1.	HDPE Pipes	IS : 4984
2.	PVC Pipes	IS : 4985
3.	LDPE Pipes	IS : 3076
4.	PE Drip Laterals	IS : 12786
5.	Emitters for Irrigation	IS : 13487
6.	PVC Conduits	IS : 9537 (Part1to111)
7.	PVC Bore/Tube Well Pipes	IS : 12818
8.	PVC Suction and Delivery line Pipes	IS : 12231
9.	PVC Moulded Pipe Fittings	IS : 7834 (Part1toVIII)
10.	PVC Fabricated Pipe Fittings	IS : 10124 (Part I to XIII)

11.	HDPE Moulded Pipe Fittings	IS : 8008 (Part I toVII)
12.	HDPE Fabricated Pipe Fittings	IS : 8360 (Part I toIII)
13.	HDPE Film	!S :10889
14.	LDPE Film	IS : 2508
15.	PE Bags	IS : 9738
16.	PE Milk Pouches	IS : 11805
17.	Edible Oil Pouches	IS : 12724,IS: 11352
18.	PE Film for Water Proofings of Roofs	IS : 7290
19.	Polyester Film for Capacitors	IS : 5361
20.	HDPE Woven Sacks	IS : 6340,IS:8069,IS:9755
21.	HDPE Woven Tarpaulins	IS : 7903
22.	HDPE Woven Fabric	IS : 6899
23.	PE Monofilament for Fishing Net	IS : 6347
24.	Nylon Monofilaments	IS : 1847
25.	Nylon Cord, Tapes & Threads for Aeronautical	IS : 4227,4228,IS:4229
26.	PE Ropes	IS : 8674
27.	PE Cane	IS : 5378
28.	PVC Asbestos Floor Tiles	IS : 3461
29.	PVC Flexible Flooring	IS : 3462
30.	PS Wall Tiles	IS : 3463, IS:4112
31.	Plastic Flooring and Wall Tiles	IS : 3464
32.	HDPE Milk Crates for Satchets	IS :11584
33.	HDPE Milk Crates for Glass Bottles	IS : 9907
34.	PP Milk Grates for Satchets	IS :13289
35.	HDPE Buckets	IS : 3730
36.	HDPE blow moulding containers	IS : 7408 (General) IS :10840 (Vanaspathi) IS : 6312 (Transport) IS : 9754,IS:12512 (Pesticides)

37.	HDPE Jerry Cans	IS : 7394 (Petroleum)
		IS : 7959 (Foam Compounds)
		IS : 7803 (Pharmaceutical)
38.	ESCR Test for PE Blow Moulded Containers	IS : 8747
39.	Compability Test for plastic Containers:	IS : 7551
40.	PE Potable Water Bottle	IS : 8688
41.	PE Water Tanks	IS : 12701
42.	Plastic Containers for Auto Batteries	IS : 1146
43.	HIPS Sheet	IS : 5210
44.	PVC Rigid Sheet	IS : 6307
45.	PVC Flexible Sheet	IS : 2076
46.	Laminates	IS : 1998
		IS : 2036 (Phenolic)
		IS : 2046 (Decorative)
47.	GRP Squatting pan	IS:11246
48.	Plastic Water Closet seats and Covers	IS : 2548(P I & 2)
49.	PVC Water Stopper	IS :12200
50.	PVC Rainwear	IS : 4761
51.	PVC Insulation and sheath of Electric Cables	IS : 5831, IS : 694
		IS :1554,IS:3961 (PII& V)
52.	XLPE insulated PVC cables	IS : 7098
53.	PE Insulation and Sheath of Electric Cables	IS : 6474,IS:1596
		IS : 3961(P IV)
54.	Adhesive Insulating Tapes	IS : 2448
55.	PVC Tapes	IS : 7809
56.	Pressure sensitive Adhesive PVC Tapes	IS : 3676
57.	PVC Sandal	IS : 6721

58.	Solid PVC Soles and Heals	IS : 6719
59.	PVC Boots	IS : 12254
60.	PVC Ventilation Tubing	IS : 3768
61.	EPS Foam	IS : 4671
62.	PUR Flexible Foam	IS : 7888
		IS : 7933(Mattresses)
		IS : 8255(Vehicle)
63.	PUR Rigid Foam	IS : 12436, IS:11239(P1 to14)
64.	Polyester Film	IS : 5361
65.	Actylic Sheet	IS : 7569
66.	Melamine Table Wares	IS : 9220
67.	Plastics for Food Packaging	IS : 10171
68.	HDPE Wash-Bowls	IS : 5322
69.	Laminated Collapsible Tubes	IS : 12007
70.	PE Air Bubble Film	IS : 12787
71.	PVC Bottle for Edible Oils	IS : 12883
72.	PET Bottle for Edible Oils	IS : 12887
73.	PET Bottle For Liquid Pesticides	IS : 13123

INDIAN STANDARDS FOR FOOD CONTACT PLASTICS

1.	Polyethylene for its safe use in contact with foodstuffs, pharmaceuticals and drinking water	IS :10146-1982
2.	Positive list of constituents of polyethylene in contact with foodstuffs, (with Amendment No.1)	IS :10141-1982
3.	Polypropylene and its copolymers for its safe use in contact with foodstuffs, pharmaceuricals and drinking water	IS :10910-1984
4.	Positive list of consituents of polypropylene and its copolymers in contact with foodstuffs, pharmaceuticals and drinking water	IS :10909-1984

5.	Polyvinyl chloride (PVC) and its copolymers for its safe use in contact with foodstuffs, pharmaceuticals and drinking water	IS :10151-1982
6.	Positive list of constituents of polyvinyl chloride (PVC) and its copolymers in contact with foodstuffs, pharmaceuricals and drinking water	IS :10148-1982
7.	Styrene polymers for its safe use in contact with foodstuffs, pharmaceuricals and drinking water	IS :10142-1982
8.	Positive list of constituents of stryrene polymers in contact with foodstuffs, pharmaceuticals and drinking water	IS :10149-1982
9.	Methods of analysis for the determination of specific and/or overall migration of constituents of plastic materials and articles intended to come into contact with foodstuffs	IS : 9845-1986
10.	List of pigments and colourants for use in plastics in contact with foodstuffs, pharmaceuticals and drinking water (with Amendment No.1)	IS : 9833-1981
11.	Specification for ionomer resins for its safe use in contact with foodstuffs, pharmaceuticals and drinking water	IS :11424-1985
12.	Positive list of constituents of ionomer resins for its use in contact with foodstuffs, pharmaceuticals and drinking water	IS :11435-1985
13.	Specification for ethylene/acrylic acid (EAA) copolymers for its safe use in contact with foodstuffs pharmaceuticals and drinking water.	IS :11704-1986

ASTM TEST METHODS FOR PLASTICS

(ASTM-American Society for Testing and Materials)

1.	Density and specific gravity	ASTM D 792
2.	Bulk (apparent) density for powder	ASTM D 1895
3.	Density gradient column for film	ASTM D 1505
4.	Volatile matter	ASTM D 3030
5.	Melting point	ASTM D 2117
6.	Compression test	ASTM D 395
7.	Chemical resistance	ASTM D 543
8.	Water absorption	ASTM D 570
9.	Carbon black content	ASTM D 1603
10.	Dimensional Stability	ASTM D 1204,D 1042
11.	Acetone Extraction	ASTM D 2587
12.	Heat aging	ASTM D 794,D1870,D 3045
13.	Sieve analysis	ASTM D 1705
14.	Moisture vapour transmission rate	ASTM E 96
15.	Mould Shrinkage	ASTM D 955
16.	Film shrinkage	ASTM D 2732, D 2838
17.	Artificial weathering xenon lamp based	ASTM G 26
18.	Out door weathering	ASTM D 1435
19.	Specimen preparation - Injection moulding (Thermoplastics)	ASTM D1897
20.	Specimen preparation - Injection moulding(thermoplastics)	ASTM D 3419
21.	Specimen preparation - Compression moulding (thermoplastic)	ASTM D 1929
22.	Specimen preparation - Compression moulding (thermosets)	ASTM D 790,D 956
23.	Tensile strength	ASTM D 638

24. Flexural strength	ASTM D 790
25. Compression Strength	ASTM D 695
26. Shear strength	ASTM D 732
27. Impact strength (Izod& charpy)	ASTM D 256
28. Rockwell hardness	ASTM D 785
29. Barcol hardness	ASTM D 2583
30. Shore Hardness (A&D)	ASTM D 2240
31. Abrasion resistance	ASTM D 1044
32. Stiffness test	ASTM D 747
33. Load deformation test	ASTM D 621
34. Dynamic fatigue test	ASTM D 671
35. Creep test	ASTM D 2990
36. Dart impact strength	ASTM D 1709,D 3029
37. Dart impact-instrumented method	ASTM D 4272
38. Blocking of film	ASTM D 1893
39. Co-efficient of friction	ASTM D 1894
40. Gas permeability	ASTM D 1434
41. Folding endurance	ASTM D 2176
42. Tear resistance	ASTM D 1004
43. Tear resistance (Elmendorf type)	ASTM D 1922
44. Tear resistance (Transfer tear type)	ASTM D 1938
45. Cup flow test	ASTM D 731
46. Spiral flow test	ASTM D 3123
47. Melt flow index	ASTM D 1238
48. Torque Rheometer test (fusion point & cure of thermosets)	ASTM D 2538, D 3795
49. Capillary rheometer test (Apparent viscocity)	ASTM D 1823,D 3835
50. Heat deflection temperature	ASTM D 648
51. Vicat softening point	ASTM D 1525
52. Brittleness temperature	ASTM D 746

53.	Thermal conductivity	ASTM D177
54.	Thermal expansion	ASTM D 696
55.	Limiting oxygen index	ASTM D 2863
56.	Horizontal burning test	ASTM D 635
57.	Vertical burning test	ASTM D 568,D 3801
58.	Smoke density	ASTM D 2843
59.	Dilute solution viscosity	ASTM D 2843 (D 1243 PVC, D 1601 PE)
60.	Brookfield viscosity	ASTM D 1824
61.	Get time	ASTM D 2471
62.	ESCR (Stress cracking)	ASTM D 1693
63.	Torsion stiffness test	ASTM D 1043
64.	Torsional pendulum test	ASTM D 2236, D 4065, D 4440, D 4473
65.	Gel permeation chromotography test	ASTM D 3536,D 3593
66.	Thermal analysis (TGA, TMA, DSC)	ASTM D 3417,D 3418 D 3895,D 4591
67.	Liquid chromotography test	ASTM D 3016
68.	IR spectrophotometric test for PVC	ASTM D 2126,D 3124
69.	Gas chromotography test	ASTM D 3465,D 3749, D 4526
70.	Arc resistance	ASTM D 495
71.	Comparative tracking index	ASTM D 3639
72.	Dielectric strength	ASTM D 149
73.	Delectric constant & dissipation factor	ASTM D 150
74.	Volume and surface resistivity	ASTM D 257
75.	Insulation resistance	ASTM D 229
76.	Luminous transmittance & Haze	ASTM D 1003
77.	Gloss	ASTM D 523
78.	Clarity	ASTM D 1746
79.	Yellowness index (colour)	ASTM D 1746
80.	Refractive index	ASTM D 1925
		ASTM D 542

10

Identification of Plastic Materials

THERMO PLASTICS

ABS

ABS is an amorphous terpolymer with a specific gravity of 1.o4. It is soluble in toluene and ethylene dichloride. It burns with a yelloW flame and an acidic odour, and continues to burn after the removal of the flame source with black smoke with soot and drippings. Infrared spectroscopy is the best method for the positive identification of ABS. The same technique can also be used to further identify a percentage of each polymer in the terpolymer composition.

Acetal

Acetal is available as a homopolymer and copolymer. Both types burn with a blue flame and give off a toxic formaldehyde odour. They are both crystalline with a specific gravity of 1.41 The homopolymer can be distinguished from the copolymer by a Fisher-John melting point test. The copolymer has a lower melting point than the homopolymer. Both types are soluble in hexafluoroacetone sesquihydrate. However due to the extreme toxicity of this solvent, it is rarely used for identification purposes. A differential thermal analysis (DTA) can also be used to distinguish a homopolymer.

Acrylic

Acrylic is an amorphous polymer with a specific gravity of 1.18 Acrylic is one of the few transparent plastics used in outdoor applications. It burns with a blue flame with a yellow tip, gives off fruity odour, and does not produce smoke while it burns. Acrylic is soluble in acetone, benzene and toluene. Infrared spectorscopy is the best means of identification of this polymer.

Cellulose Acetate

Cellulose acetate is an amorphous material with a specific gravity of 1.30. It burns very slowly with a yellow flame, drips gives off an odour of vinegar, and has black smoke with soot. It is soluble in acetone, furfuryl alcohol, and acetic acid. Cellulose acetate is positively identified by infrared spectroscopy.

Cellulose Acetate Butyrate

This polymer burns with a yellow flame with a blue tip, drips, and gives off an odour of rancid butter. The specific gravity is 1.24 and is soluble in acetone and trichloromethane. Cellulose acetate butyrate is also one of the few weatherable transparent plastics.

Cellulose Propionate

The cellulose propionate is also an amorphous material like other celluoids with a specific gravity of 1.20. It burns with a dark yellow flame and an odour of burnt sugar. The material drips while burning and the drippings also burn like other celluloids. Acetone, carbon tetrachloride, and trichloromethance are the most common solvents.

Fluorocarbons (FEP, CTFE, PTFE, PVF)

Fluorocarbon plastics do not actually burn when exposed to a flame. They can be easily identified by a copper wire test which indicates the presence of fluorine by a bright green-coloured flame. The fluoroplastics have a very high melting point. PTFE has a waxy surface and a specific gravity of 2.15 Fluoroplastics are practically impossible to dissolve in any chemical.

Nylons

There are many types of nylons with a specific gravity ranging from 1.04-1.17 All types burn with blue flames and yellow tips and give off a burnt wool or burnt hair odour. Nylon self-extinguishes on removal of the flame. Phenol, m-cresol, and formic acid are the most common solvents. Different types of nylons can be identified by the Fisher-John melting point test(ASTMD789) Solubility and specific gravity tests are also used to differentiate between the types of nylons. However infrared spectroscopy is the best method for positive identification.

Polycarbonate

Polycarbonate is one of the toughest transparent thermoplastics. It has a specific gravity of 1.2 burns with a yellow or orange flame with the odour of phenol, and gives off black smoke with soot in the air. Polycarbonate is soluble in methylene dichloride and ethylene dichloride. Infrared spectroscopy is the best method of identification for polycarbonate.

Polyethylene

Polyethylene is one of the very few crystalline plastics that will float on water. The specific gravity ranges from 0.91-0.96 It burns quickly with a blue flame with a yellow tip. Polyethylene drips while it burns and gives off paraffin odour similar to a burning candle. Polyethylene is impervious to most common solvents. However, it can be dissolved in hot toluene or hot benzene. Infrared spectroscopy is used to confirm the identity of polyethylene.

Polyphenylene Oxide (PPO)

PPO has a specific gravity of 1.06 it burns with a yellow-orange flame without driping and gives off an odour of phenol or burning gas. It exhibits self-extin guishing characteristics. PPO is soluble in toluene and dichloroethylene. Like other polymers, PPO can be identified by infrared spectroscopy.

Polypropylenes

This polyolefin family polymer has a specific gravity of 0.88 and floats on water. It burns with a blue flame with a yellow tip and gives off acid odour similar to diesel fumes. The material is soluble in hot toluene. Polypropylene is positively identified by infrared spectroscopy.

Polystyrene

Polystyrene is an amorphous plastic with a specific gravity of 1.09 It burns with a yellow flame and gives off the odour of illuminating gas or marigolds. The material burns and drips, creating a dense black smoke with soot in the air, also dripping continues to burn. Polystyrene is soluble in acetone benzene, toluene and ether. Polystyrene is often modified with rubber to improve its impact strength. These different types of polystyrenes can be identified by infrared spectroscopy.

Polysulfone

This self-extinguishing amorphous thermoplastic has a specific gravity of 1.24 It burns with an orange flame gives off the pungent odour of sulfur, and produces black smoke with soot in the air while it burns. Polysulfone is soluble in methylene chloride.

Polyurethane (Thermoplastic)

The generally easy-ignite plastic burns with a yellow flame with a faint odour of apple. It produces black smoke. Thermoplastic polyurethane is soluble in tetrahydrofuran and dimethyl formamide. The specific gravity of this material is 1.2.

PVC

This self-extinguishing amorphous plastic has a specific gravity of 1.2 - 1.7 It burns with a yellow flame and green tip, and gives off the odour of hydrochloric acid and white smoke. Tetrahydrofuran and methylethyl ketone are common solvents for PVC. PVC can be easily identified by the copper wire test which indicates the presence of chlorine by a bright green flame. There are many different types of vinyl polymers such as a polyvinyl acetate,polyvinylidene chloride, and ethylene vinyl acetate. The type of vinyl can be positively identified by infrared spectrometric techniques.

Thermoplastic Polyester

Thermoplastic polyester burns with a yellow flame with a blue edge, and as it burns it drips and gives off black smoke with soot. The characteristic odour is one of burning rubber.

THERMOSETTING PLASTICS

Diallyl Pthalate (DAP)

DAP compound's specific gravity ranges from 1.30-1.85 depending upon the type of filler. It burns with a yellow flame, produces black smoke, and gives off the faint odour of phenol. It is self-extinguishing in nature and is difficult to ignite.

Epoxy

The specific gravity of epoxy compounds range from 1.10 - 2.10. It burns with a yellow flame and gives off a black smoke that gives off pungent amine odour. Different types of epoxies can be characterized by infrared spectroscopy and thermal analysis.

Melamine Formaldehyde

This self-extinguishing thermoset has a specific gravity of 1.47 - 1.8. It burns with a yellow flame with a blue edge and gives off a fishlike odour. The material swells, cracks, and turns white at the edges of a burnt section. Melamine formaldehyde is soluble in acetone and cyclohexanone.

Phenol Formaldehyde

Phenol formaldehyde burns with a yellow flame and gives off the odour of phenol. Depending upon the type of filler, it may or may not be self-extinguishing. Phenolic compounds are only available in dark colours. The specific gravity ranges from 1.30 - 1.90 Phenol formaldehyde is soluble in acetone and acetic acid.

Polyesters

Polyesters burn with a yellow flame with blue edges and produce black smoke with soot in the air. They continue to burn without dripping after the removal of the ignition source and give off a sour cinnamon odour. The specific gravity ranges from 1.30 -1.50.

Silicones

Silicones burn with a bright yellow flame without odours and continue to burn after the removal of the flame source. The specific gravity range from 1.05 - 2.82. The positive identification is made by an infrared spectrometer.

Urea Formaldehyde

Urea formaldehyde burns with a yellow flame with a greenish blue edge. It gives off strong odour of formaldehyde and the material usually swells and cracks as it continues to burn.

Solubility of Plastics

Polymer	*Solvent*	*Nonsolvent*
Polythylene polybutene-1, isotactic polypropylene	p-Xylene* , trichlorobenzene* , decane* , decalin*	Acetone, diethylether, lower alcohols
Polybutadiene, Polyisoprene	Aliphatic and aromatic hydrocarbons	Acetone, diethylether, lower alcohols
Polysturene	Benzene, toluene, chloroform, cyclohexanone,	Lower alcohols, diethyl butyacetate, carbon aisulfide ether (swells)
Polyvinyl chloride	Tetrahydrofuran, cyclohexanone, methylethy-lketone, dimethylformamide	Methanol, acetone heptane
Polyvinyl fluoride	Cyclohexanone, dimethylfor mamide	Aliphatic hydrocarbons, methanol
Polytetrafluroe-thylene	insoluble	

cont.....

Polyvinyl acetate	Benzene, chloroform, methanol, acetone, butylacetate	Diethylether, petroleum ether, butanol
Polyacrylates and polymethacrylates	Chloroform, acetone, ethyll acetate, tetrahydrofuran, toluene	Methanol, diethylether petroleum ether.
Polyacrylonitrile	Dimethylformamide, dimethylisulfoxide, concentrated surfuric acid.	Alcohols, diethylether, water, hydrocarbons
Polyvinyl alcohol	Water dimethylformamide*, dimethyl sulfoxide*	Hydrocarbons, methanol acetone, dithylether
Cellulose	Aqueous cupriammonium hydroxide*, aqueous zinc-chloride, aqueous calcium-thiocyanate	Methanol, acetone
Methylcellulose (trimethyls)	Chloroform, Benzene	Ethanol, diethylether, petroleumether
Carboxymethyl-Cellulose	Water	Methanol
Polyamides	Formic acid, conc. sulfuric acid, dimethylformamide, M-cresol	Methanol, diethylether, hydrocarbons
Polyurethanes (uncrosslinked)	Formic acid, y-butyrolactone, dimethyiformamide, m-cresol	Methanol, diethylether, hydrocarbons.

11

Recycling-an Industrial Approach

The plastic industry has experienced phenomenal growth during the last decade. Today plastics is an industry – an industry greater than steel and aluminium combined. Plastic are now used in every segment of our industry and in the life of every one of us. They are found either in the form of products like containers, buckets, chairs carry bags and food packing or in combination with other materials as a part of transporation vehicles, computers, tools, medical equipments, sports items etc.

The significant increase in plastic products has effected a similar increase in plastic disposal. The plastic waste contribute to the solid waste stream by about 7% by weight and possibly twice that by volume. Since major portion of country's solid waste goes to landfill, the amount of plastics in this stream is considered as a contributing factor to country's increasing solid waste burden because of its non-boidegradable nature. This is further complicated by the fact that landfill sites available are getting filled. Hence, the attention is now been focussed to recycle all plastics solid waste and to foster the market for recycled material.

Recycling Routes

In the space of few years, recycling has developed into a single most important and contentious issue facing the plastics industry. The plastic recycling is a vital element of an integrated waste management approach because it conserves natural resources and decreases waste disposed in landfill.

Flammability Tests of Plastics

Chart - 1

Film	*Density range (gm/cc)*	*Flamma bility (self extin-guishing)*	*Colour*	*Behaviour*	*Odour*
Polyethylene	0.910-0.965	No	Top yellow Bottom blue white smoke	Melts and drips	Burnt wax
Polypropylene	0.900-0.915	No	Top yellow Bottom blue white smoke	Melts and drips	Burnt wax and acrid
PVC	1.28-1.38	Yes	Yellow orange with green edge	darkens, softens & decomposes	chlorine
PVDC	1.68	Yes	As above with green spurts	Black, hard residue	chlorine
PVA	1.21-1.33	Yes but slowly	Yellow with grey smoke	Swells, softens & turns brown	Pungent
Poly carbonate	1.2	Yes	Yellow orange with black smoke	No drips decomposes	Pleasant
Polyester	1.38	No	Yellow black smoke	No drips, softens, burns steadily	Pleasant
Polystyrene	1.04-1.09	No	Yellow orange Black, shoots	No drips, softens	Floral, (Sweet)
Nylon	1.06-1.14	Yes	Blue, yellow top	Melts, drips and froths, rigid drips	Burnt Hair
Cellophane	1.48	No	Yellow, Orange, Grey & Smoke	Burns fast and complete burnt area brittle	Burnt Paper
Cellulose acelate	1.28-1.32	No	Yellow with blue base	Melts burns quickly & leaves beads	Burnt Vinegar
Cellulose Nitrate	1.35-1.40	No	Yellow	Burns at once and fully	Acrid

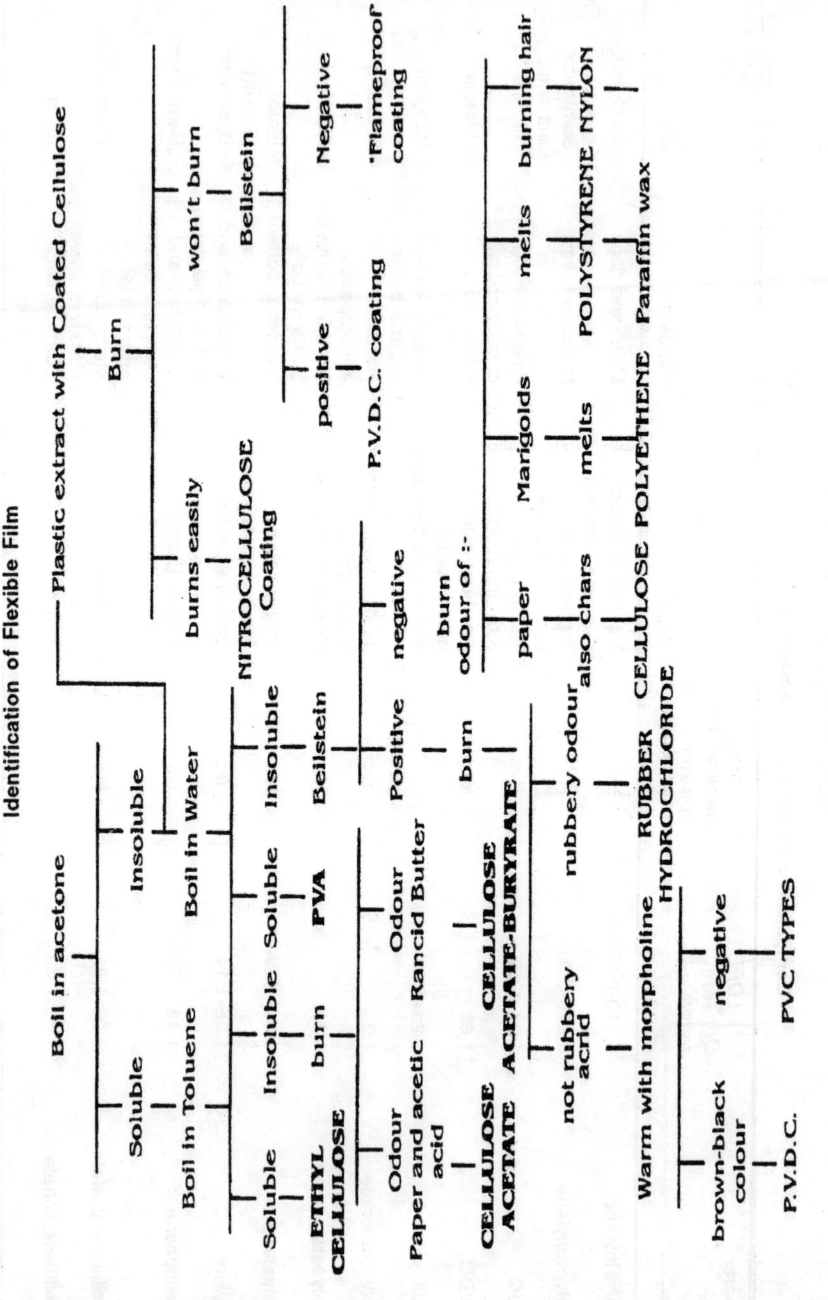
Identification of Flexible Film
Boil in acetone
Soluble
Insoluble
Boil in Toluene
Boil in Water
Plastic extract with Coated Cellulose
Soluble
Insoluble
Soluble
Insoluble
Burn
burns easily
won't burn
ETHYL CELLULOSE
burn
PVA
Beilstein
NITROCELLULOSE Coating
Bellstein
Odour Paper and acetic acid
Odour Rancid Butter
Positive
negative
positive
Negative
P.V.D.C. coating
'Flameproof' coating
burn
burn odour of :-
CELLULOSE ACETATE
CELLULOSE ACETATE-BURYRATE
paper
Marigolds
melts
burning hair
not rubbery acid
rubbery odour
also chars
melts
POLYSTYRENE
NYLON
RUBBER HYDROCHLORIDE
CELLULOSE
POLYETHENE
Paraffin wax
Warm with morpholine
brown-black colour
negative
P.V.D.C.
PVC TYPES

Comparative Properties of Major Plastic Films for Packaging

Property	Unit	LDPE Blown Films Heavy Duty	Milk Pouch	General Purpose	LLDPE Blown Films Heavy Duty	General Purpose	Octene	HDPE FILM	HMHDPE HM	TQPP FILM
Melt flow Index 190°C, 2.16 Kg. 190°C, 5 Kg.	GM/10 Min	0.20	0.50	4.0	(Butene) 1.0	(Butene) 2.0	on Hexene 1.0	0.15	0.05	—
Density	GM/CM³	0.920	0.920	0.922	0.919 to 0.920	0.919 to 0.920	0.918	0.952	0.948	0.9
Melting Range	0_C	108-112	105-110	105-110	126-128	126-128		130	130	210
Tensile Strength at break.	Kg/Cm² MD	260	220	180	400	350	550	360	460	560
	TD	240	200	160	300	260	400	330	430	385
Elongation at Break	% MD	400	350	250	600	700	550	600	550	500
	TD	600	550	400	750	750	750	650	600	550
Dart Impact Strength (F50)	Gms (38 Micron thick film	225	170	80	130	120	275 to 480 (25 Mirron Thick)	130	140	Not Tested.
Elmendor Tear Strength	GMS/Mill MD	200	180	190	230	290	430	50	30	30
	TD	230	240	250	490	460	750	225	240	
Transparency & Gloss		Low	Medium	Very Good	Low	Good	Medium	Low	Low	Very Good.
Draw Down (Minimum Thickness)	Microns	48.50	40	15	9-10	6-8	8-10	20	5	10-12
Coefficient of Friction		0.25 to 0.28	0.16 to 0.18	0.16 to 0.18	0.25 to 0.25	0.16 to 0.18	0.20	Not Tested	Not Tested	0.15 to 0.17

In plastic industry, basically three main approaches are employed for recycling viz.

I. Physcial recycling
II. Chemical recycling
III. Incineration

I. Physical Recycling

This technology is widely used in India. It involves the collection, separation, cleaning, size reduction and melt processing of waste by a conventional manner.

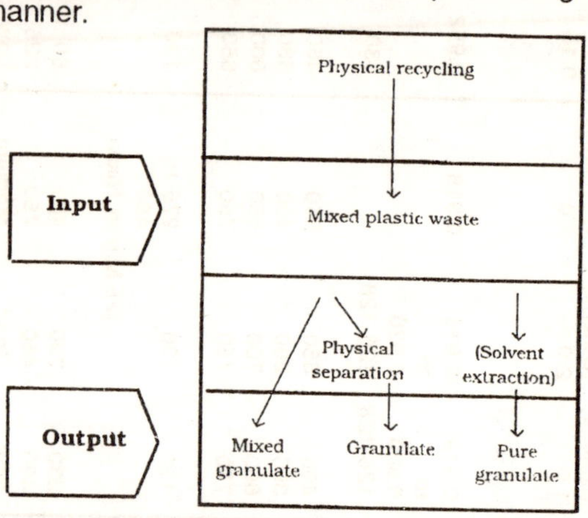

Nearly 1000 tonnes of solid waste is recycled everyday in this country. The pattern of waste collection transfer and recycling practiced in this country is schematically shown below.

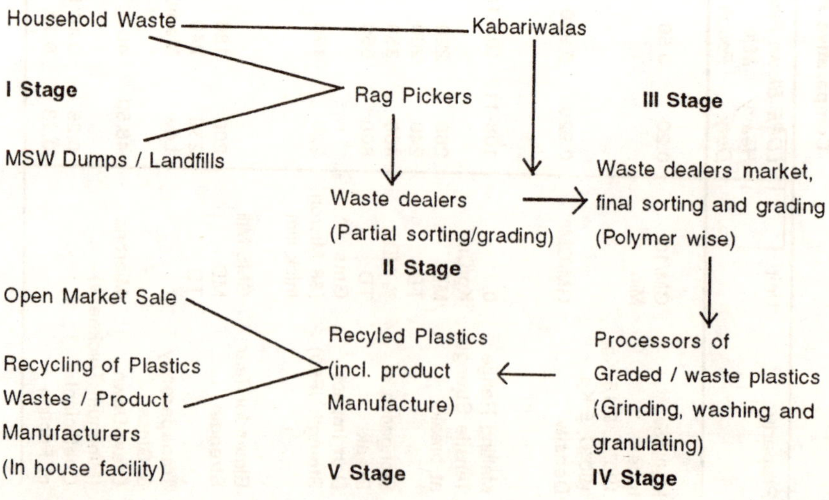

(a) **Physical Recycling - Sorting Techniques**

Till yesterday, greatest challenge to plastics recycling industry was to sort the mixed plastic waste stream. However, today sorting techniques with greater accuracy acceptability and speed have been developed and made into actual use. The most important technologies used for sorting plastic waste are :

1. Sink - float technique
2. The electrostatic separation process
3. Centrifugal system
4. Froth floatation technique

Sink-Folat Technique

A sink-float system was developed to separate different plastics by their difference in densities. The separation was done using an elutriation column and water as a sole parting medium. A schematic of sink-float system is as shown below :

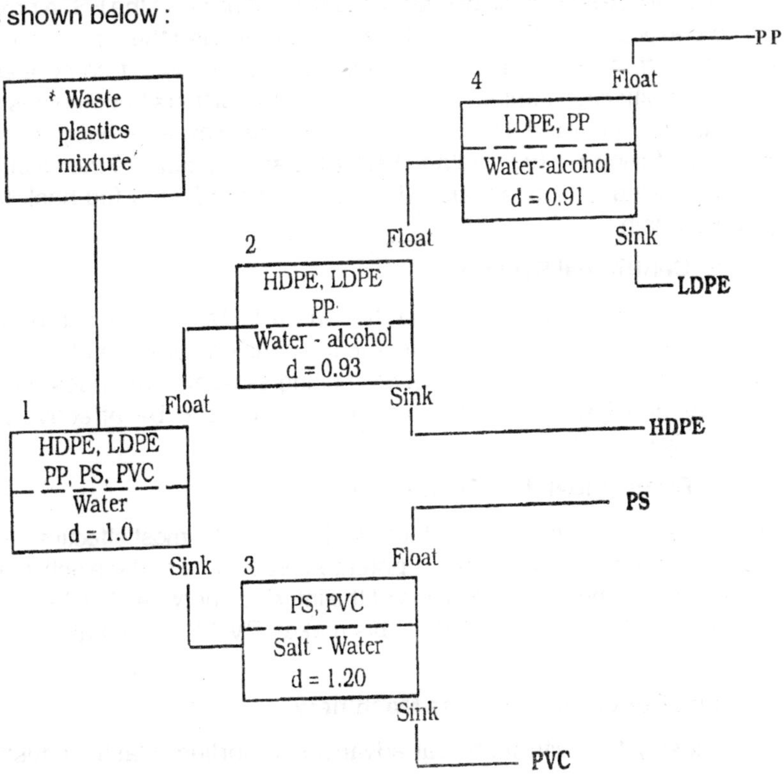

2. Electrostatic Separation Process (ESTA)

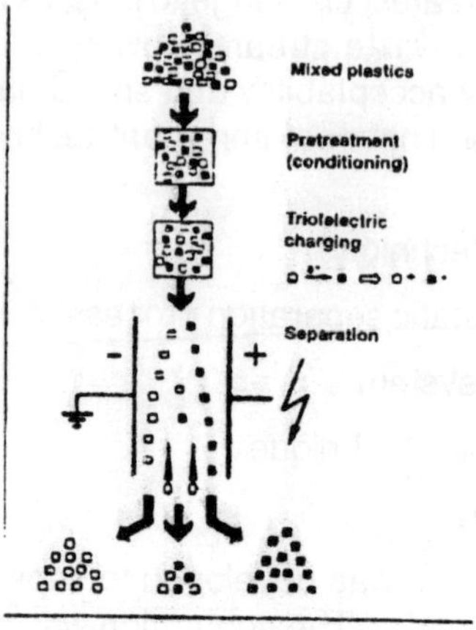

The above schematic diagram shows the principle of the ESTA process. Mixed plastics are first subjected to pretreatment and then given opposite charge by friction. When the particles come into contact some electron pass over with each contact so that the contact partners become positively or negatively charged. Particles treated in this way are charged so that when free falling in a high voltage field, they are deflected to the electrodes and separated. The unseparated middle part product is fed back to the process again.

3. **Centrifugal System**

In this process, mixed plastic waste is fed into a centrifuge in suspension. The turbulence within the suspension separate plastics from each other. If the process is repeated using several centrifuges and with different densities, different types of plastics can be effectively and selectively separated.

4. **Froth - Floatation Technique**

For PET recycles froth floatation technique is the most effective method to separate PVC and PET. In this patented process, a surface active agent is used to alter the surface tension of the interface between PVC and water so that air bubble clings to PVC. This makes PVC float and allow it to be removed.

I.b.) Recycling - Process Machinery

Closely tied with technical advances in sorting, plastic industry all over the world is concentrating more on large scale industrial plastic recycling plants. Schematic sketch of a typical industrial plant to separate pure PVC from PVC waste is shown below :

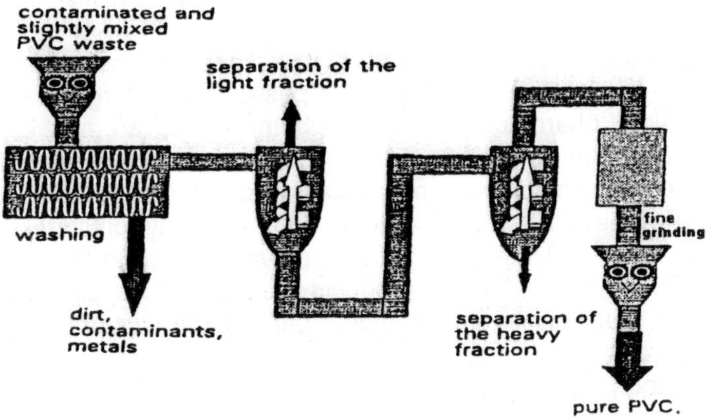

Once sorted, plastics waste are then fed into a typical recycling plant to granulate the waste. A recycling plant to granulate the sorted plastics waste is shown as below :

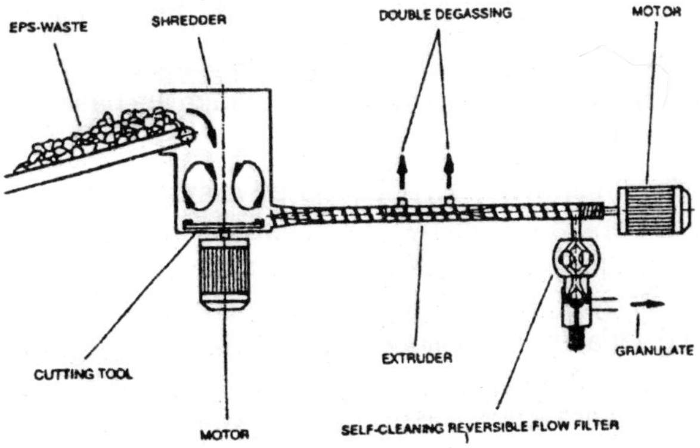

I.c.) Physical Recycling - Indian Scenario

The plastic recycling in this country has to focus mainly on plastics waste produced from packaging industry. There are number of reasons for this, Plastics packaging is considered a significant component of the solid waste stream. Plastics in packaging has attained substantial growth in the last few years and will continue to grow delivering increasing volume of waste to be recycled. Packaging has an estimated life cycle of less than a year and in many cases, only for a few days. As a consequence, plastics packaging continuously enter into the solid waste stream on short turnaround time. This, together with the visibility and the volume, has made the plastics packaging an easy target for environmental criticism.

Similarly, more and more consumer product disposals like containers, bottles for mineral water, bottles for pesticides / detergents / edible oil / cosmetics / pharmaceutical items, chemicals etc. are now continuously entering into the solid waste stream. These are currently found in residential household and made out of polymers like polyethylene terephthalate (PET) polyethylene (PE), Polypropylene (PP), Polyvinyl chloride (PVC) and polystyrene (PS). Apart from these polymers used in the fabrication of components part of finished products such appliances, furniture, luggage, housing, electrical items, automobile parts etc. also contribute to the solid waste system. These polymers are mainly ABS, acrylics, nylon, polycarbonate, polyurethanes, phynalic, film reinforced unsaturated polyesters. Hence, primary focus of recycling activity should be concentrated more on these types of polymers.

I.d) Physical Recycling - Techniques

Polyethylene Terephthalate (PET)

Recycling of PET soft drink bottles began soon after their introduction. The most commerical recycling system depend on floatation or hydrocyclone system to separate PET from HDPE. One of the serious contaminations in PET recycling is the adhesives used to attach the base HDPE cup and the label to PET bottles.

Today, most PET is reclaimed by a system that washes PET and HDPE and separate them by their difference in densities. Another method is solvent floation process which is similar to conventional floatation method but followed by a series of float/sink steps using chlorinated solvents. An interesting variation on the floatation or hydrocyclone process is the addition of a step that granulate PET bottles cryogenically. Because adhesive contamination are embrittled at cryogenic temperature whereas PET is not, the adhesive contaminations are removed as fine powders.

During the recycling of PET, the reprocessor must avoid adding any cleaning agents like caustic soda or detergent containing caustic soda in the washing step. These components are used in the process of removal of lables. They help to dissolve or disperse the adhesives. These alkaline compounds can be entrapped in PET granules during the granulation stage. Eventually, the recycler may produce a clear PET granule but when extruded, the dried PET recycled PET become discoloured and hazy. The greatest challenge to the PET recycler is the contamination of PVC. As little of 1 ppm level of PVC in PET can discolour PET. Similarly, contamination of HDPE should be eliminated as HDPE is incompatible with PET.

Polyolefins (PE & PP)

The basic commerical process of recycling of polyolefins are straightforward. The material is first sorted, cleaned and reduced into a manageable particle size. The flakes are then extruded by a single screw extruder and then pelletized. These recycled granules are normally mixed with virgin material in definite proportions to make an acceptable product of good quality.

Polyvinyl Chloride (PVC)

Since most of the PVC is used for building applications, consumer product disposables like bottles, films or sheets are normally found in the municipal solid waste. Although PVC and PET can be easily separated from HDPE and PP by water floatation, sorting of PVC and PET is difficult. Once separated, PVC can be recycled by granulating the washed and dried flakes by incorporating some more stabilizers or lubricants. Inhouse recycling of PVC is more predominant in the calendering and pipe extrusion industry.

Polystyrene (PS)

The polystyrene products are normally separated into different categories depending upon the fabricated form of polystyrene resin beofre recycling it, viz.,

1. Extruded form sheets
2. Moulded form cups
3. Injection moulded or thermoformed product
4. Custom modified shapes

Once the feedstock is separated and cleaned for contamination, polystyrenes are then granulated, washed with water containing a detergent. The granules are heat-dried to remove water and then pelletized. In the case of expanded polystyrene (EPS) waste, they are densified before extruding into pellets. The actual densification of EPS is usually accomplished by total form boards. The densification is done by heating the polymer and then by applying pressure to collapse the cell structure. The product is then pelletised as usual.

Industrial and Engineering Plastics

Most of the engineering/industrial plastics waste found in the municipal solid waste are products of ABS, nylon, polyurethenes or acrylics. The ABS is normally remelted and granulated. ABS polymers can be used several by properly stabilising with antioxidant. The PUR foam are normally decomposed by hydrolysis and glycolysis to form polyols suitable as partial replacement of virgin polyols. In another recycling process, the foam is first chopped and coated with binder such as isocynate prepolymer. The foam binder mixer is then placed in a mould and compressed. By varying the compression pressure, foam density of various values can be prepared.

Nylon products are normally depolymerised. Nylons are first solubilised with high pressure steam and then continously hydrolised with super-heated steam to produce caprolactum monomer. PET can also be depolymerised into its monomer. PET is treated with excess of water at high temperature in the presence of sodium acetate as catalyst produce TPA and EG. Alternately, PET can be treated with excess of methanol to produce DMT and EG. If PET is treated not wiht water, but with excess of glycol, a transesterification reaction take place. The polyols thus produced can be subsequently treated with unsaturated dibasic acid or anhydrides to produce unsaturated polyesters. Polyols made with diethyl glycol (DEG) can produce PURs. The major source of PET for glycolysis rejection to produce PURs is PET film waste generated by desilvering industry and film manufacture. Acrylics are normally depolymerised to the monomer. Acrylics scraps are also regrinded to fine particles and are used as blasting media to remove paint and coating from the metallic surfaces.

The recylcing technology available for thermoset resins like epoxy or phenolic polymers and limited. They are normally incorporated as fillers in thermoplastics, thermoset resins for non-critical applications.

II. Chemical Recycling

To date, chemical recycling is viewed as the most promising long term option. Chemical recycling yield monomer from polymers and they are again polymerised to give pure polymer.

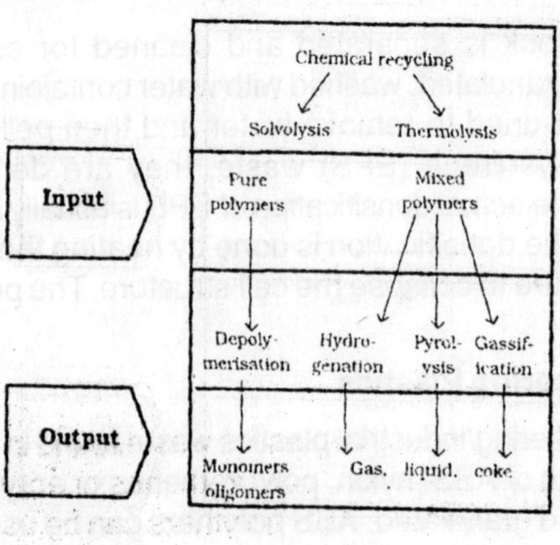

Depolymerisation techniques and purification are adopted to get high purity monomers. Unlike mechanical recycling the technique does not have the problem of contamination and incompatibility. A typical chemical recycling plant for plastic waste is an shown below :

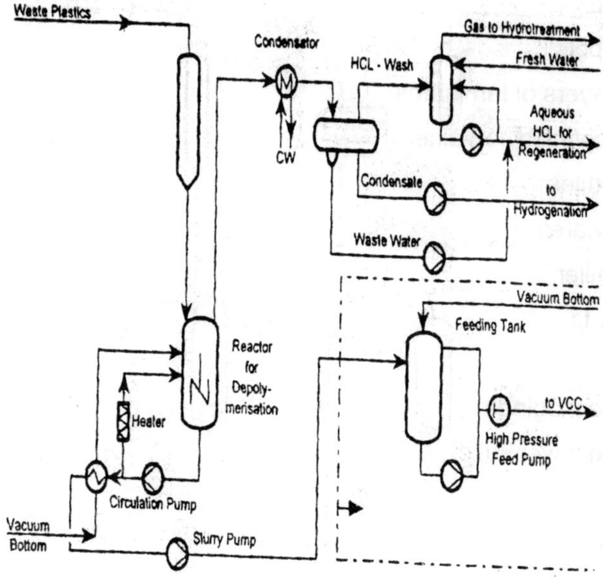

III. Incineration

European plastic industry see incineration with energy recovery more widely accepted in a way of dealing with municipal solid waste. The incineration drastically reduce the volume of waste by 90%. The energy produced in the incineration plants are now currently used for producing steam and electricity.

Potential Recycled Plastics Products

PS :

★ Office equipment

★ Display and advertising

★ Toys

★ Plastic wood

★ Horticulture

★ Waste bins

- ★ Building insulation
- ★ Packaging
- ★ Soil stabilisation

PP / PE:

Flowerpots

Inner layers of laminates

Blow moulded containers

Geotextiles

Housewares

Cable filler

Car parts

Fibres

Tank packagings

Cooling tower salts

Fences

Pallets

ABS :

- ★ Car parts (dashboards, trim, raditor, wheel covers, seat components etc.)
- ★ Computer housings
- ★ Telephones
- ★ Luggage
- ★ ABS foil for furniture
- ★ Office furniture

Nylon :

- ★ Semi-finished plastics (rod, sheet and tube)
- ★ Furniture fittings (handles, knobs etc.)
- ★ Building products
- ★ Lawnmower parts
- ★ Blends/alloys

- Brushes (monofilament)
- Technical mouldings
- Tool handles
- Office furniture

PVC :

- Window and cladding profiles
- Furniture extrusions
- Rainwater pipe
- Drainage
- Tank linings
- Exhibition and display stands
- General purpose thermoforming
- Electrical conduit
- Flooring
- Roof tiles
- Footwear

Indian Recycling - The Present Status

In India, though a part of unorganised sector, recycling industry has developed into a parallel business. The recycled plastics waste are converted into a range of consumer items which are economically priced to meet the need of the common man. Despite the sympotic existence, the link between the plastics producers, processors, and recyclers are weak. Not only plastics recycling industry are not guied and controlled, neither were any study undertaken to define the recycling technology.

The recycling industry should be convinced about the viability of sophisticated technology and machinery under Indian condition.

- We need to formulate and environmental education awareness programme to project the facts and technical information for the benefit of producers and customers.
- The Bureau of Indian Standards should include the guidelinés for use of recycled plastic waste for technically and socially adaptable applications.

★ The individual plastics product should be marked with code number for their identification.

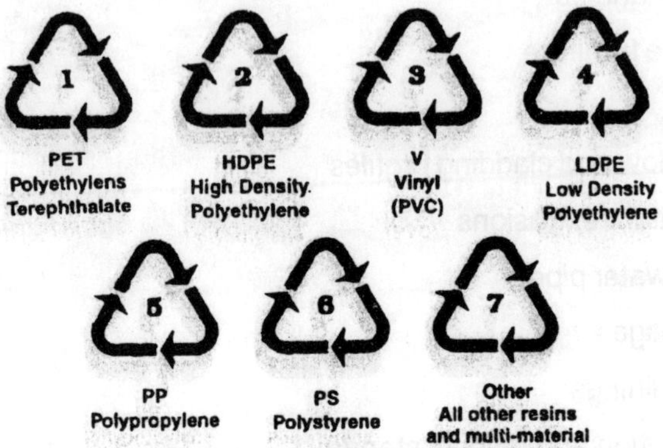

12

Additives for Polymers

INTRODUCTION

Additives is a very important term used in plastic processing technology. However the term is vague in itself but a specific characteristic is assigned to a particular additive. Their requirement may be far cost reduction, to improve certain mechanical or chemical properties or to make easy processing. Thus the role of additives are wide resulting their importance relating better processing and better desired properties of final product.

Additives are imcorporated into plastic formulation before or during processing or too the surface of finished product after processing. Their primary purposes are to modify the behaviour of plastics during processing or to impart useful properties to fabricated plastic articles.

DEFINITION

In general additives may be difined as any substances incorporated into plastics formulations to improve processability or add desired mechanical, optical, thermal or chemical properties. Thus the bulk properties of a polymer can after be after considerably by the incorporation of additives.

CHARACTERISTICS

Following are the main characteristics of additives :

1. They can alter the bulk properties of the polymer.
2. Physically they may be solids, liquids, rubbers or gases.
3. They may be Plasticizers, Lubricants, Flame retarders, colourants, cross linking agents etc.
4. They should be mono, bi or unifunctional that means one additive provide one or more than one function.

CRITERIA

In general Additives should have following properties :

1. They should be effecient in their function.
2. They should be stable under processing condition.
3. They should be stable under service condition.
4. They should not bleed or bloom.
5. They should be non toxic and not impart taste or order.
6. They should be cheap.
7. They should be adversely affect the properties of Polymer.

CLASSIFICATION

Additives are multifunctional and can be classified into four basic groups based on their function :

1. Polymerization Aids -

(a) Catalyst
(b) Curing Agents
(c) Free Radical Initiators
(d) Solution Modifiers

2. Processing Aids -

(a) Lubricants
(b) Blowing Sgents

3. Stabilizers -

(a) Heat Stabilizers
(b) Heat Stabilizers
(c) Preservatives
(d) U-V Stabilizers

4. End-Use Modifying Additives -

(a) Antistatic Agents
(b) Coupling Agents
(C) Plasticizers
(d) Flame Retardents
(e) Fillers
(f) Reinforcers
(g) Colourants

1. POLYMERIZATION AIDS

Either in thermoplastic or in thermosetting plastics, polymerization. Aids are incorporated to alter, initiate or modify polymerization. These aer incorporated to improve the polymerization and increase the rate also. Important polymerzation aids are -

(A) *Catalyst :* Catalyst is defined as any chemical substances which alter the rate of polymerization without itself being chemically changed.

Catalyst generally done the activation energy necessary for chemical reaction, and thus the rate of reaction increases. This is accomplished through the association of one or more of the reactants with the catalyst.

The catalyst is generally choosen for a specific monomer and polymerization technique-

Example :

1. Ziegler Natta Catalyst – Used for the formulation of HDPE, LLDPE, PP (Polyalifinic group)
2. Naoh (Sodium Hydroxide) – used to achieve polycondensation of Nylon 4 and Nylon 6
3. Cromium Trioxide (Metal Oxide Catalyst) also called Philips and standard oil Catalyst-used to produce HDPE & LLDPE by Phillips process.

(B) *Curing Agent :* These are chemicals used in thermosetting material to cause cross linking. Curing agents caused the ends of the thermoset monomer to join, corming long polymer chain and crosslinking.

Example :

N- Amino ethyl, Pipraging-uses are curing for epoxy Alkanol amine, Benzyl dimethyile amine, solfonil die amyline-Curing agent for epoxy resin.

(C) *Free Radical Initators :* There ae also responsible for enitiating the formation of free-radicals in a reactions. Free-radicals formation is the first step in addition polymerization. Thus there additive also play the role of polymerization aids.

Example :

1. Acetyl peroxide
2. Acetyl acceton peroxide
3. Die-t Butyle peroxide

(D) *Solution Modifiers :* These are chemicals used to control the milecular weight of the polymer and help in keeping or retaining the polymer insolation. They may Catalyst, curing agents and free radical initiators or chane transfer agents.

Examples :

1. Formic Acid
2. Amonia
3. Amonium Accetate
4. Calcium Carbonate

(ii) **PROCESSING AIDS** – This is an important class of additives incorporated into plastic to improve and make easy the processability of the later. The important processing aids are -

A. LUBRICANTS – These are the ingradiants added with the plastic resins for three basic reasons-

1. In order to prevent the friction between the resin and the processing equipment ease the flow of the plastic composition during melt processing.
2. To provide internal lubrication for the polymer resin.
3. Inorder to prevent the plastic from sticking to the mould surfae during processing.

Types of Lubricant

There are two types of lubricant

(a) Internal Lubricant

(b) External Lubricant

a. Internal Lubricant

They are low molecular weight material (i.e. Flow promoter) and are active at the inter molecular level "between Polymer chains."

Function : Internal lubricants reduce melt viscosity and improve flow but offer little metal release.

e.g. Used for PVC Amine, Waxes, Glycerol ester etc.

b. External Lubricant

External Lubricants functions on the surface of the molten polymer between the polymer & the surface of the processing equipment.

Function : External lubricants reduce melt viscosity but also provide metal release and affect fusion time more drastically than internal lubricants.

e.g.i) Graphite- Used for Nylon.

(ii) *Stearic Acid*- Used with PVC in order to stop material sticking.

B. BLOWING AGENT – Blowing Agents are also known as foaming agents and are used to produce porous polymers i.e. Cellular/foam plastics. The cellural foam is the farm in which polymer matrix is filled with gas filled cells which may or may not be intercommunicating.

The amount and type of blowing agents influences the density of the finished products and it's structure.

Mainly the Blowing agents used industrially include –

(i) Physical Blowing Agents (PBA)

(ii) Chemical Blowing Agents (CBA)

1. Physical Blowing Agents

The physical Blowing Agents are gases and liquids which are soluble in molten polymer under processure, upon depressurization. They volatilize to form the cellular components of the plastic.

The Liquid blowing agents are typically solvents with low boiling points. For example : Aliphatie hydrocarbons and their fluaro.

2. Chemical Blowing Agents

They are almost all solids with sufficient heat chemical blowing agents decompose to generate gas which expand the plastic by farming bubbles within the resin. Chemical blowing agents are added tot he plastic process in the same manner as colour concentrates or other additives. Loading levels are normally in the range of about 0.5% to 2.5% by might of polymer and density reductions of about 50-60% are common.

The Chemical Blowing Agents decompose to farm gasses products which produce the cells and residues. This residues may remain in the product or it may be washed from the product. Following are the main advantages of chemical blowing agents :

- ★ It can be mixed with polymer at the room temp. Hence no special equipment is required.
- ★ Generally they are self nucleating.
- ★ They may be farmulated with other additive to meet specific processing requirements.
- ★ Most chemical blowing agents are stable under normal storage conditions.

Examples :

(i) AZ (azodicarbamide) Widely used for PVC exothernic CBA

(ii) ABFA (azobisfarmamide) - Most popular CBA which decomposes at temp 230° c and accounts 90% of the total Blowing Agent market.

(iii) P.P. - Oxybis (Benzeno sulfonyo by dragide)

OBSH - gasses N2 & H2 O - polymeric residue which is non toxic.

STABILIZERS

Stabilizers are additives which are incorporated into the plastics to protect them (Later) from degradation which may be caused by oxidation heat microorganism as U - V radiations.

The Stabilizers include :

(a) Antioxidants

(b) Heat Stabilizers

(c) Preservative

(d) U - V stabilizer

(a) Antioxidant are chemical compounds which are incorporated at low concentrations into polymer systems to inhibit polymer oxidation and its resulting effects at ambient or elevated temperature.

Classification and Mechanism

Antioxidents may be classified as either primary or secondary depending upon the mechanism of stabilization.

Primarly antioxidants are free radical scavangers. They terminates chain reactions.

Produce by the degradation of polymer during processing storage of use.

The secondary antioxidants also known as "SYNERGISTS" destroy hydroperoxides which are the source of free radicals. The synergists convert peroxides to non - radical stable product.

Examples :

The basic chemcial groups of antioxidants include :

phenolics ★ Primary Aromatic amines I Antioxidants _ used in elastomeric system case of PC, ABS, HIPS.

Thio ethers I Secondary

Phosphites I Antioxidants- used in Polyolefinic systems PU, ABS, HIPS. Significance : Antioxidants are more significant in order to protect the polymer during processing, compounding, production and end use.

- They protect the polymer from discolouration loss of glass or tansparancy, surface chalking and cracks. Loss of impact strength alongwith and tensile strength.

Most antioxidants are consideration- hazardous and therefore accepted for food packaging and other applications by FDA.

- They extend the service life of the polymer ambient temp and increase the stability of the polymer at the high temp.

(B) **Heat stabilizers :** These are the chemicals which inhibit or refard the degradation of halogenated polymers and co polymers. Thus their application is restricted to halogenated polymers only. They are extensivelly used in PVC.

Mode of action

These additives are acid acceptors which react with HCL formed during processing and eliminate its ability to further degrade the polymer.

The major chemical groups of heat stabilizer include :

(a) Mixed metal stabilizers

(b) Tin organic (i.e organotin)

(c) Lead based systems (Low cost)

(d) Antimony mercaptides

Examples :

Ba-cd (mixed metal) used to stabilizer most flexible PVC.

Ba-zn/CA-Zn- used in drinking water bottles.

- Organation – To stabilizer most rigid PVC including pipe, profile, sheets etc.

(b) *Preservatives* – They prevent the biological degradation of plastics by micro organism such as bacteria, fangi and yeast.

Most polymers are highly resistance to microbial degradation however many additives incorporated in polymer such as Plasticizers, Lubricants and Fillers are more susceptible to attack by micro organism.

Specific chemical groups which are susceptible to microbial degradation include amides, esters and urathanes. PVC and Polyurathanes are major consumers of biocides.

In general plastic which are subjected to moist environment and intended far long term service life have higher requirements for preservatives.

Examples :

(i) Capten, Falten (Chlorinated Nitrogen - Sulphur Hytrocytes) - Fungicides used in PVC.

(ii) Tributylin Flrroide and Tributylin Oxide – Anti-Bacterials and Anti Fungal used in PVC.

(e) U - V Stabilizers – U _ V Stabilizers inhibit or reduce degradation of polymers resulting from U _ V radiation. The u - v radiation causes breakage of chemical bonds.

The Plastics intended for outdoor application require U - V stabilizer. Most of the U - V stabilizers important stability by two mechanisms absorption and / or quenching.

The basic chemical groups of U - V stabilizer are -

Benzophenones |

Benzotriazoles | act as a absorptions

Nicket organics - act as a quencher.

Over 75% of the U - V stabilizers consumption in plastics is in polyolefin (mainly PP & HDPE) the next largest consumer is PV.

Examples :

Benzophenones - Most widely Benzotriazole

Hals (i.e. Hindered Amines).

13

Get Virgin Quality From Reprocessed

Gone are the times when a supplier would charge a price on cost plus basis. Price is no more under your control. But the costs still are. Your survival thus depends how prudently you spend. Prudence lies in saving cost without sacrificing quality. We came across an Indo-American company, SB J Von whose products help the plastics industry do just that. This article first talks about on little background of the company, followed by its product range and lastly its marketing network.

The World of SB J Von

SB J Von Compounders Pvt. Ltd. is an Indo-American Joint venture Company based in Ahmedabad manufacturing Thermoplastic Rubber (TPR) Compounds. Its parent company J-Von is an ISO 9001 organisation and is a market leader worldwide in the TPR Industry for over 25 years. Since its inception, SB J-Von Compounders, has made a name for itself in the industry as suppliers of quality TPR Resins with a wide variety of properties and colours.

This has been possible due to the state-of-the-art manufacturing facility set up in Gujarat over sprawling 6 acres. To retain its leadership in the TPR industry, the company has extensive fac8ilities for developing new processes and products. The company is in the process of setting up a world class Product Application, Research & Development facility at their plant premises to cater to worldwide research needs of J Von. In line with its futuristic philosophy, the company has retained best professionals in the industry to provide the customers with the best of products and services.

Range of TPR compounds currently manufactured include :

Thermoplastic Olefins. (TPOs).

Thermoplastic Elastomers. (TPEs).

Thermoplastic Vulcanizates. (TPVs).

The Company also provides facilities for compounding of polymer hlends As per customer specifications.

The Company Provides TPR Compounds for the following applications.

1. Compact Footwear soles.
2. Blown Footwear soles.
3. Grips raw material.
4. Eraser compounds.
5. Toys material.
6. Impact Modifiers for Plastic Industry.
7. Cable sheathing compounds.
8. Extrusion grades for linings.
9. Compounds for sheet extrusion.
10. Compounds for Blown film and others.

Why TPR ?

TPR is now becoming a material of choice the world over, and is slowly replacing toxic materials like PVC.

In addition to being much more environment, machine, and operator friendly, TPR enjoys inherent advantages like :

- ✓ Complete Recyclability of process scrap
- ✓ Ease of Processing on existing plastic/rubber processing equipment
- ✓ Rubber-like Look and Feel
- ✓ Low Temperature Crack Resistance
- ✓ Low Specific gravity (0.7 - 0.98)
- ✓ Non - Toxicity
- ✓ Equipment & Operator friendly
- ✓ Excellent mould dedinition
- ✓ Controlled Shrinkage
- ✓ Easy colourability
- ✓ Low inherent colour
- ✓ Anti - skid properties

PRODUCTS TO MATCH REPROCESSED QUALITY WITH VIRGIN

1. Impact Modifiers

These are of two types, one for polyolefins industry, suitable to be added with LDPE, LLDPE, HDPE,.MDPE, PPHP, PPCP, RCP, Filled PP and other for Polystyrene industry, mixed with GPPS, HIPS, ABS, SAN, PC. An average 4-6% (depending upon type and % age of reprocess) addition in 70 - 100% reprocessed matches the quality of reprocessed with that of virgin. Alternatively, addition of 1-2% enhances greatly the impact strength of virgin polymers.

A. Hercuprene Olefinic Modifier

The Product

Hercuprene is a TPO (Thermoplastic Olefinic) based customized modifier. It has properties and feel similar to rubber. The company has developed customized grades of this material to be used as impact modifiers in a wide range of applications.

These compounds help you to adjust and fine-tune the properties of your product. Addition of these compounds, in small quantities (2-6%) will increase the toughness and the impact strength of your end product to a large extent. They also improve the crack resistance of your product. it is of special relevance to articles with high degree of filler loading.

Areas of Application

These compounds significantly improve the impact properties of the following Materials :

- ✓ Polyethylene (PE)
- ✓ LDPE
- ✓ LLDPE
- ✓ MDPE
- ✓ HDPE
- ✓ Filled PE
- ✓ PE Reprocess
- ✓ Polypropylene (PP)
- ✓ Homopolymer.
- ✓ Random Copolymer.
- ✓ Impact Copolymer.
- ✓ Filled PP.
- ✓ Reprocess PP.

These compounds disperse easily into the polymeric matrix and improve the flow behaviour during processing. The dispersed rubber particle size goes down to micron level due to added compatibilizer in the compound and thus significantly improves the impact strength of the ultimate product. It does not hamper significantly other mechanical properties like tensile strength, flexural strength etc. It has low inherent colour and does not hamper the colour of the end product.

Hercuprene resins are highly recommended for both **Injection Moulding** as well as **Extrusion Products.** They are especially effective in moulding of filled PP and HDPE. They also allow higher filler loading, thus helping in cost reduction.

Recommended Dosage : 2 – 6 % (according to Customer Requirements).

Advantages

The advantages of using Hercuprene are manifold, the prime among them being :

- ✓ Increases Impact Strength
- ✓ Increases Elongation at Break
- ✓ Allows Higher Filler Loading
- ✓ Improves Crack Resistance
- ✓ Allows Higher Reprocess Utilization and thus Reduces Cost
- ✓ Eliminates the problem of Process Scrap
- ✓ Improves Product Durability
- ✓ Reduces in process Breakage
- ✓ Upgradation of Scrap
- ✓ Improves Environmental Stress Crack Resistance (ESCR) of PE
- ✓ Little Adverse Effect on Processing Performance
- ✓ Addition of Hercuprene to Film Grade HDPE (independent of manufacturing process) reduces the Performance Anisotropy Caused by Unbalanced Processing Conditions.

This product has proven its effectiveness in moulded articles like :

- ✓ Blow Moulded Containers
- ✓ Large Crates and Containers
- ✓ Electronic & Kitchen appliance bodies
- ✓ Moulded Furniture
- ✓ All other moulded articles

Test Results

Testing has been carried out on an Izod Impact Tester as per method ASTM D 256.

Material	Impact strength J/ m
PP (60% + Talc (40%)	44.1
PP (60%) + Talc (40%) + IM (4%)	57.6
PP (60%) + $CaCO_3$ (40%)	40.0
PP (60%) + $CaCO_3$ (40%) + IM (4%)	62.0

Thus the use of this impact modifier is two fold. It can either be used as an additive to your product to improve product performance or it can be used to increase the filler loading / process scrap content in your product. It can also help reduce wall thickness, thus reducing article weight and further reducing costs.

This product offers you improved products, lowered costs and complete usage of your in-plant process scrap.

Note : Can be added just like masterbatch.

B. Hercuprene Styrenic Modifiers

The Product

Hercuprene is a Styrene based elastomer. It has properties and feel similar to rubber. The company has developed customized compounds of this material to be used as impact modifiers in a wide range of applications in the same fashion as elaborated for polyolefins.

These compounds help you to adjust and fine-tune the properties of your product. Addition of these compounds, in small quantities will increase the toughness and the impact strength of your end product greatly. They also improve the crack resistance of your product.

Areas of Application

These compounds significantly improve the impact properties of the following Materials :

- ✓ Polystyrene (PS).
- ✓ High Impact Polystyrene (HIPS).
- ✓ Styrene-Acrylonitrile (SAN).
- ✓ Acrylonitrile-Butadiene-Styrene (ABS).
- ✓ All Styrenic Blends & Alloys.
- ✓ Reprocess of PS, HIPS, SAN, ABS.

These compounds disperse easily into the polymeric matrix and improve the flow behaviour during processing. The dispersed rubber particle size goes down to micron level due to added compatibilizer in the compound and thus significantly improves the impact strength of the ultimate product. It does not hamper significantly other machanical properties like tensile strength, flexural strength etc. It has low inherent colour and does not hamper the colour of the end product.

Hercuprene resins are highly recommend for both Injection Moulding as well as Extrusion Products.

Recommended Dosage : 2–5% (according to Customer Requirements.)

Advantages

The advantages of using Hercuprene are manifold, the prime among them being :

Increase Impact Strength

- ✓ Increases Elongation at Break
- ✓ Increases Elongation at Break
- ✓ Allows Higher Filler Loading
- ✓ Improves Crack Resistance
- ✓ Allows Higher Reprocess Utilization and thus Reduces Cost
- ✓ Eliminates the problem of Process Scrap
- ✓ Improves Product Durability
- ✓ Reduces in process Breakage

This product has proven its effectiveness in moulded articles like :

- ✓ TV Cabinets.
- ✓ Wall clock bodies.
- ✓ Electronic appliance bodies.
- ✓ Thermoformed & Vacuumformed Cups & Glasses.
- ✓ All types of containers and boxes.
- ✓ All other moulded articles.

Test Results

1. Testing has been carried out on HIPS using method ASTM D 638, on a Universal tensile testing machine with a draw speed of 5 mm / min.

Specimen Sample	Tensile Strength (KG/CM2)	% Elongation At Break
Virgin HIPS (100%)	219.00	49.0
Virgin HIPS + 3 % IM	203.00	56.0
Regrind HIPS + 1.5 % IM	204.00	56.0
Regrind HIPS + 3.0 % IM	175.00	60.0
Regrind HIPS + 5.0 % IM	154.00	65.0

2. Testing has been carried out on an Izod Impact Tester as per method ASTM D 256.

Material	Impact strength J / m
HIPS	230.00
HIPS + 5 % IM	300.00
ABS	320.00
HIPS + 35 % IM	500.00

Thus the utility of this impact modifier is two fold. It can either be used as an additive to your product to improve product performance or it can be used to in increase the filler loading / process scrap content in your product. It can also help reduce wall thickness' reducing article weight and further reducing costs.

This product offers you improved products, lowered costs and complete usage of your in-plant process scrap.

Grades

Grade	*Appearance*	*Application*	*Rate/Kg*
SBJ/OSG/1026	Opaque	PS, HIPS, SAN ABS General Purpose.	100.00
SBJ/OSI/1010	Opaque	PS, HIPS, SAN ABS Injection Moulding.	100.00
SBJ/OSI/1015	Opaque	PS, HIPS, ABS Injection Moulding.	115.00
SBJ/OSE/1000	Opaque	PS, HIPS, SAN ABS Extrusion.	100.00
SBJ/TSM/1026	Transparent	PS, HIPS, SAN ABS General Purpose.	220.00

Note : Can be added just like masterbatch.

2. Other TPR Based Products

A. Eraser Compounds

SAMPLES

Injection moulding grade   Extrusion grade

The Product

SB J-Von has developed excellent grades of eraser compounds for use by eraser/stationary manufacturers. It is based on SBS (Styrene-Butadiene-Styrene triblock copolymer), which is an extremely versatile material. It is completely non-toxic and lightweight. Some of the more prominent features of the eraser compounds are :

✓ Developed for the 1st time in India based on TPR

✓ Excellent Erasing action

✓ Negligible Dust Generation

✓ Lasts longer

✓ PVC - Free, Non - Toxic material

✓ Suitable for use by young children

✓ Does not harden or turn yellow over long duration

✓ Easy colourability and low inherent colour

✓ Can be easily scented

✓ Complete recyclability of process scrap

✓ Excellent Melt Flow and Shape Retention Properties

✓ Extreme ease of Processing on all existing equipment

✓ Available in Extrusion & Injection Moulding grades

Physical Properties

Property	*Method*	*Unit*	*Eraser*	*Compound*
			Extrusion Grade	Injection Moulding
Hardness	ASTM D-2240	Share-A 10 sec	60 ± 2	60 ± 2
Density	ASTM D-1238	Gms / cc	1.54+ 0.02	1.40 + 0.02
MFI	ASTM D-792	Gms/ 10 mins(Cond P)	3.0 + 1.0	8.0 +1.0
Packing	25 kgs HDPE woven sacks			

Processing Temperatures : 165 - 175° C on all conventional equipment.

✓ Custom grades with hardness as per customer requirement will also be supplied.

SBS Grades

Opaque(Natural)... Translucent(Natural)... Blown(Natural)

SEBS Grades

Opaque(Pigmented) Translucent(Pigmented) Blown(Pig.)

The Product

In Today's World of Ergonomic design, soft touch grips have achieved great importance. A well-designed grip successfully reduces required effort, calling for lesser muscular fatigue and providing more precise control. It also immensely improves comfort and the handling of product. This has been a well-documented fact as a result of numerous scientific studies. With these developments in mind, SBJVon has developed a wide range of Gripper Compounds for the folllowing applications :

- ✓ Pen & Pencils
- ✓ Toothbrush & Razors
- ✓ Kitchen Appliances
- ✓ Hand & power tools
- ✓ Two - Wheelers & Bikes
- ✓ Utensil & Serving Bowls
- ✓ Knife & Peeler handles
- ✓ Exercise Equipment
- ✓ Umbrella handles
- ✓ Cricket abts, Hockey sticks
- ✓ Sports Racquets
- ✓ Cameras, Camcorders, etc.
- ✓ Crates
- ✓ Suitcases & Soft Luggage
- ✓ Torch Grips
- ✓ Spectacle Frames And Others

These compounds are available in a wide range of properties and colours according to customer specifications. Grades based on SBS as well as SEBS compounds , which give excellent appearance, feel, texure and surface finish are available. A custom grade based on TPVs is also available.

Physical Properties :

Property	*Method*	*Unit*	*Griper* Minimum	*Compound* Maximum
Hardness	ASTM D-2240	Share-A 10 sec	60 ± 2	60 ± 2
Density	ASTM D-1238	Gms / cc	1.54+ 0.02	1.40 + 0.02
MFI	ASTM D-792	Gms/ 10 mins(Cond P)	3.0 + 1.0	8.0 +1.0
Packing	25 kgs HDPE woven sacks			

Processing Temperatures : 165 - 175°C on all conventional equipments Custom grades with upto 85 A shore Hardness are available.

14

Specialty Additives and Masterbatches

Specialty Additives and Masterbatches are today used very frequently in today's plastic industry by processors and the recommended by all the plastic experts. Masterbatch industry is itself a big industry in India, as there are approx 20 players are in organized and about 50–70 masterbatch manufacturers are in India. Especially in Nothern and West region of India masterbatch people are present and providing solutions to the Plastic processors and manufacturers in all-over India, Masterbatches and Additives are also exported to our neighbouring countries like Bangladesh, Pakistan, Nepal, Sri Lanka and Bhutan. In India this Additive and Masterbatch Industry is grown to such a stage that it not only provides processing solutions to the Industry but also find ways to replacing costlier imported chemicals and additives. There is approx. 1200 MT's market is present in India for Masterbatches and Additives.

The Role of Additives & Masterbatches in Processing

Additives and Masterbatches are agents used to get following advantages in Plastic.

- Smooth Processing
- Colouring Agent
- Process Controller Agent
- Flexibility Provider
- Filler Loader Enhancer

Types of Masterbatches & Additives

There are following types of available masterbatches & additives.

1. ANTIFIBRILLANT MASTERBATCHES
2. SLIP & ANTIBLOCK MASTERBATCHES

3. ANTI - OXIDANT STABILISERS MASTERBATCHES
4. PROCESSING AID
5. MOULD RELEASE AGENT
6. FLAME RETARDENT MASTERBATCHES
7. DESSICANT MASTERBATCH
9. ULTRA VIOLET STABILISERS
10. COLOR MASTERBATCHES

ANTIFIBRILLANT MASTERBATCHES

Basically Antifibrillant Masterbatches are used in PP Fibers and Tape Production. Such masterbatches are well dispersed low dust masterbatch in nature. The reason for adding a $CaCo_3$ (Calcium Carbonate) masterbatch to PP for the extrusion of fibers and tapes, sometimes also referred as Raffia, is to facilitate processing. The tapes and fibers are used for products like heavy duty woven sacks or big bags (semi bulk containers of usually 750 kgs to 1 mt).

The process for making the tapes can be described in following steps:

I. Extrusion of a flat PP sheet/film. In this film the masterbatch is already incorporated at a typical level of 2%.

II. The film or sheet is slit using knives to form tapes. The influence of knife wear by the $CaCo_3$ may be an issue brought up by the customer. Usually the customer decided for a standard masterbatch as this product is has a lowest cost and provides the most favorable total costs.

III. The tapes are stretched with a specific force while receiving a temperature treatment. During the stretching process the PP molecules are oriented and align themselves in the machine direction increasing the strength of the tapes very considerably. The transverse strengths of the tapes decrease strongly, leading to fibrillation of the tapes. In other words the tapes become more or less a bundle of smaller individual fibers. Breaking of these fibers can result in a very 'hairy' exterior of the tape, which would make further processing very difficult. Machine blockage or defective end products may be the result. The $CaCo_3$ masterbatch helps to reduce the breaking of the fibers, and gives therefore better properties of the tape, especially for further processing.

IV. The tapes are wound on bobbins, for transfer to the weaving machines.

V. On the weaving machines, the PP woven bags or big bags are made. Sometimes, the woven fabric is coated with a PE layer to increase the barrier properties of the packaging material.

The presence of LLDPE in the masterbatch is believed to add to the anti-fibrillation and extrusion properties of the PP tapes. Some customers insist on using PP based $CaCo_3$ masterbatches. For more sophisticated PP tape and fiber applications, finer particle masterbatches may be used. These products use more costly raw materials are substantially more expansive to produce. This market is however estimated to be very small.

SLIP & ANTIBLOCK MASTERBATCHES

SLIP FUNCTION

The function of slip additive is to make the surface of the more slippery, e.g. give it a lower coefficient of friction. This is often required for films that are later on used on automatic packaging lines. Lines speeds can be increased when the film has the "correct" of coefficient of friction. This properly must be optimized and must lie between certain border values for an efficient operation.

The active ingredient is mixed with the polymer but is not really compatible with the polymer. Therefore after the extrusion the active component will start to migrate to the surface. One at the surface the active ingredient will fulfill its function of making the surface more 'slippery'. The migration process takes time. Therefore immediately after extrusion the film will not yet have its final properties. Depending on the type of active ingredient used and the ambient temperature is the faster this process will go. There are two types of active ingredients, Oleamide, which is fast migrating ingredient and Erucamide, which is a slower migrating component.

ACCURATE DOSING

The addition rate of the masterbatch is important to control very precisely. Variation in dosage may give irregular distribution of how slippery the surface is in different parts of the film surface.

FILM THICKNESS

A thin film usually needs a higher dosage in percentage of masterbatch than a thick film. As in the end all the ingredient will arrive at the surface, a thin film needs more masterbatch to arrive at the same coefficient of friction than a thick film. Dosage percentages have to be calculated as in function of the volume of the film.

PRINTING PROPERTIES

The efficiency and the effectiveness of the printing inks depend strongly on the surface tension of the film produced. Slip additives will change those properties as a function of the time. For this reason it is critical to know the surface properties at the moment of printing.

Surface treatment of the film surface is often used to enhance the adherence of the printing ink to the surface of the polyethylene film. Having slip additives at the surface of the film will usually increase the level of treatment needed to get an acceptable result.

Sometimes when the film is printed soon after the extrusion (in line printing) and the adherence of the printing ink to the film is not good enough, for instance when the treatment was irregular because of the defective equipment, the migrating slip additive may 'push' the ink from the surface.

The ink can then be easily wiped off, sometimes even by hand. It is important to make the customer aware of this to avoid problems.

For the extrusion of HDPE film usually no slip additive are added. The combination of the stiffness of the film and the surface properties and the internal additive used in the HDPE production, give the film surface the right kind of properties.

ANTIBLOCK MASTERBATCHES

An anti-block masterbatch is designed to alter the film surface properties to allow easy opening of bags or to increase the coefficient of friction of a film. The anti-block masterbatch is a mineral filler material, ehich forms very small irregularities at the surface of the film. In this manner the so-called 'mirror' effect can be avoided between two flat layers of the film. Two very flat film surfaces act like mirrors when put on top of each other and will tend to stick together (this is called blocking of films), as all the air in between has been eliminated. Such surfaces can only be separated by using a lot of force. The irregularities at the surface to stick together, which is called 'anti-blocking'. Ease of opening of bags is again especially used in household bags and gas for industrial high-speed packaging lines.

Dosing high levels of a coarse particle antiblock may make the surface more rough, and perform as an 'anti-skid'. This property of anti-block masterbatch is especially used for applications like industrial bags.

Sometimes such type of masterbatches are used for cleaning extruders. For instance when changing colour this masterbatch speeds up the process of change, thus reducing the amount of reject and change-over material.

ANTI-OXIDANT STABILISERS

PROCESS STABILISATION

Antioxidants are used to stabilize polymers during their conversion to end products against the effects of degradation of the polymer by a longer exposure to higher temperatures. Using an anti-oxidant prevents or reduces the appearance of gels, pips etc. resulting from thermal degradation and will therefore enhance the quality of the film.

Especially 'older' converting equipment with sub optimal design increases the risk of thermal degradation, due sub optimal flow of the resin (pockets), resulting in longer than necessary residence times of the resin in extruder and excessive shear contitions, will both tend to result in defective parts when the resin is not properly stabilized. The result may be excessive scrap rates representing high monitory loss for the converter. The total costs of the production of a product go down, stabilization pays !

STABILISATION AT MACHINE STOPS

Resins are particularly degraded by temperature when extruders are being stopped and then restarted or kept in non-running condition during a longer period of time. Contamination of the extruder by degraded polymer sticking to the inside of the barrel, often accumulating in places where the flow is low. Often it may take many hours to get rid of this problem (gels, burned particles, streaks etc.) after the production line restarted. This occurs for instance after a week-end stop. The result may be a lot of scrap product.

Additing a higher percentage of anti-oxidant (4 - 5%) just before the machine is stopped usually decreases the problem radically, When using a proper stabilization the machine can often be restarted without loss of production even after a prolonged stop. The productivity gain and the reduction of scrap is substantial and 'pays' for the additional costs of stabilization.

THERMAL STABILISATION OF CABLE JACKETING

When cables are coated with polyolefin's, this is done at high extrusion speeds and relatively high temperatures. The risk of degradation of the polymers is high under those conditions. The presence of metal (Copper) : increases the risk polymer degradation, resulting in extrusion defects and weak spots in cable jacketing. Cables have a long service life. The defects in the cable usually appear only after they have been in use for some time. Replacing cables is a very expansive exercise. Therefore it pays to stabilize the cable properly with a specialized anti-oxidant.

PROCESSING AID

Processing aid masterbatches are designed to drastically improve the quality and appearance of extruded products and help to considerably boost the output of extruders when operational limits have been reached.

MELT FRACTURE

At high throughput rates an extrudate may take on a rough, irregular appearance resembling shark skin. This is attributed to the physical breakdown of the melt-fracture.

Melt-fracture occurs when the shear stress of the melt exceeds its shear strength e.g. In an extrusion die where, due to a substantial reduction in channel width, a sudden increase in the shear rate occurs. Fracture occurs at a critical shear rate which is dependent on the die entry geometry and melt viscosity. Melt at the surface near the die walls is moving more slowly than in the bulk. On exiting the die surface melt undergoes rapid stretching as it attempts to equilibrate its velocity with that of the bulk melt - this rapid stretching manifests itself as melt fracture.

LLDPE or LLDPE rich blends with LDPE and high molecular weight HDPE are more difficult polymers to extrude at higher speeds on the older extruders, which were designed to convert LDPE. When the limitations of the extruder are reached, extrusion defects tend to start to appear. This may be the 'orange pell' or the 'shark skin' effect. A more scientific description of these phenomena is the term 'melt fracture'. melt fracture occurs as a result of irregular flow at the surface of the extruded product. The molten polymer will tend to stick to the metal parts of the extrusion head.

THE FUNCTION OF A PROCESSING AID

Using a processing aid only to just overcome the melt-fracture problem is usually not supported by a sufficient economic advantage. But the processing aid masterbatch offers more. A considerable higher output of the extruder: 30 – 40% increases have been observed, less back pressure and energy consumption keeping a good quality product are very worthwhile advantages of using a process and masterbatch. New, usually heavy investments in new equipments can be postponed, and therefore a substantial increase in the profit potential of the existing extrusion lines can be achieved. Under those circumstances a process aid starts to pay off in a big way. Usually the largest benefits are seen on the older type of extruders currently in use in the plastic converting industry.

HOW TO APPLY A PROCESS AID MASTERBATCH ?

When starting up the extrusion operation a 35–50% mix of masterbatch and resin must be used during about 20 minutes. The moment the backpressure stabilizes the machine is 'prepare". The preparation is needed to cater the metal parts of the extruder with the active ingredient in the masterbatch.

After this, a percentage of 1 = 2% needs to be adde4d to maintain the coating intact. The material, which was used to apply the initial coating, is not lost ! This product can be recycled and used as a 'masterbatch' at one third to half of the original strength depending on the concentration used during the initial coating of the extruder body and die.

The additional rate and therefore the costs can be fine tuned using the backpressure as a measure.

MOULD RELEASE MASTERBATCH

Mould Release Agent masterbatch are used to demould an injection moulded product at higher temperatures without distorting the article. Therefore the cycle time can be increased substantially.

FLAME RETARDANT MASTERBATCH

Flame retardant masterbatches substantially increases the flame retardancy of a polyolefin resin.

DESSICANT MASTERBATCH

Desiccant masterbatch eliminates problems resulting from a too high water content in a compound or resin. Those problems can demonstrate themselves amongst others in the form of surface defects on moulded or extruded products, or lacing defects in thin film. These kinds of problems often occur when using recycled resins in film or extrusion processes.

ANTISTATIC MASTERBATCH

Antistatic masterbatch is used in applications, where for instance the attraction of dust on film surfaces or on blow moulded bottles is a problem for the customer. The promotional appeal of the product is usually.

ULTRA VIOLET STABLISATION MASTERBATCH

Such types of masterbatches are responsible for the ultra violet protection to the products and videly used by the film manufacturers.

15

PVC Compounding

I. COMPOUNDING FUNDAMENTALS

Compounding PVC essentially involves adding to the base PVC resin the components that will allow it to be processed into a finished product with desired properties, at minimum cost. The "families" of materials that will be chosen will probably fall into one of the following classifications, each of which is discussed here :

a. Plasticizers
b. Stabilizers
c. Lubricants
d. Impact modifiers
e. Processing and resins
f. Fillers
g. Colorants
h. Miscellaneous (antistatic agents, tackifiers, antiblocking agents foaming agents, flame-retardants, fugicides, odorants)

If one were to take PVC resin as it is received from the manufacturer and attempt to process it by normal conversion techniques (calendering, giving off hydrogen chloride, discoloring, and sticking to the equipment. The results could be described only as disastrous. Adding to the PVC resin the proper type and amount of plasticizer, stabilizer, lubricant, pigment, and so on (as outlined above) results in a compounded mixture that can subsequently by processed on properly designed equipment into a satisfactory finished product. In simplest sense, compounding can be defined as the mixing to homogeneity of PVC resin with the other components required for processing and performance. The homogeneous mixture of materials can be subsequently fed to processing equipment, providing a uniform, controlled product at maximum rates of production.

II. PROCESSING EQUIPMENT LIMITATIONS

A fixed factor that the manufacturer must accept is the specific processing equipment available and its suitability for producing a given item made of PVC. A plastics processor may be expert at extruding polyethylene profiles; but an attempt to process formulated PVC on the same equipment might run into difficulties. The processor might then go to the formulator or compound supplier and complafin abouth the quality of the material supplied for the job at hand. One supplier after another might be tried, in a search for the magic PVC compound that would provide the desired product. The basic problem, however, is the manufacturer's failure to recognize that the problem is with the different plastic material with its peculiar processing requirements. Whereas formula modification may help in some instances (and a poorly formulated compound may not run on the best of equipment), difficulties can be expected, for example, if processing is attempted on an underpowered short-barreled extruder with unsuitable screw and die design. The most expert formulator can't help in such a situation.

III. FORMULATING OF PLASTICIZED VINYL COMPOUNDS

In formulating for any given vinyl application, three factors must be considered :

1. suitability for application;
2. suitability for processing equipment; and
3. economics.

A. Choosing Raw Materials

To satisfy these requirements for a flexible PVC compound, the formulator chooses from the following groups of raw materials:

Resin	Plasticizer
Stabilizer	Filler
Lubricant	Colorant

1. Resin

The primary factors to be considered in choosing a resin for flexible PVC are molecular weight, bulk density, and plasticizer absorptivity. Other factors that can be important, depending on the specific process or application, are particlesize distribution, dry flow, gel and contamination levels, electrical characteristics, residual monomer content, heat stability, and clarity. For plastisol applications, which require a dispersion resin, rheological properties as measured by both low shear (Brookfield) and high shear (severs) techniques must be considered.

However, brief discussions of some of these properties and their importance in choosing the proper resin for a given application or process.

Resin molecular weight is probably the single most important property to be considered. Mechanical properties, such as tensile and tear strength, will improve with increasing resin molecular weight. On the other hand, resins of low molecular weight will provide lower melt viscosities and can thus be processed more readily. Therefore the choice of resin molecular weight is often a compromise between desirable properties and ease of processing. In general, as plasticizer concentration decreased for optimum processing.

Certain forming processes require relatively low melt viscosities (e.g., injection molding) and in such instances, resins of lower molecular weight than what might be used for calendering or extrusion will be chosen.

Resin bulk density and plasticizer absorptivity are generally inter related and can affect processability. A resin with high bulk density offers the advantage of larger batch sizes during preblending as well as potentially faster rates of extrusion from powder blend. Such resins may tend, however, to have relatively poor plasticizer absorptivity, so that difficulties in blending may occur with high plasticizer content or with polymeric plasticizers. Dry-blendability will also generally tend to worsen with decreasing resin molecular weight. The formulator will generally prefer the resin that has the highest bulk density that will still give the degree of dry-blendability required for a particular process.

If a finished product is to be extruded directly from powder blend, then particle-size and dry-flow characteristics become of interest. The percentage of "fines" in the resin should be controlled from lot to lot to ensure consistent fusion characteristics and thus uniform extrudability. Dry-flow rates should preferably be high to obtain maximum production rates and to prevent "bridging" in the hopper or conveying system.

By the term heat stability, most vinyl chemists actually mean a resin's response to given stabilizer system or type. If the formulator is "locked in" to a given stabilizer system or type, he will look for he will look for a resin that will provide the best possible results with that system. It should be recognised that stabilizers can often be tailored to provide optimum response with various resins.

Considering electrical characteristics or clarity becomes important when the compounder requires such properties in the finished product. A resin's suitability for such applications is generally determined in a final formulation.

2. Plasticizer

The type and amount of plasticizer used will have the most significant effect on the compound's properties and processing characteristics.

The most important groups of plasticizers with which the formulator will work are outlined below.

a. Phthalates

The most versatile and widely used group of plasticizers are the phtatlates, produced by causing phthalic anhydride to react with alcohols. They provide an outstanding compromise of good compatibility, excellent processing behaviour, low temperature flexibility, low volatility, heat and light stability, and availability at relatively low cost. They may be considered the starting point in all vinyl formulation work.

The alcohols most commonly used to manufacture phthalate esters are butyl, hexyl, octyl, onoyl, decyl, undecyl, tridecyland benzyl, the aliphatic alcohols may be either straight-chained or branched. Mixtures of various isomers and alcohols are often used instead of a single alcohol.

b. Aliphatic Diesters

Esters of aliphatic dicarboxylic acids (adipates, azelates, sebacates) give excellent low-temperature flexibility to PVC. They also give that nebulous property called hand and drape to sheeting compounds and thus are popular for use in vinyl drapery materials. As with the phthalate series, volatility, compatibility, and solvation can be varied by choice of alcohol.

c. Phosphates

Esters of phosphoric acid are used as plasticizers in applications requiring flame resistance. The commercially available and most commonly used phosphates are the tri-aryls (based upon aromatic structures such as cresol, isopropyl phenol, tert-butyl phenol, and phenol), the tri-alkyls (based upon aliphatic alcohols such as octyl or decyl), and mixed alkyl-aryl phosphates (based upon combinations of the foregoing groups).

d. Epoxides

Epoxy plasticizers are widely used for their benefical effect on a vinyl composition's heat and light stability. They are stabilizing adjuncts, displaying a synergistic effect with most matallic stabilizers, especially with those containing cadmium or zine. The epoxidized oils (soybean and linseed) are considered nontoxic and are characterized by low volatility and performance.

e. Polymeric Plasticizers

Reaction of a dihydric alcohol (glycol) with a dicarboxylic acid results in a polyester of high molecular weight. Most such polyesters are chain-terminated with a monocarboxylic acid to provide the polymeric plasticizer.

Polymeric plasticizers are noted for their low volatility and resistance to extraction by various media. They are valuable in formulating high-temperature electrical insulation and in preparing vinyl compounds that will not mar or attack other polymers, and compounds that must resist oil or solvent extraction. Drawbacks of the polymerics include their high viscosity, low rate of solvation, poor low-temperature properties, and relatively high cost.

f. Secondary Plasticizers

In the vinyl field, secondary (or extender) plasticizers are defined as materials with relatively limited compatibility that are ordinarily used in combination with a primary plasticizer, such as DOP. Besides limited compatibility, secondaries often provide other undesirable characteristics such as poor heat or light stability, or high volatility; their effect on these properties should be carefully evaluated. Secondaries may be used for specific processing or end-use performance requirements; they are mainly used for reducing cost, however.

g. Specialty Plasticizers

many other plasticizers besides those outlined above have been developed over the years, and find application depending on economic factors, commerical availability of new raw materials, and specific requirements of the vinyl industry.

3. Stabilizer

Under the effect of heat or light, unmodified polyvinyl chloride will degrade, resulting in loss of physical properties, discoloration, and evolution of hydrogen chloride. To minimize or eliminate these effects, a stabilizer must be added to the vinyl formulation. Hundreds of stabilizers and stabilizer combinations are available to the vinyl formulator. Although some are identified by their chemical composition, the large majority are sold as proprietary products or mixtures of materials.

The compounder will choose among the following families of materials for stabilization of flexible vinyls.

a. Tin Mercaptides

On a pound-for-pound basis, organotin mercaptides represent the most powerful vinyl heat stabilizers available. They provide excellent long-term stability, good initial color, and crystal clarity. Yet because of the undesirable characteristics they lend to many finished products, tin mercaptides are seldom are used in the United States for stabilizing plasticized vinyls. Among their disadvantages are the objectionable odor they impart to the finished product, their poor light-stabilizing action, and their tendency to cross-stain (i.e., to form colored metallic sulfides) when in contact with any salts of lead, antimony, or cadmini present in the processing plant or in adjacent vinyl products.

b. Tin Carboxylates

The nonmercaptide organotin stabilizers have limited use in plasticized vinyls. Although organotin carboxylates provide outstandfing clarity, they are expensive and relatively inefficient. They have largely been replaced by barium-cadmium combinations.

c. Barium-Cadmium Soaps

The barium-cadmium soaps generally consist of mixed or coprecipitated salts of barium and cadmium with a fatty acid such as lauric, myristic, or stearic acid. Many of the proprietary materials available also contain antioxidants and other additives to provide improved stability. The soaps are generally used in conjunction with a phosphite stabilizer. Soap systems generally provide excellent long-term stability, good color control, and moderate transparency. Their primary drawbacks lie in their tendency to show moderate staining in the presence of sulfides (formation of yellow cadmium sulfide) and in their tendency to plateout on equipment.

d. Barium-Cadmium Liquids

Barium-Cadmium liquids can be described as the workhorse of the vinyl industry for stabilization of flexible stocks. They provide excellent heat and light stability and can be used for manufacture of crystal clears as well as opaques. The liquids are less prone than the soaps to plateout and sulfide-stain and they are generally less costly.

e. Barium-Cadmium-Zincs

Barium-Cadmium liquids or soaps are often combined with zinc organic salts. Such barium-cadmium-zinc combinations have proven especially effective for stabilizing highly filled stocks. Zinc, by its presence, can also provide almost complete protection against cadmium sulfide staining.

f. Leads

Lead compounds are widely used for stabilizing electrica compounds and for the processing techniques that require outstanding long-term heat stability. Use of lead salts is generally limited to opaque applications. Primary disadvantages are toxicity and severe tendency to sulfide-stain.

g. Organic Stabilizers

In the United States, organic stabilizers are generally adjunct materials, used in combination with metallic stabilizers. Organic phosphites are the most commonly used and they display a synergistic effect with many metallic systems. They are an integral part of most barium-cadmium liquids and are generally recommended for separate addition with most barium-cadmium soap stabilizers.

Antioxidants are included in many of the proprietary stabilizer systems. They are sometimes added separately by the formulator, however, especially in compounding electrical formulations, where incorporating an antioxidant such as Bisphenol "A" can markedly improve the retention of physical properties on elevated-temperature aging of the vinyl compound.

h. Nontoxic Stabilizers

Markets exist for flexible PVC in the food packaging and medical fields. In the United States, most nontoxic stabilizers used in flexible formulations consist of selected organic salts of calcium, magnesium, and zinc, in combination with approved organic adjuncts such as antioxidants, polyols, and epoxides. Such nontoxic stabilizers are generally not as efficient as the stabilizers based on barium-cadmium or lead; nonetheless, they provide sufficient stability for a wide range of processing techniques and applications.

4. Other Compounding Additives

In addition to the basic compounding materials - resin, plasticizer, and stabilizer - the formulator must be concerned with fillers, lubricants, and pigments and also such special-purpose additives as fungicides and flameproofing agents.

Assuming that the compound to be manufactured is not clear, the compounder may wish to add a filler. Most fillers sell in the two- to eight-cent-per-pound price range and thus can exert a significant effect in minimizing compound cost. Fillers have a higher specific gravity than either polyvinyl chloride resin (specific gravity 1.40) or plasticizers (specific gravity 0.85 to 1.25). The specific gravity of the most commonly used filler, calcium carbonate, is about 2.7. Adding filler will therefore increase the compound's specific gravity, which inturn will influence product yield. Thus, one should determine the cost of vinyl/compound on the basis of volume cost.

B. THE PROPERTIES TO BE TESTED AFTER COMPOUNDING

We have indicated that compounded PVC is a versatile plastic; that is, properties can be varied over a wide range depending on the specific formulating components chosen. Thus, the properties that can be tested and that are of interest to the formulator of flexible PVC are :

Hardness ASTM D1706	Tensile Strength ASTM D638
Modulus of elasticity ASTM D638	Elongation ASTM D638
Low-temperature performance	Volatility ASTM D1203
Heat stability	Light stability
Electrical properties	Clarity
Toxicity	Chemical resistance
Permanance	Stain resistance
Flammability	Fungal and bacterial resistance
Barrier properties	Melt viscosity

C. TECHNIQUES FOR FORMULATING PLASTICIZED VINYL

Various properties, then can be achieved with flexible vinyl and also with the formulation components that are available for attaining these requirements.

There are specific techniques the formulator can use, in a step by step, systematic manner, to achieve the processing and product properties desired. The number of different vinyl formulations designed to meet all possible requirements is infinite. No attempt can be made even to begin to list so-called typical formulations. There is no such thing as a typical formulation; all compounds are extremely specific in requirements and processing. Instead of making a compendium of viny formulations, we show here by several specific examples how a compounder can use the tools available to him to attain desired properties.

Example

Product :	General - purpose vinyl film.
Production :	Intensive hot fusion and calendering.
Requirements :	Good all-around performance, translucent, 85 Durometer, flame-retardant.

The first step is to determine that an 85-Durometer compound can ba achieved using 47 parts of DOP (the most commonly used plasticizer and the starting point in most vinyl formulations). Thus, step 1 in formulating gives :

1.	PVC	100 parts
	DOP	47 parts

For the plasticizer content chosen, a medium-molecular-weight resin will be suitable in most instances. With higher plasticizer content, resin molecular weight sould be higher; for stiffer compounds, a resin of lower molecular weight might prove the best. If obtaining sufficient steam pressure in a plant were a problem, a somewhat lower-molecular-weight resin than usual would be selected.

For calendering, barium-cadmium liquids have proved effective and economical stabilizers; they also allow a clear or translucent end product. Lead stabilizers might contribute too much to opacity and they generally do not provide the degree of initial colour control required for high-speed calendering. Tin stabilizers, due to their high cost and undesirable side effects, are not widely used in flexible PVC formulating. Thus, 2 parts of a barium-cadmium liquid are chosen, in a concentration typical of what is required for normal processing. Higher speeds and higher temperatures, however, might necessitate higher stabilizer concentrations.

Since the barium-cadmium liquids provide little lubricating action, a lubricant must be added. Stearic acid as a lubricant is effective and low in cost, and also helps the heat-stabilizing effectiveness of many barium-cadmium liquids. About 0.5 part is typical for calendering.

2.	PVC (med. MW)	100 parts
	DOP	47
	Ba-Cd liquid	2
	Stearic acid	0.5

Because of the heat- and light-stabilizing effectiveness of epoxy plasticizers, especially with barium-cadmium stabilizers, 3 to 5 parts of an epoxy plasticizer is added to the formulation, replacing an equivalent amount of DOP. An epoxidized soybean oil would be the most common choice.

3.	PVC (med. MW)	100 parts
	DOP	42
	Epoxidized soya oil	5
	Ba-CD liquid	2
	Stearic acid	0.5

Since the compound should be flame-retardant, either a phosphate plasticizer or antimony trioxide should be incorporated. Since antimony salts are prone to sulfide-staining, a generally undesirable trait in calendered film, a phosphate would be chosen. The most commonly used phosphates are the triaryl and alkyl diaryl esters. The choice depends largely on the relative importance of low-temperature flexibility and flameproofing agent than the more aliphatic alkyl diaryl phosphate. The latter, however, provides significantly better low-temperature flexibility. Assuming that low-temperature flexibility is not an important requisite, a triaryl phosphate such as the tricresylester (TCP) will be incorporated at a level of 10 – 15 parts. For this illustration, the 15-part level is chosen.

Since the product is to be translucent, a small amount of a low-opacity filler can be added to reduce cost and to achieve translucency. Ablout 10 phr of calcium carbonate will accomplish this without seriously affecting physical properties.

Through the use of tricresyl phosphate, low-temperature performance will be adversely affected. The formulator may wish to compensate partially for this (even though it is not part of the specification) by using an eposy tallate (rather than an epoxidized soybean oil) in the compound or a straight-chain rather than a branched-chain phthalate. Such a choice might be based on economic considerations.

The formulation now reads

4.	PVC (med. MW)	100 parts
	DOP	27
	TCP	15 parts
	Epoxy tallate	5
	Calcium carbonate	10
	Ba-cd liquid	2
	Stearic acid	0.5

Examination of Formulation 4 in the laboratory will indicate that the various formulation steps taken to achieve some of the required properties may have modified other desirable characteristics. It will be noted that the compound is harder than it was originally (since TCP is less efficient than DOP). It will also be noted that incorporating TCP has worsened heat stability, perhaps to the extent that 2 phr of the barium-cadmium liquid will not provide sufficient stability for the processing.

To adjust the hardness, the DOP content should be increased, and the amount of increase can be determined by laboratory evaluation. An increase of about 4 parts of DOP is needed to bring the hardness reading back to 85.

The stability of phosphate-plasticized systems can be improved by adding a barium-cadmium soap to the formulation. The compound is now

5.	PVC (med. MW)	100 parts
	DOP	31
	TCP	15
	Epoxy tallate	5
	$CaCO_3$	10
	Ba-cd liquid	2
	Ba-cd soap	1
	Stearic acid	0.5

While adding the barium-cadmium soap has compensated for the poor heat stability TCP introduced, using a soap may now have raised two other problems. Since the soap is lubricating, the compound may now be overlubricated, and a reduction in stearic acid content may be necessary. In addition, barium-cadmium soaps have a tendency to plateout on calender rolls. To overcome plating out, a small amount of silica may be added. The final formulation is thus

6.	PVC (med. MW)	100 parts
	DOP	31
	TCP	15
	Epoxy tallate	5
	$CaCO_3$	10
	Ba-cd liquid	2
	Ba-cd soap	1
	Stearic acid	0.3
	Silica	0.5

The preceding formulation should be prepared in the laboratory to check for exact Durometer required and degree of translucency and flameproofing obtained. Minor final adjustments in formulation can then be made.

Example 2

Product :	Sheeting for outdoor upholstery use.
Production :	Intensive powder mixing plus flat die extrusion.
Requirements :	Low-temperature flexibility, resistance to water extraction, resistance to migration into clothing, opacity, light stability, resistance to fungi, 75 Durometer.

The required Durometer is obtainable with about 62 phr DOP so the starting point is

1.	PVC	100 parts
	DOP	62

One of the requirements of the formulation is resistance to migration into clothing which could eventually cause stiffening of the vinyl. Experience has shown that the use of polymeric plasticizers will help to reduce such plasticizer loss. Polymeric plasticizers are expensive, however, and they generally exhibit poor low-temperature performance. Thus, the formulator will not want to use more than is necessary to do the job.

To determine the amount of polymeric needed to reduce migration to a satisfactory level, the formulatore may devise accelerated migration tests into absorbent materials such as a silicate, or may prepare a controlled series of compounds and run use tests on various pieces of furniture in the field. An educated guess may be all that is necessary. The path chosen will depend on the test facilities available and the amound of time available to make a choice.

For this example, it can be assumed that the formulator has found that replacement of 20 parts of DOP by an equal efficiency concentration of a medium-molecular-weight polymeric plasticizer will give the migration resistance desired. Thus, the formulation now is

2.	PVC (med. MW)	100 parts
	DOP	42
	Polymeric plasticizer	24

Since the particular polymeric plasticizer chosen is less efficient than DOP, it is necessary to use 1.2 parts of polymeric to replace 1.0 part of DOP to maintain equal hardness.

Incorporating the polymeric plasticizer has now worsened low-temperature properties, perhaps to the point that will not allow the compound to pass whatever low-temperature specification exists. Thus, the plasticizer system must again be modified to improve low-temperature performance. Two routes are open :

1. use an adipate, an azelate, or a sebacate; or
2. replace part or all of the DOP by a normal alcohol phthalate. The second approach is probably best, since the phthalate is likely to have less of an adverse effect on extraction properties than the highly mobile and migrating aliphatic esters will. Some

improvement in water extraction resistance will also result if the normal alcohol phthalate is used.

Assuming the use of a mixed normal-octyl normal-decyl phthalate with an efficiency value of 0.95 compared with DOP, the formulation now reads.

3.	PVC	100 parts
	NONDP	40
	Polymeric plasticizer	24

An experienced formulator might have foreseen the need for using a low-temperature plasticizer and would probably have run the migration tests in combinatin with NONDP instead of DOP.

Since heat- and light-stability are important factors, an epoxy plasticizer should be used. An epoxidized soybean oil, which displays permanence properties similar to many polymerics, might be the best choice and could be used to replace an equal efficiency amount of the polymeric. Assuming an efficiency value (compared with DOP) of 1.05 for the epoxy and 1.2 for the polymeric, 5 parts of epoxy would replace 6 parts of polymeric (to the nearest whole part).

Assuming that 20 parts of calcium carbonate filler can be used while still exceeding minimum tear and tensile strength requirements, the formulation now reads

4.	PVC (med. MW)	100 parts
	NONDP	40
	Polymeric	18
	Epoxy soya	5
	$CaCO_3$	20

Since the compound is fairly soft and the product requires good tear and tensile strength, a high-molecular-weight resin will be chosen. Since the sheeting is to be extruded from dry blend, and since it contains polymeric plasticizer and a relatively high plasticizer level, the resin should be one with high plasticizer-absorption properties.

A barium-cadmium or barium-cadmium-zince stabilizer will probably be selected. In combination with the epoxy present, light stability will be satisfactory for outdoor use, especially in combination with highly opaque and light-stable pigments. Stearic acid will again be the lubricant of choice, So that the formulation is now

5.	PVC (high MW, high absorption)	100 parts
	NONDP	40
	Polymeric plasticizer	18
	Epoxidized soybean oil	5
	$CaCO_3$	20
	Barium-cadmium liquid	2
	Stearic acid	0.5

All the plasticizers used in this formulatin are subject to attack by fungus. Thus, a fungicide must be added, since fungal resistance is part of the product requirement. Some fungicides adversely affect heat stability, so that it may also be necessary to modify the stabilizer system, perhaps by adding a phosphite stabilizer or increasing the barium-cadmium content, or both.

The final formulati, which must now be checked in the laboratory and adjusted if necessary, is

5.	PVC (high MW, high absorption)	100 parts
	NONDP	40
	Polymeric plasticizer	18
	Epoxidized soybean oil	5
	$CaCO_3$	20
	Barium-cadmium liquid	2.5
	Phosphite stabilizer	0.5
	Fungicide	1.0
	Stearic acid	0.5

Choice of the proper type and amount of light-stable and nonmigratory pigments completes the formulation.

Some very common & general formulations of PVC can be discussed catergorically in the tables given below. It will give a clear idea to us, how a PVC product can be formulated to get choicable end product:

Table - 1

PVC Pipe Formulations

Variable ingredients dependent on applications

Application	*Ingredient*	*Twin-screw*	*Single-screw*
Telephone duct	Acrylic lubricant processing aid	0.75	1.0
	or High-efficiency acrylic, mod. acrylic impact modifier	2.0	2.0

	or CPE		
	calcium carbonate	20 to 30	20 to 30
Electrical conduit	Acylic processing aid	0.75	1.0
	or High-efficiency acrlic processing aid	00.5	0.75
(Small diameter)	High-efficiency acrylic mod. acrylic impact modifier or	4.0	4.0
	High-efficiency MBS	3.0	3.0
	impact modifier or CPE	5 to 6	5 to 6
	Calcium carbonate	10	10
Irrigation pipe	Acrylic processing aid	0.75	
	or High-efficiency acrylic processing aid	0.5	
	High-efficiency acrylic or mod. acrylic impact modifier		
	TiO_2	7.0	
	Calcium carbonate	0 to 5	

Table - 2

PVC Conduit Pipe Formulations

	Twin-screw	*Single-screw*
Constant ingredients (for all pipe types)		
PVC resin (K=67, 68; IV=0.92)	100	100
Tin stabilizer	0.4	1.2
Calcium stearate	0.8	1.5
parafin wax (165° C)	1.2	0.8
TiO2	1.0	1.0

Variable ingerdients dependent on applications		
Pressure		
Acrylic processing aid (or high-efficiency acrylic processing aid)	0.75 (0.5)	1.0 (0.75)
calcium carbonate	0 to 5	0 to 5
DMV		
High-impact efficiency MBS or ABS (or CPE)	1 to 2 (3)	1 to 2 (3)
Calcium carbonate	0 to 5	0 to 5
Sewer		
Calcium carbonate	0 to 5	0 to 5
Drain		
Acrylic lubricant	0.75	1.0
Calcium carbonate	20 to 40	20 to 40

Table - 3

Window Profile Formulations

	Twin-screw	*Single-screw*
Tin stabilized		
PVC resin (K=67; IV=90)	100	100
Acrylic, mod, acrylic, or CPE impact modifier	5 to 6	5 to 6
Acrylic processing aid	1	2.5
Acrylic lubricant processing aid	0.5 to 1.0	0.5 to 1.0
Tin stabilizer	1.5	2.0
Calcium stearate	1.2	1.0
Parafin wax (164'F)	1.0	0.75
TiO_2	8 to 12	8 to 12
Barium/cadmium stabilized		
PVC resin (K=67; IV=0.90)	100	100
Acrylic, mod, acrylic, or CPE impact modifier	5 to 6	5 to 6
Acrylic processing aid	1	1.5
Acrylic lubricant processing aid	0.5	0.5
Ba/Cd stabilizer	3.0	4.0
Alkyl-aryl phosphate	0.5	0.5

Calcium stearate	1.0	--
Ester wax	0.5	--
Glyceryl monostearate	0.4	2.0
$TiiO_2$ 7.0	7.0	7.0
$CaCO_3$ (fine particle size, coated)	5.0	5.0

Table - 4

Interior PVC profile Formulations

	Twin-screw	*Single-screw*
PVC resin (K=67; IV=0.90)	100	100
High-efficiency, low die swell MBS or acrylic impact modifier	6 to 10	6 to 10
Acrylic lubricant processing aid	1.0	1.0
Tin stabilizer	1.5	2.0
Calcium stearate	0.8	0.8
Parafin wax (165' F)	1.2	0.7
Calcium carbonate	3 to 5	3 to 5
Pigments	As needed	

Table - 5

PVC Siding Formulations

	Twin-screw	*Single-screw*
PVC resin (K=67; IV=0.92)	100	100
Acrylic, mod, acrylic, CPE		
Impact modifier	5 to 6	5 to 6
Acrylic processing aid (or high-efficiency acrylic processing aid)	1 (0.5)	2 (1.5)
Acrylic lubricant processing aid	0.5	0.5
Tin stabilizer	1.6	2.0
Calcium stearate	1.3	1.0
parafin was (165' F)	1.0	1.0
TiO_2	10 to 14	10 to 14

Table - 6

Cellular PVC Profile Formulations

	Twin-screw	*Single-screw*
PVC resin (K=62; IV=0.80)	100	100
Paraloid* KM-318Fa	8 to 9	8 to 9
Azodicarbonamide	0.5	0.5
Tin stabilizer	1.5	1.5
Calcium stearate	0.8	1.0
Parafin wax (165' F)	1.0	0.8
Calcium carbonate	0.1	—
Pigments	As needed	

Table - 7

Extruded PVC Sheet and Film (Single-Screw)

	Clear	*Opaque*	*Non-stress whitening clear*
PVC resin (K=60 to 62, IV=0.67 to 0.80)	100	100	100
High impact effeciency or ABS impact modifier	10 to 12	—	MBS —
High impact efficiency MBS crease whitening resistant	—	—	10 to 15
General-purpose MBS (or ABS) impact modifier	—	8 to 12	(6 to 10)
Acrylic processing aid (or high-efficiency acrylic processing aid)	2.0 (1.6)	2.0 (1.6)	2.0 (1.6)
Acrylic lubricating processing aid	1.0	1.0	1.0
Tin stabilizer	2.0	2.0	2.0
Montan ester wax	0.4	—	0.4
Glyceryl monostearate	0.75	—	0.75

Calcium stearate	--	2.0	--
Parafin wax (165' F)	--	0.7	--
Blue toner	0.0004	--	0.0004
TiO_2	--	As needed	--

Table - 8

Calendered PVC Sheet and Film Formulation - Second Alternative

	Clear	*Opaque*	*Non-stress whitening clear*
PVC resin (K=60; IV=0.76)	100	100	100
MBS or ABS impact modifier	10 to 15	--	--
High-efficiency impact modifier	--	--	10 to 15
General-purpose MBS or ABS (or acrylic or high-efficiency MBS or ABS impact modifier)	--	8 to 12	(6 to 10)
Acrylic processing aid (or high-efficiency acrylic processing aid)	2.0 (1.6)	2 (1.6)	2.0 (1.6)
Acrylic lubricant processing aid	0.5 to 1.0	0.5 to 1.0	0.5 to 1.0
tin stabilizer	2.0	1.6 to 2.0	2.0
Glyceryl monostearate	0.5 to 0.8	0.5 to 0.8	0.5 to 0.8
OP wax	0.2 to 0.4	0.2 to 0.4	0.2 to 0.4
E wax	0.05 to 0.2	0.05 to 0.2	0.05 to 0.2
Blue toner (1% in PVC)	0.06	--	0.06
TiO_2		As needed	

Table - 9

PVC Injection Moulded Pipe Fitting Formulation

	Type I/type I improved (cell class 12454/13454	*Type II (cell class 14333)*
PVC resin (K=57 to 61; IV=0.68 to 0.79)	100	100
High-efficiency. MBS, ABS impact modifier; (CPE)	1.0 (3.0)	3.0 (0.75)
Acrylic processing aid (or high-efficiency acrylic processing aid)	1.0 (0.75)	1.0 (0.75)
Acrylic lubricant processing aid	0.5	0.5
Tin stabilizer	1.5	1.5 to 2.0
Calcium stearate	0.5	0.5
Parafin wax (165' F)	0.5	0.5
TiO_2	1.5	1.5

Table - 10

High-Flow PVC Injection Moulding Formulation

	General purpose	*Exterior use*
PVC resin (K=52; IV=0.57-0.60)	100	100
High-efficiency. MBS or ABS impact modifier	10 (or 12)	—
(or low die swell MBS or ABS impact modifier)		
High-efficiency acrylic impact modifier	—	10 to 12
Acrylic processing aid	1.5 to 2.0	1.5 to 2.0
(or high-efficiency acrylic impact modifier)	(1.2 to 1.7)	(1.1 to 1.7)
Acrylic lubricant processing aid	1.0 to 1.5	1.0 to 1.5
Tin stabilizer	2.0	2.2
Glyceryl monostearate	2.7	2.7
Polyethylene wax	0.3	0.3
TiO_2	As needed	10 to 12

Table - 11

Extrusion Blow-Moulding Rigid PVC Containers

Ingredient	*Formulation*
S-PVC[a], K 57	100 parts
Acrylate impact modifier	10.0 phr
Ingredient	Formulation
Process aid	2.0 phr
Octylthiotin stabilizer[a]	1.5 phr
Internal lubricant	0.6 phr
External lubricants	0.7 phr

[a]Suspension PVC

[b]D-n-octyltin-S S' - bis (isooctylmercaptoacetate)

Crystal-clear food-contact bottles

Ingredient	*Formulation*
M-PVC[a], K 57	100 parts
MBS, impact modifier	8-14 phr
Di-n-octylthiotin stabilizer[b]	1.5 phr
Lubricant based on a long-chain fatty acid ester	0.8 phr
Lubricant based on a fatty alcohol	0.2 phr
Amide wax (acrawax C, Advawax 280)	0.2 phr

Table - 12

Clear Bottles Good on Taint and Odour

Ingredient	*Formulation*
S-PVC, K 58	100 parts
Paraloid KM 522 (impact modifier)	10 phr
Paraloid K 120N (process aid)	1.0 phr
Butyltin stabilizer[a]	1.5 phr
Glyceryl monostearate	0.7 phr
Partially modified montan ester wax	0.3 phr

[a]Di-n-butyltin-S,S'-bis (isooctylmercaptoacetate)

Table - 13

Blow-Moulded Bottle Formulations

General-purpose A		*Calcium/zinc (Europe) ribbed bottle*	
PVC (K value 58)	100.0	PVC (K value 58)	100
Butyltin stabilizer	1.5	Calcium stearate or behenate	0.35
Acrylic processing aid	1.5	Zinc octoate (23% zinc)	0.10
Glyceryl monooleate	0.5	Epoxidized soya oil	5.5
OP wax	0.2	Loxiol G15	0.5
Toner (1% in PVC)	0.06	Stearoyl benzoyl methane	0.3
Clear MBS or ABS impact modifier	12.0	OP wax or PED 191	0.25
		Loxiol G78	0.15
General-purpose B		Toners (1% in PVC)	0.065
PVC (K value 58)	100.0	Acrylic processing aid	0.3
Butyltin stabilizer	2.0	Clear MBS impact modifier	8.0
Glyceryl monoestearate	0.5		
OP wax	0.2	Ca/Zn (U.S.) 16 oz. Boston round PVC (K Value 58)	100.00
Acrylic processing aid	1.0	Ca/Zn package stabilizer	2.00

Table - 14

Acrylic lubricating processing aid	1.0	ESO	4.0
Toner (1% in PVC)	0.06	Acrylic processing aid	1.5
Clear MBS or ABS impact modifier	12.5	Stearoyl benzoyl methane	0.3
		Glyceryl monooleate	0.5
		OP wax	0.2
		Tris (nonylphenyl) phosphate	0.5
		Clear MBS impact modifier	12.0
		Toner (1% in PVC)	0.07

Table - 15

Blow-Moulded PVC Bottle Formulations

	General purpose tin	*Food grade octyltin*	*Food grade Ca/Zn*
PVC resin (K=58; IV=0.72)	100	100	100
Clear MBS or ABS impact modifier	12 to 14	12 to 14	12 to 14
Acrylic processing aid	2.0	2.0	2.0
Acrylic lubricant processing aid	0.5 to 1.0	0.5 to 2.2	---
Tin stabilizer	2.0	2.0 to 2.2	---
Ca/Zn stabilizer	---	---	2.0
Glyceryl monostearate	0.5	0.5	0.5
Montan ester wax	0.2	0.2	0.2
Benzoyl stearoyl methane	---	---	0.3
Alkyl-aryl phosphite (food-approved)	---	---	0.5
Epoxidized soya oil	---	---	4.0
Blue toner (1% in PVC)	0.06	0.06	0.07

MINERAL WATER BOTTLE

Table - 16

CA-ZN Formulation (Mineral Water)

Ingredient	*Formulation*
S-PVC, K57	100
Kane Ace B modifier or equivalent	10.0
Kane Ace PA 20 process aid or equivalent	0.5
Expoxidized soyabeen oil	5.0
Saturated partial easter of glycerine	1.2
Easter of montanic acid	0.4
Calcium stearate	0.16
Stearoyl benzoyl methane	0.15
Zinc stearate	0.14

Table - 17

CA-ZN Epoxy Recipe for 1 Liter Bottle

Ingredient	*Formulation*
S-PVC, K 58	100
MBS-impact Modifier	8
Epoxidized soyabean oil	5.5
Acrylic processing aid	0.5
Glyceryl ester of montanic acid	0.50
Di-stearyl pentaerythriotol disphosphite (antioxidant)	0.30
Calcium stearate	0.25
Zinc octoate	0.17
Stearoyl benzoyl methane	0.12

Table - 18

PVC Bottle for Shampoo

PVC (0.75 to 0.9 IV)	100
Acrylic processing aid	1 to 5
MBS impact modifier	8 to 15
Organotin mercaptide stabilizer	1.5 to 3.0
Lubricants	0.5 to 2.0
Tinting agent	As required

Table - 19

Shoe Soles

PVC resin	100 (K-value around 70)
Plasticizer	70-90
Heat stabilizer	03-08
Lubricant	02.0
Pigment	As required
Fillers	As required

Test for Compound

Heat Stability	:	50 minutes at 180°C
Plasticizer Volatility	:	Loss of < 2% in 100°C heating test over a period of 24 hours
Solvent Leaching	:	Leaching of plasticizer takes place if sole comes in contact with solvents and oils
Processing Temperature Range	:	160-180°C

Table - 20

Floor Coverings/wall Coverings

	Floor Covering	*Wall Covering*
Foam Layer		
Paste grade Resin (K-value 65-70)	100-70	100
Micronised Suspension resin	0-30	--
Plasticizer	55	65
Azodicarbonamide	2.5	3-4
Stabilizer (or Kicker) (Tin Carbodylate/Ca-Zn Liquid Stabilizer)	0.5-2.5	1-2.5
Filler (Calcium Carbonate)	10-35	0-10
Titanium Dioxide	5	5-10
Foam Layer		
Paste grade resin (K-Value 75-80)	80-60	100
Micronised suspension resin	20-40	--
Plasticizer	40	55
Tin Stabilizer	1-2	1-2

Table - 21

Typical Light Stable Formulation

PVC resin	100
Ester Plasticizer	30 to 80
Epoxy Plasticizer	3 to 5
Calcium Carbonate	0 to 5
Ba-Cd-Zn Stabilizer	2 to 4
Phosphite Stabilizer	0.5 to 1.0
UV absorber	0.1 to 1.0
Fatty acid or ester lubricant	0.3 to 1.0

Table - 22

Carbon Black Properties

Property Black	Furnace Black	Channel Black	Thermal
Average particle size (mm)	13-75	10-30	150-500
Surface area (N_2BET) (m_2g)	25.500	100-1125	6-15
Oil absorption (cm^3/g)	0.70-1.85	1.0-5.7	0.3-0.5
pH	3.3-9.0	3.0-6.0	7.0-8.0
Percent Volatiles	1.0-9.5	3.0-17.0	0.1-0.5

Table - 23

Comparison - Titanium Dioxide and Zinc Oxide

Property	*Titanium*	*Dioxide*	*Zinc Oxide*
		Anatase	*Rutile*
Average particle size (micron)	0.3	0.2-0.3	0.2
Density (g/cm')	3.9	4.1	5.6
Refractive	2.55	2.76	2.01
Tinting Strength	1200	1600	210
Oil absorption (ab/100 lb)	18-30	16-48	10-25
Hardness (Mohs)	5-6	6-7	4+

Table - 24

Potable - Water Pipe

(EXTRUDED FROM DRY BLEND)

PVC (0.9 to 1.0 IV)	100
Processing aids	1 to 5
Impact modifier	0 to 10
Calcium Carbonate	0 to 10
Alkytin or antimony mercatide	0.3 to 2.0
Calcium stearate	0.5 to 1.5
Paraffin Wax	0.5 to 1
Pigment	1 to 2

Table - 25

General Purpose Vinyl Film by Calendering

(Parts)

PVC (med MW)	100
Dop	31
Exopy tallate	5
Phosphate	15
CaCo3	1.0
Ba-Cd liquid	2
Ba-Cd Soap	1
Stearic acid	0.3
Silica	0.5

Table - 26

Sheeting for Outdoor Upholstery

(Parts)

PVC (high MW, high absorption)	100
$C_{7,9,11}$ mixed aliphatic phthalate	40
Polymeric Plasticizer	18
Epoxidised soyabean Oil	5
CaCo3	2.0
Barium-Cadmium liquid	2.5
Phosphite stabilizer	0.5
Fungicide	1.0
Stearic acid	0.5

16

Compounding of PVC Pastes

PVC Pastes are paste-like suspensions of PVC polymer particles in plasticiser. A paste containing polymer dispersed in plasticiser, with stabilisers and others additions is also called plastisol. When the paste contains volatile solvent also as part of the dispersion medium in addition to the plasticiser, it is known as organosol. The solvent is removed ultimately and this is the disadvantage and restriction in the organosols. But they are useful low initial viscosity but a hard final products with low plasticiser contents is desired, which is not possible with plastisols. A plastigel is the plastisol containing some thickerning agent to increase the viscosity and inconsistancy varies from that of butter to putty and may be highly thixotropic.

Plastisols

Plastisols are basically suspensions having high concentration of the suspended resin. They are useful forms of PVC compounds as they are liquids thus can be readily processed for number of applications. On heating at the right time during processing, they are irreversibly converted to very highly viscous solutions of polymer in plasticiser. This phenomenon is known as 'gelling'. These solutions on solidify, giving plasticised PVC product.

It can be seen that rheology of the PVC pastes is of profound importance. The plastisol should have the right rheological properties for application and these should remain constant during storage. Also the gelation should proceed at the right and controlled rate. It has been that all this is a complex matter and depends on the nature and composition of the paste.

Compounding Ingredients of Plastisols

PVC plastisols just like other PVC compounds contain the polymer, plasticiser, stabiliser, colourants, fillers and external lubricants. Sometimes special additives such as antistatic agents or blowing agents etc., may also be incorporated depending on the end use properties desired. Solid compounds and plastisols are different in their physical state and processing. In pastes polymeric modifiers and internal lubricants are not added; and viscosity modifiers, diluents and thickness are incorporated. The major compounding ingredients for plastisols are given on following pages.

PVC Polymers

Paste polymers should be resistant at room temperature to the plasticisers user, this makes the paste stable. For good gelation polymers should have good affinity for the plasticisers so that they dissolve in them at the appropriate temperature during gelation. Paste polymer are usually of to plasticiser attack at room temperature. The preferable particle size ranges from 0.5 to 2 microns. To lower plastisol viscosity, a part of paste polymer is replaced by suspension-type polymer or co-polymer ranging in particle size from 80 to 140 microns. These co-polymers or homopolymers have a non-absorbant particle surface. Minimum plastisols viscosity is achieved at a combination of 50 per cent dispersion resin with 50 per cent blending resin concentration. This viscosity effect is rather permanent and in some cases the ageing properties of the paste may be improved. Viscosity reducing extender polymers are used for coating, spraying and rotational casting operations.

Suspension homopolymers with absorbent surface increase the viscosity sharply and ageing properties deteriorate, due to absorption of some plasticiser into the extender-polymer particles, they are also sometimes used for special purposes.

Plasticisers

The plasticisers selection as usual depends on the end use properties desired, but in the case of plastisols this also depends on paste viscosity, rheological characteristics, and gelation properties desired. Initial viscosity of the plastisols is very much affected by the bulk viscosity of the plasticiser. The solvating power of the plasticiser has also some effect in increasing the viscosity. Polymer mixtures impart, physical and end use properties, intermediate between those imparted by them individually. Monomeric type plasticiser very quite extensively in oil viscosity and solvent power thus affecting paster viscosity, they are frequently used in pastes. Polymeric plasticiser have higher oil viscosities, they raise the paste viscosity, increase gelation times and temperatures and improve viscosity stability. Low temperature plasticiser have quite low oil viscosities, hence they are suitable for low viscosity pastes, and increase viscosity stability due to limited resin solvent power. They increase gelation times and temperatures. Epoxy soyabean oil plasticiser have similar effects to those of the polymeric plasticisers. Extender type plasticisers have low solvent power hence they improve paste viscosity and increase gelation times and temperatures.

Phthalates impart medium viscosity at room temperature, with low or medium setting temperatures. For rotational casting they should be used in high concentration or should be mixed with plasticiser giving high setting temperatures. DBP can not be used alone, due to its volatility and good solvating properties which promote ageing. DDP is useful because of the high setting temperature (about 105'C) it imparts. DIDP is a slow slovating plasticiser giving good ageing properties with longer times and higher temperatures of fusion. Phosphates imprat low setting temperatures and some dilatency, them produce plastisols of medium viscosity. Low temperature plasticisers are good for rotational casting as they promote a large drop in viscosity with increasing temperature. Citrates are useful for pastes for their effect on the setting temperature which may be adjusted by such plasticisers.

Stabilisers

The criteria for selection of stabilisers is same as that with solid PVC compounds. With pastes liquid stabilisers are preferred. The stabilisers selection depends on the physical properties and processing requirements of the pastes. Solid stabilisers increase the paste viscosity whereas the liquid ones decrease it. Basic lead carbonate dibasic lead phosphate give excellent heat and light stability. Basic lead carbonate is commonly used for opaque compounds. Calcium stearate is best for transparent ones and should not be used at more than 1 per cent level. It should be remembered that stearates increase initial viscosity and viscosity on ageing, so they should be used with care. Light stability of any system can be improved by adding 1 per cent phenyl salicylate.

For the selection of stabiliser, the concerned chapter may be seen. Mould may be of copper or alloys hence those stabilisers which may cause discolouration in the presence of copper should be avoided. Strong basic and sulphur containing stabilisers should not used. Some colourants such as lead chromate and antimony trioxide, also may exert some stabilising effect. Iron containing have pigments have antistabilising effect hence with them particularly stabiliser are added. The heat stabiliser concentration depends on the process requirements of the applications, generally 3.0 phr level is considered to be satisfactory. The liquid Ba/Cd/Zn types are the most common type of stabilisers.

Fillers

Just like in solid PVC compounds fillers are used here also to lower the cost and increase the hardness. In pastes they increase the viscosity of the pastes and reduce the shelf-life. Fillers increase the hardness the hardness tackness of the films obtained from pastes but adversely affect the physical properties. They sometimes give the correct degree of translucency and life-like appearance of soles. Calcium carbonate, silicates and asbestos are the most commonly used fillers. Silica gel, barytes, gypsum alum, wood flour etc. are also used. Fillers, depending upon the oil absorption value, lower the tensile properties, increase hardness, lower flexibility and increase processing temperatures.

The particle size of the fillers should not be too small as finer particles yield higher viscosity. Various fillers in the increasing order of oil absorption value are : Barytes (16), State powder, Dolomite, whiting (36), china clay, silica, veryfine china clay, and water ground mica (79). Usually not more than 30 phr of fillers are used in general pastes and 20 phr in pastes for rotational casting. Very high filler loading cause a whitening effect upon the compound when it is bent.

Colourants

Iron oxide pigments are strong, have good light stability and are cheep but can not be used for high temperature applications. Cd/selenide pigments have good light and heat stability, and chemical resistance but have weak colour intensity. Organic colours are strong, sharp and bright with fair heat stability but are costly with poor light stability and may change colour with pH. Some colourants have effects on reheological properties. Pigments such as phthalocyanine greens, blue and some blacks can cause high paste viscosities. Colourants are usually incorporated into pastes by means of a predispersed pigment-plasticisers paste. Paste is best prepared on a 3-roll paint mill using a small quantity of a polymeric plasticiser as the grinding medium to give mill tack, this gives better dispersion.

Thickners

Thickening agents or thickeners are used in thixotropic plastisols and plastisols. To convert normal pastes into thick plastigels various thickening agents may be added. Tgese thixotropic gels and plastisols are used for one-dip coating, for non-drip coatings and for spreading processes to reduce penetration. Fillers like very fine whitings and carbon blacks have thickening properties. Bentonites and aluminium stearates are good thickeners. The plasticiser is pregelled with the agent and the resultants product is used to prepare the paste. This is done by dispersing the agent in the plasticiser and warming to get a clear solution (usually at 115'C). A marked increase in viscosity takes place and after cooling. The plasticisers is ready for use. In the case of aluminium stearate a 25 per cent pregel solution is made in the plasticiser. The amount on plastisol being about 2 to 10 per cent. DOP and

DOS can easily be pregelled in this way but TTP can not be. For higher plasticiser content more thickening agent is required.

Other Additives

Sometimes it so happens that for particular end use properties certain plasticiser system and plasticiser polymer ratio is used resulting high paste viscosities; to overcome this certain surface active agents, such as polyethylene glycols etc., are added in low quantities (usually 1 per cent), which are known as viscosity depressants. They usually retard the ageing of the paste. Diluents are the organic solvents used to reduce the viscosity, mainly in organosols. Other minor additives are, antistatic agents, fungicides, fire retardants and odourants etc.

Organosols

Organosols are plastisols containing a volatile diluent. Diluent is added to lower the paste viscosity. The ratio of resin to plasticiser depends mainly on the physical property requirement of the final product, such as hardness, flexibility and abrasion resistance etc.

Compounding Ingredients

Compounding ingredients used in organosols as those with plastisols and same criteria of selection applies here also but extra care has to be taken in selecting the volatile diluent. Diluents are frequently very poor solvents for the resin. Aromatic hydrocarbons such as white spirit, ketones such as white spirit, ketones methyl ethyl ketone and methyl isobutyl ketone, alcohols, glycol ether and chlorinated hydrocarbons have been used as diluent. During the processing they are volatilised off. Paste viscosity can thus be controlled by diluent; hence higher levels of viscosity increasing ingredients such as polymeric plasticisers and fillers may thus be used.

This organosols can solve various processing problems but have the problems of fire hazard, toxicity, solvent recovery problems porous films and also cost factor. Organosols should, as far as possible, be avoided in preference to plastisols.

Preparation of Pastes

With old type standard resins grinding is necessary but with paste polymers paste mixer are sufficient. It should be remembered that sufficient shearing action should be there to produce satisfactory dispersions. This applies to both plastisols and organosols. With organosols the final paste viscosity are much lower than those with plastosols. Typical organosol viscosities are from 2000 to 6000 cps, hence high-speed Disc Impeller type mixer is usually used.

All the dry components of the compound such as pigments, fillers, stabilisers etc., should be predispersed in a small quantity of the plasticiser. Usually 1 to 3 parts of plasticisers to 1 part of dry material is sufficient. This is best done on 3-roll mill or by ball milling. The polymer is placed in the mixer with the plasticiser just sufficient to form a paste and into this the predispersed dry components are added. This ensures mixing at the maximum shear. The frictional heat will be generated and temperature should not be allowed to exceed 30'C. Otherwise the plasticiser will start to attack the polymer and the ultimate viscosity will be higher. Water cooling may be done. Mixing is done for 10 to 30 minutes, after this 'thick mixing' the remaining plasticisers, the diluent if any, is gradually added. This 'thin stage mixing' may be done for about 1 hour. Various suitable mixing for this purpose are : poly type mixers, dough mixers, disk impellers and high intensity mixers. In general vertical stirr type mixers (anchor, paddle or propeller) and planetary mixers are considered to be good enough. The use of efficient mixers designed for paste mixing will reduce the chance of the formation of lumps and aeration etc.

During the mixing operation air is entreapped in the mix, as dispersed bubbles. For sprayable plastisols and plastisols containing blowing agents removal of bubbles is not necessary but for the preparation of clear transparent cast articles, films, dip coatings and slush moulded products, this air should be removed, Plastisols being more viscous than organosols entrape more air. For thin fabric coating etc. also no deaeration is required. For thick pastes deaeration can be done by applying vacuum. For thinner pastes keeping standing for 24 hours may be sufficient. With organosols deaeration is unnecessary.

Gelation

When a PVC paste is heated, the viscosity drops at first, then it rises sharply and finally a solution of PVC in plasticiser is obtained. This whole process of conversion of PVC paste into a uniform solution or gel of PVC in plasticiser is know as Gelation. The stage of high viscosity is known as 'pre-gel'. The pre-gel state is utilised for multiple dipping process, intermediate stages are pre-gelled and the whole layer is then fully gelled at the appropriate temperature. The pre-gel is quite cohesive but mechanical properties are very poor. For gelation the temperature should be at least 160'C for best physical properties in the final product. Heating above this, reduce gelation time but a high temperature will cause some plasticiser loss and decomposition.

For good process control it is essential to know whether gelation has been complete or not. Some physical properties such as tensile strength, hardness etc. ,are very good indicators but the teste for these are quite laborious. Solvent test is very good for the purpose. In this test a strip of the finished article such as PVC coated glove is suspended in ethyl acetate (solvent) and number of minutes for PVC to start 'flaking' are determined. Poorly gelled PVC coating start flaking earlier. In solvent tests of kind, PVC may be taken to be completely gelled if no flaking occurs specified time, usually anything from 5 to 20 minutes depending on the severity of the test.

APPLICATIONS OF PVC PASTES

In this section various uses and methods of application of PVC pastes or unit operations are being given.

1. Slush moulding
2. Rotational Moulding
3. Spraying
4. Coating
5. Organosols

ROTATIONAL CASTING FORMULATION FOR DOLLS AND PLAY BALLS

PVC Paste Polymer (K 65)	100 parts
DAP	40
DMP	50
Ca/Ba liquid stabiliser	3

COMPOUNDING OF PVC LATICES

Various types of compounding ingredients for PVC latices are used. Some ingredients affect latex properties such as its stability etc. , other affect the end properties such as heat stability and physical properties etc., of the final PVC product. The former type of ingredients are known as latex property modifiers and latter ingredients are known as polymer property modifiers. These will now be discussed in details :

Latex Property Modifiers

Under this category come latex stabilisers, wetting agents, thickeners, antifoaming agents and pH modifiers etc.

Latex Stabilisers

Stabilisers are added to the latices to ensure adequate chemical and mechanical stability. Protective colloids and surface active agents improve stability. Wetting properties of the latex compound, water sensitivity of the dried film etc., influence the choice of the suitable stabiliser.

Surface Active Agent

The addition of surface active agents reduces the surface tension and thus increases the wetting power of the system. This helps the penetration of fibrous substrates during coating but with increasing quantity of surface active agent, sensitivity of the dried film to water and foaming increases. Wetting agents are aniounic and non-ionic infectants which reduce surface tension and increase wetting. They increase the resistance of latex to instability under high shear and mono-or polyvalent cations. Excess of wetting agent will cause too much foaming and increase of water soluble salts in the final film. Anionic wetting agents such as ethylene oxide/fetty alcohol condensation products give very good protection against the chemical destability of high concentration of mono-or polyvalent ions which destroy the latex particles, negatively charged protective colloids causing coagulation. Anionic wetting agents increases the mechanical stability of the latex. Protective colloids such as casein impart stability of the latex under high shear. Alkyl sulphosuccinates and polyoxyethylene alkyl phenol derivates are good wetting agents.

Dispersing agents are also surface active agents which promote deflocculation of pigment particles and prevent agglomeration. These also should be kept to minimum level as final film gets weaker with higher levels. In sone cases, to prevent future agglomeration of particles, very small amount of a wetting agent is necessary to be added.

Defoaming Agents

These are also known as antifoamers. As the name indicates these material are added during latex compounding to reduce the formation of foam. Defoamers are added to the final compound to break up any existing foam. Some surface active agents increase the formation of foam whereas other act as antifoamers but not as defoamers. Both silicone and non-silicone based antifoams are available and are used in concentrations varying from 0.05 to 0.5 per cent based on latex.

Thickners

Latex systems usually do not require additives to alter viscosity but thickners are added to prevent the setting of heavier ingredients such as pigments and to obtain proper coating viscosities. Natural thickners such proteins and casein etc. are not that popular as they are prone to attack by microbes such as fungi and bacteria. Cellulose derivatives such as CMC, and polyacrylates are the popular thickners. Polyacrylates are more efficient than cellulose derivatives, and thus in their case sedimentation is minimum. These thickners are used as 2 to 5 per cent solutions. They are usually used in quantities varying from about 0.4 to 0.6 parts per hundred of dry PVC.

To obtain best dispersion and maximum efficiency latex should be added slowly to the thickener with slow constant agitation. Another method is that of master batching. Thickener, in this method, is mixed thoroughly with small portion of the latex mix and this mixture is then incorporated with the main latex batch, giving maximum efficiency. When large batches of highly filled latex are prepared, thickener may be added directly, effectiveness depending on the agitator efficiency.

pH Modifiers and Buffers

pH of the PVC latices vary form 8.5 to 11. Hence the pH of the dispersions, emulsions and solutions to be added to latex, should be atleast 7 to 8. If this not possible then the pH of the latex should be raised and buffered to prevent destabilisation. In any case strongly acid material should not be added to anionic latices. The most popular pH modifier is ammonium hydroxide, it does not cause flocculation when added in conventrated form. On drying it evaporates. Though strong alkalis such as sodium and potassium hydroxides are sufficient in small quantities, in solutions of above 5 per cent conventration cause flocculation. Unlike ammonium hydroxide, they remain in the latex film adversely affecting water resistance. Sodium bicarbonate and alkali phosphates may also be used as pH modifiers.

Phosphates such as trisodium phosphate (TSP) and sodium hexa meta phosphate are the buffering agents usually employed. Phosphates reduce the effects of sharp changes in pH. They also sequester the calcium, zinc and magnesium cations and aid dispersion of solids, thus increasing the stability of the latex mix. Ethylene diamine tetra acetic acid is very good requiestering agent and in even very small quantities prevents the precipitation of stabiliser soaps by calcium, magnesium and zinc ions, but it is not a good buffering agent and is rather costly.

Polymer End Properties Modifiers

The ingredients discussed above balance the emulsion properties for processing and do not much affect the properties of the end product. On their own the PVC latices dry out to give hard thermoplastics product which is not of much use. Hence many ingredients are added. PVC latices usually have 30 to 50 per cent PVC by volume which increases to 70 per cent on evaporation of water without any structural changes but on further evaporation position become different and complex. Softer particles coalesce easily but hard particles do not. Softer particles give strong network due to autohesion but hard particles require higher temperature and pressure for the same effect. In presence of plasticiser autohesion occurs readily as particles get softened.

Various compounding ingredients which modify the polymer end-use properties are heat stabilisers, plasticisers, fillers, pigments and anti-blocking agents.

Heat Stabilisers

As with other PVC compounds a heat stabiliser is sometimes necessary in PVC latex mix. They are required to retard of prevent decomposition during processing and during services file, only when high temperatures such as 150oC over are encountered for extended period of time. Various types of heat stabilisers are available, but they should be capable of being dispersed in water by a ball mill or should be capable for being emulsified in water (if they are liquid) so that the danger of flocculation is avoided. It should also be quite efficient and should be compatible with the latex mix. Liquid stabilisers containing metallic salts or soaps may be soluble in the latex. When solubility occurs metallic cation may be formed injuring the stability of the latex.

A stabiliser effective insolid PVC compound may not be necessarily effective in the latex mix, dur to the influence of water, emulsifiers and dispersing agents, Organo-tin compounds especially when used with an epoxy secondary stabiliser/plasticiser are quite good heat stabilisers for PVC latex mixer. Good results are obtained at the level of 4 parts per hundred of PVC resin (dry). Heat stabiliser emulsion should be added to the latex, at an early stage during compounding, with constant slow stirring.

Plasticisers

Latex resin particles are very much finer than the particles of resin in solid compounds hence they require lower plasticiser content. The reasons for introducing plasticiser in latices are similar to those with solid PVC compounds. They reduce hardness and increase flexibility. For better plasticising action the plasticiser should be compatible with the PVC and its molecular weight should be low, but with lower molecular weight volatility and migration problem increases. DOP, DIOP and DAP have good alround performance with economy but phosphates such as TCP has good flame retardancy, low volatility but low efficiency and colour stability on ageing. TXP has greater performance. Plasticiser should usually be added to the latex as oil-in-water emulsion. This requires equipment of high speed and shearing action. Simple mixing will not give a fine enough plasticiser emulsion to provide efficient absorption and absorption of the plasticiser particle by the extremely small PVC particles in the latex.

Fillers

Fillers are ioncorporated to reduce cost, provide opacity, increase hardness and reduce tack. Whiting clays, barytes, silica and mica are the most common fillers used in PVC latex mixers. When used at about 20 phr they modify the PVC film without much adversely affecting the physical properties. Water absorptivity or water demand of the filler is a very important point. It depends on particle size, shape and moisture level of the filler. It should be added as dispersion in water, the concentration of which depends on; the water demand of the filler, its moisture content and total solid desired in the finished compound. Every tatex has a critical limit (CPVC) above which if filler loading is increased, physical properties, such as elongation, drop sharply.

Whitings and clays are quite economical where mica is costly. Whitings are soft, clays are harder and micas have high hardness. For coatings barytes have good covering power. But have greater tendency to settle, addition of small amounts of fine silica reduces this tendency. Filler dispersion should have particles of as fine size as possible and for this a collid mill may be used.

Pigments

Pigments are used to improve the appearance. Oxides of iron, zinc or copper should be avoided as these metallic ions sometimes catalyse the decompositions of PVC, hence pigments should be chosen with care. For nastel shades a white base should be incorporated. Titanium dioxide is best for this purpose but lithopone and blance fixed could also be used. Organic pigment are usually satisfactory for coloured compositions. These pigments etc., should be dispersed in aqueous medium before addition to the latex many of the processing considerations given above under the head of fillers apply to pigments also.

Antiblocking Agents

Blocking means the tendency of the coating, or the film of the plastic to adhere to itself or any other material with which it comes in contact. It occurs with soft internally plasticiser PVC latices or those with a high proportion of plasticiser. It has been seen that fillers reduce tackiness and blocking. Usually filled latices do not require antiblocking agent. Best antiblocking filler is; finely divided silica which is sufficient in proportions upto 20 phr with minimum effect on transparency, Blocking may also be climinated by adding a paraffin or amide waxes emulsion into the latex mix. The low compatibility of waxes in PVC reduce tack and blocking by blooming, if wax concentration is below 10 per cent, physical properties of the PVC remains unaffected. There are other methods also of preventing blocking apart from changes in compounding.

Coalescing aids (Volatiles)

Coalescing aids are volatile PVC solvents which when added to the latex assist in film-forming properties. Butyl carbitol acetate, methyl carbitol and butyl cellosolve acetate etc., are such additives. Volatile additives may also be added to control pH.

Handing and Processing

PVC latices do not have freeze-thaw resistance they should be stored at above 5_0C but over 40_0C. They should not be stored for more than 3 months and should be buffered and adjusted to pH of about 10. PVC latex should be periodically stirred to prevent sedimentation. Mild steel or concrete tanks coated with phenolic resin are good for storage. If pumps are to be used they should be centrifugal type with open impeller, wide clearance and low rmp.

Mixing

For low viscosity latices high speed mixing equipment, such as used with PVC solutions, are used but for viscous latex systems; or for preparing other dispersions for compounding of latex ball mills and/or colloid mills may be used.

Dipping

Objects to be coated by PVC latex are usually at room temperature. For good dip coating the latex-mix should be of high low shear viscosity, high low shear ratio, high hot melt viscosity and evaporation of water should be high.

Coating

Latex systems have low viscosities hence with them high shear viscosity problems are not encountered. Usually the lower shear viscosity requires correction. Latices have low solid (usually less than 50 per cent) contents, hence much of the coating weight has to be removed as water. As there are not film formers usually in the latex, it is necessary to heat develop film properties. For spreading with knife or roll coaters on loose weave, tight weave and continuous surface water evaporation rate, depends on the heat supplied, but for strand coating fast evaporation rate is required.

Spraying

In the ase of PVC latices slush moulding and rotocasting are not important. Before applying high temperature fusion, sufficient times should be allowed to completely evaporate the water otherwise the surface film will crack or blisters will form. The final film properties of the latex-based coatings depend mainly on time and temperature of cure. PVC latices are not used for applications which require adhesion with metal surfaces.

Compounding of PVC Solution & Adhesives

Compounding of vinyl solutions is not an important aspect but for special applications some compounding ingredients may be required.

Plasticisers

Plasticisers are sometimes incorporated in the solutions to give greater flexibility to the final film. Monomeric phasticisers are very useful but for outdoor use they are not good, from the permanency angle. Phosphate plasticisers are also not suitable for outdoor use as they have low heat and light stability. Polymeric plasticisers have very good performance and stability. Their high viscosity is not a disadvatage here as solutions have high solvent content. When baking method is used epoxy plasticiser may be used for giving good heat stability. Extender type plasticisers are not used in solutions, as they have poor light stability. Amount of plasticiser used should not exceed 10-15 per cent, as larger quantities give tacky films and poor adhesion to metals. Most commonly used plasticisers are DOP and TCP.

Stabilisers

The amount, and type of stabiliser used will depend on the method of processing, end use and the type of the resin. If heating is not necessary and films are not exposed to light, stabilisers need not be used. Thus for baking type system stabiliser is required. Sulphur containing organotin stabilisers are very useful for resin solutions stabilising. Phenyl salicylate is a good light stabiliser. Metal soaps should not be used as they cause blooming and loss of adhesion. Basic lead carbonate may be satisfactory if transparent films are not required. The shelf-life of the reactive type resin may be improved by the addition of 1 per cent prolylene oxide or epichlorohydrin before packing.

Fillers

Fillers, lower-the cost, increase-hiding power of the coating and total solids. But due to the presence of impurities, such as iron, they may adversely affect the heat and light stability and may cause porosity in the film.

Pigments

They should not be used at more than 20 per cent level in the solutions otherwise the film properties will seriously deteriorate. Pigments containing iron and zinc should be avoided as they adversely affect heat stability. Resins are of usually acidic nature hence the pigment, with basic impurities or with basic metals, have low compatibility. Use of pure pigment is recommended. The reactivity of the pigment may be reduced by incorporating small amounts of malic or malonic acids. TiO_2, lithopone or white lead should be used in small quantities. Usually 8-15 per cent level of organic pigments is needed for adequate depth of colour.

Lubricants

They are not required but small amount of a wax may be incorporated to increase surface slip.

Plasticiser is incorporated into the solution by stirring in or by mixing into the resin with the help of a 2 - roll mill. Stabiliser can be incorporated with a 2 - roll or may be dispersed in a slow evaporating solvent using a differential 3 - roll mills, but it is desirable to add the pigment directly to the resin itself and then dissolve in solvent. The milling temperature should not be allowed to exceed 75'C, in this method it will be better add dispersing aid such as blown castor oil.

As mentioned slight heating, during the dissolution of the resin the solvent is helpful and gives clear solutions. Wetting of the resin, with the diluent (if any) before adding the true solvent, eliminates the danger of gelling. Solvents used are usually of highly inflammable type hence due care should be exercised and process vessels should be equipped with tight fitting covers to prevent solvent loss due to evaporation. Vessels should be made of stainless steel, glasslined steel or aluminium as mild steel catalyses resin decomposition and increases gel formation. Agitators used should be of disk impeller type or paddle type as the solutions have low viscosity.

Methods of Application of Solutions

Vinyl solutions are applied by brushing, spraying or by roller coating. Dipping is not favoured, as the solutions have low viscosity and solid content. In dipping process rapid gelling, after withdrawl, is required so that flowing does not take place. Solutions similar to those used for spraying may be used but higher solids and some quantity of quick drying solvent should be used. With solutions slush-moulding and rotocasting are not important methods. In the case of spraying the evaporation rate of the solvent is very important as too rapid evaporation gives a dry spray, and slow evaporating solvent will cause sagging an vertical surfaces. Hence kethylethyl ketone with toluene or xylene is preferred, diacetone alcohol and ethyl and butyl acetate are useful as thinners.

In roller coating, the large surface areas of the rollers cause excessive solvent evaporation resulting in drying out the rollers, hence solvents with slow evaporation rate should be used. In the case of brushing method, to reduce the solvent action of the top coat on the under coat, strong solvents, such as methyl isobutyl ketone and cyclohexanone etc., should be used with maximum possible proportion of diluents such as xylene.

Applications of Solutions

Vinyl resin solutions are used in protective coatings, decorative coating and adhesives etc. Protective coatings for industrial applications require good chemical resistance. They are used for coating of metals, plastics, wood and other surfaces. Vinyl coating are good for metal containers. Iron or tin plate is first coated with the resin by spraying or roller coating, which is then backed. Plate is then formed into containers. The film of coating has good toughness and adhesion to the metal surface. These coatings are resistant to chemicals, oils, greases and food materials. Vinyl coated paper gives food labels, here baking at moderate temperature gives a good gloss. Resin solutions are useful in, printing inks for PVC printing, and cable industry.

For all these applications good adhesion to the surface is a must, and selection of the vinyl resin for the purpose is an important point. It has already been discussed. The compatibility of the other ingredients, particularly the pigmens, with resin, and their effect on the metal adhesion should also be kept in mind. A general purpose vinyl solution formulation is given below :

Vinyl resin	15 parts
DOP	3
Methyl isobutyl ketone	30
Toluene	30
Propylene oxide	0.2
Phthalocynine green	12
Titanium dioxide	3

DOP is a general purpose plasticiser; methyl isobutyl ketone is a true solvent and toluene is a diluent. Propylene dioxide improves the containers life and shelf-life of the solution. Titanium dioxide and phthalocynine green are pigments.

The following resin solution is a metal finish formulation :

Vinyl resin	7.5

Alkyd resin		18
Titanium dioxide	23	
Antimony oxide	2.5	
Cyclohexanone	10	
Methyl isobutyl ketone	14.5	
Xylene	24	
Dryer	0.1	

Alkyd resin gives good coat properties. Antimony oxide is good heat stabiliser and pigment. Cyclohexanone and methyl isobutyl ketone act as solvents whereas usual xylene is a diluent. Dryer used is any of the usual type.

Adhesives

The adhesives may be considered here from two angles, first the use of vinyl resin in adhesives for sticking PVC to itself or other surface and use of other adhesives for sticking PVC to various surface. The adhesives may contain PVC or vinyl copolymers in solution form. In vinyls polyvinyl acetate and polyvinyl butyral are the important resin for use in the adhesives. Vinyl ehtyl ether adhesives are used for pressure-sensitive adhesives and vinyl butyral resins are useful for the manufacture of safety glass. Vinyl ethyl ether resins are light in colour, adhere to many surfaces and can be easily formulated. They have good flexibility, resistance to ageing and have low toxicity. Polyvinyl methyl ether (PVM) is water soluble and useful for remoistenable adhesives. Polyvinyl ethyl (PVE) and polyvinyl isobutyl (PVI) ether resins are soluble in other solvents such as cyclohexanone ethyl acetate and benzene of toluene etc. Some examples are given below :

An example for transparent cellophane backed tapes :

PVI (high viscosity)	80 parts
PVI (low viscosity)	20
Ester gum	.5

It is dissolved in heptane as 20% solution. PVM has excellent adhesion to hard, glossy printed magazine surface, the following adhesive is good for adhering paper lables to magazine :

Bentonite (less than 200 mesh)	2 parts
PVM	22
Water	72

Vinyl butyral resins have excellent impact strenght with excellent adhesion to glass and have good clerity. The following formulation is an example of adhesive for interlayers for safety glass :

Polyvinyl butyral resin	100 parts
Dibutyl cellosolve adipate	40
PVM	5
Water	0.6

Coating based on vinyl butyral resins maintain film integrity in water. These resins are tough, flexible and slock-resistant.

Polyvinyl acetage (PVA) adhesives are adaptable to high speed machinery in paper converting and packaging fields and are also used in wood glues. PVA gives the household "white glue". PVA adhesives are now used in bookbinding, paper bags, milk cartons, drinking straws, envelopes, gummed tapes, folding boxes, foils, film and paper board, cigarette tips, padding, automobile upholestry, pencils, leather binding and the tile cements etc. Paper pad and binding glue is given below as an example, this has reference to U.S.Patent no 23,87,967.

Polyvinyl acetate emulsion (55% solids)	1 gal
Dibutyl phthalate (DBP)	0.5 lbs
Glycerin	2 oz

Phthalate acts as plasticiser and glycerine works as humeatent preventing the cracking of the glue line.

17

Expanded Polyethylene

INTRODUCTION

It is a well known fact that all commercial product are generally exposed to a hostile environment in varying degrees, during its transfer from manufacturing factory to the ultimate consumers. These hazards could be classified as under :

1. Mechanical hazards - eg. handling, transportation, abrasion, stacking etc.
2. Climatic hazards-Rain, hot weather, cold weather, humidity etc.
3. Biological hazards-Insects, rodents etc.
4. Social hazards-Theft, statutory regulations, customer appeal etc.

Hence selection of a packaging material requires knowledge and trials to overcome the first three hazards, for determining the properties that can possibly match the needs of a particular product at a reasonable cost packaging.

In our country, it is incumbent to provide a good package cushioning to most of the products during transportation to protect them form the hazards like jolting, abrasion, scratches and even breakage which are a common occurance.

The market for polymeric foams with present day environment is continuing to grow rapidly throughout the world. The cellular polyolefins offer many unique properties such as light weight, toughness, flexibility, shock, vibration sound absorption besides cushioning comfort feartures. More important properties are excellent electrical and thermal insulation properties and a high degree of moisture resistance. Polyolefins offer a range of polymers

Table - 1

Typical Properties of Polyolefins I

Properties	Units	Polypropylene Homo- polymer	High density Co polymer	Low-and Medium Polyethylene	Ethylen/ density Bunnhed Linem	polyethylene	vinyl acetate copoly-
mer							
Specific gravity	kg/m²	900-910	890-905	952-965	917-932	918-940	922-943
Melting point	°C	160-175	150-175	130-137	98-115	122-124	103-108
Tensile strength at break	MPa	31-41	28-38	22-31	83-31	13-28	15-28
Elongation at break	%	100-600	200-700	10-1200	100-650	100-965	300-750
Tensile modulus	MPa	1140-1550	900-1090	1070-1090	170-280	260-520	48-200

that offer from properties from semi rigid polypropylene homo polymer to soft ethylene/ester copolymer. The properties of foam made from these polymers are listed in Table - 1.

The present polyethylene foam industry is predominantly dominated by the low density polyethylene products such as sheets, tubes, net, planks and several other fabricated products tail or made to suit specific needs

The highly expanded polyethylene foams are potentially the most inexpensive of all cellular plastic and have become increasingly popular cushioning material to provide a protective packaging to most commercial items.

PROCESS

All foamed plastics or cellular plastics are commonly referred to as expended plastics. Expanded plastics have a cell structure distributed throughout the entire mass. A cell consists of a void formed during the manufacture of foam. This cell is closed partly or completely by cell walls. Unlike an open cell (e.g. Flexible polyurethane foam) a closed cell is totally closed and not interconnected with the other cells via the gas phase.

RAW MATERIALS

Basically, the starting materials for foam manufacture are the polymer, blowing agent and some additives. While polymer is solid phase, the gaseous phase is derived from the blowing agent, which is normally a gaseous material or decomposable solids. While expansion with a decomposable solid blowing agent is a chemical phenomenon, the expansion of the liquid polymer with a gaseous agent is only a physical change.

BLOWING AGENTS

There are two types of compounds which are used for foaming polymers. These are called blowing agents-chemical blowing agents and physical blowing agents.

CHEMICAL BLOWING AGENTS (CBA)

Of the various chemical compound experimented so far, only a few compounds such as Azodicarbonomide (ADCA) or Benzene sulfonyl hydrazide is more suited for the production of low density PE foam since it has the highest gas yield in comparison to other chemical blowing agents. CBA assists in liberating the gas as a result of chemical reaction. CBA are all solids.

PHYSICAL BLOWING AGENTS (PBA)

Selection of a physical blowing agent is very important in as much as it should be odourless, nontoxic, inert in liquid phase, and low boiling volatile liquids such as aliphatic and halogenated hydrocarbons (including CFCs) low boiling alcohols, either ketones, aromatic hydrocarbons.

These blowing agents must also meet other requirement such as;

a. It is an inert material in the liquid phase and must not affect the physical or chemical properties of the polymer.

b. It should mix easily with foaming formulations.

c. It should be non-corrosive.

d. It must be highly volatile to heat reaction and must have a lower rate of diffusion in polymer than air.

e. It must be environmentally safe.

Chlorofluorocarbons (CFCs) have been widely used in manufacture of foamed polyurethane and later in the polyolefin foams, because of its incumbustibility and low toxicity besides its lower coefficient of thermal conductivity than are and other gaseous compounds.

CFC

CFCs or Freons as they are commonly called are gradually being phased out as blowing agents for foam and in other applications as well because of its ozone depletion problem. It has been convincingly accepted that Freons do react with and destroy ozone in the stratosphere, resulting in increase of ultraviolet radiation which is most harmful for human life.

India has also signed the Montreal Protocol agreement which makes it compulsory for all countries to phase out the freons production and its usage.

BUTANE

For the manufacture of Expended Polyethylene, butane particularly isobutane has been more widely used now-a-days in view of its easy availability and economics. However its high flammability and combustibility requires several measures of precautions to be undertaken all through the stages of storage tanks, pumps compressor, instrumentation and modifications in equipment.

Other Additives

In addition to blowing agents, nucleating agents are also added to obtain a more uniform cellular structure in product.

Open and Closed Cell Foamed Plastics

Foamed polymers are, broadly, classified into two categories of open and closed cell structure. Generally polyurethane foam has an open cell structure while polyethylene foam has a closed cell structure.

Open-cell foamed materials have very high absorptive capacity for moisture and water, a higher permeability to gas and vapour, less effective insulation capacity for heat or electricity. It has, however, a better capacity to absorb and damp sound. In open cell structure, the gas phase is air and it helps the displacement of air easily to facilitate breathing which is commonly experienced by everybody in P.U. foam or pillows.

Highly expanded polyolefin foam are classified, generally, in three broad groups namely ;

a. Non-Crosslinked foam

b. Crosslinked foam

c. Moldable foam beads.

Non-Crossedlinked Foam

This is manufactured by an extrusion process which is not only simple but economical. A low density PE the most suitable material for the extrusion process in as much as it can be made into foam sheets having a wide range of densities (19 - 150 kgs/M^3).

In this extrusion process, the polymer is mixed with a volatile blowing agent which is injected under pressure into mixing section of the extruder. The mixture is then cooled to foaming temperature when it comes out of the molten die orifice. The cells are nucleated as the melt is decompressed during its travel through the die land. The cells grow rapidly as the melt comes out of the die. The foamed sheet is cooled and then aged for sometimes till it stabilizes.

A thin sheet takes atleast 5-7 days to age while a thicker plank if extruded directly will take some weeks to stabilize.

Crosslinked Foam

The know-how for crosslinked foams were originally designed by four Japanese companies namely; Sekisui, Toray, Furukhawa and Hitachi. Since then world over have been producing this product with any one of the technologies from them. Crosslinked foam are manufacture either by high-energy radiation or with the help of chemical peroxides. Of the two, radiation method is very expensive due to high capital investment. Peroxide foam process is less expensive and requires no additional equipment in the process and is suited for lower rate systems only.

The process consists of mixing the proper quantity of polymer chemical provide and blowing agent inside an extruder or any mixer like Banbury type. Uniform small cells on the product can be guaranteed only with the proper dispersion of peroxide DCP-Dicumyl Peroxide and the blowing agent ADCA. Care should be taken to avoid both premature crosslinking and premature decomposition. After a through mixing polymer melt is shaped into sheet or slabs which are transferred into a mould. In this method the expended polymer-gel is heated under pressure to decompose the peroxide and crosslink the polymer in an overn for expansion. The oven design is most critical in this method. Upto the cross-linking stage, the processes remain same as under:

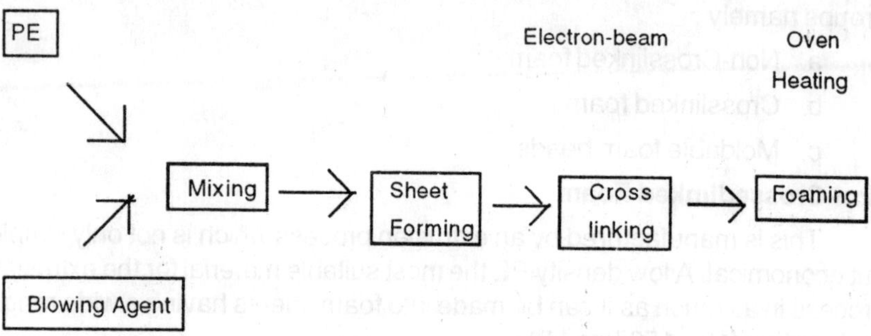

Fig. 12.0 Radiation Cross-Linking of Polyolefin Form Sheet Process

Both the process of radiation crosslinking and chemical crosslinking have certain advantages and disadvantages and disadvantages.

Radiation crosslinking has advantages of higher production, quality of product and flexibility of food stock selection. It also can give a thin sheet with a fine cell structure, and smooth surface finish. Whereas chemical crosslinking process has a low investment risk and can yield thicker and more thermoformable products.

Mouldable Foam Beads

Similar to crosslinked PE, polyolefin foam beads are also manufactured either by any one of the four process developed by the companies namely BASF, KANEGFUCHI, JSP and Sekisui. Each of these processes has its merits and demerits. Normally the expansion ratio in this process is also lesser than the other methods. In India, this process is popular with Expanded Polystyrene manufacture.

Properties

The cellular expanded polyethylene foams exhibit almost all the inherent properties of the low density polyethylene polymer. It is tough, flexible, light in weight, moisture resistance, and resistance to most corrosive chemicals. Expanded polyethylene foams have low density, semi-rigid/flexible closed cell and weather-stable, characteristics. They also exhibit the basic polymer properties such as non-hygroscopic, non-water absorption, non-corrosive, excellent mould resistance temperature stability over a wide range between-40° to 70°C and good mechanical properties.

Antistatic Property

It is known fact that conventional polyethylene films have inherent static charges that attract atmospheric dust to its surface. With the incorporation of blowing agent, Expanded Polyethylene foam is fairly antistatic and bags/pouches made from EPE can be conveniently used as dust protection covers for many electrical or electronic items. With addition of special antistatic masterbatch, effective antistatic property in EPE (in pink colour as per international standards) can be obtained for protection of products which are highly sensitive to static discharges.

Fire Retardant Property

Expanded polyethylene foam which is made from low density polyethylene is not easily combustible and it takes time to ignite it. It burns slowly without any emission of toxic gases. Fire-retardent grades can be made available for many special applications.

Density

The density of foam, which is related to the degree of expansion, has a major influence on the physical properties of the cellular product. The mechanical properties generally increase with the increasing density of the foam if other variables are constant. Most physical characteristics of the polymer foam is directly related to the density.

Size of Cells

The size of the cells can have a fair degree of influence on the properties of forms even if the density, closeness of cells, chemical composition remain same. The coefficient of thermal conductivity of foams increases when the cell size increases because there are more paths for heat transfer by radiation and convection. An increase in the cell size comes a rise in youngs modulus of foams.

Thermal Conductivity

The composition of the gasphase in the cells in foam plays an important part in determining the thermal conductivity of the product. In fact the thermal conduction through gas phase contributes to the overall thermal conductivity of cellular foam material. Hence it is ideal to have a gas having low thermal conductivity.

PE foam has a low thermal conductivity similar to expanded polystyrene but its very low water-vapour transmission rate and flexibility makes it more suitable as a thermal insulation material for most insulation applications for low temperature service conditions.

TEMPERATURE RANGE

The recommended temperature range for all such cellular plastics used insulation applications is given as under :

Table - 2

Material	*Min.temperature*	*Max. temperature*
Expanded Polyethylene	– 40°C	70°C
Expanded Polystyrene	– 200°C	80°C
Polyurethane Foam	– 200°C	150°C
Phenolic Foam	– 200'C	130°C

Generally, any packaging or insulation material undergoes stress deformation during transportation, usage and operation. Expanded polyethylene being a flexible material takes the stress or elongation and can still recover without breaking.

Expanded Polyethylene is an ideal cushioning material in as much as it has fair resilience, good tensile strength, fair vibration-damping characteristics, low creep and a fair compression set. Its ability to withstand multiple impact is considered superior to all other foam cushioning materials.

Creep curves (thickness loss under constant compressive strain at 22.88°C) are also superior to polyurethane but not as good as EPS. Expanded Polyethylene has several other characteristic such as elongation, and resiliency to return to near original thickness after deformation from strain damp vibrational impacts which are all its favour to consider it as a better packaging material especially for fragile or heavier articles.

Fabrication Versatility

EPE foams are available in sheets, planks, in varying thickness and sizes and can be conveniently fabricated to suit specific requirements of an industrial consumer. Such conversion facility can be set up with a low investment with only a few machinery, tool equipment and working tables etc. Power requirement is also very low as also the space required for fabrication even a small area of anywhere between 500 and 1000 sq. ft will be adequate, the equipment required for such fabrication includes :

1. Hot air gun
2. Impulse heat sealer

3. Hot wire cutter
4. Clinking knife
5. Band saw
6. Micro meter
7. Plywood sheet/kraft board sheets
8. Adhesives and peel-off paper
9. Tables/drawing board/drawing instrument box etc.

Products from fabrication include cutlengths, bags/pouches dust covers, L pads, corners, buffers etc.

Laminate Products

EPE's excellent heat sealability has yielded several sophisticated laminates making not only a composite packaging but also a material with special appearance, strength and effectiveness of the product. laminates will generally ensure total moisture barrier properties since any pinhole that were existent earlier on the substrates, will be completely sealed. Also the substrate imparts reinforcement to the flimsy foam product and serves as a good back-up support material that helps in applications of newer markets. Other substrates which are ideal for lamination with Expanded Polyethylene include the following :

- ★ Brown kraft paper
- ★ High density HM film
- ★ LDPE film
- ★ Hessian cloth
- ★ LD polyethylene woven cloth
- ★ Aluminium foil etc.

High density high molecular polyethylene film laminated to EPE is becoming a more popular packaging material not only in other countries but also in our country. Laminated products serve as a good lining material for shoes, handbags, ladies bags, valets, diaries, toys and several other items.

Paper laminated foam sheets are popular in Western countries as mailer bags that enable documents or drawings to reach in good condition during postal transit or provide long term storage and protection.

Applications

The market for EPE foam Products has been registering a growth pattern of over 10-15% in several countries like North America, E.E.C,

Japan and some of the European countries. Other countries like Latin America, Brazil, Argentina, Mexico, Taiwan, South Korea and India are developing foam materials in a big way as the production facilities have come up during 5-10 years. In India, there are five units established already for EPE and their total installed capacity is far higher than the demand in the country.

The EPE foam markets have grown particularly in the following segments.

1. Cushion packaging
2. General package wrap
3. Thermal insulation
4. Automotive
5. Sports goods
6. Shoes and chappals
7. Carpet underlay
8. Shock and sound absorption
9. Toys and Novelties
10. Roof waterproofing & construction.

Cushion Packaging

EPE is more suited than other materials in cushion packaging where energy absorption is the most important property. It is good for products having a fragility factor between 20 and 100 g. EPE can provide protection against repeated impact during transportation hazards and is thus considered better than EPS moulded cushioning. Although EPE is more expensive than EPS is more expensive than EPS for the same size, the optimum package design offsets the increased cost of the material.

Also fabricated corner pads, L pads and case inserts from EPE sheets/planks facilities protection against higher loadings and ensure safe transit of goods. In India C-Dot approved companies have been sending their Exchange cabinets like RAX or MAX to far off places with the help of EPE corners & pads.

Automotive Use

In the automotive industry, EPE has been replacing both EPS and PU foam sheets employed earlier in jeeps, cars, bus bodies and airconditioned coaches.

Table - 3

Comparison of Properties of Armour (EPE) V/S EPS and rigid pur or Automotive applications

Material	*Density gms/cm³*	*Thermal conductivity K.cal/M.hr°C*	*Tensile strength kg/cm²*	*Compression strength*	*Elongatin %*	*Water absorption*	*Fatigue resistance*	*Thickness recovery*	*Corresive effect*	*Aging resistance*
Armour' Expanded Polyethylene	0.030	0.027	3.00-7.5	0.15-0.20	40-65	Nil	Good	Good	Nil	Excellent
Expanded Polystyrene	0.020	0.027	1.50-3.2	0.7-1.40	Negligible	Low	Poor	Poor	L0ow	Fair
Rigid Polyurethane	0.033	0.015	2.50-5.5	0.6-1.80	Nil	High	Good	Good	Low	Good

The properties such as thermal insulation, flexibility, ease of installation and excellent elongation property have led to this switch-over to EPE sheets. EPE has several advantages over other insulation materials. A comparison of properties is given in the table below :

Similarly the airconditioning industry have also opted for the use of EPE sheets to insulate the airconditioners but also employ them for ductlining applications.

Pipe insulation is another area of major applications of EPE in as much as its flexibility and resilience are preferred over rigid foams.

Shoes/Sports Goods

EPE foam sheets have served to provide cushion comforts in shoes and chappals. Unlike PU foam, EPE does not absorb water (e.g. during rainy season) Saddlery applications also call for EPE sheets in higher thickness for adequate cushion effect and longer life.

Sportgoods also call for similar comfort and softness in Gymnastic mates, landing pads, wall pads and several other paddings like gloves, shoulder pads legguards etc where the foam's capability of energy absorption is utilized. Crosslinked PE has made inroads into this field of sportgoods.

Many industrial applications have been developed of late, for use of EPE in gaskets, vibration pads and grommets which require high density material.

Carpet Underlay

In this Application, EPE has replaced the conventional coir mats used as underlay in carpets. Coir mats have poor shelf life and also absorbs moisture. EPE foam underlay is an ideal solution to get a longer life for the expensive carpets.

18

Expanded Polystyrene

INTRODUCTION

Expanded Polystyrene is a generic term for Polystyrene and Styrene copolymers, supplied as a compound with physical blowing agents and other additives which can be processed into low density (0.7 to 10.0 lb/cuft) foamed articles. The most common form of this product is crystal PS beads containing pentane as a blowing agent. The processing of EPS into foamed article consists of several unique steps and is a unifying corrective of a broader category of plastic resins including mouldable foam poly olefins and copolymers. EPS type materials can make products as diverse as coffee cup, an energy absorbing bumper for an automobile or a 300 cuft with foam block. Major end uses for EPS are disposable drinking cups, packaging and thermal insulation.

1. MANUFACTURING PROCESS

A. Diffusion of blowing agent into Polystyrene.

The first Patent (British Patent 605, 863 (1948) on the preparation of expandable Polystyrene containing Volatile Hydrocarbon applied for in Great Britain, teaches the soaking of polystyrene particles,held in a cheese cloth bag in a solution comprising a non solvent,petroleum ether (90-99x 0.1%) and a solvent(10-15) such an action yields ethyl acetate benzene. At 20.25°C impregnation is complete within 0.5 to 12 h depending on particle size and composition. A mixture of diethyl ether and ethanol is also claimed to render polystyrene expandable after 3 days of soaking non volatile additives may be added in the polystyrene, hastening its impregnation by n-pentane and avoiding the use of solvenator.cited additives are rubbery iso butylene polymers, rubbery-diene polymers (eg SER) fatty acid salts or esters (eg.

steorates),organic insoluble pigmentsand inorganic pigments smaller than 0.5 microns in diameter.

polystyrene (3 round to 3-20 mesh) stirred with equel nos.of n-pentane for 24 hrs.absorbed 4.7% by weight, for 48 hours. 7.8%;however the presence within the polystyrene of 1% of intimately mixed $CaCo_3$ of particle size of 0.1 micron increased the 24 hrs. absorption of n-pentane to 7.8%. Although these modification of polymer effectively decrease the absorption time, they also increase the rate at which n-pentane diffuses out of the polymer, thereby shortening shelf life.

B. The Quenched Pellet Process

The Quenched Pellet Process consists of expanding a mixture of polystyrene and additives, chilling the extrudate to avoid foaming and chilling into particles of desired size.

The following features were disclosed in the patent :

a. Extrusion into a water bath at 50 PSI.

b.. Extrution into a water bath to cool the strand instantly to below 50°C at atmospheric pressure.

c. Holding the quenched pellets at an elevated temperature (50°C to the plastifying temperture) to relieve orientation strain.

The quenched pellet process was developed primarily for the incorporation of colourants. Several modification and improvment of the apparatus to make the quenched pellets have been made. extrusion through a die made lined with PTFE to broaden the permissible temperature range of extrusion; and conveyor system for continuously passing the freshly chopped pelletes through a normalizing bath to relieve orientation strain at 65°C-80°C; an extruder to fecilitate mixing of pentane with polystyrene; and replacement of the water bath by chilled roll contaning grooves in which extrudet was cooled. Orientation strain were also relived by very short exposure (.5-15 sec.) above the sheet plasticising temperature. various finaly divided solids $CaCo_3$ may be used to the extruder as call nucleating agent for making seton expensive P.S.

The blowing agent for most commercial polyestyrene (expendable) consist of hydrocarbons obtained from the perform boiling range of petrleum. Expendable polystyrene typically contain about 6.3 to 7.3% pentane. For each composition there is an optimum amount of blowing agent for complete foaming adding only slightly more (i.e. for 1 part per 100 of polymer) the etire amount leads to such undesirable properties as expandable foam collapse, and excessive cell size are formed. The tolerable amount of blowing aagent decreases with the M -wt of the polymer. A practicable volume of n-pentane (6.5% by wt) for foaming is identical with the pie determined compressibility of an expandable polystyrene.

Table 1

Loss of n-pentane in hr. from Expandable Beads at varying temperature.

Temperature Loss wt%	*from Beads with n-pentane content of*			
	4%	5%	6%	7%
35°C	0.0	0.0	0.0	0.0
45°C	0.0	0.1	0.1	0.1
52.5°C	0.0	0.1	0.1	0.1
65°C	0.0	0.1	0.1	0.9

Extrusion Process

As n-pentane is very much volatile, so we have to maintain a very low extruder temperature which is difficult to carryout. To simplify the process we will use a blowing agent which has much higher decomposition temperature than n-pentane is used and it enables to extrude it smoothly at elevated temperature.

(i) Polystyrene (amorphous)

(ii) Blowing agent (chemical type)

(iii) Nucleating agent

(iv) Aromatic oil (Processing aid)

The details are as under :-

(i) Amorphous Polystyrene having a molecular weight in the range of 1,00,000 to 1,90,000. Stereo regular polystyrene has a very high Melting point about210°C, so it can not be taken due to processing difficulties.

(ii) Blowing agent to be taken Azo bis formamide [ABFA]–1 to 2.5 per.

(iii) Nucleating agent.

0.3% citric Acid + 0.1 to 0.3% $NaHCO_3$.

Processing Temperature

The processing temperature will be in the range of 140-150°C.

Table 2 Blowing Agents in Plastics

Name	Structure	Trade name	Manu-	Decomposition temp. in air &	Decomposition temp. in plastic	Gasyield ml/gm
Azo bis formamide	$2NCON{=}CON_2$	Kemprere	NPI			
		(Cekigeb AZ	UC			
	(Genitron AC		FICL	195-200°C	160-200°C	220
	(Azocel		F			
	CH_3 CH_3	(Ponfor	B			
AIBN	NC–C–N=N–CN	(Polyzole AZDW	NDI			
	CH_3 CH_3	(Genetron AZDW	FICL	115°C	90-115°C	130
	(Ponfar N		BB			
	Vazo		DP			
Diazoamine-benzene	H_5-NH-N=N-N_5	DAB	ACC	105°C	95-100°C	115
N-N" Dimethol						
N-N" Dinitroroterephthalimole		Nitrosan	DP	105°C	90-105°C	126
N-N" Dinitroroplentamethylene tetramine		(Opex 931100	NPI			
		(Unicel ND, NDX	DP	195°C	130-190°C	265
		(Vulcacel BW	IC!			
		(Profor B-13	B	146°C	115-130°C	85
		(CD-50				
Benzene 1,3 disnlphonsi-tydrazide						
diplensl Sulphon						
3-3" disulphonsl SO_2 hydrozides	$(SO_2NHNH_2)_2$	Profor D-33	B	148°C	120-130°C	110

NPI : National Polychemicals Inc; Wilmington; UC-Uniroy. 1 Chemical Division - Nag, toc Conn; B-Farbenfabriken Bayer Leverkusen, Germany.
FICL : Fisons Indunfrids Chemicals Ltd; Longhborough England.
ACC : National Asiline div. Allied Chemical Corporation Newyorks Nc.
DP : Dupnt; F- Fair mount Chemical Co. Inc, Newyork N.J.

Among these blowing agents Azo bis formamide (ABFA) is of major interest. ABFA and its residue are non toxic, odourless non discolouring and non standing. The storage stability of ABFA is unexcelled, unlike other foaming agents, it does not support combustion and plasticisers, it disperse easily in all elastomers and plastics. Since the gas yield of ABFA is highest of all commercially available organic foaming agents, the material is economical to use.

In general, the processing of foaming foamable compounds follows closely the operating procedures established for foam products.

Careful consideration must be given to means of obtaining a homogeneous distribution of the foaming agent in the plastic compound. This can be convenientyly achieved by adding the foaming agent in the form of dispersion in a vehicle compatible with the basic resin.

The properties of cellular plastic are, to a great extent, determined by the processing step during which the decomposition of the blowing agent occurs. At this point, the thermoplastic resin must possess the proper viscosity or the regired degree of crosslinking to retain the liberated gas. However, high viscosity modulus polymer may have restricted drgree of expansion.

Effect of Cell Nucleating Agent

With cell nucleating agent the produced foam will be coarse, brittle blistered extrudate of very high density.

Sodium bicarbonate and citric acids serves the purpose.

GENERAL PROCESSING PARAMETERS OF POLYSTYRENE

Polystyrene is generally extruded at a temperature of 175 - 230°C (Polymer-temperature) cylinder temperature may be as high as 340°C.

Polystyrene is generally extruded in an extruder having L/D ratio 17 : 1 to 30 : 1.

Some Properties of Polystyrene

Density	1.04 gm/cc
Vicet Softening Point	108°C
Tensile yield	6400 lb force/in_2
Elongation at break	1.5%
Tensile Modulus	4.7 x 10^5 lpf/in^2
Izod impact	0.25 ft Lbf/in of nitch

Relative Case of fabrication – Excellent.

Table 3

Avg. Mechanicai Properaties of P.S. foam at 23.9°C.

Avg. Density	*Avg. Cell*	*Strength PSI*			*Modulur*		
	Size	*Compressive*	*Tensile*	*Shear*	*Compressive*	*Bending*	*Shear*
0.18lb/ft3	28 (mills)	30	70	35	1000	2200	1100
3.3 "	6 "	120	225	65	6000	2000	875

Properties are to be measured (After foaming)

Compressive strength and compressive modulus. According to ASTM. D 1621 - 64.

Tensile strength according to ASTM.D 1623 - 64

Shear strength and shear modulus according to ASTM. C 273 - 53

Flexural Strength and bending modulus according to ASTM. C 203-58

Water absorption

Generally it varies from 0.03 to 0.05 lb/ft^2.

Thermal Conductivity or K factor according to ASTM C 177- 63

Coefficient of expansion according to ASTM D 696 - 44

Dielectric Constant

It varies between 1.19 at 60 Hz & 1.02 at 1 MHz.

Vol Resistivity

generally - 3.8 x 10^{13}

Applications

(i) Packaging.
To reduce damage, shipping weight and labour cost.

(ii) Cups for hot drinks.

(iii) Insulation boards.

(iv) In cold storage, refrigeration & housing insulation.

(v) Picnic coolers, ice buckets, components of refrigerators and air conditioners, display toys.

19

Speciality Plastic Compounds & Masterbatches

INTRODUCTION

Masterbatches are colour concentrates produced by blending colour pigments with a polymer and extruding the mixture, which is than cut into pellets. A significant advantage of master batches is that special additives can be added to them to impart ultra violet stabilisation, and anti-block, anti static or fire retardant properties of the plastic. Masterbatches are added to the plastic base in the percentage of 1% to 3% by weight, depending on the required tone and opacity subsequently, the base is processed.

It is proposed to manufacture speciality plastic/polymer compounds and colour masterbatches. These products find extensive use in household appliance industry, agriculture, power, electrical, electronics, refrigeration, packaging and footwear industries.

PRODUCT

Masterbatches are available mainly under two categories :

1. Masterbatches for colouration of Plastic - Coloured Masterbatch.
2. Masterbatches for enhancing specific properties - Additives Masterbatches.

Coloured Masterbatches

Colour concentrates offer the user a clean, easy to handle, and economical means of getting a wide range of colours with a single inventory of the let down resin, processing is also easier and less messy than with either dry or liquid colourants since the produce is in solid form mainly pellets similare to that of the plastic raw materials.

Special colorant ranging from pearlescent, metallic, fluorescent and phosphorescent pigments are also available.

Colour masterbatches include dyes or pigments and are mainly white, black or specific colours or shades including special colours like metallic, flouresent and pearlscent.

Additive Masterbatch/Speciality Compounds

Additive masterbatch are special purpose masterbatches which enhance the properties of plastic products. These are of different types including UV Stabiliser, Antistats, Antioxidants, Antiflibrilantion, Antiblocking, Cling Additive, Impact modifier and multi-functional masterbatches.

Market

Compounding Industry has emerged as a specialised intermediary industry catering to the plastic processors. The speciality Plastic/Polymer Compounding and Masterbatches are the components for manufacturing various plastic materials. The properties of Compounded plastic may be different from those of the base polymers used in them. Thus the application of compounding is normally dependent upon the kind of end products proposed to be manufactured. The application of these items is mainly in the manufacture of extruded profiles, bottles, wire and able footwear window profiles, etc. Thus for manufacturing furniture items, office equipment items, electronic industry items manufacturing high impact and tough applicances and tailor made product, the specialty compounded plastic is used. The purpose of using the compounding is for imparting the properties required in the end product.

The colour or white Masterbatches have also specific end use such as producing white pigmented or co-extruded films for milk packaging, multilayer laminated film and various moulding appliances. The colour Masterbatches are useful for producing a standardised product of required colour like black for irrigation piping, tarpaulins, films used for covering reservoirs, canals etc.

Masterbatches are used in various plastic processing operations such as in injection moulding, extrusion, blow moulding etc. Generally for products like synthetic fibres, thin films, jelly filled cables etc. special masterbatches are required. The market share of different types of masterbatches is as under :

White masterbatches	:	33%
Black masterbatches	:	25%
Colour masterbatches	:	33%
Additive masterbatches	:	20%

Polymer wise share of masterbatches are polyethylene (64%), Polypropylene (20%), Polystyrene (10%), PVC (25%) and Balance 3.5% for other plastics.

Similarly sector wise demand of masterbatch is maximum in packaging (55%) followed by Moulding (17%), Fibre (15%), Wire & Cables (3%) and Balance (10%) in others.

Assuming a penetration of 3% the demand for masterbatches will grow upto 78,000 tons by the turn of the century, as the demand of masterbatches, plastic blends & Alloys is closely linked to the demand for Polymers and resins.

Suggested Capacity

It is proposed to manufacture 1800 MT of masterbatches and speciality compounds per annum in this profile.

Land & Building

The unit requires about 6000 sq. mtrs. of land with covered area of 3000 sq. mtrs.

Raw Materials

Major raw material required for the project include Low Density Polyethylene (LPDE), High Density Polyethylene (HDPE), Poly Propylene (PP), Polystyrene, PVC. Acrylonitrile Butadiene Styrene polymer (ABS), Ethyl Vinyl Acetate (EVA), Linear Low Density Poly Ethylene (LLDPE), specially plastics like Polycarbonate. Polyacetyls, Carbon Black, Additive Chemicals, Fillers etc.

Besides above miscellaneous ingredients will also be required. Some of the raw materials are to be imported.

The annual requirement of raw materials are as under :-

1.	Polymer (PE/PP/PS/PVC/ABS/EVA)	1100	MT
2.	Titanium Dioxide & Special Additives (Imported)	200	MT
3.	Colour pigments, Additives & Fillers (Indigenous)	500	MT

Utilities

The unit will require a total connected load of 300 KVA. Water requirement is about 1500 KL per annum.

Manufacturing Process

The manufacturing process consists of pre-mixing of various raw materials in a High Speed Mixer. Alternatively, manual mixing is also done sometimes depending on the volume and nature of the product. The premixing is followed by mixing in a Compounding Extruder at specified temperature, speed and time span. The maintenance of particularet temperature or speed would depend on the raw materials being mixed and the ultimate product to be manufactured. The said mix of compound is thereafter fed to melt feed. Extruder through Die Plate for conveying and simultaneous cutting as well as palletising in an underwater Palletizer. Alternatively, the compound coming out of compounding extruder can be palletized directly. The slurry is then fed to the dryer for the purpose of separating water and pallets. The water goes into recycling tank, whereas dry pallets are conveyed through the top outlet into the Sizing Vibrator, which separates undersized and oversized palette. The required palette of the unit size are thereafter fed to the Bagging System for packing and subsequently making them ready for shipments.

Plant & Machinery

1. PVC compounding line complete with palletizers
2. General purposes & engineering plastic compounding line
3. D.G. set
4. Compressor
5. Conveying and bagging system
6. High speed mixers
7. Kneader mixer
8. Testing equipment

Personnels

The unit requires to employ about 75 persons including staff for office and factory for prodaction, supervision and administration.

Estimated Cost of the Project

The project cost for setting up a unit manufacture 1800 MT per annum to is estimated to Rs. 665 lakhs as follows :

		Rs. in Lakhs
1.	Land & site development	25.00
2.	Building	100.00
3.	Plant & machinery	325.00
4.	Technical know-how and engineering fees	25.00
5.	Other misc. fixed assets	30.00
6.	Preliminary & preoperative expenses	50.00
7.	Margin money for working capital	65.00
8.	Contingencies	45.00
	Total	665.00

SUGGESTED MEANS OF FINANCING

1.	Long term loan	445.00
2.	State cash subsidy	30.00
3.	Promoters capital	190.00
	Total	665.00

20

PVC Compounds

INTRODUCTION

Polyvinyl chloride (PVC) is used in numerous household and industrial applications ranging from children's toys, household wares to power cables.

To get these products out of PVC, it is not possible to use PVC as such, since PVC in isolation is susceptible to decomposition due to heat, light and oxidation. A number of chemicals are mixed with PVC to make it suitable for processing with required change in properties.

The purpose of compounding is to combine the resin and other additives into a homogeneous state for processing. Then these compounds can be used for the manufacture of finished products. It is quite impossible to process PVC resin without the addition of certain compounding ingredients such as heat stabilizers and fubricants. The main problems is to obtain used for compounding are high speed mixer, ribbon-blenders and extruders. PVC compounds in general may be divided into two groups i.e. Granulated Compound where the mix is fused and extruded in pellets form, and dry where the resultant compound is often in free flowing powder form.

Product

PVC is the most versatile thermoplastile material commercially available in a variety of compounded forms to cover a wide range of hardness and flexibility applications. It possesses physical strength and resistance to water and chemicals. In general PVC materials are difficult to ignite and have self-extinguising characteristic when the flame is withdrawn. However, PVC resin is liable to degradation on heating and is very tricky material to process unless properly compounded. This places a great dea of responsibility on the compounding technologist.

The PVC mixed with other chemicals to make it suitable for processing is termed as a PVC compound. The various constituents which are added to PVC to make its compound are stabiliser, plasticisers, modifiers, lubricants etc. The compounding is a homogeous product of PVC resin and additives. PVC compounding is done for various purposes such as for casting, cabling, tubing, shoes etc. The percentage of various components of PVC compound varies depending on the end use applications of the compound.

Market

PVC compounds are in demand in following areas :-

1. Wire & cable insulation and sheeting
2. Flexible calendering of sheets
3. Shoe & chappal compound
4. Rigid sheets, bottles etc.

PVC compounds are used extensively in pellet as well as in Dry Blend form. There is a demand of PVC compounds for a large variety of applications viz pipes, tubing, cables, shoes, films, sheetings, moulded goods etc. With the increase in production of PVC and installation of additional conversion capacity, the demand for PVC compounds is likely to grow substantially.

Suggest Capacity

It is proposed to have a minimum economic capacity of 360 MT per annum.

Land & Building

The unit requires about 1000 sq. mtrs. of land with covered area of 600 sq. mtrs.

Raw Materials

The annual requirement of raw materials for the manufacture of 360 MT of PVC compound per annum is as under :-

PVC resin	240	MT
Dioctyl phthalate	60	MT
Chlorinated paraffin wax (49%)	14	MT
Filler	40	MT
Stabilizer	9	MT
Lubricant	3.5	MT
Pigment	2.5	MT

Utilities

The unit will require a total connected load of 60 KVA. Water requirement is about 900 KL per annum.

Manufacturing Process

Dry Blend PVC resin in added to high speed mixer and the stirrer is run for few minutes in order to remove any moisture/volatile matter. Requisite quantities of plasticizer stabilizer, pigment, fillers are then added. Due to high speed rotation of the stirrer, sufficient high temperature is generated in the mixing unit. Lubricant may be added in the end approximately at a time when temperature is 10°C below the final temperature. Blender is then switched off and the compound, mix is allowed to cool in cooling trays. The compound can be directly processed on conversion machine.

Sorne of the typical formulations of PVC compounds are as under :-

1. For Rigid Pipes

PVC resion (50 - 60 K value, suspension grade)	100.00	parts
Tribas lead sulphate	5.00	parts
Calcium stearate	1.00	part
Paraloid K-120 N (acrylic modifier)	3.00	parts
Stearic acid	0.50	part
Pigments	0.50	part

2. For Bottle Blowing

PVC Resin (50 - 60 K value)	100.00	parts
Octyl thiotin	1.00	part
Epoxydised soybean oil	0.50	part
Paraloid K - 120 N	4.00	parts
Calcium stearate	1.00	part
Stearic acid	0.50	part

3. For Blown Film

PVC suspension resin	100.00	parts
Dioctyl phthalate (DOP)	56.00	parts
Chlorinated paraffin wax	4.00	parts
Stearic acid	0.50	part
Calcium stearate	0.50	part
Pigments	0.50	part
1 Vaxol EN	3.00	parts
Ba/Cd stabiliser	3.00	parts

4. For Flexible Hose Pipes

PVC resins (K - 70)	100.00	parts
1 Vaxol EN	3.00	parts
Dioctyl phthalate	40.00	parts
Chlorinated paraffin was	5.00	parts
Ca/Ba stabiliser	3.00	part

5. For Mineral Water Bottle

S-PVC. K - 57	100.00	parts
Kane Ace B modifier or equivalent	10.00	parts
Kane Ace PA 20 Pracess aid or equivalent	0.50	parts
Expoxidized soybean oil	5.0	parts
Saturated partial easter of glycerine	1.2	parts
Easter of montainic acid	0.4	parts
Calcium stearate	0.16	parts
Stearoyl benzoyl methane	0.15	parts
Zinc stearate	0.14	parts

Plant & Machinery

1. High speed mixer
2. Automatic feed mechanism
3. Twin screw extruder with die face cutter
4. Cooling & palletizing equipment
5. Air compressor
6. Testing equipment

Personnels

The unit requires to employ about 35 persons including staff for office and factory for production supervision and adminstration.

Estimated Cost of the Project

The project cost for setting up a unit to manufacture 360 MT of PVC compound per annum is estimated to Rs. 99 lakhs as follow :

		Rs. in Lakhs
1.	Land & site development	7.00
2.	Building	20.00
3.	Plant & machinery	35.00

contd....

4.	Other misc. fixed assets	7.00
5.	Preliminary & preoperative expenses	10.00
6.	Margin money for working capital	15.00
7.	Contingencies	5.00
	Total	99.00

Suggested Means of Financing

		Rs. in Lakhs
1.	Long term loan	66.00
2.	State cash subsidy	11.00
3.	Promoters capital	22.00
	Total	99.00

21

Polymer Alloys, Blends & Composites

INTRODUCTION

In this profile, mineral filled thermoplastic compounds and mineral masterbatches are proposed to be manufactures. The tailor made composites can be manufactured as per the specific requirements of end users.

PRODUCT

With blending of different polymers or elastomers and fillers achieving superior strength, durability and other properties comparable to any metal, wood or other material of construction. It is proposed to manufacture following products :-

1. **Mineral Filled Thermoplastics**

   Calcium, talc and mica filled compounds having 20% to 70% fillter leval and are used in ferniture, electrical appliances and consumer drables.

2. **Mineral Masterbathes**

   These masterbathes are filled with 60% to 70% fillers in a plastic carrier. Masterbatches are used in woven sock industry, box strapping and BOPP films.

3. **Misc. Masterbatches**

   Viz colour masterbatches, process aids, UV stabilizers, synthetic paper made from LLDPE/HMHD as substitute for natural pulp based paper.

Market

The average growth rate in the area of plastic compounds which has been around 10%-15% per annum, is now estimated to be around 20%-25%

per annum. Such compounds & masterbatches have a ready market and for the elastomeric modified compounds and alloys the market is devloping very fast.

Those polymer blends and alloys are in demand in following areas:-

1. Furniture
2. Electronic appliances
3. Consumer durables
4. Woven sacks
5. Box strapping
6. BOPP films
7. Synthetic paper etc.

SUGGESTED CAPACITY

An installed capacity of 7800 MT per annum is proposed in this profile.

LAND & BUILDING

The unit requires about 5000sq. mtrs. of land with covered area of 2500 sq.mtrs.

RAW MATERIALS

The annual requirement of raw materials is as under :-

Polymers (PP,PE,PS,ABS,EPDM)	:	3350	MT
Minerals (Tals,Calcium Carbonate)			
Asbestosm, Mica & Glass Fibre	:	4530	MT

UTILITIES

The unit will require a total connected load of 350 KVA. Water requirement is about 1500 KL per annum.

MANUFACTURING PROCESS

Depending upon the end application, the raw materials,polymers, minerals and additives are blended in the blender and fed to twin screw extruder & other compounding machines by accurate dosing of individual ingredients. Thoroughly mixed ingredients come out of die head and pelletised in pelletising system. These pellets are segregated and packed.

PLANT & MACHINERY

1. Twin Screw Extruder Compounder
2. Kneader
3. High Speed Mixer
4. Thermoplastic Extruder with Granulater

Personnels

The unit requires to employ about 85persons including staff for office and factory for production, supervision and administration.

ESTIMED COST OF THE PROJECT

The project cost for setting up a unit to manufacture 7800 MT, Biends & composites per annum is estimated to Rs.1050 lakhs as follows:

	Rs in Lakhs
1. Land & site development	25.00
2. Building	75.00
3. Plant & machinery	450.00
4. Other misc.fixed assets	125.00
5. Preliminary & preoperative expenses	80.00
6. Margin money for working capital	225.00
7. Contingencies	70.00
Total	1050.00

SUGGESTED MEANS OF FINANCING

	Rs. in Lakhs
1. Long term loan	700.00
2. State cash subsidy	30.00
3. Promoters capital	320.00
Total	1050.00

22

XLPE Cable Compound, Jelly Filled Telecommunication Cable Compound & Sheating Compound

INTRODUCTION

Polymeric compounds and co-polymers are required as source materials for cables of all types including power cables, XLPE cables, and telecommunication cables.

PRODUCT

It is proposed to manufacture following compounds :-

XLPE Compounds : These are silane grafted polymeric compounds. XLPE compounds are LDPE based filled with 2.5% carbon black suitable for low and medium voltage insulation.

Jelly Filled Telecommunication Cable Compounds : These compounds are based upon medium density polyethylene.

FRLS Compound : These are fire retardant low smoke zero halogen compounds used for making FRLS sheathing of PVC/XLPE Cables.

MARKET

XLPE COMPOUND

XLPE compound are used for power and control cables. Due to non-availability of such compounds the production & demand of XLPE cables have been restricted. Besides domestic demand there exists export market in Middle East and South East Asia.

MDPE COMPOUND

Jelly filled communication cables required MDPE compound and this compound has so far been imported. Now with the importance given to Telecom Sector, its demand is also growing.

FRLS COMPOUNDS

FRLS compounds are in demand for the manufacture of fire detardent sheathings for PVC/XLPE power cables where hazards of fire is envisaged.

SUGGESTED CAPACITY

It is proposed to produce 7200 tones of all types of compounds per annum.

LAND & BUILDING

The unit requires about 15,000 sq. mtrs. of land with covered area of 7500 sq. rntrs.

RAW MATERIALS

The annual requirement of raw materials to produces 7200 TPA of compounds will be as under :-

LDPE	:	4000	tons
HDPE	:	2700	tons
SILANE	:	45	tons
PLASTICIZER	:	85	tons
ADDITIVES/FILLERS	:	370	tons

UTILITIES

The unit will require a total connected load of 1000 KVA. Water requirement is about 1500 KL per annum.

MANUFACTURING PROCESS

XLPE COMPOUND

In this process a special grade of polyethylene is selected and then with the help of tailor made machinery a grafting process is undertaken.

In the grafting process all the feed materials PE, silane, Antioxidants & Initiator are added in specific doses to the extruder where the reaction take a form silane grafted PE compound which is pellestised, graded and packed in special moisture proof bags.

Similarly, masterbatch is prepared by compounding an organotion catalyst with special PE in specific ratio through the extruder pelletised and packed.

MDPE COMPOUND

The process involves blending of two grades of polyethylene of high and low density with desired melt flow index and compound with the requisite additives to prevent from ageing and to add superior flow characteristics through extruder specially designed for the purpose.

FRLS & LOW HALOGEN COMPOUNDS

In this process EVA, PE or other hydrocarbon rubber are compounded with flame retardant chemicals & other additives following the normal process or grafting technology with silane to finally produce the compound in pellet form.

Flame retardant grades are also produced by addition of fire retardant chemicals.

PLANT & MACHINERY

1. Single Screw Extruder with Accessories
2. Twin Screw Extruder with Accessories
3. Laboratory Extruder
4. Strip Cutter
5. Packing Unit
6. Testing Equipment

PERSONNELS

The unit requires to employ about 70 persons including staff for office and factory for production supervision and administration.

ESTIMATED COST OF THE PROJECT

The project cost for setting up a unit to manufacture 7200 tons compounds per annum is estimated to Rs. 2300 lakhs as follows :

		Rs. in Lakhs
1.	Land & site development	30.00
2.	Building	300.00
3.	Plant & machinery	900.00
4.	Technical know-how and engineering fees	120.00

Contd....

5.	Other misc. fixed assets	375.00
6.	Preliminary & preoperative expenses	200.00
7.	Margin money for working capital	300.00
8.	Contingencies	75.00
	Total	2300.00

SUGGESTED MEANS OF FINANCING

		Rs. in Lakhs
1.	Long term loan	1500.00
2.	State cash subsidy	30.00
3.	Promoters capital	770.00
	Total	2300.00

23

Thermoplastic Rubber (Elastomer) Compound

INTRODUCTION

Thermoplastic Rubber Compounds are the meeting point between the plastic material transformation technology and the vulcanised elastic characteristics.

TPR is block co-polymer based on SBS and polystyrene with the easy processing characteristics of thermoplastics.

PRODUCT

TPR is a thermoplastic which has a very good processibility with rubbery structure and good abrasion resistance. This compound, being very light in weight, has many other tailor made properties which are suitable particularly for shoe industry. Besided shoe industry TPR, with little variation in formulation an be made suitable for tyre and cable industries also.

TPR has following special properties :-

1. Excellent ozone, UV & weather resistance
2. Excellent processibility
3. Excellent elasticity & tensile strength
4. High heat resistance, from minus 50°C to 100/130°C.

MARKET

The present demand of TPR in India is partially met by the recently started production by National Organic Chemical Industries Limited and few others. Balance requirement is met by import.

With the use of better resins and more appropriate formulations our TPR is going to be lighter in weight and therefore more economical to the user industry, resulting in good acceptance and demand.

Due to the special qualities TPR is replacing vulcanised rubber in industrial parts, sports goods, shoes (upper and lower) medical goods and it can be reprocessed also.

SUGGESTED CAPACITY

The minimum economic capacity for the manufacture of TPR compound is 600 MT per annum.

LAND & BUILDING

The unit requires about 500 sp. mtrs. of land with covered area of 300 sq. mtrs.

RAW MATERIALS

The requirement of raw materials for the manufacture of 600 MT of TPR compound is as under :-

Styrene Based Resin (Imported)	400	MT
Polystyrene	100	MT
Plasticizers/Process Oils	10	MT
Pigments (Viz Yellow HR, Red 2B Toner)	30	MT
Additives like Antioxiants, Coupling Agents & Stabilizers	20	MT
Fillers (Viz. Calcium Carbonate, Talc)	90	MT

UTILITIES

The unit will require a total connected load of 175 KVA. Water requirement is about 300 KL per annum.

MANUFACTURING PROCESS

The manufacturing process of TPR is as under :-

Raw materials and fillers are fed in the kneader through the hopper, along with other additives e.g. antioxidants, coupling agents, stabilizers etc. This kneader has specially designed screw for proper mixing.

This mixed lump is then automatically carried to the extruder with the help of inbuilt conveyor. The material is further mixed and extruded in the extruder.

Extruded material comes out of the Die and cut buy Die face cutter, into rounded granules.

These granules are fed to separator cum dryer where pure granules are separated from impurities and its moisture is also removed.

The finished pure granules and weighed and packed in plastic bags.

PLANT & MACHINERY

1. Linear Containers Mixer Type Kneader
2. Twin Screw Extruder
3. Die-face Cutter
4. Separator cum Drier
5. Weighing & Packing Machine

PERSONNELS

The unit requires to employ about 20 persons including staff for office and factory for production supervision and administration.

ESTIMATED COST OF THE PROJECT

The project cost for setting up a unit to manufacture 600 MT of TPR compound per annum is estimated to Rs. 100 lakhs as follows :

		Rs. in Lakhs
1.	Land & site development	5.00
2.	Building	15.00
3.	Plant & machinery	30.00
4.	Technical know-how and engineering fees	5.00
5.	Other misc. fixed assets	10.00
6.	Preliminary & preoperative expenses	5.00
7.	Margin money for working capital	25.00
8.	Contingencies	5.00
	Total	100.00

SUGGESTED MEANS OF FINANCING

		Rs. in Lakhs
1.	Long term loan	65.00
2.	State cash subsidy	10.00
3.	Promoters capital	25.00
	Total	100.00

24

Masterbatches

INTRODUCTION

Plastics consumption in India has been growing at a very fast pace. As the awareness to use plastics in differentend uses increase, plastics manufacturers and processors are faced with the task of providing reliable and consistent products. The masterbatch industry in India has kept pace with this growth by producing tailormade masterbatches/colour concentrates. With continuous advances in both pigments and additives technology, the masterbatch manufacturers have to continuously innovate to provide colour concentrates economically.

Thermoplastics are mostly colourless. They are transparent, translucent and opaque. These thermoplastics need to be coloured to increase their aesthetic appeal which gives the end product a better market acceptability. Various types of pigments and colours can be incorporated in plastics to get the required colour and properties. Similarly, different types of additives can be incorporated in plastics to enhance/modify them to suit a particular end application.

Methods of Manufacture

Thermoplastics can be coloured by any of the four following process.

- ★ Dry colouring
- ★ Precoloured plastic granules
- ★ Extrusion
- ★ Use of masterbatches/colour concentrates

Today, it is universally acknowledged that the use of masterbatches is the most convenient way of colouring plastics. In masterbatches, pigments/ additives in high concentration are predispersed in a suitable carrier resin such as LDPE, LLDPE or PP and extruded into pellets. The dispersing of the pigments in the carrier resin a carried out in special equipment such as banbury, continuous mixers, co-kneaders, twin screw vented extruders having mixing elements, etc. Modern technology has ensured that the best way of producing a good masterbatch is on a continuous mixer or twing screw extruders which may be co-rotating or counter rotating depending on the type of product to be manufactured. The masterbatch is then mixed at a desired Let Down Ratio (1 to 15%) in the virgin plastic raw material and tumble mixed and directly processed by various processing techniques to produce the desired end product.

Advantages in Processing

These are :

- ★ Elimination of dust and dirt of dry colours. Thus, the health hazard to workers is eliminated. All masterbatches are environment-friendly.
- ★ Greater colour quality than dry colours/pigments.

OVERVIEW

- ★ Excellent consistency of colour from batch to batch.
- ★ Easy to handle and store because of pellet form.
- ★ Excellent surface finish to the finished product.
- ★ Evenness of dispersion ensures that migration of pigments is kept to the minimum.
- ★ No loss of critical properties of the virgin polymer.
- ★ Regular size of pellet makes it possible to use in automatic volumetric feeding.

The Different Types

Broadly, masterbatches can be classified as black, white colour and additive masterbatches. Within each of these categories, there exists an enormous range of products depending on the type of pigments used, carrier resins, types of additives used, etc. It has been observed the world over that the demand potential for all these four categories is almost the same.

In India, there are more than 100 masterbatch manufacturers producing around 20,000 tons of colour concentrates per year and 15,000 tons of antifibrillation masterbatches for the woven sack industry. There is a concentration of manufacturing units in the western region due to the presence of hundreds of processing units in Maharashtra, Gujarat and Daman.

According to several studies conducted, the demand for masterbatches is expected to increase by the year 2001 to 55,000 tons and for antifibrillation masterbatches to around 30,000 tons giving a cumulative average growth rate of around 17% per year.

White masterbatches

These are the most widely used masterbatches for the colouring of plastic films. A white masterbatch contains a very high concentration of titanium dioxide pigment in the carrier resin.

There are two types of TiO2, i.e. Rutile grade and Anatase grade. Rutile TiO2 has a higher tinting strength, hiding power and chalking resistance compared to Anatase grade. Hence, for good quality white masterbatches, only Rutile TiO2 is used. TiO2 is usually coated with inorganic coatings like alumina, silica and organic coatings like siloxane. The inorganic coating gives weathering resistance whereas the organic coating increases the dispersion of the pigment in the carrier resin.

It is important to have a TiO2 with optimum inorganic and organic coating. A high level of these coatings can lead to processing problems during film production at high temperatures and may also affect the seal strength and printability. A wide range of white masterbatches from 30% TiO2 to 75% TiO2 are being produced in India. Certain grades of white masterbatches also contain calcium carbonate or other such extenders to reduce the cost.

Conventional white masterbatches use LDPE as a carrier resin so that compatibility in all polyolefins is achieved. However, carrier resins such as LLDPE, HDPE, PP or PS can also achieve desired properties. Sometimes, white masterbatches are also tinted in blue shades to meet customer requirements.

In keeping with worldwide trends, India is also going in for more sophisticated high output plants where film thicknesses are being downgauged to achieve economics without compromising on strength and other desired properties. In view of these, suitable compounding of carefully chosen TiO2 grades are necessary to achieve best quality results.

Black masterbatches

Black masterbatches are used in a variety of applications like garbage films, pipes, rotomoulded tanks, drip irrigation laterals, synthetic fibres, etc. In general, a black masterbatch contains a high concentration of carbon black, finely dispersed in a suitable resin. A wide range of carbon blacks are available depending on the particle sizes, structure of carbon black, porosity of carbon black, surface area of carbon black, etc. Carbon black in plastics can impart unique properties to the resulting products such as UV stabilisation, jetness, electric conductivity or resistance, opacity, etc. The use of carbon black in plastics for each of these properties requires an optimisation of the target performance against required mechanical properties, processing ease and production cost of the compound. The primary carbon black characteristics that affect compound performances are particle size, structure and aggregate size. Better understanding of carbon black morphology and innovations in carbon black manufacturing have led to improved processability, cleanliness and high purity of the new generation carbon black grades designed for use in some of today's most demanding plastic applications.

Carbon black masterbatches and compounds usually absorb some moisture upon exposure to air. This moisture absorption can create processing problems or surface defects in the finished product. Hence, it is advisable to predry these masterbatches before using. During the monsoon, extra care should be taken to predry these masterbatches.

Colour masterbatches

A wide range of colour masterbatches are available with varying shades,capacity,colour brilliance,heat and light stability. virtually,any colour masterbatch as desired by the user can be development by choosing the proper inorganic/organic pigments. In addition to the normal colour masterbaches, there is agrowing interest in specialeffects such as pearl, fluoroescent, metallic, granite,etc.

Masterbatches can be used without any problem even at high colouration concentrations, Experience, however, shows that pigment concentrations below about 1.5% in the masterbatch can lead to shade variations due to inadequate mixing of the two melts. Other causes of shade variations are :

- ⋆ Delayed melting of the pigmented granule;
- ⋆ Too low concentration;
- ⋆ Inadequate mixing effect of the screw;
- ⋆ Too cold running of the extruder;
- ⋆ Hence, many processors opt for 2% pigment contents in moulding applications or around 4 to 5% and even more in the case of film applications.

Both organic colours and inorganic pigments are used for colourants of plastics. The latter are usually metal oxides, mixed oxides, aluminium silicates, sulphates, sulphides and chromates. Cadmium and lead pigments are slowly being phased out due to environmental reasons.

Pearlescent pigments also belong to the inorganic pigments.

Organic pigments are subdivided into dyes, i.e. colourants soluble in plastics or colour pigments i.e. colourants insoluble in plastics.

Pigments technology is becoming quite complex and it is always adivsable to take technical heop of the pigment manufacturer before processing a masterbatch. some of the characteristics which are important are heat stability, light stability, migration resistance and suitability for food contact applications. It is desirable for the masterbatch manufacturer to check with the customer the end use and the properties sought by the customer before deciding on the pigments.

Additive masterbatches

How do we classify plastic additives? The most common way is by usage i.e. heat stabilisers; light stabilisers, lubricants, fillers, flame retardants, processing aid, etc. However, the rational way of recognising additives would be as follows :

★ Additives which improve properties;

★ Additives which help processing;

★ Additives which modify properties;

In the first group, we can include flame retardants, antioxidants, preservatives, light, heat and UV stabilisers and antistatic agents. In the second group, we can include mould release agents, lubricants, antiblock agents, processing aid and slip agents. In the last group, we can include coupling agents, impact modifiers, peroxides, chemical blowing agents and plasticisers.

Fillers are not always considered as plastic additives but it must be emphasised that certain fillers/extruders used in the right dosages can improve the mechanical properties of plastics. Overall, worldwide growth in the additives market is more than 5%. the comparatively low growth in the western countries is being offset by the very rapid growth of plastics in the countries of Asia and the Fat East, south America and Eastern Europe. This article highlights the usefulness of certain types of masterbatches which have already been well accepted in the industry or which have a high potential for growth.

Antifibriliation masterbatches

The masterbatch is used in monoaxially oriented tapes made from PP or HDPE. During production of raffia tapes by extrusion, a film is slit into tapes and then oriented monoaxially on a heated hot plate or hot air oven by stretching these tapes six to eight times. This monoaxial orientation results in the alignment of PP or HDPE crystallites in the direction of orientation resulting in high tape tenacity. However, these tapes can get vertically split due to this orientation. It is to overcome this problem of splitting/fibrillation, that the antifibrillation masterbatch is added. The antifibrillation masterbatch contains 60 tc 75% calcium carbonate in a suitable carrier resin and is usually used at a Let Down Ratio of 2 to 5%. In India, sometimes to reduce the cost of the product, this masterbatch is used at a very high LDR of 8 to 10% resulting in drastic reduction in tape tenacity, increased tape breakages and early screen choking during production besides increasing the wear and tear of the extruders. Screen chocking will also depend on the particle size, dispersion of calcium carbonate used in making a masterbatch and its dispersion in the carrier resin.

UV light stabiliser masterbatch

All thermoplastics undergo varying levels of degradation when exposed to outdoor weather resulting in loss in loss/embrittlement of the finished product. This happens due to the harmful attack of UV rays present in sunlight in the wavelength range of 200 to 400 mm.

The UV light stabiliser masterbatch contains a suitable UV stabiliser incorporated in a polyolefin carrier resin.

The loading level of the masterbatch will depend on the geographical territory where the product is being used, number of sunshine hours, altitude, etc. In general, the HALS type of UV stabilisers have been found to give the best results for prolonging the service life of extruded/moulded products such as PP outdoor chairs, FIBCs, tarpaulins, greenhouse films, crates, etc. The amount of UV light stabiliser masterbatc to be incorporated will depend upon the intensity of sunlight, thickness of the product, life expected, type of UV stabiliser used, etc.

Antioxidant masterbatch

The incorporation of antioxidant masterbatch in a base polymer prevents thermal degradation of the polymer at high processing temperatures such as experienced in rotomoulding of polyethylene, extrusion of polyethylene monofilaments, etc. Oxidation can also occur during reprocessing of plastics.

In the absence of a suitable antioxidant, the polymer will degrade at high processing temperatures resulting in yellowing/black particles, screen chocking and reduction in overall mechanical properties of the end product. Antioxidants are classified as either primary antioxidants such as hindered phenols or secondary arylamines or secondary antioxidants such as phosphides, sulphides or thioesters. In general, primary antioxidants are more expensive but give better results.

Polymer processing aid masterbatches

Masterbathches based on polymer processing aid are used during the processing of narrow molecular weight LLDPE resins in film or drip lateral applications. These resins have a very high melt viscosity due to which 100% LLDPE - based films when produced on narrow die gaps result in melt fracture or shark skin like appearance affecting quality, opticals and coefficient of friction of finished films.

Polymer processing aids are fluoroelastomers and when incorporated in desired addition levels in LLDPE prevent melt fracture during production of films or pipes. Their function is to coat the die surface during processing, accelerate the melting process and to reduce die pressure and extrusion temperature. In addition, these masterbatches also increase throughput, surface gloss and clarify or LLDPE films.

Although 200 to 300 ppm level of PPA in LLDPE is sufficient to prevent melt fracture, it is advisable to first add aroound 1,500 to 2,000 ppm level of PPA during start up for about 30 minutes till the PPA coats the die. Once the melt fracture vanishes, the addition level can be brought down to 200 to 300 ppm for the result of the production run.

Antiblocking agent masterbatches

The polyolefin films of the LDPE, LLDPE and PP types are inherently prone to blocking. Blocking is a tendency of adjacent polyolefin film surfaces to adhere to each other when brought into contact together during manufacturing such as blown film production. This caused openability problems later on during bag making. This blocking tendency of film surface can be eliminated by adding antiblocking agent masterbatch during the processing of these films. Normally, silica is used as an antiblock agent but nowadays finely ground talc is also being used. Antiblock agent also improves the print adhesion, bondability and weldability of the films.

Slip additive masterbatches

This masterbatch reduces the coefficient of friction of the polyolefin film making the film surface very smooth. This is useful in obtaining higher line speeds on a converting machine such as form, fill, sealing machine during subsequent pouch making. Slip agents are usually small mobile molecules of fatty acidamides such as oleamide or erucamide which rapidly migrate to the surface forming a thin lubricating layer. In general, at a given temperature, oleamide migrates to the surface more rapidly than erucamide. However, at a high extrusion temperature a slower migration of erucamide minimises the loss of amide during processing. This is advantageous when the film is subsequently printed and sealed. Erucamide is also preferred in a film which is to be laminated because of its lower migration tendency. One should be careful not to overdose the slip masterbatch during processing as it may lead to screw slip, poor print adhesion, poor sealing or bond strength.

Antistatic masterbatches

Because of high volume and specific surface resistance, most plastics play a pivotal role as insulating materials in the electric and electronic industries. As a result, there is a tendency to acquire a strong electrostatic charge which may couse difficulties and malfunctions like :

- ★ Accumualation of dust;
- ★ Problems in subsequent processing like wrapping and covering in packaging machines;
- ★ Fire or explosive hazards;
- ★ Interference with finishing, printing decorations, etc.

It is therefore necessary that the problems associated with static charge are minimised and if possible eliminated. This can be done effectively by using oleochemicals as antistatic agents.

The surface charge may be reduced by external spraying with a dilute solution of antistatic or an internal addition of an antistatic or an internal addition of an antisatic to the polymer. Internal antistatic agents migrate to the surface and reduce the surface resistance, partly with the action of water absorbed from air. Internal antistatic are more preferred because of their long lasting effects whereas external antistatics are removed either by abrasion or washing.

APPLICATIONS

Applications of antistatic agent masterbatches include the film sheets, moulded chairs, containers and household ware.

Flame retardant masterbatches

They are incorporated in plastics to reduce the ease with which the plastics can be ignited and reduce the rate at which the plastics can burn once ignited.

Most of the thermoplastic polymers catch fire and hence cannot be used in specialised applications such on components of aircraft, blowing materials, sophisticated electronic equipment, consumer durables, etc. Hence, the use of flame retardants has become mandatory in many end uses. Fire is caused easily by heat, fuel and oxygen. Commonly, a flame retardant works by eliminating one or more of these elements thus reducing the fire spread.

Broadly, flame retardants are classified as halogenated and nonhalogenated types. Although halogenated types are more effective flame retardants, they have other diverse effects such as toxicity and higher smoke density. Hence, many a times antimony trioxide or trihydrates of alumina are synergistically used with halogenated flame retardants to reduce smoke density and toxicity.

This masterbatch with varying formulations is available to give different flammability rating.

This class of masterbatch is one of the most promising and the growth rates are in excess of 10% throughout the world.

Nucleating agent masterbatches

Nucleating agent masterbatches are added in semi crystalline polymers such as PP to improve the clarify of the end product. Common applications are films, disposable containers, syringes, etc.

The nucleating agent of the sorbitol type when incorporated in crystalline plastic such as PP provide a large number of nucleating sites forming a greater number of small spherullites which reduces the reflection and absorption of light within a polymer matrix. This reduces the haze and increase the clarity due to increase in light transmission.

Other benefits of nucleating masterbatches are :

- Increase in gloss and surface smoothness;
- Faster moulding cycles as cooling time can be reduced to accelerate crystalline rates;
- Increase in flexural modulus and tensile strength;
- Increase in heat distortion temperature;
- Increase in dimensional stability;

Cling additive masterbatches

Cling describes the tendency of thermoplastic film to adhere to similar or dissimilar materials because of the surface properties of the film itself.

Cling may appear as a surface characteristic of the unmodified polymer material, although it is then commonly destroyed when the film is stretched as in stretch wrapping application. It may be enhanced by the addition of small quantities of suitable agents to the basic polymer.

25

Production and Filling Process of a PET-Bottle

Generally there are many different ways from the PET raw material to a completely filled PET bottle.

The material from the PET producer to the bottling factory is always delivered in one of the following three ways :

- Pet - Chips
- Pre - forms
- Empty PET-bottles

In the first and second case only the bottling factory has to deal with empty bottles, in the third case producer as well as the bottling factory have to deal with empty bottles.

Handling of empty PET Bottles

Especially the handling of these empty bottles causes difficulties in most companies.

The main problems are :

★ Low bottle weight, bad stability due to the generally very small bottom.

★ Electrostatic charging caused by transport and arranging of the bottles

★ Strong adhesion in case of newly produced bottles

Moreover the main packing material, wooden pallets and load carriers in the form of carton trays or inverted carton travs resp. flat interlayers, show very large tolerances, which naturally leads to a high pelletizer failure rate.

Especially because of these tolerances it is necessary to install buffers between the very dependable blow moulders, which use exact pre-forms or completed bottles, and the pelletizer or between the depalletizer and the bottle cleaning and filling machines. For this reason the pelletizer have to have a 20% higher performance to compensate possible failures.

This buffer used to be installed in the form of air conveyors, which, however, are only able to buffer for a few minutes despite the enormous length and the considerable space requirement.

Depending on the performance these conveyor systems used to be between 50 and 200 meters long.

New empty bottle handling and packing system

The empty bottle handling system newly developed and applied consists of 4 components :

- ★ Tray loader
- ★ Tray loop
- ★ Pelletizer reps. Depalletizer
- ★ Trays storage

1. **Tray Loader**

The tray loader is located directly behind the blow moulder in order to immediately put the bottles onto a tray, which securely carries the bottles. This arrangement in the tray corresponds to the pallet layer pattern. This tray is ideal means of transport and buffer.

This tray rules out the familiar getting stuck in the air conveyor resp. the failing over of the single bottles in the conveyors of the familiar pelletizing systems.

By loading the trays row by row a very high availability is reached since one can work with very exactly measured bottles and trays. Due to this a short buffer of a few seconds only is sufficient.

The bottles are being moved row by row. The number of rows picked up per cycle depends on the blow moulder output.

2. **Tray Loop**

After these trays are being transported on conventional roller conveyors. The tray loop replaces the customary air conveyors. In case of a 2.0 liter Euro bottle, which is placed on a 1200 x 1000 mm pallet, one tray can hold for example 120 bottles. This corresponds to a conventional air conveyor length of approximately 12 meters.

These size of the tray loops and therefore the capacity of the number of tray and bottles conveyor depends on the required buffer time.

These simple and functionally safe tray conveyors are in any case saving lots of space and money compared to the formerly required air conveyors for identical buffer amounts.

In case of a bottle output of 20,000 bottles per hour this system only requires 20 trays of approximately 1200 x 1000 mm in size instead of 200 meter long air conveyors for identical buffer times.

3. **Pelletizer**

The pelletizer picks up the completed layer from the tray and puts it directly onto the pallet reps. the layer pad. The empty tray then returns to the tray loader.

Depending on the performance the pelletizer can additionally handle layer pads, trays, inverted trays or empty pallets with a multi-functional gripper head.

4. **Installation of a Tray Storage**

The transport of bottles in trays also offers the possibility to very easily install a larger intermediate storage for the produced bottles.

This make sense if the bottling factory produces the bottles itself, but for cost reason only buys a small blow moulder, which produces in 3 shifts. On the other hand bottling factories usually only fill bottles in 1 or 2 shifts. This fact makes it necessary to bring bottles into the line addition to the blowing machine during filling and to take out the produced bottles during the non-filling phase.

Up to now this is realized with costly pelletizers and depalletizers.

The addition of a tray storage, which we are familiar with from the handling of filament bobbins is much more functional, space-saving and cost effective.

In this case simple sheft operating devices are picking up the trays from the conveyors and pushing them into the drawers of the sheft storage.

The same sheft operating devices then again take the trays out of the sheft storage and return them to the tray loop when needed.

ADDITIONAL ADVANTAGES OF THIS NEW HANDLING AND PACKING SYSTEM

1. **Discharge at several production lines**

   The palletizer is built modularly so that it

   ★ can serve several lines and additionally handle layer pads and empty pallets in case of lower performances.

   ★ can pelletizer bottles as well as handle layer pads and empty

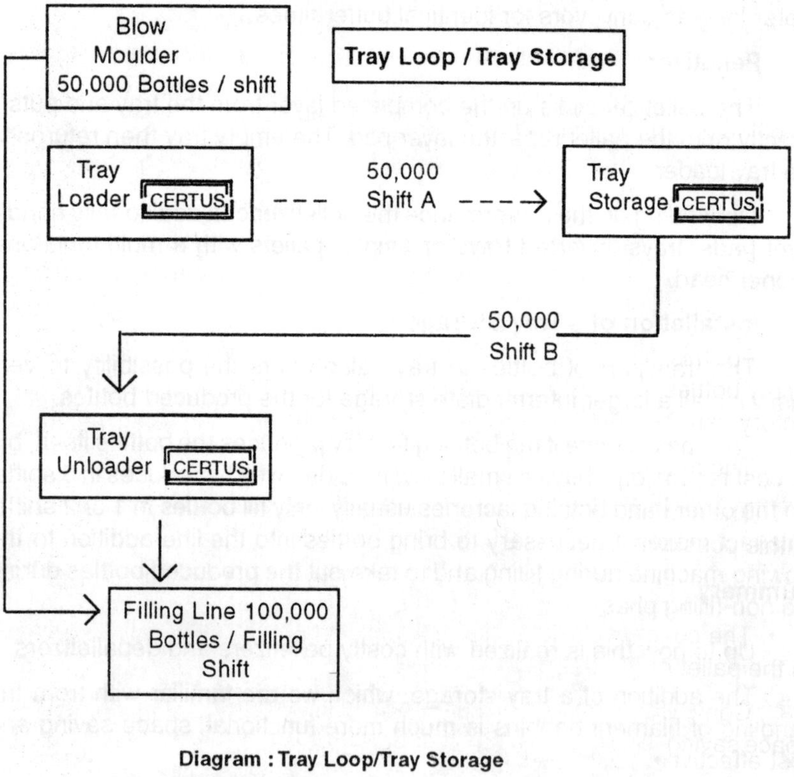

Diagram : Tray Loop/Tray Storage

☐ CERTUS manufactured products

→ Shift A ; The blow moulder produces PET-bottles. The filling line is shut off and the complete production is put storage

- Shift B : The blow moulder produces PET-bottles. Since the output capacity of the filling machine is twice as high as the blow moulder output, storage is being emptied. For this reason double capacity is now available at the filling line.

pallets in case of medium performances,

- ★ can be equipped with additional aggregates for handling of the layer pads reps. the empty pallets in case of high performances.

2. **Separation of Blow moulder and Filling Line**

For filling factories application of tray storage also makes sense between the blow moulder and the filling area.

When changing the format, filling of a new product with bottles from storage can start immediately after a change in the filling in addition to increasing the total efficiency by making use of a buffer. If bottle formats are changed frequently the very high set-up times on blow moulder are considerably compensated.

3. **Application of commercially available Plastic Trays as means of Transportation**

Especially in the soft drink market one can notice a continuously increasing application of the plastic display trays of the size of a pallet resp. a half pallet.

For this reason it would make sense in the long term to deliver the empty bottles to the filling factory already on these trays so that the filling factory can then put the filled products on the market on the same trays.

The multiple-entry trays are the then returned to the bottle producer.

The new handling system described by us would be ideal for realization of this possibility.

Summary

The concept offers absolutely safe transport from the blow moulder to the pallet or the filling line.

Conveying with trays as intermediate carrier is considerably more space saving, safer and economical compared to the conventional method.

It offers the possibility to intermediately store the bottles with simple proven storage techniques.

After all the complete system is built modularly for differing performances and for the described various different production flow methods.

26

PET Bottle Recycling

PET bottle recycling exists already for a long time Originally the PET bottle recycling was based on the use of bottles from the refill systems. The RPET was only used for fiber during the first period.

An other area that we are dedicating recourses to is finding outlets for the RPET. For the clear bottles the fiber market and in the future the bottle market (closed loop) will be big enough to absorb the growth in collection for the coming 5 years. Even without a bottle to bottle recycling there is an estimated market for RPET available of some 800 ktons by the year 2005, and the collection by then will not reach those number. However for the increasing amount of coloured bottles and (in the near future) bottles with barrier materials the market outlets can became too limited. For these products PETCORE supports product and application developments programs to overcome a future supply/demand unbalance.

As far as collection and sorting are concerned the results in PET recycling are outstanding. With an increase of approximately 50% per year the PET bottle recycling can be seen as the fastest growing plastic business.

In countries where the funding via the green dot was established growth was even much higher. AS an example, in Belgium the collection of PET bottles grew, after the funding was arranged, from 1 kton per year to 18 kton per year in a 4 years period.

Few years back, the expected collection and recycling of PET bottles in Western Europe is expected to increase from 110 ktons to 170 ktons. This brings the recycling ratio at some 16% of the virgin sales of bottles (estimated at 1000 ktons).

These growth figures create trust in the continuity of supply and opens new developments for the use of RPET in several new end use segments.

This is also reflected in the investments in new recycling processing (flake production) capacity, which to day is still higher than the supply of collected and sorted PET bottle bales.

As indicated before, PETCORE is supporting product and application development programs to find new outlets for the RPET. In the beginning of PETCORE's activities, the industry thought there were by far not enough outlets for the future RPET. Lack of understanding of the mechanics that plastic recycling industry were the main reason for this fear.

The virgin plastic sales is driven by applications that are developed (e.g.a car bumper) needing material to fit the required properties (pull).

The recycling plastic sales is driven by the (growing) availability of material for which applications are sought (push). The markets for the recycling plastic are in the first place existing applications that are served with virgin plastics, whether we like this or not.

This has consequences for the economics of a recycling business that try to deal with a new recycle material. In the beginning the sales prices are very low for reason such as, low quality, low volumes available in the beginning, lack of confidence in the continuity of supply, etc.

As far as the PET bottle recycling is concerned the economics are mainly damaged by the forced growth, caused by the EU directive targets and even higher targets in the different countries. Using the glass bottle recycling as an example with proven experience the PET bottle recycling should theoretically cost not more as DM 0,70 for collection, DM 0,30 for sorting and DM 0,35 for processing a pure flake. This would be the case if the glass iglo system would just be copied.

What's not taken into account in these prices are the innovation and technological developments that will happen as soon as a new business starts to become interesting. Good examples of automatic sorting systems to separate PET and PEN from PVC, sort on color and even per polymer type.

For the PET recycling in specific the development of a flake separation system eliminate the last bits of PVC contamination was a technological break through, to solve a major quality problem.

Since there is enough confidence now in the continuity of supply of PET bottles in Europe (50% increase per year) it is reasonable to expect the costs for PET recycling being decreased drastically over the coming five years.

The total costs for producing a good quality flake for the use in fibers (clear material) should therefore reach a level, not higher than DM 1,00 maximum. This makes the PET recycling a sustainable business.

The packaging waste management business is a specialized business, which therefore should be managed by managers with experience in the waste management industry. In practice the opposite the case. The management of the national organizations that are responsible for the implementation of the collection and sorting program are mainly coming from our own chemical industry, They might, without any doubt be the best in our industry, but they have/had no or very limited experience in the waste industry. This is one the reasons for the very high green dot values we experience in different countries. In some countries we notice now that new organizations and supermarket chains are starting to set up their own independent collection schemes in order to reduce the high green dot fees. This might stimulate the existing organization to a better control of the collection and sorting costs. We have to realize that every amount that is paid for the waste treatment is making our product in the market more expensive and leaves less money for the raw material price we can get and for sales price of the bottle. The economical situation in the PET bottle business does not allow such a waste of consumer's money. There are many reason that brought us in the situation that we are in today. The plastic industry in general never thought that the politicians would create legislation that would be so dramatic for the packaging industry. We were quite arrogant in our attitude towards the strong signals that were coming from the consumers (represented by the so-called "greens") and the politicians. But also the lack of knowledge about the possibilities in waste handling and recycling was a problem. And last but not least, lack of vision?

The PET bottle business was a good exception, being proactive by organizing itself via national Pet organizations and by the creation of European organization PETCORE.

There are of course economical and ecological limits to the mechanical recycling of PET bottle, mainly due to logistic costs in areas with a low population density. But these limits are by far not reached yet today.

In case we fail in reaching acceptable mechanical recycling quotas the economical consequences for the PET bottle business can be dramatic, varying from penalties, ecotaxes, deposit systems to mandatory refill quotas and even a ban on materials.

And if we reach high targets at unacceptable green dot levels we open the door to other more expensive raw materials that compensate their high raw material price by low waste management costs.

On the other hand, if we do it right, the PET bottle will continue the replacement of the glass bottle and the metal cans, becoming the accepted packaging material for the consumer.

We have to realise that we have to listen to the signals coming from the consumer, be proactive and also realise that waste management costs are an integral part of the final product cost.

That's why the recycling of the PET bottle is an opportunity for the PET bottle business and not a thread.

27

PET Preform and Bottle Blowing

PET Container Applications

Perhaps the most important of the plastic materials that may be oriented to improve their physical properties is "PET" , the abbreviation for Poly Ethylene Terephthalate. The familiar PET carbonated soft drink bottle, which has become an indispensable part of our lives, is made by stretch blow moulding process. The superb properties of PET make it ideal for packaging a whole host of products ranging from beverages and food products to pharmaceuticals and cosmetics.

Popular applications are :

The high strength and creep resistance of PET bottles makes them ideal for packaging of carbonated soft drinks, while their crystal clarity emphasizes the purity of bottle water. PET containers have many other advantages too, and are now used not only for beverages but also food and household products, cosmetics, pharmaceuticals and agircultural chemicals, alcoholic drink and now beer also.

Crystal clear : Products look good, pure and healthy. Sparking PET bottle attract attention.

Pure : Products teste good.

PET complies with international food contact regulations.

Safe : PET bottle are tough and virtually unbreakable. If they do fail, they split, not explode. Their high impact and tensile strength makes them ideal for carbonated products.

Good barrier : The low permeability of PET to oxygen, carbon dioxide and water means that it protects and maintains the integrity of products giving a good shelf life. PET also has good chemical resistance.

SINGLE STAGE SYSTEM

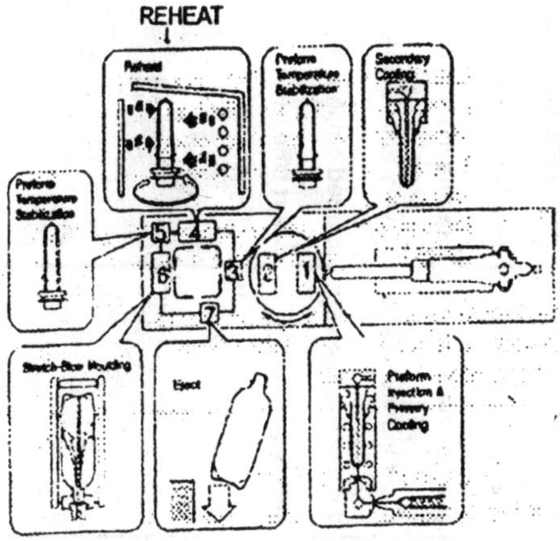

TWO STAGE SYSTEM

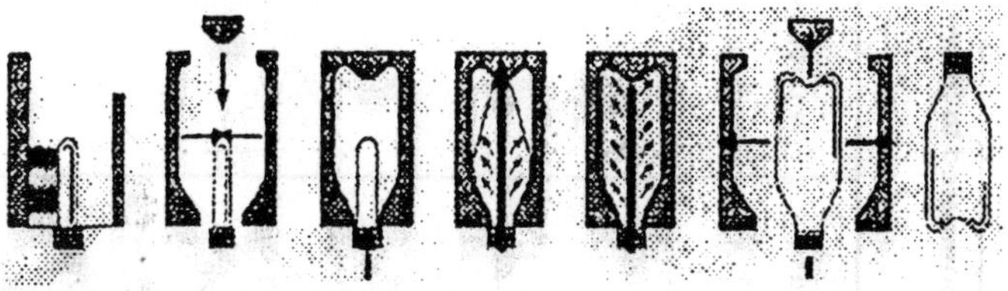

Advance of the Preform Blowing System (Two-stage System)

Compared to Integrated Systems in which injection and Blowing are carried out on the same Machine, the Two-stage Systems presents the following advantages :

Because the process comprises two separate stages, it allows making pre-forms with an injection moulding machine or buying these from a specialist manufacturer. So it is possible to optimize the injection and blowing processes and the pre-form and container quality separately.	The necessary investment is smaller,	As a maximum axial biorientation can be achieved, containers with less weight are produced.	There is no need for special skils to operate the machine since the same and the process are very simple.	High manufacturing flexibility, because starting the machine is very smiple ane is carried out in a very short time.	If offers a great versatility for making different bottle shapes.	Since this is a two-stage process, the acetaldehyde content is lower.

Lightweight : One tenth the weight of an equivalent glass pack. PET bottle reduce shipping costs, and because the material in the wall is thinner, shelf utilization is improved by 25% on volume compared to glass. High strenght, low weight PET bottles can be stacked as high as glass.

No leakage : Absolute closure integrity is possible because of the injection moulding neck finish. The absence of a weld-line in the base means that PET bottles don't leak.

Design flexibility : Suitable for bottle of all shapes, sizes, neck finishes and colours.

Recyclable : Used pet bottle can be washed, brcken into flakes and reshaped as PET bottles or employed as material for strapping, carpeting, fiber filling etc. Specially designed thickwall bottles can even be washed and refilled. PET is made from the same three elements (carbon, oxygen and hydrogen) as paper, and contains no toxic substances. When bumed, it produces carbon dioxide gas and water, leaving no toxic residues.

Popular Sizes : 20 ml to 2000 ml

MANUFACTURING PROCESSES

1. *Single stage :* Injection of preform and stretch blow of bottles (biaxially oriented) on the same machine.

2. *Two stage :* Injection moulding of preforms on Injection Moulding Machines Reheat of Preform and Blowing of Bottle on stretch-blow-moulding machine (biaxially oriented).

QUALITY REQUIREMENTS

(a) *Preform –*

- Uniform thickness
- Clarity
- No visual defects
- Correct shape and neck dimension and threads
- Residual AA Contents (Acetaldehyde)

(b) *Bottle –*

- Correct shape
- Designed thickness
- Stable bottom

– Residual AA Contents
– Clarity
– Strenght
– No visual defects

Sigle Stage Process

In single stage machine, PET granules are input and bottle/jar (final product) is output.

Preforms are made by injection process and then taken away and transferred on a cooling/reheating station and then transferred to a stretch-blow station and bottles/jars ejected in the bin/on belt.

High volume, high quality product producing machines and moulds are available renowned suppliers.

One-Step and Two-step systems compared

One-Step	*Two-Step*
Lower initial investment for a complete system.	Higher initial investment for a complete system. And yet, choosing not make preforms but to buy them can minimize initial costs.
One Conventional One-Step machines, the number of injection cavities and blow moulds is the same.	The cycle times of the two separate machines are usually different so the outputs are matched by increasing the number of injection cavities.
Traditinally considered being more suitable for low and medium volumes, and production of more technically demanding containers.	Considered to be more suitable for high volume production of less technically demanding containers such as carbonated soft drink bottles.
Conventional One-Step machines are more versatile capable of making both bottles and wide-mouth jars in a very wide variety of sizes and styles. Since container	Frequently Two-Step Machines are only capable of making bottles. (The production costs of wide-mouth

Contd....

dimensions generally determine preform specing, differences in production costs between bottles and jars are minimal.	preforms for Two-Step production are high because of the very large moulds and injection moulding that are needed.).
The thermal efficiency of One-Step process is better because the residual heat in the preforms from the injection moulding process is used for blowing.	The thermal efficiency of Two-Step process is lower since preforms are first cooled to room temprerature for storage purpose and later re-heated to the suitable blowing temperature.
Preforms are blown immediately after they are moulding, so there is no opportunity for preforms to 'age' or absorb moisture from the atmosphere, which would result in an alteration in stretch-blowing characteristic batches.	- (Relatively compact) preforms can be stockpiled to adapt to fluctuations in demand but care must be taken in controlling storage conditions to ensure consistent aging and moisture absorption of different preform. - Centralized preform production facility can be created to supply several blow moulders. - Bottle makers can make buy preforms.

One-Step and Two-Step Systems compared

One-Step	*Two-Step*
Preforms are not re-gripped before blowing so the bottles are free from scuff marks.	Preforms are normally stored before blowing and are frequently scuffed.
Since preforms are not re-gripped, a neck supporting is not essential.	A neck support ring is required to facilitate preform handling.
Conventional One-Step machines can make containers of highly oval or rectangular cross section.	Degree of ovality restricted owing to the difficulty temperature profiling the preforms.
Preform designs are different : preform wall is thicker to retain heat where stretching is wanted.	Preform wall is thinner so that it heats up faster where stretching is wanted.

TWO STAGE PROCESS

The Two-Step Process user two separate machines to make PET bottles, the first to mould the preform, and the second to blow bottle. With this approach, each machine can be optimized for the job it has to perform, making the Two-Step Process especially suitable for large volume production.

Stage 1 : Preforms are injection moulding on injection moulding machine and are stored. Very fast and precise machine-mould-pick-up robots systems are available from international names in injection moulding equipment supplies. Auxillary devices like Dehumidifier, Chillers, Mould Sweat Protector are required for good quality preforms.

Stage 2 : Preforms are fed to the heating station of stretch-blowing station and the container is blown in the blow mould and ejected in bin/on conveyor.

TWO STAGE SYSTEM

Injection Moulding Machine

Injection Moulding for Preform Moulding has special requirement of screw, stroke length and injection, refill, hold-on, back pressure, speed and pressure profiles. The thermal profile and uniformity of melt is very important for crystallization and transparency and also the strength of the bottle. The machine should give short cycle time to reduce residence time of material in barrel.

Machines to give :

(i) Good quality visible preforms

(ii) Min polymer degradation (low AA content)

(iii) Max. output.

★ Machines are available to hold mould upto 128 cavities.

★ Moulds are available in hot runner and without hot runner system (upto max. 8 cavities).

(b) Blow Moulding (Bottle)

Single/Double Cavities moulds are popular.

Dehumidification

It is very important that the resin should be free from moisture to get correct clarity of preforms and hence bottles. Hence Dehumidifier is a must.

Air Temp.	:	170 to 185_0C
Air Dew Point	:	-40oC
Heating Time	:	6 hrs

Chillers

Chillers are required to supply cooled water to moulds on injection and blow moulding machines.

High pressure compressor

For blowing bottle on automatic machine, compressed air is required at around 40 bar. Hence high-pressure compressor is required.

Blowing Station - Fully Automatic machines.

★ It has conveyorized re-heat arrangement of preforms by direct heaters and or infrared rays.

★ Auto preform loader and orienter.

Single/multiple station of blowing of bottle. This could be having or rotary table.

★ Auto ejector of bottles in bin/on belt.

★ Rate of production from 1000 bottles/hour upto 7500-9000 bottles per hour.

Renowned international suppliers offer these machines.

How are the physical properties of PET improved by stretching ?

Stretching can orient PET that is heated to a temperature where is chainlike molecules are sufficiently mobile to uncoil instead of breaking when extended. Stretching applied from two directions at right angles, as in stretch blow moulding, gives biaxial orientation. Oriented PET contains closely packed chains aligned in the directions of stretch. The material is stronger because the molecules act together instead of individually. The tensile strength of oriented PET is several times that of the unstretched, material and the impact strength, barrier and chemical resistance are also significantly improved, so bottles can be bottles can be lighter without sacrificing performance.

International trends

Internationally both single stage and two processes of large capacities are employed. However, installations of two-stage process are far more than single stage process.

Wide mouth jars, pharma bottles, kitchen storage jars are quite popular on single system machines on fast production cycles.

For mineral water, carbonated drinks, juices, bottles two stage production is popular. Now special treatment technologies are available for PET beer bottles as beer has special requirements.

The Injection Moulding Machines are holding upto 128 cavities, very efficiently cooled with hot runner systems. The cycle times are further reduced with the help of pick-up Robots and are reported upto 9-12 seconds.

The machines are advanced and have built-in features required to mould PET and get within norms quality parameters.

Blowing machines are fully automatic in feeding the preforms, heating, blowing and ejection of bottles. The output ratios are in the range of 1200 to 9500 bottles/hour in general.

Internationally stage of the art high productive machines are available.

Indian Scene

(a) Stone large scale mineral water/soft drink bottles and other bottles and jar makers have big capacity single stage and two stage high volume production machines, entire system supplied by International manufacturers.

(b) Highly scattered small bottle makers have low cost injection moulding machines running mostly non-hot runner moulds of 2 to 8 cavities and Chinese/Taiwanese/Indian semi-auto, manual low output blowing stations.

★ Do not use dehumidifier but use hopper dryer in majority of cases.

★ The quality of preforms and bottles not very good.

(c) Indian currently lacks a medium size good quality two stage machines and system for medium volume international quality preform and bottles. This vacuum is now filled by DGP Windsor PET Preform and Bottle Blowing System.

★ DGP Windsor offers small and medium scale TOTAL solutions to PET 2 stage process.

★ Injection Moulding Machines 125T, 250T and 350T clamp force in DGM and Sumitomo series for moulding preforms, giving 1000 to 3500 preforms per hour.

★ Tie-up with international brands and PET bottle blowing station in the range of 1000 to 5000 bottles per hour.

- ★ AA Contents within internationally permissible limits (4ppm).
- ★ PET preform moulds from machine suppliers suiting to tailor-made solutions.
- ★ Bottle blow-mould from machine suppliers suiting to tailor made solutions.
- ★ International tie-ups with renowned companies for dehumidifiers, chillers, high-pressure compressors and other support equipments.
- ★ Pick-up robots to reduce cycle time and avoid surface defects by falling of preforms.

Future Scene Expected

The use of PET containers is catching up in India very rapidly. The advantages of clarity and strength offered by PET containers coupled with downward trend in raw material prices, the use of PET containers is likely to be increasing exponentially in all sectors given in the beginning of this article. Also with Coke, Pepsi and other soft-drinks and Juice manufacturers expanding capacity and going for big capacities in bottled Mineral Water, the demand of PET bottles will go up exponentially in various sizes. It is certain that the demand will increase both in large and organised as well as fragmented small and unorganised sectors.

28

PET Bottles from Pre-Form PET

PRE-FORM PET which is becoming increasingly popular, the size of the container produced ranges from 500 ml. to 10000 liter.

Less material ends up in less waste. Oil bottle, are oxygen permeation sensitive, therefore the requirement is high also in terms of vacuum resistance. High side wall strength and structural design feature are important. The neck region is reduced in a minimum of material input which require short and effective heating time, a good shielding during heating and capture of the finish during blowsing operation in the blow mould.

Use for filling non carborated mineral water in 1 liters and 1.5 litres bottle wt. varied 36.5 gm to 47 gm. bottle neck dia 28 mm. - 33 mm. In case of 2 liters bottle with dia 97 mm. is European Country.

1. Use for 1.5 liters thermally stable fruit juice bottle.
2. PRE-FORM PET bottle can be used in food and confectionery.
3. It can be used for filling liquors and wine.
4. It can be used for pharmaceuticals and agro chemicals.
5. It can be used for cosmetics.

PROPERTIES

(A) Preform PET Bottles lighter, economical. Preform bottle design are more refind thereby eliminating excess material.

1. It can withstand vaccum 100 m. bar.
2. It has extremely high inter layer bond strength.
3. Total absence of solvent odour.

4. It has good flexibility and stress crack resistance.
5. Comparative lower cost.

Neck Size/Type	Available Capacity
19 mm Neck Small	30, 40, 50, 60 ml
19 mm Neck Big	100, 200 ml
25 mm Neck	50, 60, 90, 100, 140, 190, 200, 225 ml
28 mm Neck	350, 400. 500, 1000, 1500 ml
Whisky Neck	750 ml
53 mm Neck	300, 400, 500. 100, 1500 ml
83 mm Neck	780 gms., 1,1.5 Kg
100 mm Neck	1.5, 2, 3, 4 Kgs.
120 mm Neck	5.6 Kgs.

The advantages which make Padmini's Freshpet far superior.

Food Grade

100% food grade, making it non-reactive, non-toxic and odourless.

Aesthetics

Aesthetically designed, can be moulding into any shape, size and colour tint to suit your specific product requirements.

Strength

Stronger than any other in its category, it is. Eliminates the risk of loss due to breakage and survives rough handling during transportation

Weight

Lightweight, weighs 1/10th of glass. Facilitates easier handling and transportation and reduces cost.

Airtight & Leak Proof

Airtight. Not a whiff of freshness is lost. Prevents moisture from entering and prevents leakage too.

Space Utility

Has been scientifically designed to makes the most use of limited available spaces in kitchens, warehouse and retail outlets.

Chemical resistance

Padmini's Freshpet has been certified safe, for contact with food products. Has a strong resistance to greater variety of chemicals, solvents, acids, oils & fats.

ENVIRONMENT FRIENDLY

PET (Polyethyleneterephthalate) :

A.S.T.M. Index.

Inherent viscosity Test Specimen

PET Test - D 4603 (08.03)

Polymeric resin film - electrical insulation/dielectric application.

Space D 5213(10.02)

PET film/sheeting (Biaxially oriented) Space D 5047(08.03).

Molecular wt. of preform PET - 2000.

MANUFACTURING PROCESS

High powered, precision heating is applied to the preform. Optimum biorientation applied during bottle formation which guarantees a lighter packaging with superior technical and aesthetic quality.

An increased trend towards multilayer composite film that can be produced economicaly by co extrusion has been particularly noticed. In food packaging in which the mechanical and barrier properties were provided by the multilayer structure, major interest is now attracted by the sector of poly olifin film, which has so far been covered almost exclusievely by monoextrusion and the processing of blends.

The flexibility of coextrusion line continue to be of special importance for enabling a broad range of different type of composite film to be produced without the need for resulting or modifying significant parts of the line.

Composite film which uses PET (Polyesterterpthalate) as a barrier material are also being developed.

In most cases the five layer film coextrusion technology because the very thin barrier layers require adhesives for being coupled to polyolefins and for being extruded in symmetric or assymmetric five layer composite film. This is necessary to avoid high reject rates due to damage to the barrier layers and suppress the rolling effect which often is hardly controllable.

Coextrusion dies for blown film lines

The most significant criteria for evaluating a blown film coextrusion die are set out below.

1. Uniformity of the extruded layers, uniformity of the overall product across the periphery, versatility of use for overall materials, material combination and gauge ratios.
2. Low flow resistance and accessibility.
3. Channels with optimum flow conditions and no dead comers.
4. Good surface quality of the blown film.
5. Reliable rotating device and melt sealing.
6. Selection of material suitable for resisting high pressure an temperature.
7. Ability to provide internal cooling.
8. Flexibility in connecting the individual extruders to the melt feed assemblies.

In the case of 5 layers coextrusion die the 2nd and fourth layers are normally used for the adhesive but need only to be extruded at very low melt through puts (generally not more than 5% to 10% of overall melt throughout). Thus the channels and spiral distributors for these adhesive layers can be given small cross sections to save design volume and melt residence time.

Two three and five layer dies should provide possibility of preferably variable melt stream combination.

The diameter of the die outlet ranges between 20 and 100 mm.

The compact size of this die and the possibility to coextrude up to seven layers enable the die to be used in a blow moulding machine for the manufacture of six layer containers for food stuffs such as tomato ketch up..PA

Small diameter tubing is also required for food packaging film. e.g. for sausage.

Mixing section, barrier screw, etc. to the basic form of screw design are used to increase output, improve mixing, and homogeneity. However, it must stressed, although output is most important, mixing and homogeneity should not be compromised because of problems further down the melt slow i.e. feed black and automatic die.

PLANT LAYOUT

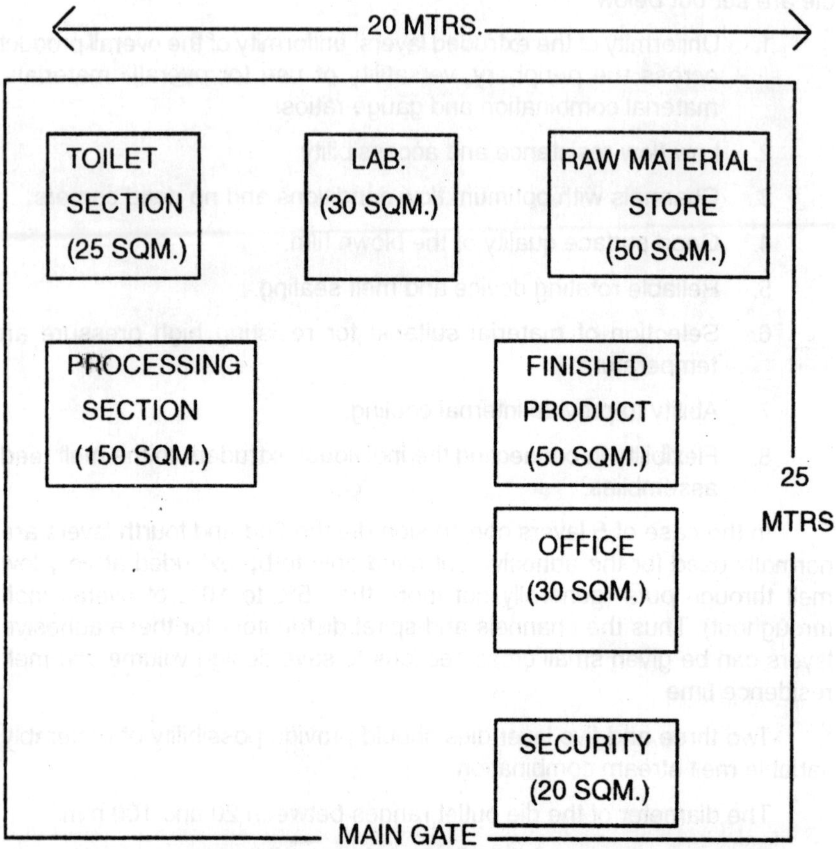

Proper initial sizing of the extruder and good homogenity of the melt through the total operating range is of importance in order to very volumetric percentages of the different layers of the co-extruded film.

2 liters bottle Preform PET wt. 42-45 gms.

29

Plant Economics of PET Bottles from Pre-Form PET

Rated Plant Capacity	=	19,200.00 BOTTLES/day Preform PET Bottles/Containers

SIZE OF EACH BOTTLES - 2 LITER

LAND & BUILDING

(Land required 500 sqm.) Rs. 11,50,000,00

PLANT & MACHINERY

1. Blow moulding machine with stretch extru. process (Cap.1000 preformPET Bottles/hr.) (size 2 litre)
2. Injection Moulding Machine for manufacturing P.P. Caps
3. Refrigeration Unit (Cap. 1 ton/day)
4. Misc. expenses

TOTAL COST OF PLANT & M/C.	Rs.	88,30,000,00
OTHER FIXED ASSETS	Rs.	08,20,000,00

FIXED CAPITAL

1. Land & Building	Rs.	11,50,000,00
2. Plant & Machinery	Rs.	88,30,000,00
3. Other Fixed Assets	Rs.	8,20,000,00
TOTAL	Rs.	1,08,00,000,00

WORKING CAPITAL REQUIREMENT/MONTH

Raw Materials

1. Preform PET resin (22 MT)
2. PP Resin (1 MT)
3. Adhesive and Plasticizer (1 MT)
4. Other raw material viz. Colour, Stabilizer, Mould releasing agent etc.)

TOTAL Rs. 19,40,000.00

TOTAL WORKING CAPITAL/MONTH

1. Raw Material	Rs.	19,40,000.00
2. Salary & Wages	Rs.	94,875.00
3. Utilities & Overheads	Rs.	2,59,000.00
TOTAL	Rs.	22,93,875.00

TOTAL CAPITAL INVESTMENT

Total Fixed Capital	Rs.	1,08,00,000.00
Total Working Capital for 3 Months	Rs.	68,81,625.00
TOTAL	Rs.	1,76,81,625.00

TURN OVER/ANNUM

By selling 57.60 Lakhs Preform PET Bottles (Size 2 Litre)

TOTAL Rs. 4,32,00,000.00

PROFIT SALES RATIO = PROFIT/SALES x 100 = 21.99%

RATE OF RETURN = OPERATING PROFIT/T.C.I x 100 = 53.73 %

BREAK EVEN POINT (B.E.P) = 45.31%

30

PET Pre-Form PET Resin

INTRODUCTION

The use of plastics of all types is increasing and will almost certainly continue to increase. The development of existing plastics and possibly the discovery of new materials will mean that in the future plastics will be used for even more purposes than they are today. Different kinds of plastics, being, processed into numerous items by three different processes as described here under.

INJECTION MOULDING MACHINES

Injection Moulding machines are designed for moulding thermoplastic materials such as pet, Polystyrene. Polythene, High Density Polythene, Polypropylene, Cellulose Acetaters, Butyrate, P.V.C. Nylonete.

BLOW MOULDING

Blow Moulding is a fast easy way to form hollow plastic items is one piece, in a single continuous cycle. 'Kumar' Hand operated blow Moulding machine has been designed for the manufacture of Blow hollow articles. Original in design, it combines the working principle of Injection Moulding and extruding.

USES

PRE-FORM PET which is becoming increasingly popular, the size of the container produced ranges from 50 ml. to 150 ml. which is further use for making required size blow moulding bottles.

Use for filling non carborated mineral water in 1 litres and 1.5 litres bottle wt. varied 36.6 gm to 47 gm. bottle neck dia 28 mm. - 33 mm. In case of 2 litres bottle with dia 97 mm. is European Country.

PROPERTIES

1. It is comparative heavier weight cylidrical type of 25 mm. diameter with 100 mm. length.
2. It has open mouth with threaded neck.
3. It is easily expanded by compressed air with specific temperature.
4. It is not reach with acid or alkali.
5. Appearance of PET Preform is very good.
6. It is transparent.

MANUFACTURING PROCESS

High powered, precision heating is applied to the preform. Optimum bi-orientation applied during bottle formation which guarantees a lighter packaging with superior technical and aesthetic quality.

Co-extrusion dies for blown film lines :

The most significant criteria for evaluating a blown film co-extrusion die are set out below.

1. Uniformity of the extruded layers, uniformity of the overall product across the periphery, versatility of use for different materials, material combination gauge rations.
2. Low flow resistance and good accessibility.
3. Channel with optimum flow conditions and no dead corners.
4. Good surface quality of the blown film.
5. Reliable rotating device and melt sealing.
6. Selection of material suitable for resisting high pressure and temperature.
7. Ability to provide internal cooling.
8. Flexibility in connecting the individual extruders to the 0 melt feed assemblies.

The diameter of the die outlet range between 20 and 100 mm.

Mixing section, barrier screw, etc. to the basic form of screw design are used to increase output, improve mixing, and homogeneity.

FOR 2 liters bottle Preform PET wt. 42 - 45 gms.

MANUFACTURING PROCESS OF PET PREFORM

Specially designed P.E.T. Injection moulding machine is used for the manufacturing of PET PREFORM.

Took P.E.T. resin and mixed with 0.1 % Plasticiser put in the injection moulding machine, where heating is applie 145°C - 170°C. Flow of plastic resign is Controlled by flow proof gear mechanism with stepless speed adjustment. There is use of two stage pressure adjustment, by the pressure molten resin pass into the preform mould cavity and formed the structure of the body which is automatically eject out ofger formation.

High precision 4 cavity Pet Perform mould can produce 20000 preforms per day of 8 hours working.

PROCESS FLOW SHEET

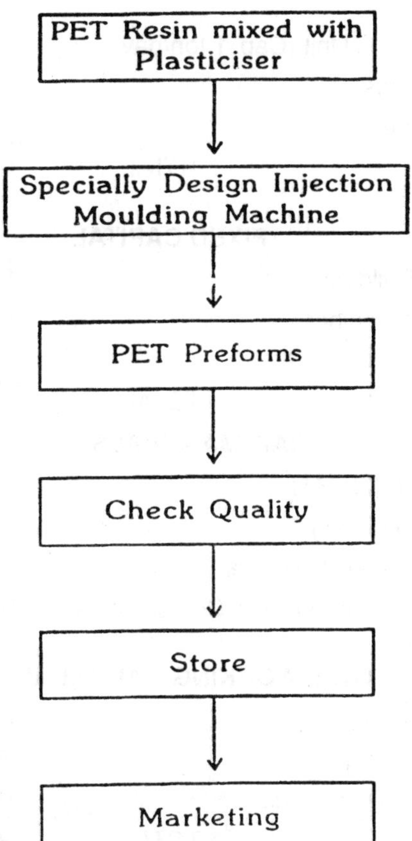

PLANT ECONOMICS

PLANT ECONOMICS OF PET PREFORMS

Rated Plant Capacity	=	20000.00 NOS./day Pet Preform
Size of PET Preform	=	500 ml.

Land & Building

(Land required 500 sqm.)	Rs.	11,50,000.00

PLANT & MACHINERY

1. Specially disign Injection Moulding Machine for manufacturing (sz-160/- 1000 SY) cap. 25000 preforms/day
2. Compressor
3. Refrigeration Unit (Cap. 1 ton/day)
4. Moulds/Dies
5. Miscellaneous

TOTAL	Rs.	46,55,000.00

FIXED CAPITAL

1.	Land & Building	Rs.	11,50,000.00
2.	Plant & Machinery	Rs.	46,55,000.00
3.	Other Fixed Assets	Rs.	8,20,000.00
	TOTAL	Rs.	66,25,000.00

RAW MATERIALS

1 PET resin (22 MT)

2. PP Resin (1 MT)

3. Adhesive and Plasticizer (1 MT)

4. Other raw materials viz. Colour, Stabilizer, Mould releasing agent etc.

TOTAL WORKING CAPITAL/MONTH

1.	Raw Material	Rs.	19,40,000.00
2.	Salary & Wages	Rs.	91,080.00
3.	Utilities & Overheads	Rs.	1,47,000.00
	TOTAL	Rs.	21,78,080.00

TOTAL CAPITAL INVESTMENT

Total Fixed Capital	Rs.	66,25,000.00
Total Working Capital for Months	Rs.	66,34,240.00
TOTAL	Rs.	1,31,59,240.00

TURN OVER/ANNUM

By Selling 60 Lakhs Preform PET		
TOTAL	Rs.	3,60,00,000.00

PROFIT SALES RATIO = PROFIT/SALES X 100 = 17.35%

RATE OF RETURN - OPERATING PROFIT/T.C.I X 100 = 47.46%

BREAK EVEN POINT = 43.25%

31

Project Profile for Pet Strech Blow Moulding Machine

(1 ltr PET Bottle)

	Rs.
Pet Stretch Blow Moulding Machine	250000
(Including One Preform Heating Oven)	
1 ltr Blow Mould (2 Cavities)	23000
Compresser (10 HP)	65000
Air Dryer	46000
Installation and Accessories	10000
Total Fixed Cost	**39400**
Working Capital Required	110000
Total Investment :	**5040000**

Statement of Profitability

	Per Hour	Per Day (22 hrs)	Per Month (25 Days)	Per Year
Standard Production (Pc)	500	11000	275000	3300000
Material Consumed in Kg. (28gm per pc)	14	308	7700	92400
Material Cost (Rs. 78/- per kg)	1092	24024	600600	7207200
Packing Cost (Rs. 0.03 per pc)	15	330	8250	99000
Labour & Other Overhead in Rs. (Rs. 0.07 per pc)	35	770	19250	231000
Total Cost in Rs.	1142	25124	628100	7537200
Total Sale Proceeds in Rs. (Rs. 2.75 per pc)	1375	30250	756250	9075000

<u>**GROSS PROFIT**</u>

Other Expenses :	**Rs.**	**Rs.**
Rent	6000	72000
Admn. & Mgt Exp.	8000	96000
Interest (16% p.a.)	6720	80640
Depriciation (20% p.a.)	6567	78800
Total	27287	327440
Net Profit	100863	1210360
NET PROFIT PER ANNUM		**1210360**

PET STRETCH BLOW MOULDING MACHINE

SPECIFICATIONS

Description	*PK - 101*	*PK - 102*	*PK - 103*
Production Capacity	500-600 Pcs. /Hr.	400-500 Pcs./Hr.	180-250 Pcs,/Hr.
No. of Mould Cavities	2	2	1
Working Air Pressure	12 kg/Cm2	12 Kg/Cm2	15 Kg/Cm2
Blowing Air Pressure	15 Kg/Cm2	18 Kg/Cm2	20 Kg/Cm2
Clamping Force	3 Tones	4 Tones	5 Tones
Air Consumption	30 CFM	40 CFM	50 CFM
Tie Bar Distance	260 mm	280 mm	400 mm
Max. Mould Opening	410 mm	425 mm	520 mm
Power Consumption	3 K W	4 K W	4 K W
Machine Dimensions (LxBxH)	1100 x 860 x 2000 mm	1140 x 890 x 2200 mm	1700 x1150 x 2140 mm
Dimensions - Preform Heater	640 x 570 x 800 mm	1030 x 690 x 800 mm	700 x 690 x 790 mm
No. of Perform Holder	33	33	16
Time for One Heating Cycle	5 Min.	5 Min.	5 Min.
Max. Product Volume	1.5 Ltrs.	1.5 Ltrs.	1.5 Ltrs.
Max. Neck Size of Product	60 mm	100 mm	120 mm
Max. Diameter of Product	120 mm	140 mm	230 mm
Max. Height of Product	350 mm	390 mm	450 mm

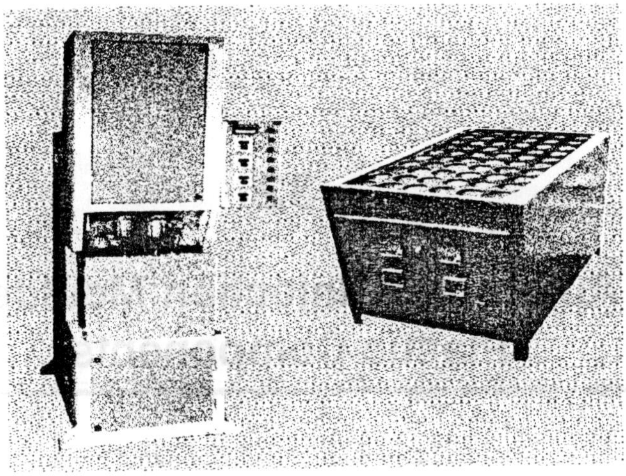

32

Automobile Injection Moulded Plastic Components

Electric lights are supplied with electricity from a storage battery. When the storage battery runs down, it can be recharged from an outside source, or from a dynamo, run from the engine. The old style 'carbon' filament in the electric globe consumed so much current that it was difficult to obtain a storage battery of a reasonable size and weight which would supply current from any length of time. The carbon filament lamp used a filament chemically treated and in a vacuum. The filament in the "Tungsten mazda" globe reduces the current consumption and is not liable to break with the unusual motor car vibration. There are three methods of furnishing electric current for car lighting.

1. By independent storage battery system.
2. By generator & battery system.
3. By an independent generator system.

Raw Materials

Propylene $(C_3H_3)_n$. A synthetic crystalline thermoplastic polymer, with molecular weight polymers are also known which are amorphous in structure, and used as gas line additives, detergent intermediates, greases, sealants, and lube oil additives; also available as a high-melting wax.

Derivation

Polymerization of propylene with a stereospecific catalyst (q.v.) much as aluminium alkyl.

Properties

Translucent white solid; specific gravity 0.90; m.p. 1680171°C ; tensile strength 500 psi; flexural strength 700 psi usable up to 250°F. Insoluble in cold organic solvents; softened by not solvents; Degraded by heat and light unless protected by antioxidants. Readily colored; good electrical resistance; low water absorption and moisture permeability; poor impact strength below 15°F; not attacked by fungi or bacteria; resists strong acids and alkalies up to 140°F; but its attacked by chlorine, fuming nitric acid, and other strong oxidizing agents. Combustible, but slow-burning . Nontoxic. Fair abrasion and good heat resistance if properly modified. Can be chrome-plated, injection and blow-molded, and blow-molded and extruded.

Film : Moulding powder; extruded sheet; cast film ; textile strength and continuous filament year; fibers with diameters from 0.05 to 1 micron and fiber webs down to 2 microns thick; low-density foam.

Uses: Packaging film; molded parts for automobiles, appliances, housewares, etc.; wire and cable coating; food container closures; coated and laminated products; bottles (with PVC); printing plates; carpets and upholstery; cordage and bristles; storage batteries; crates for soft-drink bottles; laboratory ware; toys; synthetic seaweed to encourage silt deposition; radiator grills; trays and containers for storing precision equipments; artificial grass and turfs; plastic pipe; wearing apparel (acid-dyed) fish nets.

Polystyrene : $(C_6H_5CHCH_2)n$. Polymerized styrene (q.v.), a thermoplastic synthetic resin of variable molecular weight depending on degree of polymerization.

Properties : Transparent, hard solid; high strength and impact resistances; excellent electrical and thermal insulator. Attacked by hydrocarbon solvents but resists organic acids, alkyls, and alcohols. Not recommended for outdoor use; un modified polymer yellows when exposed to light, but light-stable modified grades are available. Easily colored, molded and fabricated. Combustible and not self-extinguishing. Copolymerization with butadiene and acrylonitrile and lending with rubber or glass fiber increase impact strength and heat resistance.

Forms : Sheet, plates, rods, rigid foam, expandable beads or spheres.

Uses : Refrigerator doors; air conditioner cases;containers and molded household wares; machine housings; electrical equipment; toys; packaging; clock and radio cabinets. (As foam); thermal insulation; light construction, as in boats etc.; ice buckets, water coolers; fillers in shipping containers; furniture construction. (As spheres); Radiator leak stopper .

High Impact Polystyrene

For many applications, polystyrene may be considered to be too brittle.

This rubber modified polystyrene is an important commercial material and is commonly known as Impact Polystyrene.

High Impact Polystyrene is used in the manufacturing of advertisement displays, novelty articles, torch light cases, pens, lighting fixtures, lamp shades, false ceilings, housing for T.V., two-in-one, tooth brush, hair brush, utility brush, air conditioners front grills, etc.

Colouring

The mold is then opened to eject the molding and is closed again to receive the plasticized melt for the next cycle of operation.

Finishing

When moulding is done from the injection moulding machine. The unwanted plastic in the form of runner, fins and flash are to be removed. If the material is harder, all these products at a time depending on the capacity of tumbling barrel should be put and defining and deflashing is done. Now-a-days rotary vibratory debarring and finishing machine is available for a good finish we have to defin and deflash with rough ceramic and finish with round balls also of ceramic. For some type of product buffing is done to get a good surface finish. For buffing wax is used to polish the product.

PLANT ECONOMICS

Rated Plant capacity	=	1000.00 PCS/day
Land & Building	=	Rented

PLANT & MACHINERY

1. Horizontal Plastic injection moulding machine with shot weight,
2. Horizontal/plastic injection (semi automatic) moulding machine with shot weight, 150 gms with 7.5 HP
3. Working tools, testing equipments measuring instruments, fixtures etc.
4. Dies mould sets.
5. D.G. Set (33 KVA)
6. Air coolers

FIXED CAPITAL

1. Land & Building			Rented
2. Plant & Machinery		Rs.	8,80,000.00
3. Other Fixed Assets		Rs.	1,60,000.00
	TOTAL	Rs.	10,40,000.01

RAW MATERIALS

1. High impact polystyrene (HIP)/SAN/ acrylic polymer granules.
2. Colour master batches & other raw materials.
3. Packaging materials & misc.

TOTAL WORKING CAPITAL/MONTH

1. Raw Material		Rs.	4,00,000.00
2. Salary & Wages		Rs.	48,000.00
3. Utilities & Overheads		Rs.	54,100.00
	TOTAL	Rs.	5,02,100.00

TOTAL CAPITAL INVESTMENT

Total Fixed Capital		Rs.	10,40,000.01
Total Working Capital for 3 Months		Rs.	15,06,300.00
	TOTAL	Rs.	25,46,300.01

TURN OVER/ANNUM

1. Side indicator lamp assembly	1,00,000 pcs	
2. Parking light assembly	1,00,000 pcs	
3. Misc. plastic parts for automobile	1,00,000 pcs	
		Rs. 77,00,000.00

PROFIT SALES RATIO = 14.80 %

RATE OF RETURN = 44.74 %

BREAK EVEN POINT (B.E.P)= 47.38 %

33

Colour Master Batch for Various Plastics

These pigment concentrates or master batches are rather expensive comparitively, but the advantages usually offset the cost advantage.

The use of concentrates ensures uniform and fine dispersions of the pigment particles in the final plastic product, which result in better technical properties of the product eg. uniform electrical insulation (in cables) uniform tensile strength (in fibres) freedom from pinholes and rough surface (in thin films and thick sections), and clogging of extruder screens.

The products obtained are brighter consistant and free from specks.

The use of concentrates cuts down one heat cycle saving the polymer from thermal degradation this ensures better mechanical strength, electrical properties heatsealstrength and resistance to moisture permeation and slip or blocking.

The use of master batches ensures good flexibility of colour changes

FORMULATION

1 Formulation Black Masterbatch LDPE	**%**
- Carbon Black	25-50
- LDPE	50-25
- Ethylene - Vinyl acctate copolymer	18
- Plasticizer	5
(Di methyl phthalate or Di butyl phthalate or Di octyl phthalate)	
- Antioxidant	2

Di lauryl this di-propionate or Lecithin or Butylated Hydrodyanisole. or 2:5 di terteary butyl Hydroquinone or 2:2 melhylene bis (4 methy 6 tertiary - butyl phenol) or Do decyl gallate

Total	100 %
2. Standard packing :	25 kg in woven

3. Recommended Addition Level the percentage of Black master batch to be used depends on the grade of masterbatch selected (25-50% carbon loading) and the carbon black percentage required in the ultimate product.

Note

(i) According to indian standard specification NI 12701: 1989 the carbon black content of the compounded polythene shall be 2.5% ± 0.5%. It is required that the carbon black should be thoroughly dispersed so as to give a smooth surface to the finished moulding which must be free from any hard particles, pimples, process structure and any other imperfection.

(ii) Carbon Black at 2.5% addition level renders the polymer impermeable to sun rays

Coloured Masterbatch for LDPE

1. Formulation	%
- Pigment or Dye (as selected from list shown elsewhere in this report)	25-50
- LDPE	50-25
- Ethylene vinyl accdate	18
- Plasticizer	5

Di methyl phthalate or Di butyl phthalate or Di Octyl phthalate

- Antioxidant	2

Di lauryl this di propionate or Lecthin or Butaglated Hydroxyanisole or 2:5 Di tert butyl hydroquinone or 2,2' Methylene leis (4 methyl 6-tertiary -butyl phenol)

Total	100 %

2. Standard packing: 25 Kgs in woven bags

3. Recommended Addition Level : Polyethelene masterbatches are

recommanded to be added in ratio 2%-4% (depending on application) in the compounded coloured product.

PROCESS OF MANUFACTURE

The process of manufacture for making master batch is known as the melt compounding method. The following operations are in

(a) Pre mixing steps

(b) Extruding & granulation Pre-mixing steps

- Add resin in the blenders
- Stir the resin with the carrier resin
- Add the plasticizer
- Add the pigments or dyes
- Add the antioxidants
- Stir the mixture for 20-30 minutes till it is roughly homogenous
- Discharge the natural in trays & let it cool in air Extruding & Granulation
- Pre heat the extruder keeping 30°C above the melting point
- Slowly feed the premix to the hopper above the extruder
- Start up the extrudes & run it slowely till material comes out of the die
- Take the strands (string) coming out from the extruder die to the cutter passing through the water tank.
- Cut the stands into pellets or granules & collect these, which are ready for packing & despatch.

PLANT ECONOMICS

Rated Plant Capacity	=	1000.00 Kgs./Day
Land & Building (500 Sq. mts.)	=	Rs. 8,00,000.00

PLANT & MACHINERY

1. High speed mixer of batch size, made of stainless steel lining, air tight opening and closing system.
2. Extruder made of stainless steel, non stop magnetic chain drive system with motor

3. Pelletizer with motor special cutting blades.
4. Scrap grinder with motor cap.
5. Bag stitching machine
6. Storage bins
7. Weighing Filling machine
8. Weighing Machine Platform type
9. Laboratory testing equipment
10. Miscellaneous equipment

FIXED CAPITAL

1. Land & Building	Rs.	8,00,000.00
2. Plant & Machinery	Rs.	14,63,000.00
3. Other Fixed Assets	Rs.	4,90,000.00
TOTAL	Rs.	27,53,000.00

RAW MATERIALS

1. **For Black Master Batch**
   Carbon Black
2. LDPE
3. Plasticizer
4. Antioxidant
5. Carrier Resin Ethylene Vinyl Acetate Copolymer
6. **For Colour Master Batch**
   Colour Pigment
7. LDPE
8. Carriers Resin Ethylene/Vinyl Acetate
9. Plasticizer
10. Antioxidant
11. Packing HDPE Bags

TOTAL WORKING CAPITAL/MONTH

1. Raw Material		Rs.	12,63,260.00
2. Salary & Wages		Rs.	70,500.00
3. Utilities & Overheads		Rs.	1,20,000.00
	TOTAL	Rs.	14,53,760.00

TOTAL CAPITAL INVESTMENT

Total Fixed Capital		Rs.	27,53,000.00
Total Working Capital for 3 Months		Rs.	43,61,280.00
	TOTAL	Rs.	71,14,280.00

TURN OVER/ANNUM

1. Black Masterbatch 150000 kgs			
2. Colour Masterbatch 150000 kgs			
	TOTAL	Rs.	2,55,00,000.00

PROFIT SALES RATIO = 24.87 %

RATE OF RETURN = 89.16 %

BREAK EVEN POINT (B.E.P) = 29.28 %

34

Compact Disk

Audio signals stored on a compact disc are in high density digital format, which means that the signals recorded are an extremely accurate representation of the original audio signal. On replay, the digital information is ready by a laser beam and converted into analogue form. Since the disc is scanned by a laser beam, there is no physical contact with the disc surface, eliminating the wear found in LPs and audio tapes. The 1000th play of a compact disc will sound every bit as good as the first, a feature which LPs and tapes cannot claim.

Manufacturing Process

The process flow chart is given initially, the Master (or Blank) is made from a glass disk which is ground and polished till optical flatness is obtained. This disk is coated with a layer of photoresist whose thickness is controlled very accurately. The coating is then oven-cured, after which the disk is cut.

FLOW CHART

PREPARE BLANK

V

GRIND

V

POLISH

V

APPLY PHOTORESIST

V

CURE

V

CUT

V

ETCH

V

SILVER

V

PREPARE FATHER

V

PREPARE MOTHER

V

PREPARE SONS

V

STAMP DISCS

V

ALUMINUM COAT

V

SEAL

V

TEST

Cutting is done by a continuously operating helium-heon laser whose intensity is modulated as per the music. The laser travels from the centre of the disk to the outer edge as the master disk revolves. The exposed photoresist is developed and the areas unexposed to laser hardened. The exposed area is etched with acid. This step creates pits in the surface of the resist. These pits represent the digitised information of the audio input.

At this stage, the disk is given a thin coating of silver to make it electrically conductive. Then a few (negative) copies called "Father" are made in nickel by electroplating. From these, a number of (positive) intermediate copies called "Mother" are made. These, in turn, are used to produce a number of "Sons". Sons are used as dies to mould compact discs.

The compact disc is moulded from sheets of 1.2 mm thick from clear polycarbonate. The surface containing audio information is given a thin coating of aluminium (thickness of 10 micro metres) by metalization. This is followed by a protective coating of lacquer (thickness of 5-10 micro metres), which is sprayed on and hardened with mild heating under an infrared heater.

The side of the disc on which the identifying lable is printed, is called the label side. Information from the disc is ready by a laser at the underside, i.e., through the cover and the perspex.

The disk is sealed in a square transparent plastic sheath. This sheath acts as a protection for the disk making it less susceptible and impervious to damage during handling, from spillage, dust etc. The quality of sound remains high even after many playings unlike for records and tapes for which the quality deteriorates directly with numbers of times they are played, especially for high frequency notes.

A CD passes through 17 different positions before it reaches the optical scanner located at the end of the line. It is tested for the optical and structural properties. The quality control checks for moulding, fingerprints, reflectance levels, material deformities and other defects are carried out by one camera whereas a second camera scans the CD for refractions errors. Both cameras operate in a continuous cycle using a high pixel resolution. Scanning results are logged and printed on screen. Yield percentage and the reasons for rejected discs are updated on screen after each CD is tested.

After quality control acceptance CDs are packed for despatch.

LIST OF SUPPLIERS OF PLANT AND MACHINERY

Imported

1. DDM Netherland
2. Nimbus Records Ltd., U.K.
3. Disctronics, USA
4. OD & ME, Netherland
5. Philips Dupont Optical, Netherland

Indigenous

1. Frick India, Faridabad
2. Kirloskar Electrical, India
3. Billy Engineering, Chennai (T.N.)

PLANT ECONOMICS

Rated Plant capacity	=	16500.00 Nos./Day
Land & Building (Land 12,000 sq.mts)	Rs.	1,60,00,000.00

PLANT & MACHINERY

1. Injection Moulding Machine with all the accessories
2. C. D. Moulds
3. Metalising Machine
4. Lacquer processing machine
5. Printing Machine
6. Moving & Handling equipments
7. Stacker, Buffer, Walking Beams, Conveyers & quality control equipments
8. Temperature controllers for moulds
9. Drying and Conveying equipments
10. Compact Disc tools
11. Process Controllers
12. Air conditioning Plant
13. D. G. Set.

FIXED CAPITAL

1. Land & Building	Rs.	1,60,00,000.00
2. Plant & Machinery	Rs.	6,50,00,000.00
3. Other Fixed Assets	Rs.	2,75,00,000.00
TOTAL	Rs.	10,85,00,000.00

RAW MATERIALS

1. Polycarbonate
2. Aluminium Powder (99.99% pure EC - grade)
3. Glass Masters, Stampers, Musical Royalty etc.
4. UV Lacquer,Inks & other Consumables

TOTAL WORKING CAPITAL/MONTH

1. Raw Material	Rs.	2,26,35,000.00
2. Salary & Wages	Rs.	3,50,000.00
3. Utilities & Overheads	Rs.	7,95,000.00
TOTAL	Rs.	2,37,80,000.00

TOTAL CAPITAL INVESTMENT

Total Fixed Capital	Rs.	10,85,00,000.10
Total Working Capital for 2 Months	Rs.	4,75,60,000.00
TOTAL	Rs.	15,60,60,000.10

TURN OVER/ANNUM

By Sales of 49,50,000 Nos. Compact Discs	Rs.	44,55,00,000.00

PROFIT SALES RATIO = PROFIT / SALES X 100 = 25.73 %

RATE OF RETURN = OPERATING PROFIT / T.C.I X 100 = 73.46 %

BREAK EVEN POINT (B.E.P) = 30.79 %

35

Co-Extruded Multilayer Film and Laminated Multilayer Film

The Co-extruded multilayer (3-layers type) need to evolve a manufacturing technique whereby such systems could be produced in one single operation from Compatible-as well as incompatible materials and materials which can not be extruded led to the development of Co-extrusion.

Co-extrusion can be carried out by the blown film process or through a flat die. By these processes, it is possible to reduce the thickness of the more expensive plastic materials and the properties of two or more similar or dissimilar plastic materials can be obtained to achieve optimal product properties at lower cost. The processing of tubular composite film which can easily be made into bags for packaging, calls for a lower capital investment and hence is preferred. The flat die technique is used for the production of relatively thicker composites which are subsequently thermoformed or for extrusion coating on to various substrates. There are various materials packed in multilayer films viz; Milk, Oils, Spices, Ghee, Detergents and various other products. The industry in its search for a more effective and economic packaging system will no doubt find multilayer composites as promising substitutes.

USES & APPLICATION

1. The 3-layer Co-extruded film is used for milk packaging.
2. It is used for vegetable oil, vegetable & ghee packaging.
3. It is used for shampoo packaging .
4. It is used for packaging of Ready to eat snacks.
5. It is used in the packaging of biscuits,sweets.

6. It is used for packaging of various Lube oil.
7. It is used in Packaging of food stuffs (meat, sausage, fish, dairy products etc.
8. It is used in manufacturing of Heavy duty bags.
9. It is used as Gift wrapping material.
10. It is used in the packaging of different breweries, cold drinks, squashes, Jams etc.
11. It is used in the packing of flowers for export purposes.

Techniques of Co-Extrusion

There are primarily two routes to obtain a co-extruded laminate, that is blown film process and flat die technique.

Commercial tubular film plants consist of either two or three extruders feeding the melt to a common die. With two extruders it is possible to have upto three layer film, two layers being of the same material. The three extruders system can produce a laminate consisting of maximum five layers where two layers each are of the same material and the fifth layer is of a different one. The melts enter through different channels in the die and combine together near the exit to form a composite film. The ratio of layer thickness is adjusted by the pumping rate of individual extruders or but throttle systems incorporated in the die. Uniformity of layer thicknesses can be examined by optical microscopy or infra-red analysis. When two or more incompatible materials are required to be co-extruded to obtain a composite film, adhesion promoters or coupling agents are used in thin gauges between the incompatible material layers. Ionomers and EVA copolymers are some of the widely used adhesion promoters. More recently copolymers of ethylene and acrylic esters are also used for this purpose.

A unique blown film die has been lately developed which can generate a large number of layers of two or more polymers. This tubular die can extrude multilayer blown films having several layers with individual layer thickness less than 1000 A^0 .

There are a wide variety of plants available. The extruders are either mounted on ground or on a elevated platform horizontally or vertically. In most of the plants the extruders are mounted on an oscillating/rotating platform. The oscillation/rotation is an very slow to ensure that any possible non-uniformity of thickness in the extruded film is evenly distributed all along the width of the web. There are some plants available where the winding stations rotate and the extruders are kept stationary. Some plants provide rotating die instead of oscillating/rotating extruders to obtain similar end results. Alternatively, rotating haul-off systems are provided to obtain good quality film rolls. Most of these extrusion plants are provided with continuous automatic Screen changes for long uninterrupted production runs.

The extruders are either of conventional design or operate on autogenic (adiabatic) principle. The autogenic extruders have a short length to diameter ratio of about 12:1 and the screw has a shallow flight depth at the metering zone to facilitate the rotation at high speeds of about 650rpm to 800 rpm. These are compact, require lesser space and consume much less energy for operation. Because of the high working speeds, these extruders are likely to have high rate of wear and tear and the suitability of such plants under Indian conditions for long continuous runs is yet to be established.

Raw Materials

The raw materials required for the manufacture of multilayer film (3-layer) are LDPE, HDPE, PP, LLDPE, HM-HDPE, etc. All Plastic raw materials are available indigenously.

Manufacturing Process

The process to manufacture co-extruded multilayer film (3-layer) is very complicated and require extra precaution to be observed. For production of Co-extruded (3-layer) film complete plant consists of three extruders.

The different plastic materials are fed into all the extruders and get heated in the cylinder. The plastic granules melt due to thermal application of heat as well as shearing action in the cylinder of extruder. The melt from different extruders is conveyed forward by screw rotation. The screw subjects the material to intensive mixing inside the barrel and conveys the melt to the die in a well homogenous plasticized mass . Depending upon the speed maintained, it also meters the out put at constant rate. The molten material enters the die from different extruders forming different layers of co-extruded multilayer film. Different layers sticks each other as they emerge from the die. The film comes out of the die in usual bubble form (by passing compressed air through the centre of the die). The bubble is cooled by cooling ring and is flattened by the vertical take off unit , passes through the nip rollers which pulls the film at a certain speed. Finally, the film is wound on the winder.

PLANT ECONOMICS

Rated Plant Capacity	=		1.00 MT/day
Land & Building (Land 1500 sq. mts.)	=	Rs.	20,75,000.00

PLANT & MACHINERY

1. For C0-Extruded 3-Layer Film : 65mm
   Co-extruded 3-layer film plant with 3-screw extruders
2. Automatic cutting machine
3. Scrap grinder
4. Film winding machine
5. 4 colour flexographic printing - machine.
6. Corona treatment unit
7. For Laminating Film (Multi Layer) blown film plant with two station winder complete
8. Corona treatment unit
9. Coating lamination machine (30" - size) with accessories.
10. Single colour Rotogravure printing machine (30" size) with accessories
11. Slitting machine (30" size)
12. Compressor
13. M.S. water tank
14. Laboratory equipments
15. Genset (Diesel)

FIXED CAPITAL

1. Land & Building		Rs.	20,75,000.00
2. Plant & Machinery		Rs.	79,58,700.00
3. Other Fixed Assets		Rs.	12,50,000.00
	TOTAL	Rs.	1,12,83,700.00

RAW MATERIALS

1. For 3-Layer Co-Extruded Film : LDPE granules
2. HDPE Granules
3. Hon - HDPE granules
4. For Laminating Film : LDPE film
5. Propylene granules
6. Metallized polyester film
7. Acrylic adhesive
8. Printing ink

TOTAL WORKING CAPITAL/MONTH

1. Raw Material	Rs.	21,14,000.00
2. Salary & Wages	Rs.	1,28,125.00
3. Utilities & Overheads	Rs.	2,41,500.00
TOTAL	Rs.	24,83,625.00

TOTAL CAPITAL INVESTMENT

Total Fixed Capital	Rs.	1,12,83,700.00
Total Working Capital for 3 Months	Rs.	74,50,875.00
TOTAL	Rs.	1,87,34,575.00

TURN OVER/ANNUM

1. By sale of two-colour 3-layer Co-extruded film 210 MT.
2. By sale laminated metallized film 90 MT.
3. By sale of scraps 27.6 MT.

Rs. 4,20,90,000.00

PROFIT SALES RATIO = 18.65 %

RATE OF RETURN = 41.91 %

BREAK EVEN POINT (B.E.P) = 44.16 %

36

Egg Trays From Plastics

Packaging of various products have become a great problem in the industrial world. Almost all the products are packed in suitable container and marketed. This packing serves two purposes first is that it saves the product from destruction and on the other hand it makes these two basic facts packing techniques are developing day by day.

Among all the food products egg is a very common and important item which used in breakfast, lunch,dinner and in every refreshment. It is neither considered fully vegetarian, nonvegitarian, and hence both the classes of the people consumers use it largely.

The consumption and demand of eggs is increasing day by and the exact data of consumption can not calculated. But it can be said by studying the present market trend that the supply of eggs is less than the demand and there is wide gap in between the two which is not possible to fill in near future.

The scope of the egg is ellipsoidal and can out remain straight when kept in a plain tray or box and there are chances of cracking or breaking which spoils the egg. For this special type of trays are developed named egg trays which are used in racking the eggs in lesser space. These trays are generally made of paper pulp plasters and contains conical cavities according to the size of the egg to be racked. These trays also protects the eggs from damage by trays also protects the eggs from damage by shocking.

Raw Materials & Their Availability

The basic raw for the manufacture of plastic egg trays is PVC of good grade (K value - 57). To make the product cheaper waste plastics (thermo-plastics) are also used together with original PVC granules.

PVC resins constitute the principal input in the preparation of PVC compounds. Availability of PVC resins therefore will be the deciding factor in the performance of the industry.

Process of Manufacture

Plastic egg trays are manufactured by injection moulding process. Injection moulding is a multistep process carried out usually in a single machine in which PVC granules (usually blend of original and reprocessed granules) are melted or plasticized and injected into a mould forming a cavity of the shape and size of the desired egg trays. The mould is kept at a temperature below the solidifying point of the PVC granules, causing the injected plasticized mass to take the form of the mould cavity, and after a sufficiently long cooling time the mould is opened and the egg-trays ejected. The injection moulding process comprises four stages, each of which must be closely controlled and regulated to obtain good quality mouldings. These stages are (1) plasticizing (2) injection (3) after filling and (4) cooling mould release.

PLANT ECONOMICS

Rated Plant Capacity	=	900,000 No./Annum
Land & Building (Land 500 sq. mts.)	=	Rs. 10,52,500.00

PLANT & MACHINERY

1. Saw type injection moulding machine
2. Circulating pump pipe fittings and other accessories
3. Scrap grinder
4. High speed mixer
5. Misc. moulds for egg trays & other accessories

FIXED CAPITAL

1. Land & Building	Rs.	10,52,500.00
2. Plant & Machinery	Rs.	18,35,000.00
3. Other Fixed Assets	Rs.	3,10,000.00
TOTAL	Rs.	31,97,500.00

RAW MATERIALS

1. PVC resin
2. Dioctyl phthalate
3. Lead stabilizers
4. Lubricants
5. Colours, dyes & pigments
6. Fillers (Calcium carbonate)
7. Misc., Packaging materials etc.

TOTAL WORKING CAPITAL/MONTH

1. Raw Material	Rs.	6,30,000.00
2. Salary & Wages	Rs.	90,125.00
3. Utilities & Overheads	Rs.	73,700.00
TOTAL	Rs.	7,93,825.00

TOTAL CAPITAL INVESTMENT

Total Fixed Capital	Rs.	31,97,500.00
Total Working Capital for 3 Months	Rs.	23,81,475.00
TOTAL	Rs.	55,78,975.00

TURN OVER/ANNUM

1. By sale 6,00,000 plastic egg trays (Capacity 30 eggs.)
2. By sale of 300000 plastic egg trays (Capacity 12 eggs.)

TOTAL Rs. 1,32,00,000.00

PROFIT SALES RATIO = 18.62 %

RATE OF RETURN= 44.05 %

BREAK EVEN POINT (B.E.P) = 44.90 %

37

Ethylene Vinyl Acetate Sheet and Sole

Making of EVA (Ethylene Vinyl Acetate) sheet and sole is a new development in rubber formulations. For the compounding purposes, for EVA, rubber products, among the other ingredients, Pilene EVA 1802 constitutes a conspicuous are along with other rubber ingredients viz. SBR 1958 and natural rubber.

Polyolefins Industries Ltd. now manufactures ethylene vinyl acetate copolymer (EVA) in India and is also available for the rubber footwear manufacturing industry as PILENE EVA. Pilene EVA can be used for footwear, capable, hot melt adhesives, wax modifiers, blends with bitumen, noise absorber, injection moulding, films, masterbatches, additives as weather resistant ingredient, etc.

Rubber, either natural or synthetic, has been successfully used in the engineering fields for over a hundred years. The rubbers are very versatile and adaptable materials.

Rubber is plastic, air tight, water resistant, shock-absorbing and long wearing. These characteristics make it almost indispensable for many applications.

These outstanding physical property of rubber for the best advantage is its plasticity due to which the rubber is employed in various applications. Its weather resistivity, and carrying and cushioning features as general properties have an importance and the significance everywhere.

EVA rubber sheets are prepared by simple process known as calendering-after mixing the ingredients. The calendering machines are similar in sizes but have three, four and five rolls (bowl rolls). Other features or the machine are almost similar to that of mixing mill. The extra frictional roll (rolls) coupled in the mixing mill can be named as calender machine. In some cases, the calenders are also used as mixing mill to prepare rubber compounds.

Raw Materials

Natural Rubber :

Natural rubber is obtained from certain types of plants which yield a milky white substance when the surface is either cut or purified. The natural rubber has excellent building tack and is largely used in the compounding of sheets and belts.

S.B.R.Polymer :

Styrene butadiene rubbers are the most commonly used the general purpose synthetic rubber of today-they are produced by the co-polymerization of butadiene and styrene. Originally it has a poor tensile strength but with the addition of carbon black or other reinforcing pigments, tensile strength can be substantially improved.

Compounding Formulations for EVA (Ethylene Vinyl Acetate)

Formulation I (for EVA Sheet)

	Parts/wt. %	%
Pilene EVA 1802	70.00	31.22
SBR 1958	10.00	4.47
Natural Rubber	20.00	8.95
Zinc oxide	5.00	2.24
Stearic acid	1.00	0.45
PPt Calcium Carbonate	75.00	33.50
EVA Crumb	30.00	13.42
Dicup 40-c	3.00	1.34
ADC Blowing agent	3.50	1.56
Titanium dioxide	5.00	2.24
Colour	1.00	0.45
Total	223.50	100.00 %

Dicup 40-c = Trade mark for a series of vulcanizing and polymerizing agents containing dicumy peroxide.

MANUFACTURING PROCESS

Polymerizing agents containing as per the compounding formulation, No.1 for EVA sheet.

First of all pilene EVA, SBR 1958, natural rubber, and EVA crumb are introduced into the mastication unit, and after these ingredients are well masticated, they are introduced into the mixing mill, where other ingredients viz stearic acid, ppted calcium carbonate ADC blowing agent, titanium dioxide, & colour are added and all ingredients are well mixed in the mixing operation.

In the mixing process all the ingredients required to be mixed, are weighted out, and then mixed together either in a roller mill or in a banbury mixer.

The primary objectives of the mixing operation are.

(a) Attainment of a uniform blend of all the constituents.

(b) To get a through dispersion of the pigment, and

(c) To produce consecutive batches which are uniform in degree of dispersion and plasticity.

Mixing Mill

The standard features of this machine are that it has two rolls or either chilled iron or MS or cast iron according to the size determined by the manufacturer 10" X 24", 12" X 30", 14" X 36" and 16" X 42". It is mounted on lubricated steel bed plates, coupled with safety devices. It is driven by electrical motor.

Calendering

Compounding in the form of sheeting from the mixing rolls is fed to the calender.

In calendering, the material is formed into a thin sheet or is coated on a fabric. The calender consists of three parallel rolls arranged on above the other. The openings between the rolls are adjusted. These rolls are hollow and may be heated or cooled and driven at varying speeds. The material is fed between the top two layers. two plies, are ply from the other calender are squeezed together on the bottom roll.

After the calendering operation, talc spraying is done, followed by vulcanizing.

In the vulcanization process, dicup-40 c (vulcanizing agent) are zinc oxide are added.

This is produced by cooling, and packing of the EVA sheet.

(B) ***Manufacture of EVA Soles :***

For the manufacture of sole, as per the formulation No.2 for EVA sole (as discussed earlier in the case of EVA sheet), pilene EVA, SBR 1958, Natural rubber and EVA crumb are all introduced into the mastication unit followed by mixing operation, where other ingredients viz. stearic acid, ppt calcium carbonate, ADC blowing agent, titanium dioxide & colour are added and are well mixed. In the mixer the rubber ingredients are crushed and heated simultaneously. The temperature of the mixture is kept much below its blowing point. This is because at the boiling point oxidation will occur and destroy the rubber properties.

The rubber compound so obtained from the mixer is then melted and is left for about 15 to 30 minutes.

In compounding, the purpose is to make stocks that reach their optimum cure in a certain time at a certain temperature. This may vary from 10 minutes at 280°F to 90 minutes at 280°F, and depends on the type of finished article, which of course, influences the type of mould equipment.

Mixing operation is followed by calendering the molten rubber compound is then passed through the sheet making machine which is continuous. From one side rubber compounds enter and from the other side rubber sheet comes out. For the purpose of ultimately making EVA sole thickness of the sole being between 0.5" to 0.75" and in some cases to about 1"

After calendering vulcanization is carried out.

Vulcanization is a process where vulcanizing agent viz Dicup 40 c is added to the rubber to accomplish a high resistant, durable and high tensile strength rubber.

Vulcanization changes compounded rubber from sticky to plastic mass that melts and freezes easily to a dry elastic material with a rather wide tolerance for temperature changes. The tensile strength is increased tremendously. Solubility in solvents is decreased and the resistance to oxidation is increased.

15 to 30 minutes of vulcanization is a sufficient time. To reduce vulcanization time, zinc oxide is added.

After vulcanization, it is subjected to cooling and thus the final EVA rubber sheet is taken to the sole making unit, where soles of desired size and dimensions are made. They are packed and sent for marketing.

PLANT ECONOMICS

Rated Plant Capacity	=	5.00 MT/Day
Land & Building		**Rent**

PLANT & MACHINERY

1. **FOR EVA SHEET**
   Rubber mixing mill
2. Z-blade type mixer
3. Masticating equipments.
4. Spreading machine roller
5. Cylindrical vulcanization chambers
6. Calendering machine.
7. Boiler
8. Weighing scale.
9. Water storage tank with punch.
10. Pot mill
11. Paddle mixer
12. Dipping vats
13. Coagulating tanks.
14. Hot air oven
15. Formers and moulds.
16. Testing lab equipments, weighing balance, micrometer, hardness tester.
17. Miscellaneous tools & equipments.
18. **FOR EVA SOLES**
    Hydraulic press
19. Power operated press
20. Moulds for making soles
21. D.G.set

FIXED CAPITAL

1. Land & Building			Rented
2. Plant & Machinery		Rs.	22,85,000.01
3. Other Fixed Assets		Rs.	3,70,000.00
	TOTAL	Rs.	26,55,000.01

RAW MATERIALS

1. **FOR EVA RUBBER SHEET**
   Pilene EVA
2. SBR
3. Natural rubber
4. Zinc oxide
5. Stearic acid
6. PPt calcium carbonate
7. EVA Crumb
8. Dicup 40-c
9. ADC Blowing agent
10. Titanium dioxide
11. Colour
12. Packaging material.
13. **FOR EVA SOLES**
    Pilene EVA 1802
14. Natural rubber
15. SBR-1958
16. Zinc Oxide
17. Stearic acid
18. PPt silicon
19. PPT calcium carbonate
20. Dicup-40 C
21. ADC blowing agent
22. Packing material.

TOTAL WORKING CAPITAL/MONTH

1. Raw Materials		Rs.	54,89,455.00
2. Salary & Wages		Rs.	1,32,480.00
3. Utilities & Overheads		Rs.	1,51,200.00
	TOTAL	Rs.	57,73,135.00

TOTAL CAPITAL INVESTMENT

Total Fixed Capital		Rs.	26,55,000.01
Total Working Capital for 1 Months		Rs.	57,73,135.00
	TOTAL	Rs.	84,28,135.01

TURN OVER/ANNUM

1. EVA rubber sheet, 900 MT
2. EVA rubber soles 600 MT

TOTAL Rs. 8,46,00,000.00

PROFIT SALES RATIO = PROFIT / SALES X 100 = 16.23 %

RATE OF RETURN = OPERATING PROFIT / T.C.I X 100 = 162.96 %

BREAK EVEN POINT (B.E.P) = 17.68 %

38

Polypropylene Multifilament Spinning Yarn

Polypropylene multifilament yarns obtained as a result of spinning comprise a great number of parallel filaments which are in no way tied together. Codeusing of filament yarns into a compact form is achieved by twisting. However, yarn twisting involve a considerable labor consumption and additional industrial areas for the installation of twister.

Endeavours have been made to replace the time consuming twisting operation by treatment of filament yarns with adhesive or sizing agent. When multifilament yarns are treated with a sizing composition, thin films are formed on their surfaces which protect the yarn from separating into single filament. These film impart cohession to multifilament yarn and, provided it has sufficient elasticity, increase its breaking strength, sizing protects the yarn fluffiness during winding.

Of the classical polymers, polyester, polyamide and polyacrylnilril, polypropylene has, with the exception of certain areas, played a somewhat subordinate role in the fibre field in the past. However, in the meantime, there has been a development in respect of polypropylene which led to new views on textile products of polypropylene throughout the world. This include recognition of specific properties of polypropylene goods making it superior to other polymers.

Even in the early seventies Lurgi recognized the increasing importance of polyproplylene for textile application and developed appropriate economic processes for the various fibre products.

Uses and Application

Polypropylene filament yarns are widely used in various fields, some of uses are given below :

1. It is used for making various sizes of rope which have more strength and abrasion, resistant for general use.
2. Low denser polypropylene filaments are used in making mosquito met clothings
3. Due to resistance of water absorbity, soft in touch and durability, textured polypropylene filament yarns are used in making fabrics.
4. For marine purpose, polypropylene filament yarns are used in making line or anchor rope.
5. It is used in making filter cloth for industrial application.

Process of Manufacture

These are two ways of making partially oriented yarn (POY). In case of Melt-Spinning process for the production of POY, it is run at much higher speed and produces yarn which require little drawing. This yarn is called partially oriented yarn it is possible to use these yarns directly texturing machinewithout subjecting them to the intermediate process of draw twisting. This economizes on the production cost of PPPY the present day trend highlights the demand for texturised synthetic filament yarn for apparel use. This process imparts to the fabric such qualities as higher absorbening better cover, softer feel and greater comfort-giving properties.

In case of Melt-Spinning process for production of fully drawn yarn (FDY), it is possible to use draw equipment in melt spinning to produce a yarn which has desired level of crystallinely and orientation so that the same could be used directly for textile end uses. Such yarn is suitable for certain home textile as well as industrial end uses.

The chief raw material used in this yarn production is the polypropylene chips which is manufactured in India by the Indian Petrochemicals Limited, Baroda, in various grades the chips are stored in silos and conveyed by air and rotating drums to adjust the moisture entente is the chips to desired level.

The dried chips are then fed to a feeding silo, which under nitrogenous atmosphere feed these chips to the extruder. The chips are melted homogenised and melesed by extruder. The melted chips are passed through polymer filter and then fed to the spinning positions through melt distribution manifolds. The static mixers positioned within spinning block. The melted mass, with the help of metering pump passed through spin pack assembles consisting of sand are metallic filters and then conveyed to spinnerels to produces filaments.

The melt flow is passed through blow boxes and the yarn solidifies due to quenching action of controlled air flow, these filaments flow downwards towards winding heads. During the passage through quenching chamber, the yarn is applied with spin finish. the proposed plant will have a winding head consisting of an arrangement for testing the continually of filament arrangement and reaction of filament in case of break, an arrangement to draw the yarn with the help of godets and an arrangement to wind the yarn on packages suitable for further processing.

On account of the arrangement of godets provided on this machine, it is possible to produce fully-oriented yarn, which could be directly sold in the market for immediate use on fabric making machines such as weaving looms, warp kinitting or wett kinitting machines. Alternatively it is also possible to produce partially-oriented yarn which needs further processing. Such yarn has been found to be suitable as fed materials for present day high-speed friction draw textured machine which would incorporate into the yarn qualities desirable for production of certain types of fabrics.

PLANT ECONOMICS

Rated Plant Capacity	= 1000 Mt./Year
Land & Building (Land 10,000 sq. mts.)	= Rs. 97,00,000.00

PLANT & MACHINERY

1. Silos
2. Conveyor and Rotaling drum, Burden
3. Feeding silos
4. Nitrogen gas storage tank
5. Screw Drive Extruder with melting and arrangement
6. Distribution pipe,
7. Spinning box
8. Spinnerates
9. Blow duct
10. Jet tube
11. Take up units
12. Entagling device (goedets)
13. High-Speed friction drawing texturing machine
14. Gen. Set
15. Miscellaneous like, pipe, fittings auxiliary equipments, Tools & jigs etc.

FIXED CAPITAL

1. Land & Building	Rs.	97,00,000.00
2. Plant & Machinery	Rs.	3,42,00,000.00
3. Other Fixed Assets	Rs.	30,00,000.00
TOTAL	Rs.	4,69,00,000.00

RAW MATERIALS

1. Polypropylene chips
2. Nitrogen gas
3. Lubricants and Miscellaneous chemicals

TOTAL WORKING CAPITAL/MONTH

1. Raw Material	Rs.	50,55,000.00
2. Salary & Wages	Rs.	1,49,750.00
3. Utilities & Overheads	Rs.	1,44,000.00
TOTAL	Rs.	53,48,750.00

TOTAL CAPITAL INVESTMENT

Total Fixed Capital	Rs.	4,69,00,000.00
Total Working Capital for 3 Months	Rs.	1,60,46,250.00
TOTAL	Rs.	6,29,46,250.00

TURN OVER/ANNUM

By sale of 1000 MT of Polypropylene
Filament spinning yarn = 13,00,00,000.00

PROFIT SALES RATIO = 33.01 %
RATE OF RETURN = 68.18%
BREAK EVEN POINT (B.E.P) = 36.16 %

39

Plastic Films and Sheets with Printing (Flexo and Roto) LDPE/HDPE/PP/HM/PVC

MANUFACTURING PROCESS

PVC Sheet

The manufacturing process of PVC rigid sheets by extrusion process involves of the following operational steps :

- Drying
- Formulation
- Extrusion
- Trim and Scrap

In the vented extruder, predrying of resin is done in a hopper dryer. PVC compounds of required formulations can either be made available from market or it can be formulated in the house. In this project, it is considered that PVC compounds will be made by unit.

HM HDPE Film

HM-HDPE film is manufactured by the extrusion-blow process. The polymer is forced through a circular die by the help of an extruder to flow uniformly up and out in the shape of a tube. The die is provided with a passage to feed compressed air into the tube. At start up the ring of molten polymer is drawn together by hand and sealed to form a generally hemispherical bubble on top of the die. The internal compressed air line is opened and the bubble is hauled away at a rate of speed genrally greater than the polymer flow, thus orienting the film in the machine direction. As the bubble approaches a nip roll above the die, it is converged by wood salts, a rack of rollers or similar mechanism, to change the shape from a tubular bubble to a flat two layer sheet. While the bubble may have the same diameter as the die, it is usually blown up to 1.5 to 3.5 times of that diameter. This imparts transverse orientation. It must be noted that lower the blow ratio, lower will be the film strength.

PP Film

PP granules are fed into the hopper of an extrusion blowing machine. In the barrel, the material is pushed ahead towards the die head by rotation of the screw. Due to external heating in the barrels and the shearing action of the screw, the material coming out of the cross head die is taken on a downward take-up arrangement through a cooling system. Simultaneously, the layflat is expanded by blowing it by compressor and blown layflat is passed through the nip roller and then packed.

LDPE/HDPE Film Bags

The film suitable for the manufacture of bags is produced in form of a tube by the blown film extrusion process. In this process, a tube is extruded from an annular die and is inflated by air pressure to the desired diameter, Cooled, collapsed at the nip rolls (also called pinch rolls) and finally wound in the form of rolls. Polyethylene granules are fed into the hopper of the extruder which is heated in the barrels to form molten resin,

which flows around a mandrel inside the die and is formed into a tube. The die opening normally varies between 4 mm and 6.5 mm. The tube is usually extruded vertically upward and air is introduced through the centre of the mandrel to inflate the tube to the desired bubble size. The entrapped air is maintained in the bubble by the die at one end and by suitable wind up mechanism at the other end.

Process of Manufacture

Gravure printing process involves the transfer of ink from cells etched or engraved on a copper and chrome plated cylinder to the material being printed. The cylinder rotates in an ink fountain and the cells pick up the liquid ink. A doctor blade then wipes the excess ink from the roller, leaving ink only in the cells.

As the plastic substrate moves between the cylinder and the impression roll, ink is transferred from the cells onto the substrate in the form of the etching or an image. The number and volume of the cells control the amount of ink applied to the plastic substrate.

For colours that appear nto be solid to the eye, cells of a uniform size are used.

Various shades are created by controlling the size and volume of the cells.

Process of Manufacture

The printing section of the flexographic press consist of two cylinders and ink rollers, one of which revolves in an ink tray. other which is in contact with it, collects the ink from the first roller and transfers it on to the printing plate.

The impression cylinder and the inking rollers are of fixed size but the plate cylinder can be of any size within the range of a particular machine.

Printing adjustment consists of moving the plate cylinder to the impression cylinder and the inking rollers to the plate cylinder. Adjustments are also to be made for the lateral and longitudinal registration of colours for multi colour printing. Web tension is to be maintained by adjusting the same when the weight of roll is unwinding and winding station changes.

For multi colour printing, individual colours are applied by a series of separate printing stations.

PLANT ECONOMICS

Rated Plant Capacity	=	1200.00 KG/day
Land & Building (Land 1500 sq.mts.)	Rs.	18,50,000.00

PLANT & MACHINERY

1. Extruder
2. Extruder with eqpt.& dies
3. PVC compounding equipment
4. Air compressor
5. Cutting & Slitting equipment
6. Plastic blender mixer
7. Scrap grinder
8. Testing & quality control equipment
9. Roto gravure printing machine
10. Flexo graphic printing machine

FIXED CAPITAL

1. Land & Building	Rs.	18,50,000.00
2. Plant & Machinery	Rs.	26,80,000.00
3. Other Fixed Assets	Rs.	6,70,000.00
TOTAL	Rs.	52,00,000.00

RAW MATERIALS

1. PVC resin
2. Plasticizers (DBP,DOP,DMP)
3. Stablizers (Lead Sterate)
4. Other Chemicals
5. Colourants
6. Polypropylene granules
7. HDPE granules
8. LDPE granules
9. HM-HDPE granules
10. Printing inks

TOTAL WORKING CAPITAL/MONTH

1. Raw Material	Rs.	13,22,000.00
2. Salary & Wages	Rs.	72,250.00
3. Utilities & Overheads	Rs.	2,16,000.00
TOTAL	Rs.	16,10,250.00

TOTAL CAPITAL INVESTMENT

Total Fixed Capital	Rs.	52,00,000.00
Total Working Capital for 2 Months	Rs.	32,20,500.00
TOTAL	Rs.	84,20,500.00

TURN OVER/ANNUM

1. Receipts from Sale of Printed PVC film & Sheet 2,16,000 kgs
2. Receipt from Sales of Printed PP film products 36,000 kgs
3. Receipts from sale of printed LDPE film products 36,000 kgs
4. Receipts from sale of HM HDPE film products 36000 kgs
5. Receipts from sale of HDPE film 36000 kgs

TOTAL Rs. 2,57,76,000.00

PROFIT SALES RATIO = PROFIT / SALES X 100 = 17.88 %

RATE OF RETURN = OPERATING PROFIT / T.C.I X 100 = 54.72 %

BREAK EVEN POINT (B.E.P) = 41.20 %

40

Plastic Granules From Fresh Resin

These Plastic Granules are rather expensive comparitively, but the advantages usually offset the cost advantage.

The products obtained are brighter consistant and free from specks.

The use of concentrates cuts down one heat cycle saving the polymer from thermal degradation. This ensures better mechanical strength, electrical properties heatsealstrength andreistance to moisture permeation and slip or blocking.

MANUFACTURING PROCESS OF LDPE GRANULES FROM LDPE RESIN

1. Firstly low density polyethylene resin (LDPE) of different grade procured from the market and weighed in the quantity as per formulation.
2. Now LDPE resin is taken in a jacketed stainless steel tank and heated to 80°-90°C with constant stirring with S.S stirrer. To this add plasticizer and again continue stirring till plasticizer is dissolved. Then add to this mould release agents, lubricants, and other additive with constant slow stirring till the product become homogenized.
3. Now this resin mix compound is fed to the hopper of the extruder and is extruded through extruder die. The plastic mix compound will come out in the form of thick or thin circular strands which can be regularly cut after specific interval for desired size of granules.
4. These cut granules are passed through cold water at 15°C to 20°C to cool down and remain separate without sticking each other.
5. Now the granules are removed from waterby stainless steel strainers and loaded over separate stainless steel wire mesh trays. These trays are dried in a tray drier by regular warm air circulation.

6. The dried granules are tested for quality and packed in a suitable container with protection from atmospheric reaction.
7. Now, the granules of L.D.P.E. are sold in the market.

Plastic Filler Granules (PP)

Formulation

Ingredients		Quantity (%)
Resin (Polypropylene)	-	88
Dioctyl Phthalate	-	8
Stearic Acid	-	2.5
Stabiliser (Ba/Cd Stearate)	-	1
Antioxidants	-	0.5(2, 5 Di-tert - Butyl Hydroquinone) 100

PVC GRANULES

Formulation	%
- PVC resin	77
- Ethylene vinyl acedate copolymer	16
- Plasticizer	5
Di methyl phthalate	
or Di butyl phthalate	
or Di Octyl phthalate	
- Antioxidant	2
Di lauryl thio dipropionate	
or Lecithin	
or Butylated Hydroxyanisole	
or 2:5 Di tert butyl hydroquinone	
or 2,2' Methylene leis	
(4 methyl 6-tertiary -butyl phenol)	
Total	100 %

Standard packing : 25 Kgs bags

Process of Manufacture

The process of manufacture for making granule is known as the melt compounding method. The following operations are in a) Pre mixing steps

(b) **Extruding & Granulation**

Pre-mixing steps

- Add resin in the blenders
- Stir the resin with the carrier resin
- Add the plasticizer
- Add the antioxidants
- Stir the mixture for 20-30 minutes till it is roughly homogenous
- Discharge the mix in trays & let it cool in air

Extruding & Granulation

- Pre heat the extruder keeping 30°C above the melting point
- Slowly feed the premix to the hopper above the extruder
- Start up the extruder & run it slowly till material comes out of the die
- Take the strands (string) coming out from the extruder die to the cutter passing through the conveyor blown well chilled air.
- Cut the strand into pellets or granules & collect these, which are ready for packing & despatch.

PLANT ECONOMICS

Rated Plant Capacity = 1000.00 KGS/day

Land & Building (Land area, 500 Sq.Mts.) = (Rented)

PLANT & MACHINERY

1. High speed mixer of 50 kg. batch size, made of S.S. lining air tight opening and closing system
2. Extruder 90 mm made of SS non stop magnetic chain drive system with motor of 15 HP/1440 rpm&accessories
3. Pelletizer with motor special cutting blades
4. Scrap grinder with motor
5. Bag stiching machine
6. Air blower
7. Weighing Filling machine
8. Air chilling unit, cap: 2 Ton
9. Laboratory testing equipment
10. Miscellaneous equipment

FIXED CAPITAL

1. Land & Building	Rs.	1,00,000.07
2. Plant & Machinery	Rs.	6,30,000.00
3. Other Fixed Assets	Rs.	1,90,000.00
TOTAL	Rs.	8,20,000.07

RAW MATERIALS

1. Zinc oxide, 750 Kgs
2. Calcium carbonate (pptd), 3625 Kgs
3. Talc (white), 16125 Kgs
4. Polypropylene resin, 1000 Kgs
5. D.O.P., 1000 Kgs
6. Stearic acid, 625 Kgs.
7. Ba/Cd stearate, 250 Kgs
8. Antioxidant, 125 Kgs

9. Packaging material (50 Kgs size) 500 Bags,
10. Polypropylene scrap, 1500 Kgs

TOTAL WORKING CAPITAL/MONTH

1. Raw Material	Rs.	3,16,187.50
2. Salary & Wages	Rs.	42,875.00
3. Utilities & Overheads	Rs.	47,500.00
TOTAL	Rs.	4,06,562.50

TOTAL CAPITAL INVESTMENT

Total Fixed Capital	Rs.	8,20,000.07
Total Working Capital for 3 Months	Rs.	12,19,687.50
TOTAL	Rs.	20,39,687.57

TURN OVER/ANNUM

By sale of PP filler Master Batches

300000 Kgs = Rs. 60,00,000.00

PROFIT SALES RATIO = 11.93 %

RATE OF RETURN = 35.10 %

BREAK EVEN POINT (B.E.P) = 53.96 %

41

Plastic Injection Moulding Products

Injection moulding is one of the most important processes used in plastic articles manufacture bath in terms of volume thermo-plastics handled and the range of articles manufactured. The original injection moulding machines were similar in design to metal die casting machines, when this process was developed in 1934 for the rapid moulding of thermoplastics. During the subsequent years, especially as experience and increase in understanding of processing characteristics of plastics led to the improvements in the design of such machines, this technique has proved highly success full and to the bulk of thermoplastics are manufactured by this technique. The injection moulding machine is now a sophisticated integrated piece of equipment and includes all the mechanisms and controls required to carry out successfully each step of the injection moulding process completely in a single unit. During the past two decades the demand has grown for larger capacity machines and today its is possible to inject as much as 5 Kg of material at one 'shot'. Injection moulding process has inherent advantages of high degree of repetitive accuracy and adaptability for the production of a wide range of components. The process of injection moulding can be applied with modifications to thermosetting materials also and differs from transfer moulding in that the plasticizing chamber contains enough material to fill the mould several times.

Process of Manufactures

For the manufacture of injection moulded articles mostly, screw guided injection moulding machine is used. The advantage of this machine is that thermoplastics as well thermosets can be processed with the same machine using different dies for different product. The injection moulding process comprises four stages, each of which must be closely controlled and regulated to obtain good quality mouldings.

The re stage are :

1. Plasticizing
2. Injection
3. After filling and
4. Cooling and mould release.

PLANT ECONOMICS

Rated Plant Capacity	=	3900.00 NOS/day
Land & Building (Land 900 sq.ft.)	Rs.	1,50,000.00

PLANT & MACHINERY

1. Injection Moulding machine with all fittings Capacity 140 gm/min
2. Moulds made of hardened steel or chrome plated steel
3. Scrap Grinder

FIXED CAPITAL

1. Land & Building	Rs.	1,50,000.00
2. Plant & Machinery	Rs.	5,90,000.00
3. Other Fixed Assets	Rs.	1,70,000.00
TOTAL	Rs.	9,10,000.00

RAW MATERIALS

1. Plastic moulding powder H.D.P.E
2. Plastic scrap

TOTAL WORKING CAPITAL/MONTH

1. Raw Material	Rs.	1,86,250.00
2. Salary & Wages	Rs.	37,500.00
3. Utilities & Overheads	Rs.	37,400.00
TOTAL	Rs.	2,61,150.00

TOTAL CAPITAL INVESTMENT

Total Fixed Capital	Rs.	9,10,000.00
Total Working Capital for 2 Months	Rs.	5,22,300.00
TOTAL	Rs.	14,32,300.00

TURN OVER/ANNUM

1. By Sale of 60000 Buckets
2. 60000 Water Jugs
3. 150000 Soap Cases
4. 150000 Flower Tubs
5. 150000 Glass
6. 300000 Coffee Pots
7. 300000 Salt Pot
8. Scrap 3000 kg

TOTAL Rs. 42,45,000.00

PROFIT SALES RATIO = PROFIT / SALES X 100 = 15.04 %

RATE OF RETURN = OPERATING PROFIT / T.C.I X 100 = 44.59 %

BREAK EVEN POINT (B.E.P) = 56.58 %

42

Plastic Mat

Mat and matting industry is well established in India. Previously it was made from vegetable origin like coconut fibers, jute and cotton fibers etc. Woven fabrics were among the earliest bases used for laminating. They provide a stronger and more impact resistant product. In woven fabrics the fibrous structure is stronger because the individual fibers are longer by virtue of spinning into yarn. Continuous filament yarns of plastics are much tougher than conventional yarns of vegetable origin. The continuous filament fabrics produce tough structure that are often difficult to bond because the surface of the extruded filament is smooth, the individual filaments are in maximum geometrical close packing, and there are no ends to the filamnents to provide mechanical anchoring.

Raw Materials

The main raw materials required for manufacture of plastic mat are polypropylene or high molecular plastics. Other materials are, plasticizers, etabilizers, colours, etc. The properties of polypropylene is suitable for making mats. It has lower density, greater rigidity, greater stress crack resistance. PP has high abrasive resistance, excellent electric properties and low creep. The combination of properties given are adventageous over conventional alternatives. Polypropylene is easily available in the open market.

Process of Manufacture

The production of plastic mat is simple with automatic machine. First of all plastic yarn or straps are prepared with PP granules. These yarns or straps are woven into mats with the weaving machine. The production steps are as follows.

The polypropylene (PP) granules are fed into the hopper of the extruder. Required colour and chemicals are mixed with it. The plastic granuler gets heaterd, met and are conveyed in a homogenous plastic melt form to the die face. This is led into a water bath for quenching. The purpose of quenching is to cool the melt rapidly and hereby preserve the tougher molecular structure of the plastic material. The process helps in formation of a microcrystalline structure which is necessary for the subsequent strething steps. The water temperature of the quenching bath should not exceed 80°C and this can be controlled by the water flow rate.

The yarns/straps leaving the water bath is dried by air knite system. The strapping is then conveyed to the first goddet where orientation takes place. the amount of streching depends upon the final product to be manufactured, its thickness, width and extruder output.

Normally, the stretching is about six to eight time. the thickness, and width of the strapping is decreased by a factor equivalent to the square root of the stretch ratio. The size of the die opening and its width should be selected according to the diemensions of the streched strapping.

The strapping now passes to the orientation oven with hot air circulation inside. The temperature inside the oven is controlled between 130 to 195°C so as to meet the stretching requirements of both the finest and coarest sections. This strapping passes through the second goddet and subsequenly to the stabilization tank to recover the stressed state of the strapping. Finally, it is passed through the embossing unit and it is wound upon the core at the winding station.

For production of mat, the yarns or straps are wound on bobbins, and transferred a creel which is set on the automatic mat weaving machine. Mat is woven with the machine. It is cut into required, length and braided. The final product is packed.

PLANT ECONOMICS

Rated Plant Capacity	=	200.00 Kg./Day
Building (Land 1000 sq. mts.)	Rs.	20,08,000.00

PLANT & MACHINERY

1. Strap making machine consisting of extruder motor,gear box,barred & screw, take up units Cooling water tank, winder, panel board etc.
2. Plastic mat making machine
3. Mixer/grinder

FIXED CAPITAL

1. Land & Building	Rs.	20,08,000.00
2. Plant & Machinery	Rs.	6,00,000.00
3. Other Fixed Assets	Rs.	3,90,000.00
TOTAL	Rs.	29,98,000.00

TOTAL WORKING CAPITAL/MONTH

1. Raw Material	Rs.	4,78,000.00
2. Salary & Wages	Rs.	78,750.00
3. Utilities & Overheads	Rs.	49,600.00
TOTAL	Rs.	6,06,350.00

TOTAL CAPITAL INVESTMENT

Total Fixed Capital	Rs.	29,98,000.00
Total Working Capital for 3 Months	Rs.	18,19,050.00
TOTAL	Rs.	48,17,050.00

TURN OVER/ANNUM

By sale of 60 MT of plastic mat	Rs.	1,05,00,000.00

PROFIT SALES RATIO = PROFIT / SALES X 100 = 22.19 %

RATE OF RETURN = OPERATING PROFIT / T.C.I X 100 = 48.37 %

BREAK EVEN POINT (B.E.P) = 39.32 %

43

Pet Bottles From Pre-Form (Capsules)

Pet bottles and containers are being used to pack mineral water, edible oils, coolant, shampoos etc.

The packing Industry has undergone a revolutionary change. Conventional packing materials like tins plate, glass, paper etc. have been replaced by P.E.T.

Glass container are not suitable due to their fragile toy nature and are heavy. Metal containers are not suitable at all for certain chemicals.

P.E.T containers are light, tough, unbreakable, hygenic durable and appealing. They reduce transport cost and damages, and increase the sale appeal of the products, P.E.T. containers like glass container can be made transparent, beside they may be given different colours also. They are not affected by humidity and is chemically, Inert therefore preserve the goods as such for a long time. It is therefore, increasingly used for packing food, chemical, and other consumable items.

Manufacturing Process

The one line processing system of the machine (stretch blow molding machine) is fully automatic in the sense that a well proportioned PET or PVC or Pp materials fed through the hopper and it convert itself into a ready bottle complete in all respects. The machine is designed to heat up the material and under spiral screw and barrel plunger force feed it to the mold where a perform called parison is formed This parison is reheated to its below melting temperature and the action of compressed air it is biaxially stretched to a dimension air it is biaxially stretched to a dimension about ten times bigger than the parison dimensions. Thus, the container becomes too thin walled and very light weight. But, due to stretching it gets harder, stronger, stiffer, The wall sections re very uniform in thickness as the some are precisely controlled in the machine automatically. The more the material is stretched the stronger it becomes after solidification and cooling. When the articles get cooled, these are auto matically ejected from the machine and stored for inspection, sorting, packing or despatch.

All the reforming operators eq. (a) parison forming (b) Stretch blowing take place in well designed & constructed moulds in two have and closing and opening of the mold is effected hydraulically, The drives and heating elements are electrically electronically controlled. For Mfg. any hollow article, the homogeneous formation of prison is very much essential. This prison, then, is introduced into the mold where it is blown and stretched into the from of plastic bottle.

PLANT ECONOMICS

Rated Plant Capacity	=	1834.00 BTL/day
Land & Building (Area 250 Sq. Mt.)	Rs.	3,50,000.00

PLANT & MACHINERY

Plant & Machinery including one stage bi-axial orientation stretch blow moulding machine, Moulds for 1 ltr.. Size of bottles,chiller,dryer,compressor & accessories.

FIXED CAPITAL

1. Land & Building	Rs.	3,50,000.00
2. Plant & Machinery	Rs.	4,50,000.01
3. Other Fixed Assets	Rs.	30,000.00
TOTAL	Rs.	8,30,000.01

RAW MATERIALS

1. Pet preforms (capsules) 45850 Nos. 1 Lit., bottles (28 gms.) bottle caps purchased from open market
2. Packaging Materials

TOTAL WORKING CAPITAL/MONTH

1. Raw Material	Rs.	69,775.00
2. Salary & Wages	Rs.	26,728.00
3. Utilities & Overheads	Rs.	20,300.00
TOTAL	Rs.	1,16,803.00

TOTAL CAPITAL INVESTMENT

Total Fixed Capital	Rs.	8,30,000.01
Total Working Capital for 1 Months	Rs.	1,16,803.00
TOTAL	Rs.	9,46,803.01

TURN OVER/ANNUM

By sale of 550200 Nos of PET Bottle/Containers Rs. 19,25,700.00

PROFIT SALES RATIO = PROFIT / SALES X 100 = 14.08 %

RATE OF RETURN = OPERATING PROFIT / T.C.I X 100 = 28.63 %

BREAK EVEN POINT (B.E.P) = 64.14 %

44

Pet Pre-Form Pet Resin

The use of plastics of all types is increasing and will almost certainly continue to increase. The development of existing plastics and possibly the discovery of new materials will mean that in the future plastics will be used for even more purposes than they are today.

Process

Injection Moulding is one of the most economical and conventional methods of fabricating thermoplastic materials into a variety of simple and complex forms, to manufacture utility & industrial articles. almost every known thermoplastic materials can be processed by this technique. The process consists of feeding of a granulated solid thermoplastic material in a measured quality into an electrically heated cylinder where it melts and is intermittantly forced (injected) by high pressure in a fluid state in a closed metal mould, where it cools and solidifies. The mould is then opened, the article removed and sequence repeated. This is termed as a 'Moulding Cycle'.

The complete moulding process can be divided into four steps viz.,

1. Introduction of moulding powder into the machine
2. Plasticating or melting the material in the machine
3. Injecting the molten material into the mould
4. Cooling the article in the mould and removal of the article.

Material in the form of granules or powder is fed from a hopper in measured quantities to a cylinder electrically heated by means of band heaters. It is necessary that the material must be completely dry and free from moisture. The heat is controlled by means of an Energy Regulator. The mould is locked just below the nozzle of the cylinder as to receive the molten material. The plunger (ram) is then forced down into the feed cylinder, thereby squeezing the melted material into the closed mould, where through gates or runners it fills the cavities and forms the moulded pieces. The pressure is held for the length of time required to cool or harden the harden the material in the mould. The plunger is then moved up and the new granules introduced. As the pressure is relieved the mould is unlocked and the new granules introduced. As the pressure is relieved the mould is unlocked and the moulded pieces thus formed are ejected from mould. This sequence is repeated for continuous production.

Blow Moulding

Blow Moulding is a fast easy way to form hollow plastic items is one piece, in a single continuous cycle. It has been recognised for several years as a sound commercially promising method. This technique offers exciting new profit opportunities to manufacturers and marketers of plastic products. 'Kumar' Hand operated blow Moulding machine has been designed for the manufacture of Blow hollow articles. Original in design, it combines the working principle of Injection Moulding and extruding. By this time, our machines has been accepted as a standard machine for blow moulding.

The machine is simple in machanism and is operated by pedal Pump or Compressor. Versatile, this hand operated Plastic Blowing Machine is simple in operation, requires more practice than skill. The nozzle is easily interchangeable for different parisons required for blow moulding different items.

Here is how the Blow Moulding Machine works. Plastic granules are fed in the Cylinder and hot tubes of plastic (called parison) is extruded between the two halves of the mould. The mould closes and the tube is inflated with air until it conforms. The mould opens and the article is removed and the operation repeated continuously. Many machines are in operation throughout India and are engaged in the profitable production of toys such as Dolls, Doll bodies, animals, riding toys, base ball, bats and balls, cartoon character dispensers, model cars, aeroplanes, and hundred of similar types. The household and industrial products include milk containers, double wall bottles, cosmetics jars, squeexe containers, soap and bubble bath dispensers, mason jars, water cane, oil cane, floats for toilets, lamp shades, hollow type dispensers, umbrella Handles etc.

Manufacturing Process

High powered, precision heating is applied to the preform. Optimum biorientation applied during bottle formation which guarantees a lighter packaging with superior technical and aesthetic quality.

An increased trend towards multilayer composite film that can be produced economicaly by co extrusion has been particularly noticed. In food packaging in which the mechanical and barrier properties were provided by the multilayer structure, major interest is now attracted by the sector of poly olifin film, which has so far been covered almost exclusievely by monoextrusion and the processing of blends.

The flexibility of coextrusion line continue to be of special importance for enabling a broad range of different type of composite film to be produced without the need for resulting or modifying significant parts of the line.

Composite film which uses PET (Polyesterterpthalate) as a barrier material are also being developed.

In most cases the five layer film coextrusion technology because the very thin barrier layers require adhesives for being coupled to polyolefins and for being extruded in symmetric or assymmetric five layer composite film. This is necessary to avoid high reject rates due to damage to the barrier layers and suppress the rolling effect which often is hardly controllable.

Coextrusion dies for blown film lines

The most significant criteria for evaluating a blown film coextrusion die are set out below.

1. Uniformity of the extruded layers, uniformity of the overall product across the periphery, versatility of use for different materials, material combination and gauge ratios.
2. Low flow resistance and good accessibility.
3. Channels with optimum flow conditions and no dead corners.
4. Good surface quality of the blown film.
5. Reliable rotating device and melt sealing.
6. Selection of material suitable for resisting high pressure and temperature.
7. Ability to provide internal cooling.
8. Flexibility in connecting the individual extruders to the melt feed assemblies.

In the case of 5 layers coextrusion die the 2nd and fourth layers are normally used for the adhesive but need only to be extruded at very low melt through puts (generally not more than 5% to 10% of overall melt throughout). Thus the channels and spiral distributors for these adhesive layers can be given small cross sections to save design volume and melt residence time.

Two, three and five layer dies should provide possibility of preferably variable melt stream combination.

The diameter of the die outlet ranges between 20 and 100 mm.

The compact size of this die and the possibility to coextrude up to seven layers enable the die to be used in a blow moulding machine for the manufacture of six layer containers for food stuffs such as tomato ketchup.

Manufacturing Processes of Pet Preform

Specially designed P.E.T. Injection moulding machine is used for the manufacturing of PET PREFORM.

Take P.E.T. resin and mixed with 0.1 % Plasticiser put in the injection moulding machine, where heating is applie 145°C - 170°C. Flow of plastic resin is Controlled by flow proof gear mechanism with stepless speed adjustment. There is use of two stage pressure adjustment, by the pressure adjustment molten resin pass into the preform mould cavity and formed the structure of the body which is automatically eject out.

High precision 4 cavity Pet Preform mould can produce 20000 preforms per day of 8 hours working.

PLANT ECONOMICS

Rated Plant Capacity	=	20000.00 Nos./Day
Land & Building (500 sqm.)	=	Rs. 11,50,000.00

PLANT & MACHINERY

1. Specially design Injection Moulding Machine
2. Compresser
3. Refrigeration Unit
4. Mould/dies
5. Miscelloneous

FIXED CAPITAL

1. Land & Building		Rs.	11,50,000.00
2. Plant & Machinery		Rs.	46,55,000.00
3. Other Fixed Assets		Rs.	8,20,000.00
	TOTAL	Rs.	66,25,000.00

RAW MATERIALS

1. PET resin
2. PP Resin
3. Adhesive and Plasticizer
4. Other raw materials viz. Colour, Stabilizer, Mould releasing agent etc.)

TOTAL WORKING CAPITAL/MONTH

1. Raw Material	Rs.	19,40,000.00
2. Salary & Wages	Rs.	91,080.00
3. Utilities & Overheads	Rs.	1,47,000.00
TOTAL	Rs.	21,78,080.00

TOTAL CAPITAL INVESTMENT

Total Fixed Capital	Rs.	66,25,000.00
Total Working Capital for 3 Months	Rs.	65,34,240.00
TOTAL	Rs.	1,31,59,240.00

TURN OVER/ANNUM

By selling 60 Lakhs Preform Pet = Rs. 3,60,00,000.00

PROFIT SALES RATIO = 17.35 %

RATE OF RETURN = 47.46 %

BREAK EVEN POINT (B.E.P) = 43.25 %

45

PVC Pipes & Fittings

1. PVC pipes are recommended only for water (cold) services and not the hot water supply.
2. Rigid pvc pipes are immune to corrosion and can be used in all types of corrosive soils which generally causes external corrosion in metallic pipes.
3. The specific gravity of PVC is 1.4, i.e. (5 times less than that of mild steel). Hence rigid PVC pipes can be transported easily at a lower cost handled and shaped easily. This property permits quicker and easier installation of PVC pipes.
4. The smooth weil of the rigid PVC pipes reduces frictional loss to a minimum. It is about 40% lower than that of metallic pipes.
5. The thermal conductivity of PVC is some 2,650 times less than that of copper. This factor reduces insulation cost.
6. The coefficient of thermal expansion of rigid PVC is 5 to 6 * 10^{-5} per 1°C. This means that in a hundred feet run the length of pipeline will after by about one inch per 10°C change in temperature. Due allowance should be made, particularly in over ground pipelines, for any change in length of pipeline which may occurs during installation of when pipeline is in service.

Process of Manufacture

Rigid or unplasticized PVC pipes are made from polyvinyl chloride (PVC) which in resin form is hard and rigid material. This rigidity can be controlled by controlling the percentage of plasticizer at the time of compounding. The production of rigid PVC pipes consists of plasticizing and homogenizing PVC compound and metering through and extruder. This hot molten PVC compound is extruded by the extruder through a circular slit. This circular slit governs the size of the pipe to be extruded. Different dies are used for manufacturing different sizes of pipes.

The pipe thus extruded through the die is then passed through a vacuum sizing tank where the dimensions of the pipe can be accurately set. This also helps in the surface finish of the pipe. Vacuum sizing which is more sophisticated than other types of forming operations reduces the percentage of wastage considerably.

Twin Screw Extruders

The various design changes for the counter rotating intermeshing Twin Screw Extruders, which are predominantly used for the processing of PVC powder mixed are as follows :

Introduction of modular construction systems for entire type series.

Increasing of barrel lengths.

Increasing of the screw speed range,

Increasing the torque for the screws.

Improved drives and reduction gears,

Reliable long life radial load berings for the screw drive shafts with improved axial load bearings (cylindrical roller bearings in single and tandem arrangement).

Metallurgical optimized steel alloys for screws and barrels with special heat treatment, partly with surface protection coatings also.

The outstanding processing developments in respect of twin screw extruders are :

Introduction and improvements of barrel venting.

Lengthening of screws and thereby more clearly defined energy transfer, Improved temperature control systems for screws and barrels, Introduction of mixing zones of screws, Use of polylefins in powder from with fillers.

Extrusion Dies

The compilation of numerous computer programs to assist design calculations for melt flow channels has been a decisive contribution towards the development of extrusion dies.

Calculations and practical values permits the manufacture of dies independent of melt viscosities. The application range of one extrusion die is increased so that various thermoplastics resins at high output rates can be extruded without losing their requirements for uniformity and dimensional precision.

As far as calculation is concerned, the consideration of the extruder and die as one unit has become of increasing importance in order to calculate output rates more precisely.

Extrusion dies used for the coextrusion process have kept their unchanged position compared to the adopter technology. The dominating use concerning the extrusion of different melt viscosities at various output rates is obvious.

Extrusion Lines

The extrusion line passes through very different steps of development dependent on the product quality and the thermoplastic resin to be processed.

In general, an extrusion line can be divided into three operation section, to evaluate and to determine these section parameters with their limit values influencing the product quality.

(a) *Extrusion section :*

Feeding of the materials, extruder with auxiliary equipments.

(b) *Melt forming section :*

Die head and sizing die.

(c) *Conversion into the final product :*

Cooling and calibrating units, transport, cutting and stacking.

PVC Pipe Fittings

For manufacturing same procedure is applied as in the case of pipe manufacture. Fittings are manufactured by suing different dies meant for different kinds of fittings. These dies are fitted on the moulding machine and molten PVC is charged in them. The dies are removed and the produced form is removed and the die is again set on the moulding machine. The same process is repeated.

Elbows and T-joints are manufactured using elbow moulding machine in which molten PVC is charged in the die and compressed air is injected in the die to get the desired product.

FORMULATION FOR PVC RIGID PIPES

Ingredients	*Parts*
1. PVC	100
2. DIOP & DAP	42-50
3. Basic Lead Carbonate	5-8
4. Calcium Stearate	1
5. Mineral Precipitated Calcium carbonate	0.0.5

PLANT ECONOMICS

Rated Plant Capacity	=	1.60 MT/Day
Land & Building (Land 2000 sq.mt.)	Rs.	42,85,000.00

1. **PRODUCTION UNIT**
   High speed mixer
2. 65 mm PVC rigid pipes extrusion plant consisting of extruder, vacuum sizing unit, cooling tank, etc.
3. Dies for various sizes of pipes and other desired accessories
4. Scrap grinder heavy duty fitted with motor
5. Over head water tank with recyclin pump unit
6. Weighing Balance every type industrial model 100 gms to 5 kg 1 Kg to 100 Kg pipe storage racks
7. **MAINTENANCE**
   Small hand tools, greasing and coiling equipments
8. Chemical testing lab, consisting of chemical balance oven & eqp. testing geqps.apparatus for testing bulk
9. Instrument laboratory equipped with testing facilities for impact measurement compressive strength etc.
10. PVC Injection moulding machine

FIXED CAPITAL

1. Land & Building	Rs.	42,85,000.00
2. Plant & Machinery	Rs.	10,06,000.00
3. Other Fixed Assets	Rs.	2,13,100.00
TOTAL	Rs.	55,04,100.00

RAW MATERIALS

1. P.V.C. resin (K value 66)
2. Stearic acid
3. Stabilizers
4. Calcium Stearate
5. Filler (Precipitated Caco3)
6. Colour & Pigment

TOTAL WORKING CAPITAL/ANNUM

1. Raw Material	Rs.	2,04,94,980.00
2. Salary & Wages	Rs.	17,36,040.00
3. Utilities & Overheads	Rs.	6,46,800.00
TOTAL	Rs.	2,28,77,820.00

TOTAL CAPITAL INVESTMENT

Total Fixed Capital	Rs.	55,04,100.00
Total Working Capital for 3 Months	Rs.	57,19,455.00
TOTAL	Rs.	1,12,23,555.00

TURN OVER/ANNUM

1. Receipt by sale of 360 tons of P.V.C. pipes
2. By sale of 120 MT of PVC pipe fittings
3. Recovery from 4 MT PVC Scraps

TOTAL Rs. 3,18,48,000.00

PROFIT SALES RATIO = PROFIT / SALES X 100 = 21.74 %

RATE OF RETURN = OPERATING PROFIT / T.C.I X 100 = 61.69 %

BREAK EVEN POINT (B.E.P) = 30.23 %

46

PVC Extrusion Profiles

The extrusion profile for wire channel is used for covering open wires, cables in houses, multistorey buildings, industries, offices, Godowns and other almost every places where electric light connection is there.

Besides this other places where it is used viz. Hospitals, Libraries, School, Colleges, Clubs, Restaurants, Hotels, and in any building where wiring takes place.

It protects the open wire to be dispersed on the wall.

MANUFACTURING PROCESS OF EXTRUDED WIRE CHANNELS

The extruded electric wire channels are prepared from plastic materials by following processing steps.

1. Procurement of raw materials as white PVC granules and coloured master batches (as per the required colour by the consumer) from the suppliers.
2. Weighing and proportionating of white PVC granules and coloured master batches as per requisite quantity.
3. Feeding of the granules mix into the hopper of single screw extruder continuously.
4. Extruder with selected size of die for capping and casing side is fixed and machine is set into the operation.
5. The continuous channel or profile comes from the machine.
6. The channel or profile is air cooled or water cooled to cool the product to room temperature.
7. The channels are then cut into desired length and packed into desired length and packed into polyethene film or in any packaging material after complete quality testing.

PLANT ECONOMICS

Rated Plant Capacity	=	200 Kg./Day
Land & Building (Land 500 sq.mt.)	=	Rented

PLANT & MACHINERY

1. Manufacturing of profiles(channels) upto a width of 140 mm
2. Dies of various sizes for casing and capping (1 set)
3. Scrap Grinder
4. Water Cooling arrangement
5. Compressors
6. Water tanks (M.S.)
7. Miscellaneous equipment

FIXED CAPITAL

1. Land & Building		Rented
2. Plant & Machinery	Rs.	5,60,000.00
3. Other Fixed Assets	Rs.	1,30,000.00
TOTAL	Rs.	6,90,000.00

RAW MATERIALS

1. PVC white granules
2. PVC Masterbatches
3. Packaging materials

TOTAL WORKING CAPITAL/MONTH

1. Raw Material	Rs.	2,70,625.00
2. Salary & Wages	Rs.	13,250.00
3. Utilities & Overheads	Rs.	36,000.00
TOTAL	Rs.	3,19,875.00

TOTAL CAPITAL INVESTMENT

Total Fixed Capital	Rs.	6,90,000.00
Total Working Capital for 3 Months	Rs.	9,59,625.00
TOTAL	Rs.	16,49,625.00

TURN OVER/ANNUM

By Sale of Extrusion Profile for

Electric Wire Channel 60000 kgs. = Rs. 54,00,000.00

PROFIT SALES RATIO = 22.62 %

RATE OF RETURN = 74.05%

BREAK EVEN POINT (B.E.P) = 32.06 %

47

Computer Ribbon Cartridges

Computer ribbon cartridges one of the important item in the field of computer accessories. Without Cartrige the printing works by computers are not possible. So it is a key item, which is always required by everybody Who are using Computers.

Computer ribbon cartriges are used to encase the Nylon ribbons impregnated with oil based ink. Nylon ribbons ar remained sage till it is completely used by the operator.

It is made of PVC plastic body, so it is generally unbreakable in nature. It remain intact till its shelf life and maximum usable period.

The nylon ribbons are purchased from the market and PVC plastic Cartriges are injection moulded in by the assembler. The ribbons are fixed inside the cartriges and it is packed in polyethylene film pack to prevent it from drying or from damages.

The computer ribbon cartriges are playing a Vital role in printing of desired informations from computer. It is used to print tickets viz. rail ticket, bys tickets, flight tickets etc. It is used to print accounts, ledgers in financial institutions, companies, Banks, commercial organizations. It is used to print designs, matters by books publishers, advertising agencies, laser type set works and almost any type of Written and data print works. The quality of impressions are depending upon the quality of printing ribbon fabrics as well as Inks required for printing of matter.

Raw Materials Required

PVC granules, PVC master batches (black), Nylon ribbon impregnated with oil based ink, polyethylene film, paper Cardboard packs, labels, adhesive tapes etc.

MANUFACTURING PROCESS

1. Procure the raw materials viz.PVC Granules,PVC black masterbatches, Nylon ribbon impregnated With ink.
2. Weigh the requisite quantity of PVC granules, PVC masterbatch for product manufacturing.
3. Feed the PVC granules and masterbatch into the hopper of the injection moulding machine. The granules are melted and mixed with melted masterbatch uniformly inside the barrel and Screw assembly filled with electric heater. The molten mass is injected into the mould cavity. It is now shaped and cooled inside the mould within residential time. The mould is now opened, and the finished moulded product is ejected out. In this way 3 different parts viz. upper cover lower cover and toothed gears are injection moulded separately.
4. Now, the Nylon ribbon (size=13mmX16mts) are filled inside the plastic cartrige and toothed gear is affixed in it to control the speed of ribbon movement. The upper cover is affixed and sealed completely by manual process.
5. The finished Computer ribbon cartrige is now sealed inside the polyethene film by manual heat sealing machine to prevent drying of ink.
6. It is now packed inside the cardboard packs and sealed with adhesive tapes and then sealed in the cortons for marketing.

PLANT ECONOMICS

Rated Plant Capacity	=	5000.00 Nos./Day
Land & Building (Land 1000 sqmts)	Rs.	34,00,000.00

PLANT & MACHINERY

1. Injection moulding machine cap: 100 gms shot
2. Injection moulding machine with all accessories cap: 50 gms shot
3. Moulds
4. Compressor
5. Cooling tower
6. Heat Sealing Machine
7. Water Tank (M.S)
8. Weighing Balance
9. Laboratory Equipment
10. Tools, Jigs, Fixtures

FIXED CAPITAL

1.	Land & Building	Rs.	34,00,000.00
2.	Plant & Machinery	Rs.	23,71,000.00
3.	Other Fixed Assets	Rs.	4,60,000.00
	TOTAL	Rs.	62,31,000.00

RAW MATERIALS

1. PVC Granules
2. PVC Masterbatches (black)
3. Nylon Ribbon impregnated with oil based ink
4. Polyethene films, Cardboard packs, adhesive tapes, cartons

TOTAL WORKING CAPITAL/MONTH

1.	Raw Material	Rs.	54,62,500.00
2.	Salary & Wages	Rs.	1,88,125.00
3.	Utilities & Overheads	Rs.	2,08,000.00
	TOTAL	Rs.	58,58,625.00

TOTAL CAPITAL INVESTMENT

Total Fixed Capital	Rs.	62,31,000.00
Total Working Capital for 1 Months	Rs.	58,58,625.00
TOTAL	Rs.	1,20,89,625.00

TURN OVER/ANNUM

By sale of 1500000 Nos Computer Ribbon Cartridges

Rs. 8,25,00,000.00

PROFIT SALES RATIO = PROFIT / SALES X 100 = 11.91 %

RATE OF RETURN = OPERATING PROFIT / T.C.I X 100 = 81.24 %

BREAK EVEN POINT (B.E.P) = 30.33 %

48

HDPE/PP Woven Sacks (Bags)

HDPE oriented sacks are becoming popular through out the world. This is because they are chemically inert & are water repellent & lighter in weight. They are free & possess sufficient strength & can easily be handled. They are competitive in price with other type of bags also. Air permissible sacks made of polythene strips are used for packing potatoes, coconut etc. The only problem is that the conventional using of hooks to lift cannot be used with HDPE bags.

These bags are expected to substitute jute and craft paper bags in several areas. This would mean a considerable saving in foreign exchanges by avoiding recurring imports of multiwall paper which are at the order of Rs. 5 million per annum on one hand and on the other hand lead to an increase in foreign exchange earning in the country by releasing more jute for exports.

These bags are free and posses sufficient strength and can easily be printed. These are competitive in price with other available type of bags for this purpose.

MANUFACTURING PROCESS

Tape Making Process & Specifications Extruder

1. The single screw extruder is mounted on a heavy steel frame. Screw and barrel are made of nitrided Nitro Alloy Steel with provisions for thermocouples. Heating load is 19.5 kw. Screw is mounted on cost bearing having thrust bearing. Hopper is made of steel and capacity 45 kgs with provision for removal of granules. Drive.
2. Consist of 30 HP DC Motor with thyristor control and is connect to screw via gear box.

Cross Head and Die

Cross lead and 225 mm die are hard chrome plated & have accentring screws. It has two heating zones and load is 5 kw.

Air Cooling Ring and Blower

Specially designed aluminium cost air cooling ring has many air entries guides for air impinging on the film bubble. Blower has damper & driven by 5 MP AC motor.

Air Compressor

It is for blowing of the film & driven by 0.25 HP AC motor.

Control Cabinet

The control cabinet includes temperature controllers, thermocomples, ammetres insulation switch, voltmeter, energy regulator, fuse units, controller switches, relays etc.

Vertical Take off Tower Unit

Two wooden boards to suide the bubble into riprollers, one abonite and another rubberized and driven by 0.5 HP DC motor with gear box and rectifier control & it also has a pneumatic device for closing/opening. Tower is fabricated from steel & height 15 feet & it has platform with railing & ladder.

Preliminary Take Off

Provided with guide rollers, side slitting arrangement & multislitter.

First Goddet

It has M.S. Chrome plated rolls. The upper 3 roller are driven 300 mm dia. 600 mm long and bottom 2 rollers are free 150 mm dia. 600 mm drive is 3 HP DC motor and gear box & rectifier control. On rubberized pressure roller is mounted on the last goddet roller to avoid slippage.

ORIENTATION OVEN

This is fabricated from steel sections & sheet and with suitable insulating to minimize heat losses and thereby functioning with high efficiency.

Air flow is from high pressure to blower driven by 10 HP AC motor. Heating by electric open coild heaters & load 24 kw. Hot air recycling and solid state temp. Controllers help to maintain constant temperature.

Second Goddet

This is same as the first goddet and the only difference in drive is from 7.5 HP motor.

TABILISATION OVEN

This is same as the orientation oven and the difference is driven for air blower is 2 HP motor & heater load is 18 kw.

Third Goddet

This is similar to 1 & 2nd goddet rollers & has 2 upper roller & one bottom roller 300 mm dia 600 mm long drive is from 3 HP motor.

MASTER HEAD

Consists of two rotating drums & driven by the same drive of 3rd goddet and is useful in transferring the tapes to choose winder.

CHEESE WINDERS

It has a set of 76 units for winding tapes driven by individual torque motor. It has automatic transverse drive. Individual torque control is provided to adjust winding tension and all enable trouble free operation.

CIRCULAR LOOMS

The circular warping machinery achieves high production rate by use of multiplicity of shuttles of capacity and by the adoption of a rotary form of shuttle propulsion.

The principal operation is the circular motion of series of shuttle through an annular warp shed. This shed is derived from two large beams. The ends from which are taken under the warping platform and upwards to a circular ring through needles mounted on circular weaving head driven from a central shaft is fitted with pushed blocks equipped with bowlds. These bowlds revolve and fabric grows on passes down a central table to the take up roller a central table to the take up roller. There are other arrangements like tensioning of weave, etc. are also provided. The limiting circumference for the tubular cloth are 3-1/2 + and 58-1/2". Saint freres loom manufactured by fair hair lawson Barlooms Ltd. has two models J_2 & J_{30} J_2 & J_3 has speed limit at 130 & 520 rpm and 4 shuttles & 3 shuttles respectively.

Lamination

Since the woven fabric is in tubular form and for laminating form the machinery cost is very higher. The tubular form is cut and made into plain cloth form and then laminated using conventional plan. Then it will be stitched to make bags and then packed for sales.

Process

The process consists of three steps :

1. Production Mono-axially oriented HDPE tapes
2. Weaving of tapes
3. Bag Making
4. Finishing Operations

COMPLETE PLANT SUPPLIERS

Remica Plastic Machinery Manufacturers
2/AB Sardar Patel Ind. Estate,
Near Gujarat Petrol Pump,
Shahwadi, Narol, Ahmedabad - 382 405 (Guj.)
Ph : 5832741 Fax : 0091-79-5894234
E-Mail : remica@ad1.vsnl.net.in

J.P. Industries
1701, GIDC. Ankleshwar,
Dist. Bharuch (Gujarat State) - 393002
Ph : 02646-51083, 50194
Fax : 91-2646-50196
E-Mail : jpindank@egujarat.net

PLANT ECONOMICS

Rated Plant Capacity	=	10000.00 Nos/Day
Land & Building (Land 3000 sq. mt.)	Rs.	87,00,000.00

PLANT & MACHINERY

1. Extrusion Plant
2. Pressure transducer system
3. Water pump
4. Water storage tank.
5. Water chilling unit.
6. Voltage stabilizer to stabilize

7. **CIRCULAR LOOM SECTION/PLAIN LOOMS**
   Circular loom
8. Sizing ring 24" tubular cloth
9. Additional winder
10. Gusseting device
11. Packing bell press machine
12. Miscellaneous machine, equipments etc.
13. Quality control and lab testing equipments
14. Warping machine
15. Pirn Winder
16. Rewinding machine
17. Automatic cutting machine
18. Heavy duty stitching machine
19. 2-Colour printing machine

FIXED CAPITAL

1. Land & Building	Rs.	87,00,000.00
2. Plant & Machinery	Rs.	75,89,500.00
3. Other Fixed Assets	Rs.	8,50,000.00
TOTAL	Rs.	1,71,39,500.00

RAW MATERIALS

1. HDPE granules
2. Colorant, plasticizers and other ingredients
3. Printing Inks for HDPE Woven sacks printing

TOTAL WORKING CAPITAL/MONTH

1. Raw Material	Rs.	15.88,500.00
2. Salary & Wages	Rs.	2,94,400.00
3. Utilities & Overheads	Rs.	1,59,000.00
TOTAL	Rs.	20,41,900.00

TOTAL CAPITAL INVESTMENT

Total Fixed Capital	Rs. 1,71,39,500.00
Total Working Capital for 3 Months	Rs. 61,25,700.00
TOTAL	Rs. 2,32,65,200.00

TURN OVER/ANNUM

3000000 HDPE Woven Sacks	Rs. 3,90,00,000.00

PROFIT SALES RATIO = PROFIT / SALES X 100 = 23.47 %

RATE OF RETURN = OPERATING PROFIT / T.C.I X 100 = 39.34 %

BREAK EVEN POINT (B.E.P) = 45.10 %

49

Semiconductive Compounds and Master Batches

This project envisages for the manufacture of Semiconductive compounds and master batches for colour special for power cables of PE, PVC & rubber sheathing. Semi conductive compounds are made by mixing Semi-Conducting materials like Semi-conductors with plastic/rubber based materials to make compounds. Various Semiconductors are used in compounding materials of plastic/rubber alongwith Compounding ingredients.

Semiconductive Compounds are nothing but Compounds of plastic/rubber by mixing Semiconductors as per the formulation alongwith other compounding materials like plasticizers, stabilizers, fillers, pigment and other additives.

Master batches of plastic/rubber materials for colour special for power cables are made by similar way of compounding materials by adding various ingredients as required of PE, PVC & rubber base material.

Uses & Application

Semi-conductive Compounds are used in electronic & electrical industries as conducting materials. Various components/ parts are produced from this semiconductive compounds as per the requirements.

Master batches are used for colour special for power cables made up PE, PVC & rubber as covering material.

Manufacturing Process

The process of making semiconductive Compounds and Master

batches consist of Mixing of plastic/rubber materials with other ingredients/ additive, compounding/masterbatching the same to make final products.

Semi-conductive compounds are produced by mixing plastic/rubber materials with Semiconductor material and other additives like plasticizer, stabilizer, pigments, filler etc. in a mixing plant equipped with stirror. After mixing operation, the prepared materials are compounded in a compounding plant, jacketed with stirrer. In this process, heat is given to make final' semiconductive compounds as per the requirements and end use product making.

Master batches are also produced by mixing of plastic/rubber materials with additives like plasticizer, stabilizer, filler, pigments/colour as required in a mixing plant and then master batch is produced in Jacketed vessel equipped with stirrer.

The final products are tested and then packed for dispatch.

MASTER BATCHES FOR COLOUR SPECIALS FOR POWER CABLES

Polymer Compounding

In many commercial plastics, the polymer is only one of several constituents, and it is not necessarily the most important one. Such systems are made by polymer compounding-a term used for the mixing of polymer with other ingredients. These other ingredients or supplementary agents are collectively referred to as additives. They may include chemicals to act as plasticizing agents, various types of filling agents, stabilizing agents, antistatic agents, colorants, flame retardants, and other ingredients added to impart certain specific properties to the final product.

The properties of compounded plastics may often by vastly different from those of the base polymers used in them. A typical example is SBR, which is the largest-volume synthetic rubber today. The styrene-butadiene copolymer is a material that does not extrude smoothly, degrades rapidly on exposure to warm air, and has a tensile strength of only about 500 psi (3.4×10^6 N/m^2.) However, proper compounding changes this polymer to a smooth-processing, heat-stable rubber with a tensile strength of over 3000 psi (20×10^6 N/m^2). Since all properties cannot be optimized at once, compounders have developed thousands of specialized recipes to optimize one or more of the desirable properties for particular applications (tires, fan belts, girdles, tarpaulins, electrical insulation, etc.). In SBR the compounding ingredients can be (1) reinforcing fillers, such as carbon black and silica, such as mineral oils, fatty acids, and esters; (4) antioxidants, basically amines or phenols, which stop the chain propagation in oxidation; and (5) Curatives, such as sulfur for unsaturated polymers and peroxides for saturated polymers, which are essential to form the network of cross-links that ensure elasticity rather than flow.

Polymer applications which generally involve extensive compounding are rubbers, thermosets, adhesives, and coatings. Fibers and thermoplastic polymers (with the exception of PVC) are generally not compounded to any significant extent. Fibers, however, involve complex after-treatment processes leading to the final product. PVC, which by itself is a rigid solid, owes much of its versatility in applications to compounding with plasticizers. The plasticizer content varies widely with the end use of the product but is typically about 30% by weight.

Of the compounding ingredients, fillers and plasticizers are more important in terms of quantities used. Other additives used in smaller quantities are antioxidants, stabilizes, colorants, flame retardants, etc. The ingredients used as plasticizers, antioxidants, stabilizers, and flame retardants and their effects have been discussed previously. Fillers and colorants are described next.

Fillers

Fillers play a crucial role in the manufacture of plastics. Alone many plastics are virtually useless, but they are converted into highly useful products by combining them with fillers. For example, phenolic and amine resins are almost always used in combination with substances like wood flour, pure cellulose, powdered mica, and asbestos. Glass fiber is used as a filler for fiber-reinforced composites with epoxy or polyester resins.

Another extremely important example is the use of carbon filler for rubber. Rubber would be of little value in modern industry were it not for the fact that the filler carbon greatly enhances its mechanical properties like tensile strength, stiffness, tear resistance, and abrasion resistance. Enhancement of these properties is called reinforcement and the fillers which produce the strengthening effect are known as reinforcing fillers. Other fillers may not appreciably increase strength, but they may improve other properties of the polymer, thus making it easier to mold, which reduces cost.

Fillers used in plastics can be divided into two types: particulate and fibrous. In some instances they are added to perform one or more prime functions or to provide special properties. Asbestos, for example, provides high-temperature resistance and improves dimensional stability. Mica improves the electrical and thermal properties of all compounds. Glass fibers produce high strength. Carbon black is the only important reinforcing filler for most elastomers. It also imparts UV resistance and coloring.

Beryllium oxide-filled resins gain high conductivity without loss of electrical properties. Metal particles have been used as fillers for plastics to improve or impart certain properties. Thus, aluminium has been used for applications ranging from making a decorative finish to improving thermal conductivity. Copper particles are used in plastics to provide electrical conductivity. Lead is used because it dampens vibrations, acts as barrier to gamma-radiation, and has high density.

Colourants

A wide variety of inorganic and organic materials are added to polymers to impart color. For transparent colored plastics materials, oil-soluble dyes or organic pigments (such as phthalocyanines) having small particle size and refractive index near that of the plastic are used. Others, including inorganic pigments, impart opaque colour to the plastic. Some of the common colorants for plastics, among many others, are barium sulfate and titanium dioxide (white), ultramarine blues, phthalocyanines blues and greens, chrome greens, molybdate oranges, chrome yellows, cadmium reds and yellows, quinacridone reds and magentas, and carbon black. Flake aluminum is added for a silver metallic appearance, and lead carbonate or mica for pearlesence.

The principal requirements of a colorant are that it have a high covering power-cost ratio and that it withstand processing and service conditions of the plastic. The colorant must not catalyze oxidation of the polymer nor adversely affect its desirable properties. Colorants are normally added to the powdered plastic and mixed by tumbling and compounding on a hot roll or in an extruder.

SEMI-CONDUCTIVE COMPOUNDS

In the most general sense, the term compound semiconductor encompasses a large number of materials, most of which crystallize in either the zincblende (cubic), wurtzite (hexagonal), or rock salt (cubic) crystal structures. Prototypes of these structures are GaAs, CdS, and PbS, respectively. More exotic examples of zincblende semiconductors are $ZnSiP^2$ and Ga^2Se^3. The latter crystal is a defect zincblende structure in which one-third of the Ga sites are structural vacancies. Groups 13 and 15 (III-V) and 16 (II-VI) compounds which crystallize in the zincblende structure are of significant value for electronic and photonic device applications. The III-V nitrides, AlN, GaN, and InN, crystallize in the wurtzite structure and are being developed for blue light-emitting devices and high temperature and high power electronics. The Group and 14 (II-VI) compounds are of value primarily for photonic applications. Blue lasers have been created from ZnMgSSe alloy heterostructures. The HgCdTe alloy system has been extensively studied for infrased photovoltaic detectors CdTe has a band gap of 1.49 eV, whereas HgTe is a semimetal. Consequently, the band gap of the alloy may be varied smoothly from over 1 eV to zero. Another interesting class of materials are the dilute magnetic semiconductors. The transition-metal Mn, with a half-filled d shell, may be readily.

PLANT ECONOMICS

Rated Plant Capacity	=	33.33 MT/Day
Land & Building (Land 5 Acres)	Rs.	4,30,00,000.00

PLANT & MACHINERY

1. Mixing Plant With agitator
2. Compounding Plant Jacketed with Stirrer, Motor etc.
3. Boiler
4. Pulveriser
5. Storage Tanks Pumps & Pipelines
6. Packing Unit
7. Testing & Lab. equipments
8. Misc. equipments

FIXED CAPITAL

1. Land & Building	Rs. 4,30,00,000.00
2. Plant & Machinery	Rs. 2,90,00,000.00
3. Other Fixed Assets	Rs. 1,40,00,000.00
TOTAL	Rs. 8,60,00,000.00

RAW MATERIALS

1. **A. FOR SEMI CONDUCTIVE COMPOUND**

   Plastic/Rubber materials
2. Semi Conductor Materials

3. Additive Like Stabilizer,
   Plasticizer, Filler, Pigments etc.
4. **B. FOR MASTER BATCHES**
   PE Materials
5. PVC Materials
6. Rubber Materials
7. Plasticizer, Stabilizer, Filler, Pigments, etc.
8. Packing Materials & Other Consumables

TOTAL WORKING CAPITAL/MONTH

1. Raw Material		Rs. 3,98,00,000.00
2. Salary & Wages		Rs. 15,00,000.00
3. Utilities & Overheads		Rs. 28,10,000.00
	TOTAL	Rs. 4,41,10,000.00

TOTAL CAPITAL INVESTMENT

Total Fixed Capital		Rs. 8,60,00,000.00
Total Working Capital for 3 Months		Rs.13,23,30,000.00
	TOTAL	Rs.21,83,30,000.00

TURN OVER/ANNUM

1. Receipts by sale of 4000 MT. of Semi Conductive Compounds
2. 6000 MT of Master batches for Colour special for Power Cables (PE, PVC & Rubber)

TOTAL	Rs.68,00,00,000.00

PROFIT SALES RATIO = PROFIT / SALES X 100 = 16.51 %

RATE OF RETURN = OPERATING PROFIT / T.C.I X 100 = 51.43 %

BREAK EVEN POINT (B.E.P) = 34.48 %

50

Plastic Sutli or Polypropylene Sutli

The major raw materials required for the plastic sutli is premanufactured polypropylene granules or HDPE granules, white or different coloured.

Alternatively polypropylene resin, colour etc. are required for processing of sutli production.

Process of Manufacture

The dry polypropylene is blended with colors and dyes and fed into the extruder through the hopper. After plasticization it is extruded through the die and led into a water batch for quenching. The purpose of quenching is to cool rapidly and thus preserve tougher molecular structure. This aids the formation of a microcrystallien structure necessary for the subsequent stretching step. The water temperature should be controlled to a maximum of about 80ºC. The articles leaving the water batch should be dried by air knife or other appropriate systems. This is necessary since wet items are not heated uniformly in the stretching over and may either break or deform as a result of non-uniform stretch.

The untreated sutli from the cooling step is conveyed by a group of rotating feed rolls at a certain linear speed; the sutli is than drawn by a second group with which it is pulled by fed rolls.

The stretch ratio is the ratio of speeds of the second group of rolls to the feed rolls. it is stretch that confers the desired molecular orientation on sutli, resulting in an increase in tenacity, a decrease in elongation at break and a decrease in cross section. In general, the thickness and width of the sutli is decreased by a factor equivalent to the square root of the stretch ratio. This rule allows the thickness of the unstreached items and, consequently,the size of the die opening and its width to be selected according and its width to be selected according to the dimension of the stretched sutli. A converter must, however, find the best possible compromise between the utilization of this equipment and the characteristics most suitable to the end use of the articles.

The temperature of the stretching oven varies according to the dimensions of the instretched item, the relative stretching speed and the oven should allow a continuous heat regulation at any temperature between approximately 130 to 160°C so as to meet stretching requirements on both the finest and the coaresest sections and with the most diverse through put speed.

The stretched articles are usually conveyed through a secondoven maintained at 115-145°C, 50 as to have controlled recovery of the stressed state of sutli. The processing conditions in a typical case may be as follows.

Feed zone temperature	170-190°C
Cylinder Temperature	200-230°C
Die Temperature	215-225°C
Stretching temperature (air oven)	130-169°C
Stabilization temperature (air oven)	115-145°
Stretching ratio	6-7.5

PLANT ECONOMICS

Rated Plant Capacity	=	1 MT./Day
Land & Building (Land 500 Sq.Mt.)	Rs.	3,95,000.00

PLANT & MACHINERY

1. Screw preplasticizing type extruder with screw fitted with variable speed
2. Water circulation system for cooling
3. Stretching unit
4. Stabilization
5. Scrap grinder
6. Drycolor blending unit

FIXED CAPITAL

1. Land & Building	Rs.	3,95,000.00
2. Plant & Machinery	Rs.	6,60,000.00
3. Other Fixed Assets	Rs.	1,30,000.00
TOTAL	Rs.	11,85,000.00

RAW MATERIALS

1. Polypropylene resin
2. Colors
3. Packaging material

TOTAL WORKING CAPITAL/MONTH

1. Raw Material	Rs.	6,44,000.00
2. Salary & Wages	Rs.	33,428.00
3. Utilities & Overheads	Rs.	33,000.00
TOTAL	Rs.	7,10,428.00

TOTAL CAPITAL INVESTMENT

Total Fixed Capital	Rs.	11,85,000.00
Total Working Capital for 2 Months	Rs.	14,20,856.00
TOTAL	Rs.	26,05,856.00

TURN OVER/ANNUM

Receipt by sale of 300 ton of polypropylene sutli	Rs. 1,14,00,000.00

PROFIT SALES RATIO = PROFIT / SALES X 100 = 19.01 %

RATE OF RETURN = OPERATING PROFIT / T.C.I X 100 = 83.16 %

BREAK EVEN POINT (B.E.P) = 32.14 %

51

Disposable Plastic Syringes (Sterilized)

Syringe is an instrument which is used for injecting any liquid into the body of human beings or of animals. It consists of a cylinder and a air tight piston. These syringes are used for injecting the medicine into the body or into veins of the body which are not possible to take in through mouth because it takes much time in mixing with blood.

These syringes are available in sizes varying from 2 c.c. to 100 c.c. Most popular and commonly used sizes are 2. C.C., 5 C.C. Other sizes are also frequently used by upto a lesser extent.

Raw Material

Raw material for these syringes is only plastic of high quality. This plastic can be had from the manufacturers. All the requirement are on the theoretical grounds. In practice these quantities should be adjusted accordingly.

For 2,000 dozens, Plastics syringes of 5 C.C. the following material is required.

Plastic surgical grade	480 kgs.
Colour for scaling the syringe	1 kgs.

The composition of the compounding mixture of high density for the compounding mixture of high density polyethylene is given below.

1. HDPE	95%
2. Filler like calcium carbonate	4%
3. Lubricant	1%

For the calibration of the syringe, printing ink is required.

Manufacturing Details

The manufacturing process of plastic syringes is very simple. Only little care is required after each step. It will be better if the output of each step is checked thoroughly. Manufacturing process of plastic syringes has been described as under.

The starting step is the manufacture of barrel of cylinder of desired diameter. The plastic used for this products should contain the following properties:-

1. It should not be compressible.
2. It should be hard enough
3. Melting point should be as high as possible.
4. The plastic should be transparent.
5. It should be non reactive to the medicines and liquid to be injected.
6. Yield strength of the plastic used should be high.

On a semi-automatic plant this process is carried out in the plastic blow moulding, while in this profile we have considered an automatic plant where the plastic material of the appropriate formulations is fed into the machine.

PROCESS FLOW SHEET DIAGRAM

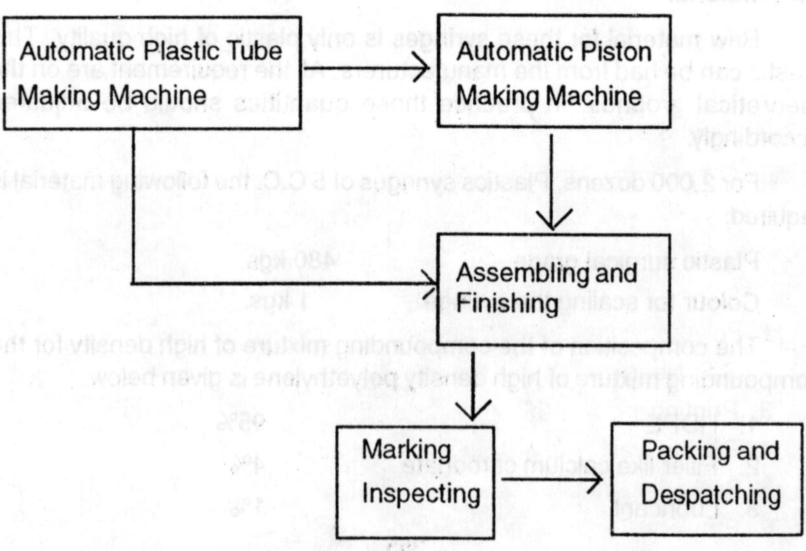

PLANT ECONOMICS

Rated Plant Capacity	=	33600.00 Nos./Day
Land & Building (Land 2000 Sq.mt.)	Rs.	21,00,000.00

PLANT & MACHINERY

1. Winder,Ferromatic injection moulding machine
2. Nozzle plate and Cap making automatic machine (vertical type injection moulding machine 20 gms shot)
3. Scrap Grinder
4. Universal Screen Printing Machine
5. Sterilization unit with Ethylene Oxide
6. Automatic Assembling machine
7. Packaging machine (Blister Pack)
8. Electronic Weighing Scale
9. One set mould for 2.5 ml. syringe
10. One set of mould for 5 ml. syringe
11. Air Compressor with 5 HP motor
12. Chilling Plant
13. Water Pump
14. Laboratory Testing equipment.

FIXED CAPITAL

1. Land & Building	Rs.	21,00,000.00
2. Plant & Machinery	Rs.	67,80,000.00
3. Other Fixed Assets	Rs.	5,35,000.00
TOTAL	Rs.	94,15,000.00

RAW MATERIALS

1. Polypropylene Granules (moulded - grade)
2. S.S. Needles
3. Printing inks
4. Rubber washer (silicon rubber)
5. Packaging material
6. Ethylene Oxide Gas

TOTAL WORKING CAPITAL/MONTH

1. Raw Material		Rs.	7,11,800.00
2. Salary & Wages		Rs.	60,875.00
3. Utilities & Overheads		Rs.	1,41,900.00
	TOTAL	Rs.	9,14,575.00

TOTAL CAPITAL INVESTMENT

Total Fixed Capital		Rs.	94,15,000.00
Total Working Capital for 3 Months		Rs	27,43,725.00
	TOTAL	Rs.	1,21,58,725.00

TURN OVER/ANNUM

1. By sale of 50,40,000 Nos. of size 2.5 ml. plastic disposable syringe
2. By sale of 50,40,000 Nos. of size 5 ml. disposable plastic syringe

TOTAL Rs. 1,99,08,000.00

PROFIT SALES RATIO = PROFIT / SALES X 100 = 24.77 %

RATE OF RETURN = OPERATING PROFIT / T.C.I X 100 = 40.56 %

BREAK EVEN POINT (B.E.P) = 50.22 %

52

Plastic Water Storage Tanks (HDPE) (Sintex Type)

Low Density Polyethylene : L.D.P.E. (density 0.91 - 0.94 gm/cm^3) melts at approx. 115°C, is insoluble at room temperature but dissolves in various solvents when molten. An increase in molecular weight distribution facilitates processing but reduces strength, toughness and resistance to environmental stress-cracking. The average molecular weight, also effects these properties. Increasing it increases the strength, toughness and melt temperature, but decreases the ease of processing and the malt Index.

High Density Polyethylene :- H.D.P.E. (density 0.94 - 0.97 gm/cm^3) is widely used for pipes and drains especially in large - diameter corrugated forms. The corrugations provide stronger walls at less thickness, which reduces the materials cost of the pipe. The high density homopolymer malts at about 135°C is over 90% crystalline and quite linear with more than 100 ethylene units per side chain. It is more rigid and harder than low density polyethylene and has a higher melting point, tensile strength and heat-deflection temperature.

Polypropylene - Can be fabricated by almost any process used for plastics.

Poly Vinyl Chloride - Rigid unplasticized PVC is stronger, with a higher tensile strength than the polylefins.

Process of Manufacture

Manufacture of Plastic tanks (sintex type) is achieved by adoption of rotational moulding process both batch type or continuous types. Most material used in the process are thermoplastics - H.D.P.E., L.L.D.P.E. & L.D.P.E. or a combination in desired proportion as required. Raw materials are ground to a 35 mesh powder. This fine particle size insures good flow into angles and undercut moulds. However particles size required is function of the material flow properties and the part to be produced. Finer particle sizes are required when thin walled sections are desired if the part to be produced has sharp radic and undercuts.

An ideal particle would be uniform in shape and have a smooth surface with a narrow particle size distribution. Now the process particle size distribution. Now the process consists of heating the powdered resin in a closed mold which is kept rotating simultaneously about two axes vertically and horizontally. The moulding operation is preferably carried out in a closed oven at a temperature of 205°C to 315°C heated by gas or molten salt. The size of the rotational molded product is limited only by the size of the oven. The mold is detached from the spider each of which is permanently affoxed at one end of a spindle. The other end of the spindle is attached to a driving hub that carries the spider with the mold through other stations of molding cycle.

Cycle time generally range from 6 to 10 minutes. Cycles as low as 2 minutes have been accomplished on the other hand extremely large parts with heavy walls may require 15 minutes or more rotation of the machine is at low speed generally in the range of 0 to 40 r.p.m. on the minor axis and 0 to 12 rpm on the major. A 4:1 rotation ratio is common and some machines do not permit variations from this. However, both variable speeds and variable ratios should be available for molding unaseel configuration.

Some machines incorporate a sintering phase between the heating and cooling portions of the cycle for chemical cross linking. Still others inject inert gases during heating to retard degradation and discoloration as well as to remove offensive odours from certain materials. Cold gas is occasionally injected internally to speed up the cooling of exceptionally thick parts. The basic process is however as outlined above. Molds used for rotational molding are generally made from cast aluminium thin sheet steel or electroformed copper to ensure maximum heat transfer through mold walls. The type of equipment used determines mold wall thickness. The recommended wall thickness is 1/4" to 1/2" for hot air and molten salt machines respectively.

Barring few limitations there is a practically no shape or size that cannot the rotationally molded. The wall thickness variations can be as low as + 5 percent of desired value and surface texture can be produced very accurately depending upon the mold finish. The process permits forming parts with a wall thickness as low as 15 mils or as thick as 500 mils, little or no draft angle is necessary since the parts are not formed under pressure and since they tend to shrink away from the mold when in order of consumption viz powdered thermoplastics, liquid plastisols and thermosets.

Rotational molding process produce SINTEX type tanks of any sizes varying from 100 litres to 10,000 litres as required even up to 25,000 litres.

The complete procedure are enumerated as follows :

1. The cavity or multiple cavity in the bottom parts of the unheated molds are charged with a predetermined weight of the polyethylene powder desired in the finished products.

2. The mold parts are clamped in place. For totally enclosed pieces. The entire mold is made of heat-conductive material. When are or both ends of the pieces are open heat-imsulating covers are used to close the mold.

3. The charged molds are placed in an over where they are heated while simultaneously rotated around two oves in planes at right angles to eads other.

Normal one temperatures are 205°C to 315°F. Ovens may be heated by various types of heat sources.

a. Infrared (gas or electrical)

b. Direct gas flame

c. Hot air

d. Molten salts.

4. The double revolving motion results in forming hollow objects in every mold cavity,the polyethylene powder being evenly distributed to form walls off uniform thickness when the resin fuses (except where heat insulating covers are used). Weight and wall thickness of the increasing or decreasing the amount of powder initially put into each lower mold easily.

5. When all the powder has formed into a homogenous layer on the inner walls of the molds are cold by spraying cold water tank or by spraying cold air preferably while still being rotated.

6. The mold is opened and the moldings are removed.

7. Molding cycle time ranges roughly from 2 to 30 minutes depending on piece size and thickness, oven temperature, the particular resin used, and the mold material.

8. The whole process consists of heating the powdered resin in a closed mold which is kept rotating simultaneously about two axes - vertically and horizontally. The molding operation is preferably carried out in a closed oven at a temperature of 205° to 315°C heated by gas or molten salt. The size of the rotational molded product is limited only by the size of the oven. Mould is preferably made of aluminium. It is rapidly cooled by spraying cold meates on the mold or by total immussion of the mold in water. The article is through removed from the mold and after engraving, printing, decorating and polishing the material is ready for marketing.

PLANT ECONOMICS

Rated Plant Capacity	=	50.00 Nos/Day
		(1000 Ltr. Capacity)
Land & Building (Land 2000 sq.mt.)	=	Rs. 35,50,000.00

PLANT & MACHINERY

1. Automatic Rotational moulding machine capable of handling complete with drives & accessories
2. Injection moulding machine for lid cover complete with all accessories
3. Grinder, Mixer & cutter etc.
4. Dies & Molds
5. Finishing & Testing Equipments, working tools & instruments
6. Tool room machineries, material handling & printing equipments

FIXED CAPITAL

1. Land & Building	Rs. 35,50,000.00
2. Plant & Machinery	Rs. 70,55,000.00
3. Other Fixed Assets	Rs. 15,20,000.00
TOTAL	Rs. 1,21,25,000.00

RAW MATERIALS

1. HDPE Polymers
2. Carbon black & dyes & pigments
3. Hinges & inserts & contingencies

TOTAL WORKING CAPITAL/MONTH

1. Raw Material	Rs.	26,66,000.00
2. Salary & Wages	Rs.	79,000.00
3. Utilities & Overheads	Rs.	1,15,800.00
TOTAL	Rs.	28,60,800.00

TOTAL CAPITAL INVESTMENT

Total Fixed Capital	Rs.	1,21,25,000.00
Total Working Capital for 3 Months	Rs.	85,82,400.00
TOTAL	Rs.	2,07,07,400.00

TURN OVER/ANNUM

By sale of 15000 Tanks (1000 lts. capacity)	Rs.	5,62,50,000.00

PROFIT SALES RATIO = 28.92 %

RATE OF RETURN = 78.57 %

BREAK EVEN POINT (B.E.P) = 28.82 %

53

Thermocole Based Disposable Glass, Cups and Plates

Thermocole based products viz. glass, cups, plates are the items used in catering which can be further discarded after use. It can be used in public places viz. Hotels, Railway Stations, Air Ports, Cinema Halls etc.

Process of Manufacture

Polystyrene is available in an expandable form (Thermocole) which can be processed by steam moulding to give light-weightarticles viz. cups, plates, glass etc.

Moulding of expandable polystyrene beads is carried out in three stages

1. Pre expansion 2. Maturing 3. Molding

Pre-expansion is achieved by heating the expandable beads in steam. This has the ual effect of increasing the pressure of the blowing agent within the beads and of softening agent within the beads and of softening the polystyrene.

The beads thus expand and the degree of expansion being controlled by the temperature and the duration of heating. Pre-expansion being controlled, by the temperature and the duration of heating.

Pre-expansion can be carried out as a batch operation or continumsty after pre-expansion the beads are allowed to cool, when the residual blowing agent a partial vaccum. At this stage the pressed between finger and thumb they collapse. During the multicellular structiure of each bead until equilibrium with the atmosphere is achieved. The beads are then resilient and do not collapse when squeezed between finger and thumb. In this condition the beads are ready for moulding to obtain plate, galss & cups since expansion of the air within the bead during the molding process can controbute to the pressure generated by the residual blowing agent and so ensure good fusion.

Maturing times normally range from 9 to 24 hours maturing can also be done in a well ventilatage siles. When maturin si complete, the pre-expended bead are transferred to the mould which is then closed and heated by injectin steam. The residual blowing agent and the air which entired the beads during maturing both expand and the polystyrene is again softened since the beads are confined in a closed mould, the expansion in volume of the blowing agent and air within the beads causes them to distort and fill the voids between the beads. Individual beads merge into the mass, giving a coherant non communicating microcellular structure. The mould is then cooled a pened and the moulding removed.

Pre-expansion can be carried out in a continuous pre-expander, by introducing a expandable beads. As beads expand they are swept upwards and out of the pre-expander. The require density is normally obtained by controlling the feed sate of expandable beads to the base of the equipment, allowing air to bleed into the steam supply to reduce the temperature or varying the height at which the pre-expandable bead a re remove.

Moulding of the shoped article such as Glass, Cups, Plates etc. is carried out in one or other of two basis methods. In the autoclave method the mold is filled with pre-expanderal beads closed and placed in autoclave. Fusion of beads is achieved by steaming for a given period at 10-20 lb/m^2 the mould is completely filled with beads. In addition a certain amount of pre compression is achieved which ensures that in the moulding operation, maximum use is made of the expansion powere of the beads to fuse completely into a homogeneous mass.

In a automative molding machine which is efficient and simple in operation the pre-expanded beads are injected into the mould by means of an air injector and then fused by steam. The mould is in two parts and the steaming starts which themold is still closing. This pre-heating avoids condensation forming during moulding. The beads are then injected and when the mould is filled steam at 15-20 lb/m^2 pressure is introduced into the male sector and at 30-40 lb/m^2 pressure into the female section. The steam from the male portion of the mould do places the air from the voids between the beads and the mould is then completley closed. Steaming is then continued until fusion of the beads is complete. At the end of the steaming cycle the steam is quickly vented to atmosphere and now the cooling is carried out by circulating cold water. Through both parts of the mould. The mould is then opened and the article ejected automatically.

The final products viz. plates, cups and glasses is now ready to despatch. Any other form or shapes are directly produced in mould in corresponding shapes and sizes.

PLANT ECONOMICS

Rated Plant Capacity	=	250.00 KG/day
Land & Building (Land 600 Sq. Mts.)	Rs.	17,00,000.00

PLANT & MACHINERY

1. Steam Boiler, Heavy Duty Horizontal type
2. Water Softening Plant
3. Continuous Prefoamer
4. Silos
5. Automatic Moulding Machine
6. Air Compressor
7. Step Down Transformer
8. Testing Equipment e.g. Specific Specific Gravity Measuring Eqpt. Thickness, Guage etc.
9. Moulds for Glases, Cups & Plates
10. Miscellaneous viz; Pumps Valves & Pipe Fittings etc.

FIXED CAPITAL

1. Land & Building	Rs.	17,00,000.00
2. Plant & Machinery	Rs.	11,55,000.00
3. Other Fixed Assets	Rs.	2,35,000.00
TOTAL	Rs.	30,90,000.00

RAW MATERIALS

1. Expandable Polystyrene Beads
2. Misc. viz; Packaging Material (Polythene) etc.

TOTAL WORKING CAPITAL/MONTH

1. Raw Material	Rs.	4,46,250.00
2. Salary & Wages	Rs.	63,595.00
3. Utilities & Overheads	Rs.	89,700.00
TOTAL	Rs.	5,99,545.00

TOTAL CAPITAL INVESTMENT

Total Fixed Capital	Rs.	30,90,000.00
Total Working Capital for 2 Months	Rs.	11,99,090.00
TOTAL	Rs.	42,89,090.00

TURN OVER/ANNUM

By Sale of Thermocole (Expanded Polystyrene) Based Disposable Mould Products, viz; Plates, Cups, Glass	Rs.	90,00,000.00

PROFIT SALES RATIO = PROFIT / SALES X 100 = 9.46 %

RATE OF RETURN = OPERATING PROFIT / T.C.I X 100 = 19.84 %

BREAK EVEN POINT (B.E.P) = 66.51 %

54

Plastic Granules

Plastic, in many applications, can do a better job at a lower cost then other materials. Each plastic should be selected on the basis of its properties. Thus, each plastic is not an answer to all problems. Here in this project report we have considered Ten Plastic materials, out of that major five thermo plastic materials have ABC, PP, L.D.P. L.L.D.P.E., OPP, OPS, Polystyrene in :

1. Injection Moulding purposes.
2. Extrusion Purposes.
3. Extruded Sheets.
4. Extruded Pipes.

Mechanical engineering applications like gears, cans bearings, brushes and valve seats.

PROCESS OF MANUFACTURE

Sorting

The plastic waste is taken for granules manufacture off contains many inpuritles like dust, mud, wires and vails, or First of all the scrap is sorted out and the wire and wail are removed these way also be removed by a magnetic separator.

Smashing

Then the plastic scrop is crushed by means of a scrap grinder or pulverizer small pieces of desired size.

Washing

The crushed material is then fed to the washing unit where it is washed with water and detergent solution and oil HCL under this process, the scrap is cleaned and is ready for the next process.

Concentration of Blending

After washing, the clean scrap is melted in a vessel by direct firing. Now add DMP (Dimethyl Phthalate) or DOP (Di-octyl Phthalate) or any other plasticizer. The ingredients are thoroughly mixed.

Now, the above mass is taken to a mixer, where solvent is 2 xylene, toluene, ethanol, cresol, Butanol etc. may be added or for the bushose, preferably a mixture or there solutions like Ethanol, Toluene and are added is requisite proportions into the melted mass and diluted. Thoroughly with the above solvents till the desired consistency of mass is obtained.

REMOVAL OF COLOUR TO OBTAIN TRANSPARENT GRANULES BY ACTIVATED CARBON TREATMENT

Now, the mass, is treated with activated carbon to adsorb all the dyes, pigments, colours owing to the scrap.

This treatment of adding solvent and activated carbon is repeated two to three times till all the colour is removed.

Filteration

Now, the abovs mass is filtered by passing through a rotary drum filter where the melted scrap is totally cleaned, the impurities being retained on the filter.

Distillation

After the removal of colours, it is introduced into a distillation column (Tray Type) to remove the solvent and when a particular viscosity of the molten mass is attained, it is withdrawn out of the distillation column by means of veir- jorew type pump.

There is solvent recovery unit attatched to the distillation column to recover the solvents is Butanol, Toluene & Xylene.

Cooling and Dehumidifying

The molten mass is sent to the cooling unit and at the same time it is dehumidified from its moisture content. The cooling is done to a temperature of 60°C before it enters the granulater.

Granulation

The molten mass cooled to 60°C is possed through the granulator (with cutting arrangement) to obtain desired sized granules.

Weighing, Filling and Packing

The granules are then weighed filled and packed by means of automatic weighing, filling and packing machine into 25 kgs. polythene packs, and stored and then sent for marketing.

PLANT ECONOMICS

Rated Plant Capacity	=	1.00 MT/Day
Land & Building (Land 210 sq.mt.)	=	Rs. 6,03,650.00

PLANT & MACHINERY

1. Extruder
2. Mixer
3. Grinder
4. Washing Machine
5. Cutter
6. Lab. Testing Equipment

FIXED CAPITAL

1. Land & Building	Rs.	6,03,650.00
2. Plant & Machinery	Rs.	2,15,000.00
3. Other Fixed Assets	Rs.	30,000.00
TOTAL	Rs.	8,48,650.00

RAW MATERIALS

1. Plastic Waste (All Category)
2. Packging Exp.

TOTAL WORKING CAPITAL/MONTH

1. Raw Material	Rs.	3,78,750.00
2. Salary & Wages	Rs.	13,310.00
3. Utilities & Overheads	Rs.	46,650.00
TOTAL	Rs.	4,38,710.00

TOTAL CAPITAL INVESTMENT

Total Fixed Capital	Rs.	8,48,650.00
Total Working Capital for 1 Month	Rs.	4,38,710.00
TOTAL	Rs.	12,87,360.00

TURN OVER/ANNUM

By selling 300 MT of plastic Granules	=	Rs.	63,00,000.00

PROFIT SALES RATIO = 12.60 %

RATE OF RETURN = 61.65 %

BREAK EVEN POINT (B.E.P) = 40.02 %

55

Cross Linked Polyethylene (XLPE) Compound for XLPE Cables

Cross Linked Poly Ethylene (XLPE) by Sioplas/Monosil method is famed by cross-linking mechanism of polyethylene by means of cross-linking/Grafting/curing catalyst in the presence of other agents viz; anti-oxidant etc. and this compounded product is used for XLPE cables which inturn are used as underground electric transmission and distribution cables in high tension lines.

Cross linked Poly Ethylene (XLPE) compound is used for XPLE Cables which are used as underground electric transmission and distribution cables in high tension lines in urban areas, in power projects and in large power-intensive industrial complexes.

Raw Material

For the manufacture of cross linked polyethylene (XLPE) compound for cables, The raw matarials are polyethylene, cross-linking/grafting/curing catalyst (Benzoyl Peroxide, etc), anti oxidant siloxane/silicone, colourants, etc.

MANUFACTURING PROCESS OF CROSS-LINKED POLYETHYLENE (XLPE) COMPOUND BY SIOPLAS/MONOSIL PROCESS SIOPLAS PROCESS

This is followed in two steps.

After the procurement of raw materials they are measured in requisite proportions as per the formulation.

In step I, 95 parts of the raw materials and in step II, the remaining 5 parts are used.

Step - 1

Polyethylene resin is melted in a stainless steel jacketed vessel and Grafting catalyst benzoyl peroxide is added and stirred well.

Benzoyl peroxide acts as a cross linking agent. To these contents requisite quantity of siloxane is added and the contents are again stirred well (Tumble Mix) for about 1/2-1 hour till a homogenous mass is obtained,

This tumble mix mass is then subjected to compounding extrusions (Chemical Process). For which compounding extruder is used for the process.

The extruder is initially heated electrically to the required primary temperature. Further heating is achieved by the mechanical work which is rendered thermoplastic by the shearing action of the screw and the adiabatic temperature rise due to compression.

The extruder essentially consist of a cylinder which is heated by electrical band heaters and in which the screw rotates. The screw is long and shallow. The feed and compression sections of the screw are formed by a gradual decrease in the root diameter of the screw to the end of the compression section with the result that the compound melt during its travel is compressed as well. At the end of the screw and between it and the die assembly is placed a breaker plate. This is a plain disc with a number of holes with a comical lead drilled through. To increase the back pressure wire gauges of 150 and 200 mesh are placed on the breaker plate, on the side of the screw. The wire gauge also acts as filter removing any extraneous contamination from the melt and also the unmelted bigger particles of compound melt from entering the die.

By the compound extrusion (chemical reaction), cross-linkable graft polymer granule, are fumed (95 Parts).

In step II, likewise, Polyethylene, curing catalyst viz; Benzoyl Peroxide, Anti-oxidant and colorant are all tumble mixed and then subjected to compounding extrusions (Simple mixing) leading to formation of master batch granules (5 Parts).

Subsequently, 95 parts of cross-linkable graft polymer granule, (from step I) and 5 parts of master batch granules (from Step II) are tumble mixed.

The final product is checked for quality, packed in suitable containers and despatched for marketing.

PLANT ECONOMICS

Rated Plant Capacity	=	30.00 MT./Day
Land & Building (Land 5000 sq.mts.)	Rs.	1,12,20,000.00

PLANT & MACHINERY

1. Mixer SS fitted with agitator & motor
2. Extruder for compounding of granules with all accessories
3. Material Handling Equipments
4. Storage Tanks
5. Pneumatic & Conveyor system
6. Lab Testing Equipments
7. Instrumentation and Process Eqpt.
8. D G Set
9. Misc.Equipments

FIXED CAPITAL

1. Land & Building	Rs.	1,12,20,000.00
2. Plant & Machinery	Rs.	1,50,00,000.00
3. Other Fixed Assets	Rs.	53,50,000.00
TOTAL	Rs.	3,15,70,000.00

RAW MATERIALS

1. Polyethylene
2. Siloxane/silicone
3. Grafting and curing catalyst(Benzoyl Peroxide)
4. Antioxidant viz; Butylated Hydroxy Anisole/Ditert-Butyl p-cresol
5. Colourants
6. Packing Material Viz;Tin Drums

TOTAL WORKING CAPITAL/MONTH

1. Raw Material	Rs. 6,04,25,000.00
2. Salary & Wages	Rs. 4,94,375.00
3. Utilities & Overheads	Rs. 4,88,000.00
TOTAL	Rs. 6,14,07,375.00

TOTAL CAPITAL INVESTMENT

Total Fixed Capital	Rs. 3,15,70,000.00
Total Working Capital for 1 Months	Rs. 6,14,07,375.00
TOTAL	Rs. 9,29,77,375.00

TURN OVER/ANNUM

By sale of XLPE Compounds 9000 MT.	Rs.78,30,00,000.00

PROFIT SALES RATIO = PROFIT / SALES X 100 = 3.90 %

RATE OF RETURN = OPERATING PROFIT / T.C.I X 100 = 32.83 %

BREAK EVEN POINT (B.E.P) = 39.95 %

56

Typical Processing Equipments

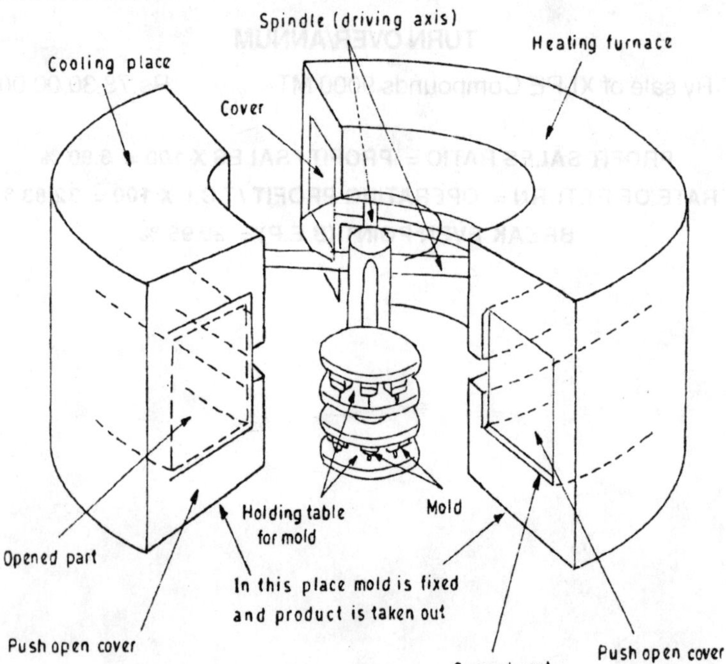

FIG. 15.1

MULTI-AXIS (4 AXES) VOTOMOULDING MACHINE

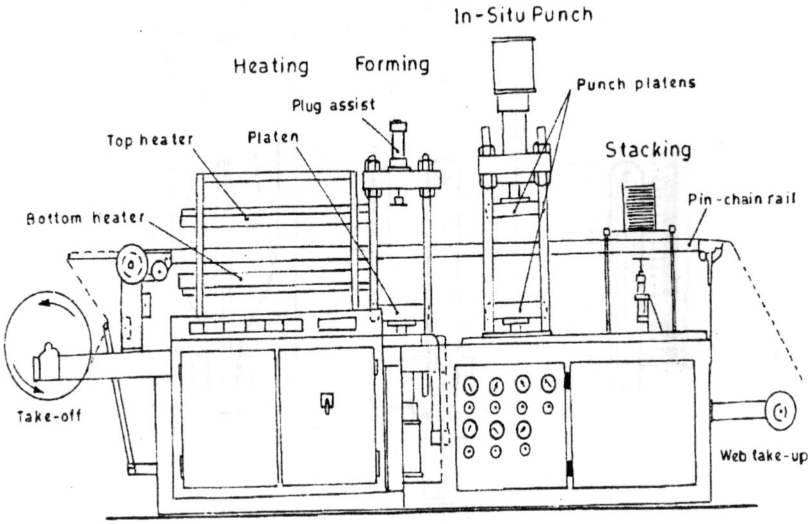

FIG. 15.2
THIN-GUAGE ROLL-FED THERMOFORMER (KIEFEL)

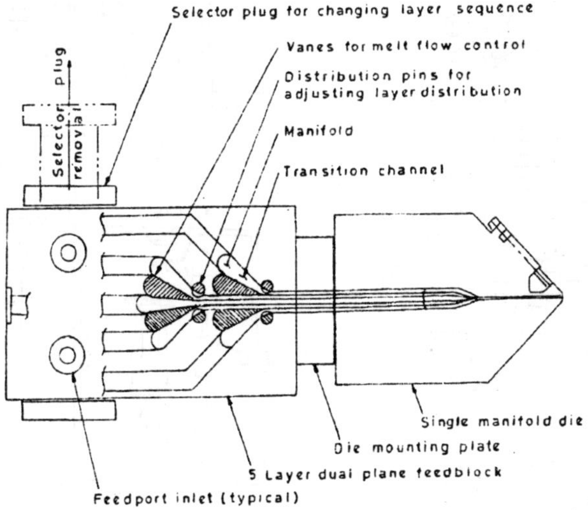

FIG. 15.3
FIVE LAYER CLOEREN FEEDBLOCK

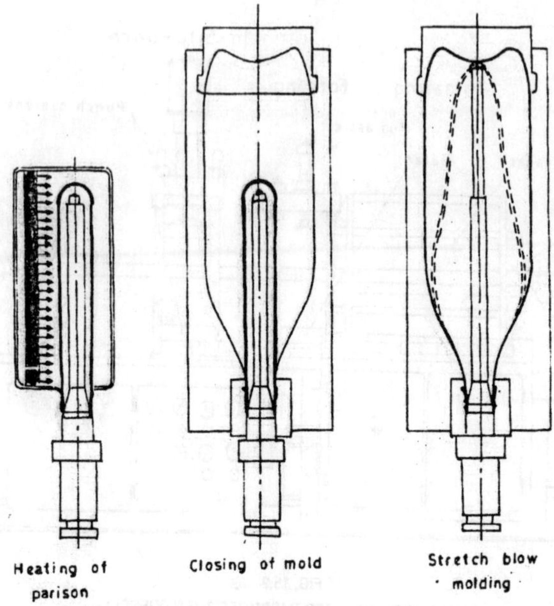

FIG. 15.4
BIAXIALLY STRETCH BLOW MOULDING OF COLD PARISON MADE BY INJECTION MOULDING

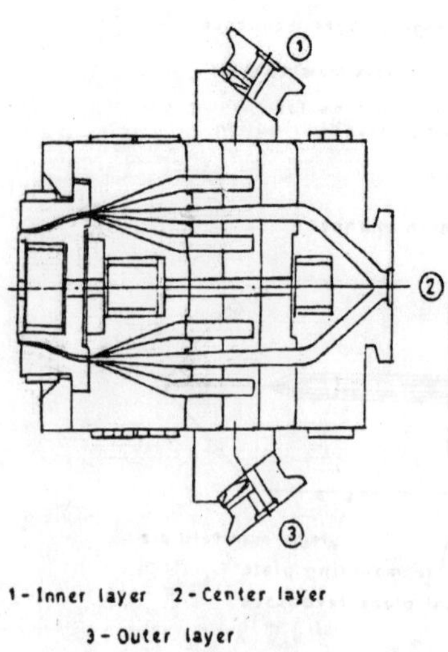

FIG. 15.5
CO-EXTRUSION DIE FOR 3-LAYER PVC PIPE

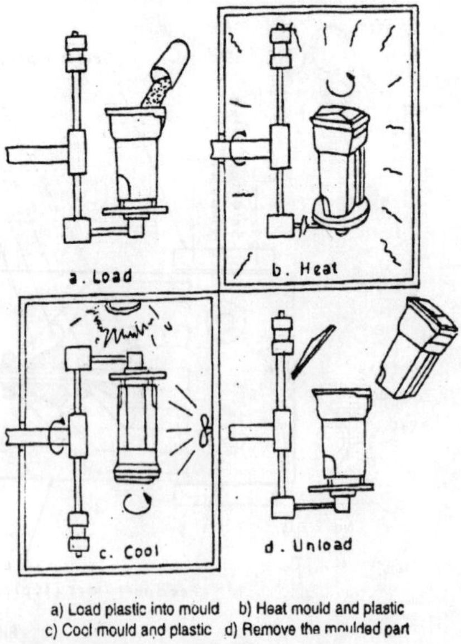

a) Load plastic into mould b) Heat mould and plastic
c) Cool mould and plastic d) Remove the moulded part

FIG. 15.6
FOUR STEPS OF ROTATIONAL MOULDING PROCESS

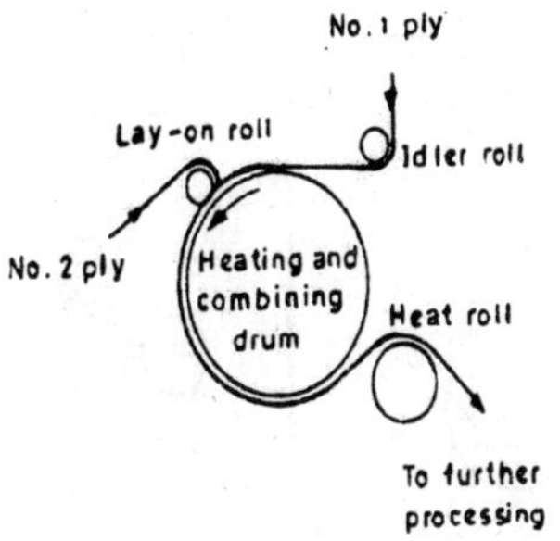

FIG. 15.7
TYPICAL TWO-PLY LAMINATION BY FUSION

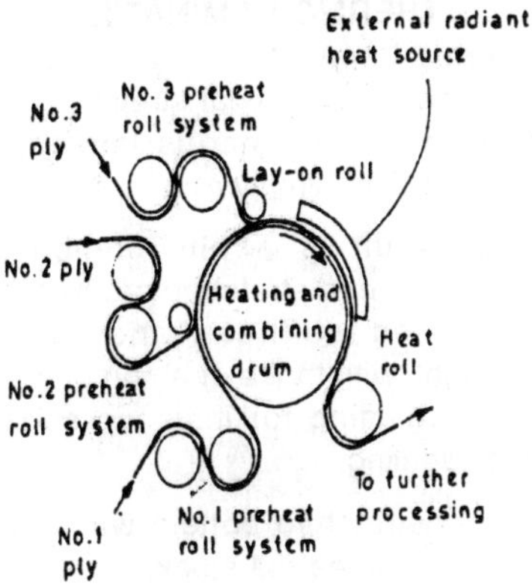

FIG. 15.8
THREE-PLY FUSION LAMINATION

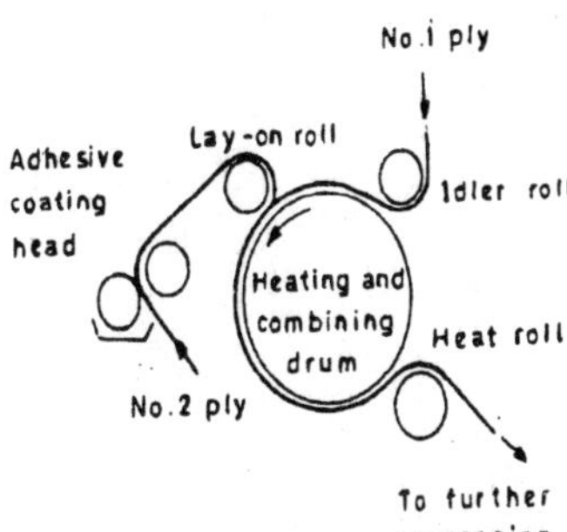

FIG. 15.9
LAMINATION BY WET COMBINING

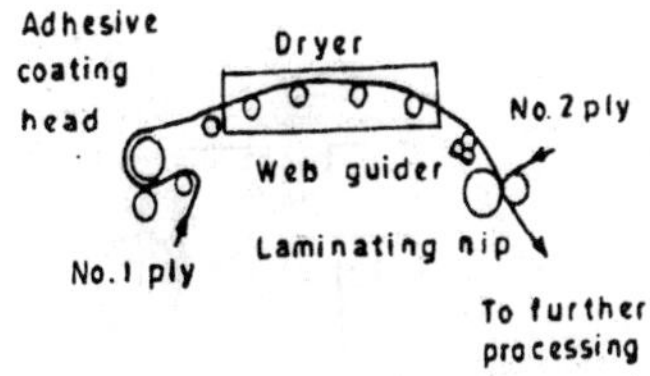

FIG. 15.10
LAMINATION BY WET COMBINING WHEN WATER OR SOLVENT IS PRESENT

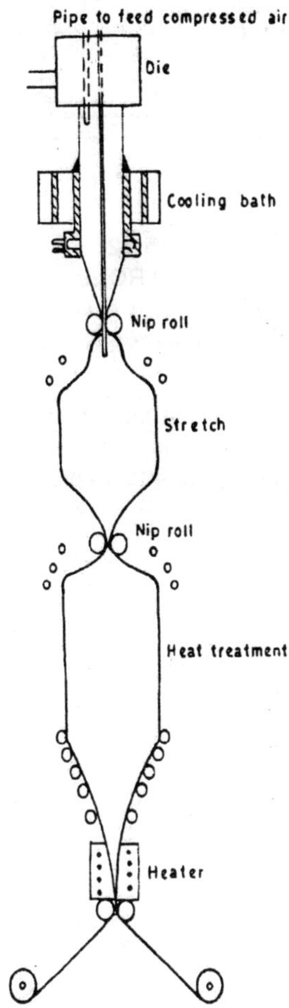

FIG. 15.11
APPARATUS FOR MANUFACTURING OF BIAXIALLY ORIENTED FILM (TUBULAR METHOD)

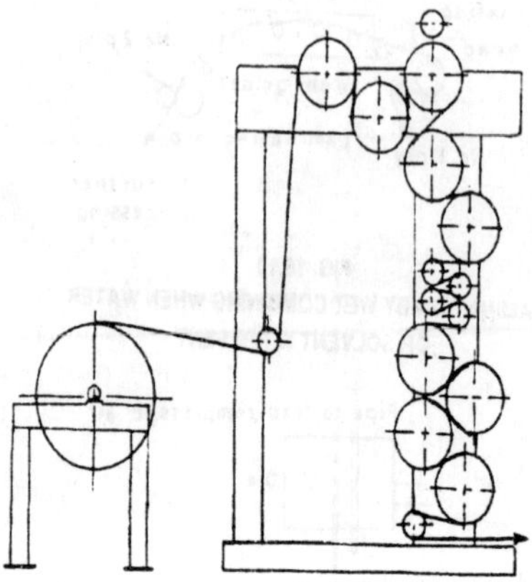

FIG. 15.12
ROLL TO ROLL

Roll to roll stretching is used on smaller size equipment for process development.

This way of off-line stretching is also used when films from various extrusion lines have to be processed.

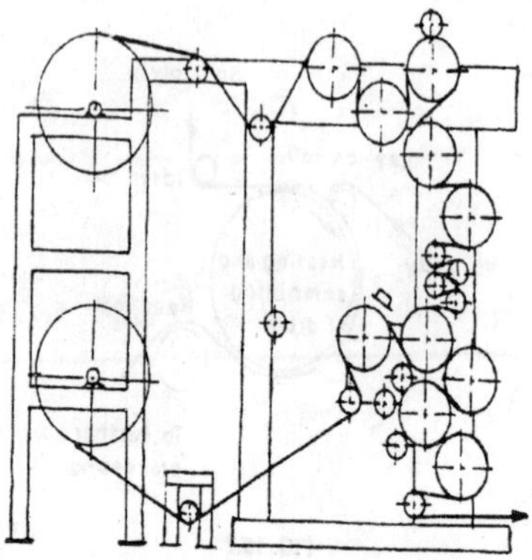

FIG. 15.13
THERMO-LAMINATING

Thermo-Laminating is a combined process of monoaxial stretching one film and simultaneous laminating another film, simply.

The result is a film combining properties of a stretched product, like increased stiffness and tensile strenght, with those of a non oriented film, providing for instance superb heat sealing.

The unstretched bottom web might also be printed roll stock.

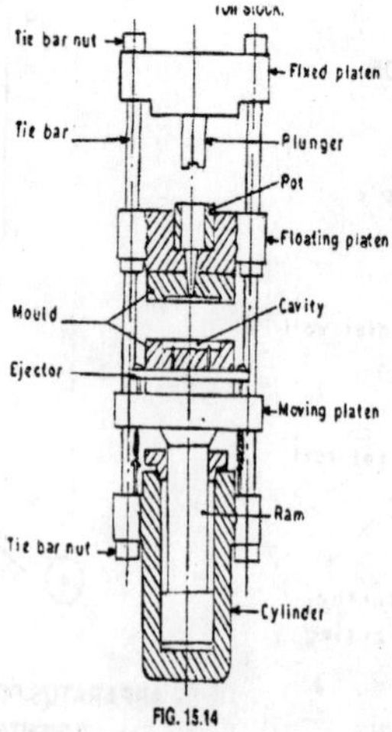

FIG. 15.14
POT TYPE (UP STROKE TYPE)

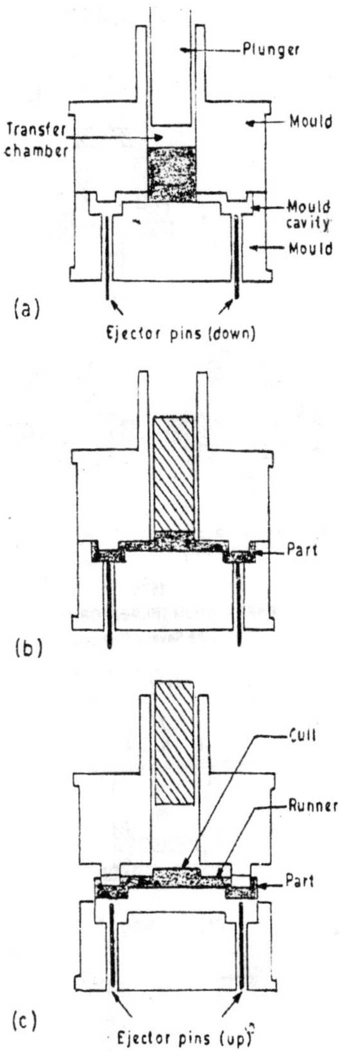

FIG. 15.15
COMPRESSION AND TRANSFER MOULDING PROCESS

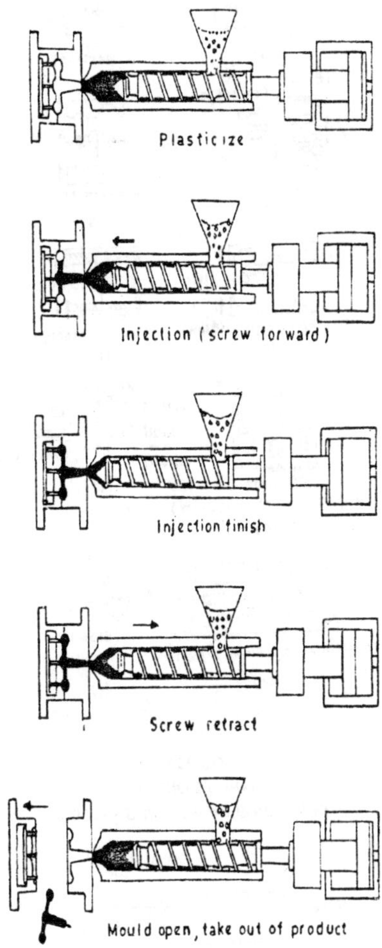

FIG. 15.16
INJECTION MOULDING PROCESS

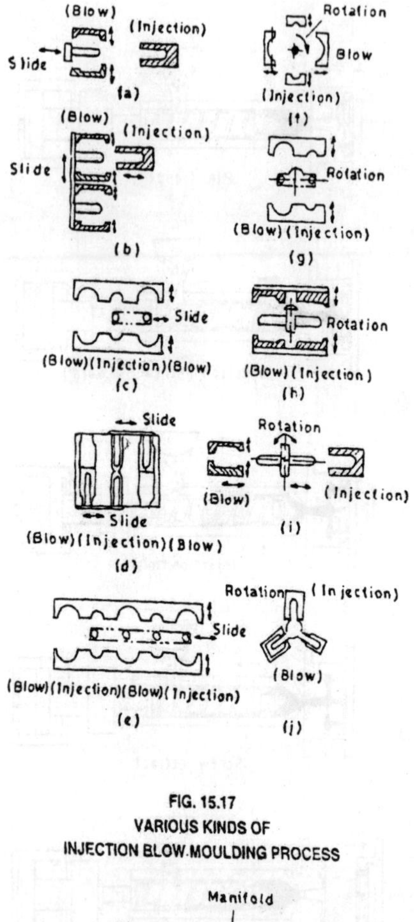

FIG. 15.17
VARIOUS KINDS OF
INJECTION BLOW MOULDING PROCESS

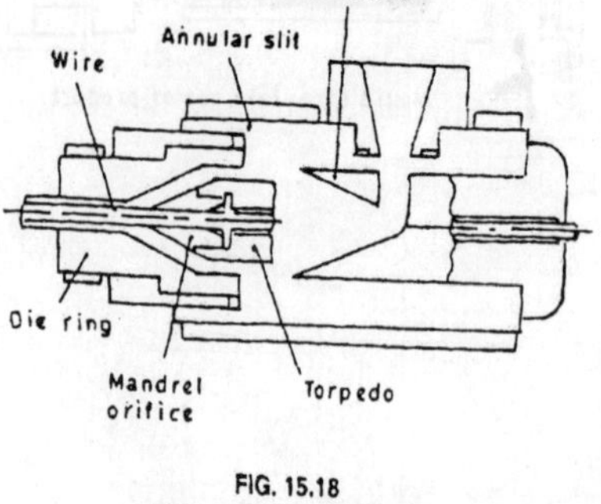

FIG. 15.18
WIRE COATING PROCESS

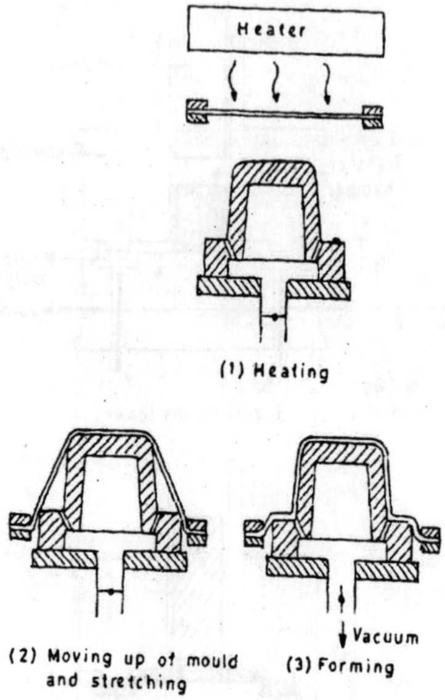

FIG. 15.19
DRAPE VACUUM THEMORFORMING
(One of the Several Methods)

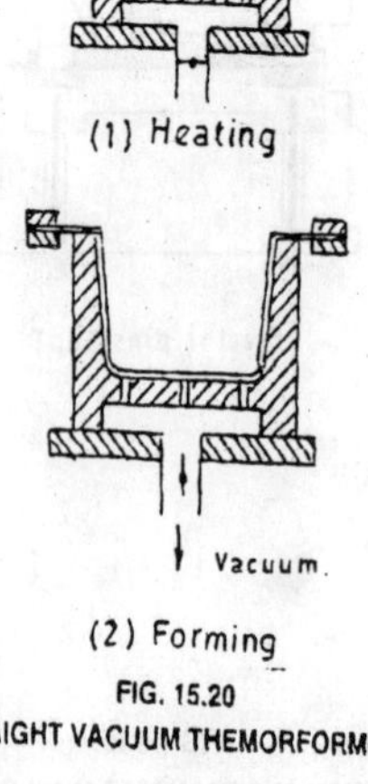

FIG. 15.20
STRAIGHT VACUUM THEMORFORMING

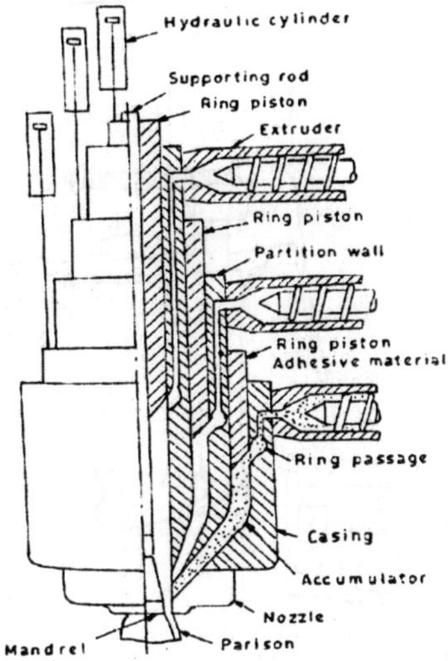

FIG. 15.21
CONSTRUCTION OF DIE FOR MULTI-LAYER BLOW MOULDING

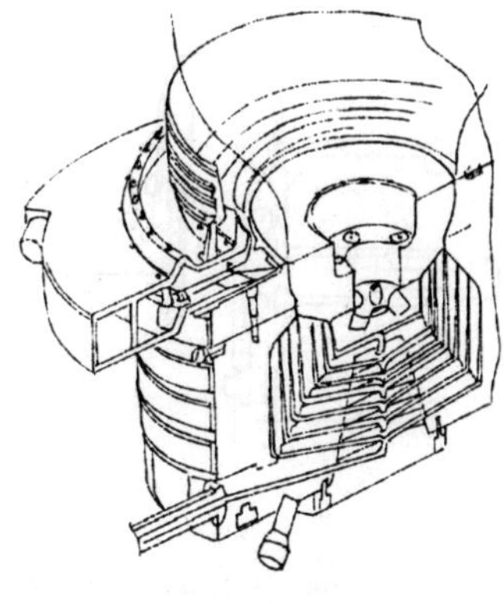

FIG. 15.23
7 LAYER OPTIFLOW BLOWN FILM DIE

Computer designed flow channels minimise polymer residence time in both oscillating and stationary Gloucester Dies. This virtually eliminates gel problems and speeds product changes. Gloucester's innovative taper lock self aligning design cuts innovative taper lock self aligning design cuts downtime by permitting simple die cleaning at the processor's plant. The easy to reach non-rotating dies minmise string-up and adjustment time.

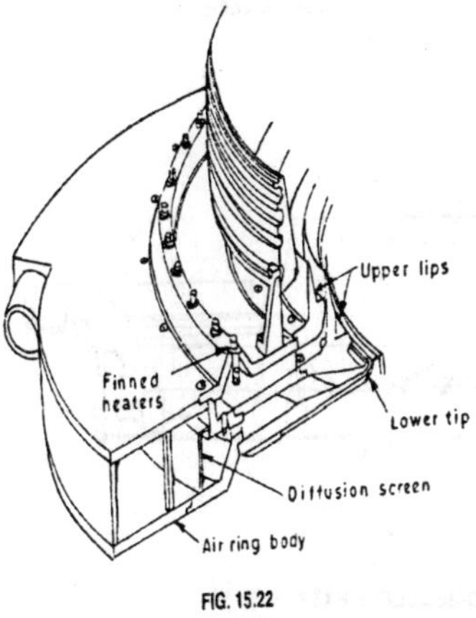

FIG. 15.22
AIR-RING

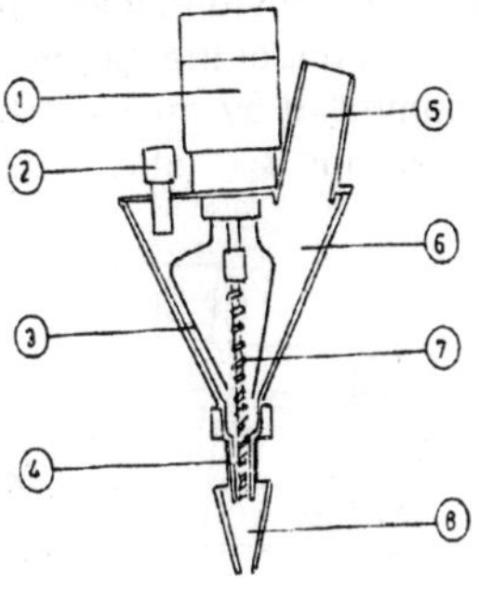

1. Drive mechanism 2. Level control 3. Stirrer
4. Filling tube 5. Product inlet 6. Hoppar
7. Filling screw 8. Discharge funnel

FIG. 15.24
FILLING SYSTEMS (AUGER FILLER)

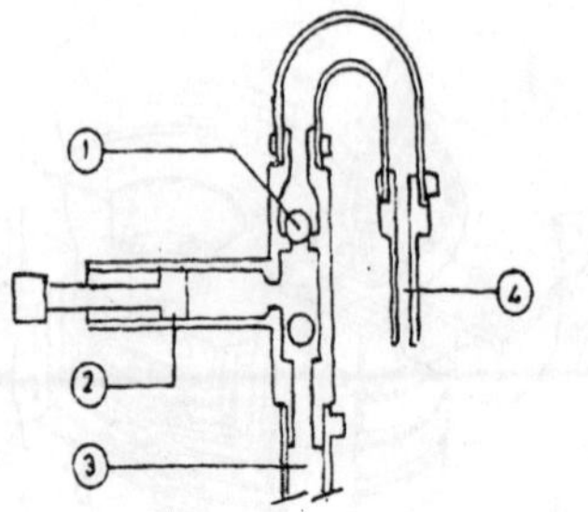

1. Ball valves 2. Filling piston 3. Inlet pipe 4. Outlet pipe

FIG. 15.25
FILLER FOR LIQUIDS

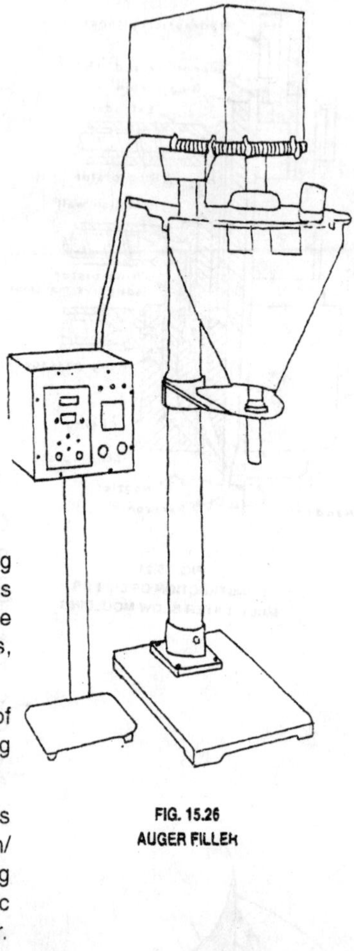

FIG. 15.26
AUGER FILLER

Auger Filler is a versatile powder filling machine for dosing free flowing as well as non free flowing powders, like Pharmaceutical powders, Ground spices, ground Coffee, Milk powders etc.

The machine operates on the principle of positive Displacement Screw operating under constant head.

The precisely designed Auger displaces the product through funnel into the pouch/ container held under the funnel. The filling cycle is controlled by an Electromagnetic Clutch/Brake unit & Photoelectric sensor.

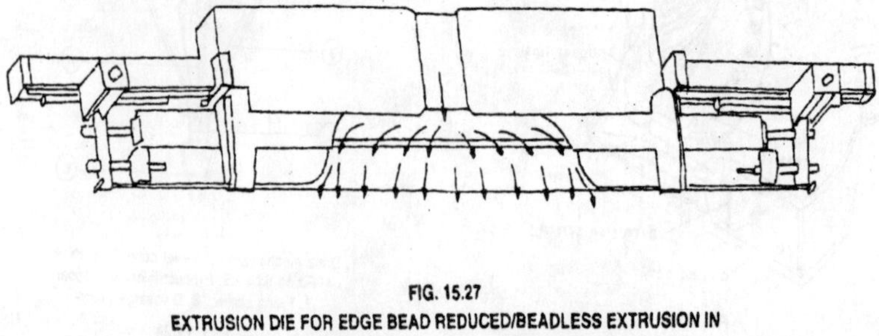

FIG. 15.27
EXTRUSION DIE FOR EDGE BEAD REDUCED/BEADLESS EXTRUSION IN THE EXTRUSION COATING AND LAMINATION PROCESSES

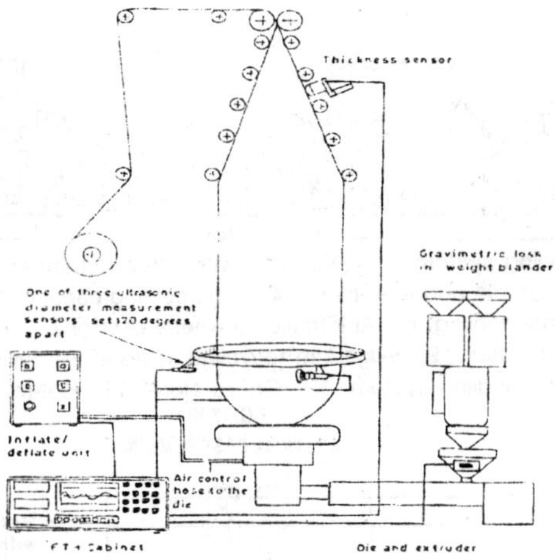

FIG. 15.28
INTEGRATED FILM CONTROL SYSTEM

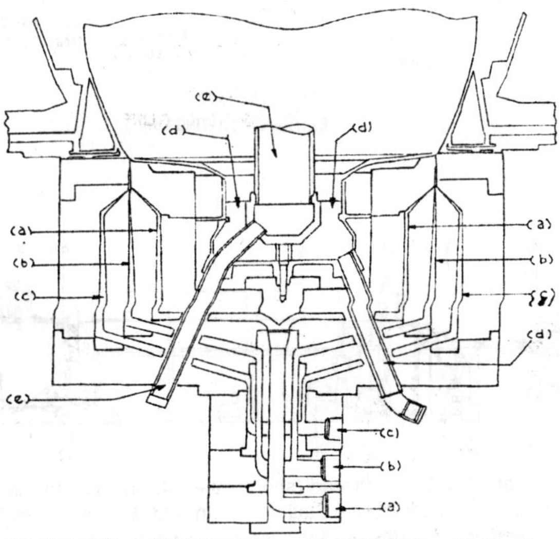

(a) INNER LAYER (b) MIDDLE LAYER (c) OUTER LAYER (d) AIR-INLET
(e) AIR-OUTLET

FIG. 15.29
A FIVE LAYER CO-EXTRUSION DIE HEAD

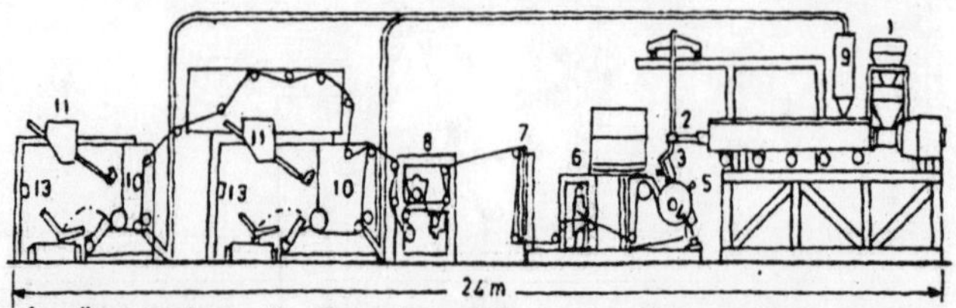

1. Gravimetric feeding system 2. Extruders with screen changes and adapters 3. Automatic extrusion die and feed-block 4. High cooling capacity chill roll 5. Blowing air knife for additional cooling 6. Automatic thickness control 7. Oscillating web-guide 8. Corona treatment station 9. Edge trim recycling system 10. Winding station 11. Automatic shaft handling system 12. Core's store 13. Hot-melt gluing station

FIG. 15.30

A TYPICAL CAST FILM LINE

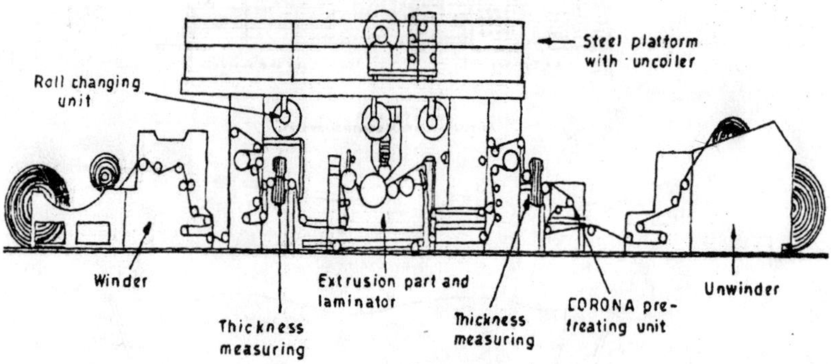

FIG. 15.31

EXTRUSION COATING LINE

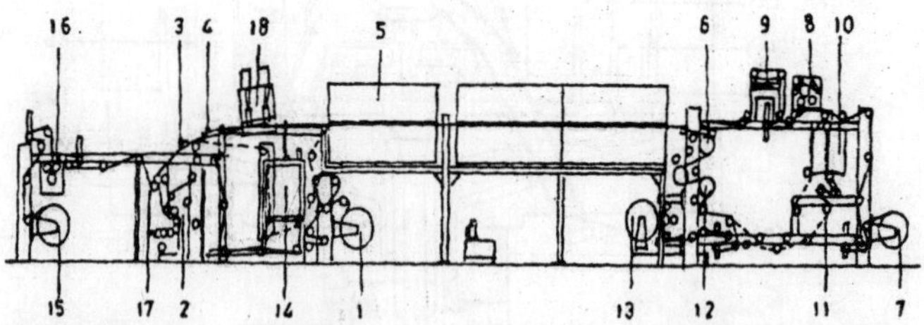

1. Unwind 2. Coating unit 3. Infrared (short wave) 4. Infrared (medium wave) 5. Floatation dryer 6. Dry laminating station 7. Unwind 8. Corona station 9. Edge guide unit 10. Remoistening device 11. Cooling cylinders 12. Cooling cylinders 13. Rewind 14. Election Beam unit 15. Unwind 16. Corona station 17. Wet laminating station 18. UV processor system

FIG. 15.32

A TYPICAL COATING AND LAMINATING LINE

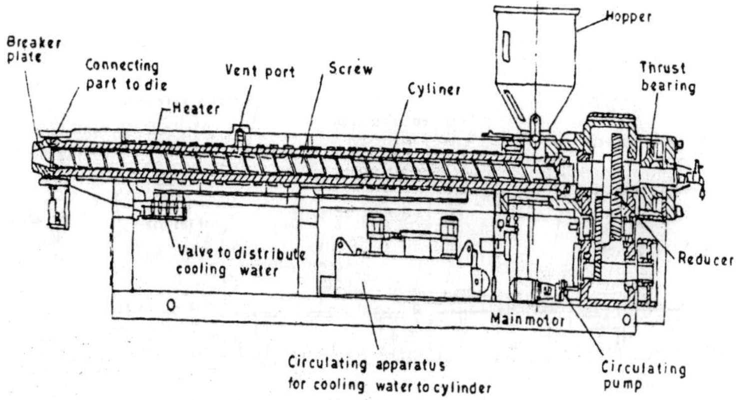

FIG. 15.33
SINGLE SCREW EXTRUDER (VENT TYPE)

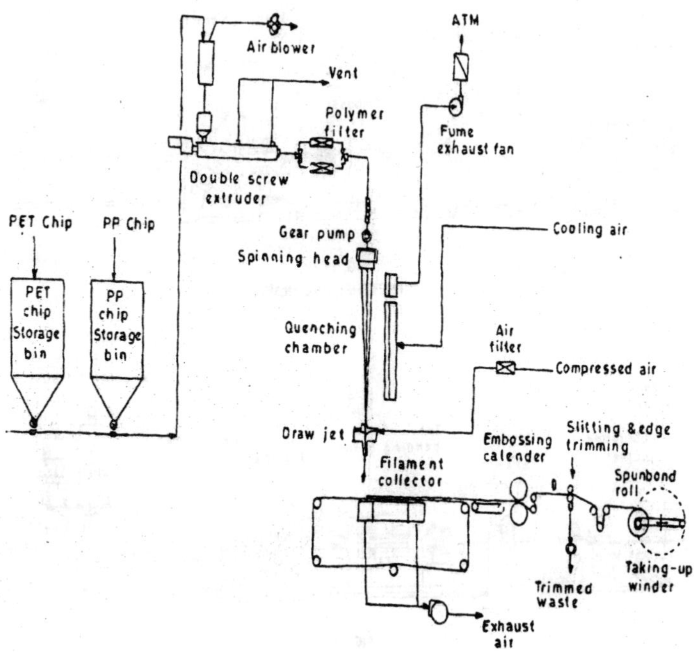

FIG. 15.34
PP & PET SPUNBOND PLANT (NON-WOVENS)

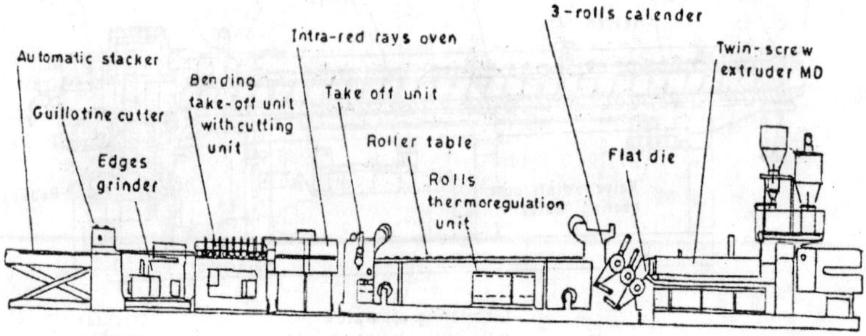

FIG. 15.35

CORRUGATED SHEET (PP)

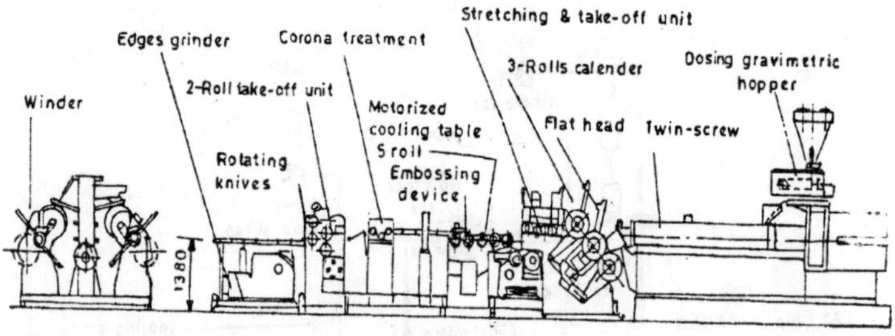

FIG. 15.36

STRETCHED PVC FILMS

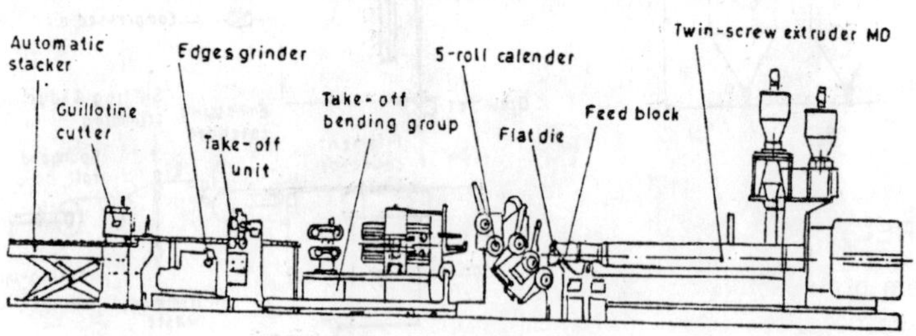

FIG. 15.37

EDGE BOARD PROFILES UNIT FOR PACKAGING

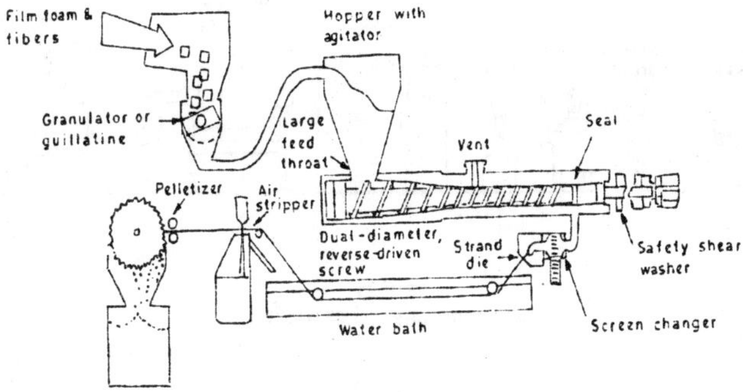

FIG. 15.38

EXTRUSION SYSTEM GEARED FOR RECLAIM

Flow low bulk density scrap, this system has dual-diameter screw driven from the discharge end. This allows 72 : 1 compression ratios and eliminates ram suffers. The extruder is available in outputs of 300-3,000 Lbs/Hr.

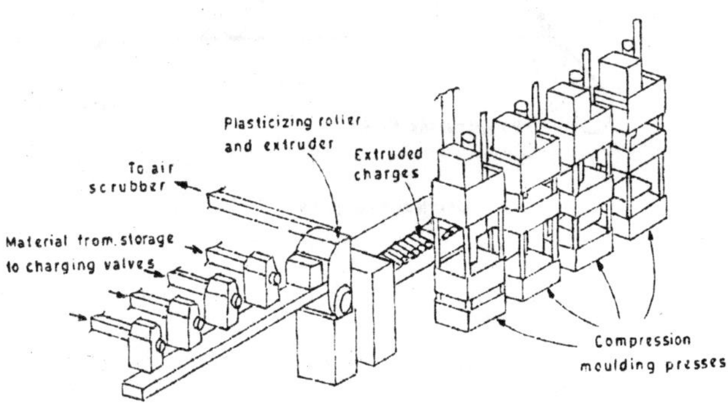

FIG. 15.39

RECYCLOPLAST PRODUCES SHEET USING 50% SCRAP

This system granulates commingled scrap and plasticates it with a 50% PE or PVC resin carrier. Continuously extruded charges are fed to compression moulding presses that produce sheet. This technology can be licensed through Innovative Plastics Products, Inc., Atlanta, Ga.

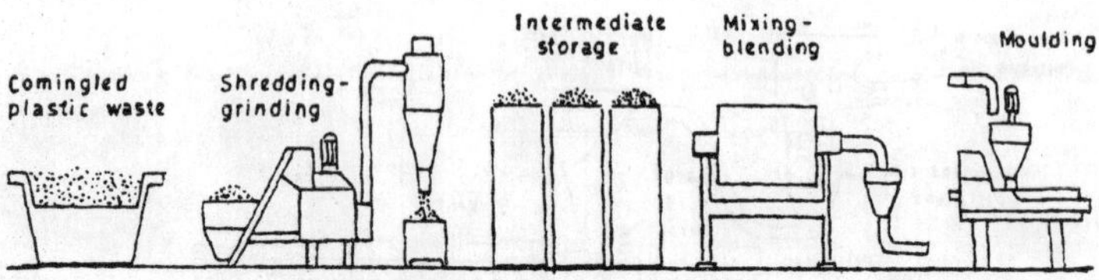

FIG. 15.40
RECYCLING OF PLASTICS WASTE

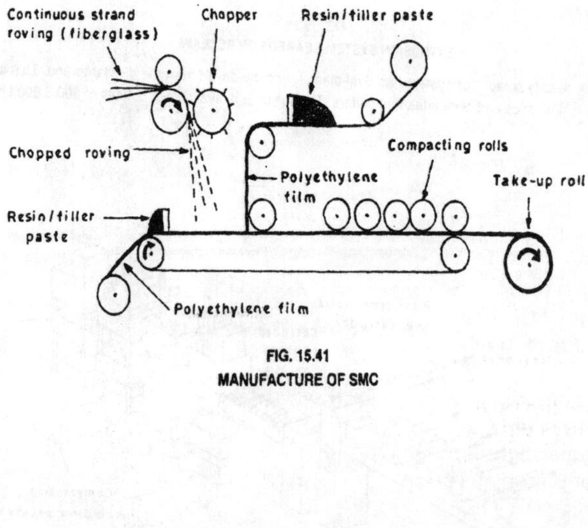

FIG. 15.41
MANUFACTURE OF SMC

57

Suppliers of Raw Materials

PLASTIC MANUFACTURING CHEMICALS

Carbon India
152-153, Ajmeri Gate
Delhi -110006
Tel :+ 91 (0)11 23236666
Fax : +91 (0)11 23237383

Demaco Polymers Ltd.
B-1/G-3, MCIE
Mathura Rd.
New Delhi -110044
Tel : + 91 (0) 11 26959424
Fax : + 91 (0) 11 26959112
E-mail:
demaco@ndf.vsnl.net.in

High Polymer Labs Ltd.
803, Vishal Bhavan, 95
Nehru Place
New Delhi -110019
Tel : + 91 (0) 11 26431522
Fax : + 91 (0) 11 26474350
E-mail: hpll@hpl-group.com

Hindustan Rasayan Pvt. Ltd.
705, Vikram Towers
Rajendra Palace
New Delhi -110008
Tel : + 91 (0) 11 25750215
Fax : + 91 (0) 11 25789698

Industrial Coatings & Adhesives
A-679/A, Shastri Ngr.
Delhi -110052
Tel : + 91 (0) 11 23551487

J K Paper Co.
19, Gagan Vihar
Trans Yamuna
Delhi -110051
Tel : + 91 (0) 11 25717773

KLJ Polymers & Chemicals Ltd.
KLJ House, 63, Rama Marg
Najafgarh Rd.
New Delhi -110015
Tel : + 91 (0) 11 25459706
Fax : + 91 (0) 11 25459709
E-mail : klj/delhi@dartmail.
dartnet.com

Rubber-Chem Corp.
9, Rehman Mkt.
Sadar Bazar
Delhi -110006
Tel : + 91 (0) 11 27771174
Fax : + 91 (0) 11 23552019
E-mail:
rubber@ndf.vsnl.net.in

Sungrace Polychem Pvt. Ltd.
3/123, Karan Gali
Vishwas Ngr., Shahdara
Delhi -110032
Tel : + 91 (0) 11 22202206
Fax : + 91 (0) 11 22448279

Yin Enterprises
B-14, Inder Puri
New Delhi -110012
Tel : + 91 (0) 11 25738562
Fax : + 91 (0) 11 25726682

Ajay Plastic Chem Inds
Shed No.C1/1901-20
Phase-IV, GIDC Est.
Vapi, Gujarat-396195
Tel : + 91 (0) 260 24341

Apex Petrochemicals Ltd.
2nd Flr., Gaekwad Chmbrs.
Nr. Gendigate
Vadodara, Gujarat-390017
Tel : + 91 (0) 265 471505

Cosmos Chemicals
760, GIDC Est.
Makarpura
Vadodara, Gujarat-390010
Tel : + 91 (0) 265 642064

Gujarat State Fertilizers & Chemicals Ltd.
Polymers Unit, P.O. Petrofils
Vadodara, Gujarat-391347
Tel : + 91 (0) 265 373341
Fax : + 91 (0) 265 372794
E-mail: gafcpu@gsfcho.
xeebdq.xeemail.com

Shreeji Chem
Plot No. 2210, Nr. Post Office
GIDC Est.
Ankleshwar,
Gujarat-393002
Tel : + 91 (0) 2646 52476

BASF India Ltd.
Rhone-Poulenc House
S K Ahire Marg
Mumbai
Maharashtra-400025
Tel : + 91 (0) 22 24930703
Fax : + 91 (0) 22 24941612

Dow Corning Singapore Pte. Ltd.
India Liaison Office
1102, Maker Chmbr. V
221, Nariman Point
Mumbai
Maharashtra-400021
Tel : + 91 (0) 22 22820194
Fax : + 91 (0) 22 22828110

High Grade Industries
904, Bldg. No. 13
Indra Darshan, Phase-I
Shree Swami Samarth Ngr.,
Off Link Rd., Oshiwara
Mumbai
Maharashtra-400053
Tel : + 91 (0) 22 26396233
Fax : + 91 (0) 22 26244082

Hindustan Organic Chemicals Ltd.
A Govt. Of India Enterprise
Harchandrai House
81, Maharshi Karve Marg
Mumbai
Maharashtra-400002
Tel : + 91 (0) 22 22014118
Fax : + 91 (0) 22 22059533
E-mail:
hoclras@bom3.vsnl.net.in

Indofil Chemicals Co.
Industrial Products Divn.
Nirlon House
Dr. Annie Besant Rd.
Worli, Mumbai,
Maharashtra-400025
Tel : + 91 (0) 22 24937391
Fax : + 91 (0) 22 24935667
E-mail:
indofil@giasbm01.vsnl.net.in

Indu Nissan Oxo Chemical Industries Ltd.
Maker Bhavan No. 2
18, New Marine Lines
Mumbai
Maharashtra-400020
Tel : + 91 (0) 22 22051938
Fax : + 91 (0) 22 22060633
E-mail:
inocil@bom3.vsnl.net.in

Kesar Petroproducts Ltd.
7, Nagin Mahal, 2nd Flr., 82
Veer Nariman Rd.
Churchgate
Mumbai
Maharashtra-400020
Tel : + 91 (0) 22 22040181
Fax : + 91 (0) 22 22046206
E-mail:
global.power@gems.vsnl.net.in

Super Chlorides Pvt. Ltd.
74/78, Prashant Chmbrs.
Bhandari St.
Mumbai
Maharashtra-400003
Tel : + 91 (0) 22 23447650
Fax : + 91 (0) 22 23413935
E-mail: chawala@vsnl.com

Eddy Chemical Pvt. Ltd.
F 43-44, Phase-VII
Focal Point
Ludhiana, Punjab-141010
Tel : + 91 (0) 161 674963
Fax : + 91 (0) 161 675307

Mittal Udyog
F-474, Phase-II
Indraprastha Indl. Area
Kota, Rajasthan-324005
Tel : + 91 (0) 744 424397
Fax : + 91 (0) 744 500748
E-mail:
info@metalsoaps.com

Thirumalai Chemicals Ltd.
Lakshmi Towers, 1st Flr.
48, N Usman Rd., T Ngr.
Chennai
Tamil Nadu-600017
Tel : + 91 (0) 44 8255289
Fax : + 91 (0) 44 8257637

Uniroyal Chemicals Ltd.
Plot No. 4,
R & D Defence Cly.
Sikh Village
Secunderabad
Andhra Pradesh-500009
Tel : + 91 (0) 40 7847482
Fax : + 91 (0) 40 7811343
E-mail:
bvrajul@hd1.vsnl.net.in

Vinyl Chemicals Pvt. Ltd.
6-3-252/37/G/6
3rd. Flr., Erramanzil Cly.
Hyderabad
Andhra Pradesh-500082
Tel : + 91 (0) 40 3318971
Fax : + 91 (0) 40 3316735
E-mail:
vinyl@cityonline.com

MASTERBATCHES

Eles Vinyl
D 26, Phase-IV Extn.
Jeedimetla
Hyderabad
Andhra Pradesh-500018
Tel : + 91 (0) 40 3092311

Master Blends (I)
Plot No. 35, IDA
Kattedan
Hyderabad
Andhra Pradesh-500077
Tel : + 91 (0) 40 4015009
Fax : + 91 (0) 40 4742418
E-mail:
madimpex@hd1.vsnl.net.in

Sunplast Industries
Plot No. D-84/6
IDA, Block B, Autonagar
Visakhapatnam
Andhra Pradesh-530012
Tel : + 91 (0) 891 516218
Fax : + 91 (0) 891 567126

Unitech Plastics Pvt. Ltd.
M-49, Adityapur Indl. Area,
Phase-IV, Gamaria
Jamshedpur, Bihar-832108
Tel : + 91 (0) 657 200142
Fax : + 91 (0) 657 200042
E-mail:
uniplast@satyam.net.in

Prayag Polymers Pvt. Ltd.
2468, Prayag House
Nalwa St.,
B/h Imperial Cinema
Paharganj
New Delhi-110055
Tel : + 91 (0) 11 23623772
Fax : + 91 (0) 11 23543773
E-mail:
prayag@del2.vsnl.net.in

Aalekh Polymers Pvt. Ltd.
8/30, Indl. Area, Kirti Ngr.
New Delhi-110015
Tel : + 91 (0) 11 25195193
Fax : + 91 (0) 11 25195195

Allied Industries
A-2/3, Phase-I
Mayapuri Indl. Area
New Delhi-110064
Tel : + 91 (0) 11 25144619
Fax : + 91 (0) 11 25140705
E-mail: allied@vsnl.com

Alok Industries
Phase-II, C 65/1
Okhla Indl. Est.
New Delhi-110020
Tel : + 91 (0) 11 26832222
Fax : + 91 (0) 11 26927392
E-mail:
alokb99@mantraonline.com

B L & Sons Ltd.
604, Indra Prakash, 21
Barakhamba Rd.
New Delhi-110001
Tel : + 91 (0) 11 23755263
Fax : + 91 (0) 11 23755264

Gazal Industries
Gazal House, 50/15
Swarn Park, Mundka
New Delhi-110041
Tel : + 91 (0) 11 5472815
Fax : + 91 (0) 11 25183108

Indian Friction Material Engg. Co.
F-186/52, Dilshad Cly.
Delhi-110095
Tel : + 91 (0) 11 22127363
Fax : + 91 (0) 11 22118986
E-mail: fricmart@bol.net.in

J K Plastics
WZ-2A, Hind Ngr.
Chowkhandi Rd., Tilak Ngr.
New Delhi-110018
Tel : + 91 (0) 11 25100543
Fax : + 91 (0) 11 25434886
E-mail:
jkplastics@mantraonline.com

J K Polycolours
WZ-1, Hind Ngr.
Chowkhandi Rd., Tilak Ngr.
New Delhi-110018
Tel : + 91 (0) 11 25100543
Fax : + 91 (0) 11 25434886
E-mail:
jkplastics@mantraonline.com

KLJ Group
KLJ House, 63
Rama Marg, Najafgarh Rd.
New Delhi-110015
Tel : + 91 (0) 11 25459706
Fax : + 91 (0) 11 25436264
E-mail: delhi@kljindia.com

Neetu Plastics Pvt. Ltd.
149, Rajdhani Enclave
Pitampura
Delhii-110034
Tel : + 91 (0) 11 7180130
E-mail:
ajay@neetuplastic.com

Nitto Polymers Pvt. Ltd.
RZ-22A, Mahavir Enclave
Palam Rd.
New Delhi-110045
Tel : + 91 (0) 11 25034806
Fax : + 91 (0) 11 25034221

Polyblends India Pvt. Ltd.
C-30, 1st Flr.
Opp. Fire Stn.,
Mansarovar Garden
Kirti Ngr.
New Delhi-110015
Tel : + 91 (0) 11 25939269
Fax : + 91 (0) 11 25930923
E-mail:
polyblends@hotmail.com

Prayag Polytech Pvt. Ltd.
2468, Prayag House
Nalwa St.,
B/h Imperial Cinema
Paharganj
New Delhi-110055
Tel : + 91 (0) 11 23523773
Fax : + 91 (0) 11 23543773

S S Polymers
K-54, Udyog Ngr.
Indl. Area, Rohtak Rd.
New Delhi-110041
Tel : + 91 (0) 11 25472125
Fax : + 91 (0) 11 25476962

Advance Colourants Ltd.
123/B 1, GIDC, Phase-I,
Opp. Torrent Lab Vatva
Ahmedabad
Gujarat-382445
Tel : + 91 (0) 79 5831444

Anand Polymers
3016, GIDC, Phase-I
Vatva
Ahmedabad
Gujarat-380023
Tel : + 91 (0) 79 8592371
Fax : + 91 (0) 79 5830471

Colo Plast
Plot No. 194 & 195, GIDC
Vithal Udyognagar
Gujarat-388121
Tel : + 91 (0) 2692 36142
Fax : + 91 (0) 2692 36070

Daman Plastic Pvt. Ltd.
Shed No.19
Modern Ind.Est.
Zari Causeway Rd.
Kachigam
Daman, Gujarat-396210
India
Tel : + 91 (0) 236 52671

Kalpana Industries Ltd.
653/1/43
Comnath Co-op. Ind. Soc. Ltd.
Dabhel
Daman, Gujarat-396210
Tel : + 91 (0) 236 52682
Fax : + 91 (0) 236 52137

Plastichemix Industries
6, Kirti Towers, Tilak Rd.
Vadodara, Gujarat-390001
Tel : + 91 (0) 265 424241
Fax : + 91 (0) 265 422129
E-mail:
plastichemix@satyam.net.in

Prism Finance Ltd.
1, 2nd Flr.
Fountain Place Cmplx.
Nr. Mithakhali Six Rds.
Ahmedabad
Gujarat-380015
Tel : + 91 (0) 79 6421239
Fax : + 91 (0) 79 6401121

Swastik Enterprises
Old CDA Bldg., 15-16
Basement, Jawahar Marg
Indore
Madhya Pradesh-452007
Tel : + 91 (0) 731 285090
Fax : + 91 (0) 731 369327

ALA Chemicals Ltd.
Mahalaxmi Chmbrs.,
3rd Flr., 22
Bhulabhai Desai Rd.
Mumbai
Maharashtra-400026
Tel : + 91 (0) 22 24920280
Fax : + 91 (0) 22 22950447
E-mail:
scanand@giasm01.vsnl.net.in

Bajaj Plastics Ltd.
D-1, MIDC, Hingna
Nagpur
Maharashtra-440028
Tel : + 91 (0) 712 36512
Fax : + 91 (0) 712 36510
E-mail:
ngp@nagpur.dot.net.in

Bankim Industries
28, Ramgopal Indl. Est.
Dr. R P Rd., Mulund (W)
Mumbai
Maharashtra-400080
Tel : + 91 (0) 22 25618509
Fax : + 91 (0) 22 25644828

Bhulani Plastics
1/1, Perumal Mudali St.
Kondithope
Chennai
Tamil Nadu-600079
Tel : + 91 (0) 44 5265908

Madras Polymoulds
108, Royapettah High Rd.
Mylapore
Chennai
Tamil Nadu-600004
Tel : + 91 (0) 44 4993775
Fax : + 91 (0) 44 4990908
E-mail:
mdspoly@md3.vsnl.net.in

Uttam Plastopack
34/1, Wall Tax Rd.
Chennai
Tamil Nadu-600079
Tel : + 91 (0) 44 5221937
Fax : + 91 (0) 44 5385947

Gajindra's
D-14, Sect. 2
Noida
Uttar Pradesh-201301
Tel : + 91 (0) 120 4529046

Newgen Speciality Plastics
C-451, Sect. 10
Noida
Uttar Pradesh-201301
Tel : + 91 (0) 120 4547853
Fax : + 91 (0) 120 4456440
E-mail:
newgenpoly@vsnl.com

Vivek Polychem Pvt. Ltd.
H-44,45, Site-I
Panki Indl. Area
Kanpur
Uttar Pradesh-208022
Tel : + 91 (0) 512 691170
Fax : + 91 (0) 512 692731

Engel India Machines & Tools Ltd.
Polymer Divn.1,
Taratala Rd.
Kolkata
West Bengal-700053
Tel : + 91 (0) 33 4787233

Vibgyor Masterbatches Pvt. Ltd.
594, Urla Indl. Est.
Raipur
Chhattisgarh-493221
Tel : + 91 (0) 771 323355
Fax : + 91 (0) 771 326974
E-mail:
vibgyor@bom6.vsnl.net.in

GRANULES : POLYPROPYLENE (PP)

AMI Plastic
5, Ajay Co-op. Indl. Est.
Opp. Dena Bank, Nagarvel
Hanuman Rd., Rakhial
Ahmedabad
Gujarat-380023
TEL : + 91 (0) 79 2741123

Indian Petrochemicals Corporation Ltd.
A Govt. Of India Undertaking
P.O. Petrochemicals
Vadodara, Gujarat-391346
Tel : + 91 (0) 265 373144
Fax : + 91 (0) 265 373163
E-mail:
pac@wilnetonline.net

Mansi Plastics Pvt. Ltd.
A2/25, GIDC
Somnath Indl. Est.
Daman, Gujarat-396210
Tel : + 91 (0) 236 52725

P I Polymers A Divn. of P.I. Industries Ltd.
237, GIDC
Panoli, Gujarat-394115
Tel : + 91 (0) 6471 72105
Fax : + 91 (0) 6471 72313
E-mail:
mgupt.piilpnl@narmada.net.in

Synergy Multibase Ltd.
103, Synergy House
Subhanpura
Vadodara, Gujarat-390007
Tel : + 91 (0) 265 382078
Fax : + 91 (0) 265 382077

TIPCO Plastic Corp.
Plot No. 115/2
B/h Bhagwati Foundry
GIDC
Odhav, Gujarat-382415
Tel : + 91 (0) 79 2871267

Vishal Plastic Industries
C-1/B, 1943/C
GIDC Est.
Halol, Gujarat-389350
Tel : + 91 (0) 2676 21556

Hunny Enterprises
Shop No. 40-41
2H, Park Mkt., NIT
Faridabad, Haryana-121001
Tel : + 91 (0) 129 5411696

Machino-Montell India Ltd.
Plot # 2, Sect. 33, N.H. 8
Delhi-Jodhpur Highway
Gurgaon, Haryana-122001
Tel : + 91 (0) 124 371902
Fax : + 91 (0) 124 371904
E-mail: mmi@vsnl.com

S K Plastic Works
9, Phase-II, Sipcot
Hosur, Karnataka-635109
Tel: + 91 (0) 4344 60054
E-mail : skpw@hotmail.com

Chhattisgarh Plastics Pvt. Ltd.
M-6, Farishta Cmplx.
Raipur
Madhya Pradesh-492001
Tel : + 91 (0) 771 535509

Borouge Pte. Ltd.
101/102, A N Chmbrs.
Turner Rd., Bandra (W)
Mumbai
Maharashtra-400050
Tel : + 91 (0) 22 26431702
Fax : + 91 (0) 22 26431705

Hame Agencies Pvt. Ltd.
Udyog Bhavan, 4th Flr.
Walchand Hirachand Marg
Mumbai
Maharashtra-400001
Tel : + 91 (0) 22 23523994
Fax : + 91 (0) 22 22619044
E-mail:
hame@bom3.vsnl.net.in

Rajiv Plastic Industries
House No. 490-B, XXIII
Gali No. O, Janakpuri
Ludhiana, Punjab-141003
Tel : + 91 (0) 161 650470

Gugaya Plastics
Kalipatty Post
Thiruchergodu Salem
Main Rd., Attayampatty
Namakkal
Tamil Nadu-637501
Tel : + 91 (0) 4288 38294

Iqbal Plastics
118, Pulianthope High Rd.
Chennai
Tamil Nadu-600012
Tel : + 91 (0) 44 5322036

Haldia Petrochemicals Ltd.
1, Auckland Place
Kolkata
West Bengal-700017
Tel : + 91 (0) 33 2812611
Fax : + 91 (0) 33 2471361

B L & Sons Ltd.
604, Indra Prakash, 21
Barakhamba Rd.
New Delhi-110001
Tel : + 91 (0) 11 23755263
Fax : + 91 (0) 11 23755264

GRANULES : POLYVINYLCHLORIDE (PVC)

Unitech Plastics Pvt. Ltd.
M-49, Adityapur Indl. Area,
Phase-IV, Gamaria
Jamshedpur, Bihar-832108
Tel : + 91 (0) 657 200142
Fax : + 91 (0) 657 200042
E-mail:
uniplast@satyam.net.in

Arihant Plastic India
340A/20, Gali No. 1A
G T Rd., Friends Cly.
Indl. Area, Shahdara
Delhi-110095
Tel : + 91 (0) 11 2144399
Fax : + 91 (0) 11 2154399
E-mail: pragati1@vsnl.com

Ess Ess Enterprises
487/18, School Rd.
Peera Garhi
New Delhi-110041
Tel : + 91 (0) 11 5572702

KLJ Group
KLJ House, 63, Rama Marg
Najafgarh Rd.
New Delhi-110015
Tel : + 91 (0) 11 5459706
Fax : + 91 (0) 11 5436264
E-mail: delhi@kljindia.com

Jyoti Polyvinyl Ltd.
Haripreet Apts, 2nd Flr.,
33-B, Anandnagar Soc.
Productivity Rd.
Vadodara, Gujarat-390007
Tel : + 91 (0) 265 333953
Fax : + 91 (0) 265 335954

M M Plast (I)
39, Kamal Sahakari
Audyogik Vasahat Ltd.
Nr. Sukhramnagar
Uttam Dairy Rd., Rakhial
Ahmedabad
Gujarat-380023
Tel : + 91 (0) 79 2730060

Sai Shakti Polymers
2A/2B, Tirupati Indl. Est.
Opp. Rabbani, Somnath Rd.
Daman, Gujarat-396210
Tel : + 91 (0) 236 253270
Fax : + 91 (0) 236 256273

Pee Kay Polymer
354, Friends Cly.
Rly. Rd., Pravesh Marg
Faridabad, Haryana-121002
Tel : + 91 (0) 129 5268644
Fax : + 91 (0) 129 5279778

Avinyl Polymers Pvt. Ltd.
65/1, 2nd Flr., Mission Rd.
Bangalore
Karnataka-560027
Tel : + 91 (0) 80 2221761
Fax : + 91 (0) 80 2237018

Sankhla Industries
147, 9th Main, Phase-III
Peenya Indl. Area
Bangalore
Karnataka-560058
Tel : + 91 (0) 80 8395260
Fax : + 91 (0) 80 8394200
E-mail:
sankhla@giasbg01.vsnl.net.in

DCW Ltd.
3rd Flr., Nirmal
Nariman Point
Mumbai
Maharashtra-400021
Tel : + 91 (0) 22 22871914
Fax : + 91 (0) 22 22028838
E-mail: ho@dcwltd.com

Dubreuil Pressman Ltd.
505, Raheja Centre
Nariman Point
Mumbai
Maharashtra-400002
Tel : + 91 (0) 22 22821969
Fax : + 91 (0) 22 22042496

Finolex Group
26/27, Mumbai-Pune Rd.
Pune, Maharashtra-411018
Tel : + 91 (0) 20 7475963
Fax : + 91 (0) 20 7472224
E-mail : finolex@vsnl.com

K K Plastic
30, Unique Indl. Est.
Dr. Rajendra Prassad Rd.
Mulund (W)
Mumbai
Maharashtra-400080
Tel : + 91 (0) 22 25600799
Fax : + 91 (0) 22 25642577
E-mail:
kkgroup.chandan@gems.vsnl.net.in

Reliance Industries Ltd.
3rd Flr, Maker Chmbrs. IV,
222, Nariman Point
Mumbai
Maharashtra-400021
Tel : + 91 (0) 22 22831633
Fax : + 91 (0) 22 22042268

Desana Polymers Pvt. Ltd.
G-29, RIICO Indl. Area
Nokha
Bikaner, Rajasthan-334801
Tel : + 91 (0) 151 825312
E-mail : ruppoly@vsnl.com

Gajindra's
D-14, Sect. 2
Noida
Uttar Pradesh-201301
Tel : + 91 (0) 120 4529046

Sanco Plastics Pvt. Ltd.
3/1/23 Site-4
Indl. Area, Sahibabad
Ghaziabad
Uttar Pradesh-201010
Tel : + 91 (0) 120 4773747
Fax : +91 (0) 120 4773949
E-mail : sanco@bol.net.in

Khatuja Cable Co.
Indl. Area, Bhanpuri
Raipur
Chhattisgarh-493221
Tel : + 91 (0) 771 562234
Fax : + 91 (0) 771 562600

COLOURS : PLASTIC OR MOULDING COMPOUND

Devarsons Industries Ltd.
443, GIDC Indl. Est.
Nr. Water Tank
Odhav, Gujarat-382415
Tel : + 91 (0) 79 2871092
E-mail: devarson.coldyes@gnahd.global.net.in

Orient Paint Industries
Plot No. 4
St. No. 4, New Rohtak Rd.
Anand Parbat Indl. Area
New Delhi-110005
Tel : + 91 (0) 11 5725526

Shree Nathji Dyestuffs
R-60/1, Model Town-III
Delhi -110009
Tel : + 91 (0) 11 27133896
Fax : + 91 (0) 11 27444651
E-mail: jatin@satyam.net.in

Devarsons Industries Ltd.
443, GIDC Indl. Est.
Nr. Water Tank
Odhav, Gujarat-382415
Tel : + 91 (0) 79 2871092
E-mail: devarson.coldyes@gnahd.global.net.in

Electro Polychem Ltd.
AG 26
Aisa Lynwood, No. 26, EVK
Sampath Salai, Vepery
Chennai
Tamil Nadu-600007
Tel : + 91 (0) 44 5386369

Kromatik & Insulants Pvt. Ltd.
D-8, Indl. Est.
Mogappier (W)
Chennai
Tamil Nadu-600058
Tel : + 91 (0) 44 6243432
Fax : + 91 (0) 44 6359220
E-mail:
ratna@md3.vsnl.net.in

Tamilnadu Pigments Pvt. Ltd.
A-6/3, SIPCOT Indl. Cmplx.
Cuddalore
Tamil Nadu-607005
Tel : + 91 (0) 4142 39565
Fax : + 91 (0) 4142 39525
E-mail:
tnblue@md3.vsnl.net.in

PLASTIC INKS

Kinnari Printing Technologies Pvt. Ltd.
P.O. Box No. 17821,
14, Aroto House, 3rd Flr.,
Above Pooja Blood Bank
P K Rd., Mulund (W)
Mumbai
Maharashtra-400080
Tel : + 91 (0) 22 25907156
Fax : + 91 (0) 22 25681284
E-mail:
kinnari@bom3.vsnl.net.in

Rainbow Ink & Varnish Manufacturing Company Ltd.
133-C, Vakola, Santacruz (E), Mumbai
Maharashtra-400055
Tel : + 91 (0) 22 26183974
Fax : + 91 (0) 22 26116704
E-mail:
rainboink@bom3.vsnl.net.in

Numerators India
Mendu Compound,
3/6 Marris Rd., Aligarh
Uttar Pradesh-202002
Tel : + 91 (0) 571 509056
Fax : + 91 (0) 571 502156

HDPE POLYMERS

Avantika Packaging Pvt. Ltd.
B-262, Phase-I, Okhla Indl. Area, New Delhi-110020
Tel : + 91 (0) 11 26816032
Fax : + 91 (0) 11 26812139
E-mail:
ravimeattle@hotmail.com

Vishal Plastic Industries
C-1/B, 1943/C, GIDC Est.
Halol, Gujarat-389350
Tel : + 91 (0) 2676 21556

Hunny Enterprises
Shop No. 40-41
2H, Park Mkt., NIT
Faridabad, Haryana-121001
Tel : + 91 (0) 129 5411696

S K Plastic Works
9, Phase-II, Sipcot
Hosur, Karnataka-635109
Tel : + 91 (0) 4344 60054
E-mail: skpw@hotmail.com

Rupam Industries
Nr. Telegram Office, 54
Nandlal Pura, Indore,
Madhya Pradesh-452004
Tel : + 91 (0) 731 531959
Fax : + 91 (0) 731 430575

Borouge Pte. Ltd.
101/102, A N Chmbrs.
Turner Rd., Bandra (W)
Mumbai
Maharashtra-400050
Tel : + 91 (0) 22 26431702
Fax : + 91 (0) 22 26431705

Josh Plastics
No. 216, Sathy Rd.,
Sivanandha Puram
Saravnampatty P.O.
Coimbatore
Tamil Nadu-641035
Tel : + 91 (0) 422 866347

DSM EPP Surlon India Ltd.
54/11, Site-IV
Indl. Area, Sahibabad
Uttar Pradesh-201010
Tel : + 91 (0) 120 4772546
Fax : + 91 (0) 120 4775764
E-mail:
skumar@del2.vsnl.net.in

Hind Polymers
P-22, Swallow Lane
Kolkata
West Bengal-700001
Tel : + 91 (0) 33 2425953
Fax : + 91 (0) 33 2426182
E-mail: mslhp@vsnl.com

PLASTIC MOULDING COMPOUNDS

Prayag Polytech Pvt. Ltd.
2468, Prayag House
Nalwa St.,
B/h Imperial Cinema
Paharganj
New Delhi-110055
Tel : + 91 (0) 11 23523773
Fax : + 91 (0) 11 23543773

Takkar Industries
A-95, DDA Sheds, Phase-II
Okhla Indl. Area
New Delhi-110020
Tel : + 91 (0) 11 26840412
Fax : + 91 (0) 11 26311442

Vinyl Products
9/51, Indl. Area, Kirti Ngr.
Delhi -110015
Tel : + 91 (0) 11 25933173
Fax : + 91 (0) 11 25458142
E-mail:
ashish-gupta@vsnl.com

Riviera Polymers Pvt. Ltd.
203, N R Hse.
Opp. Popular Hse.
Ashram Rd., Ahmedabad
Gujarat-380009
Tel : + 91 (0) 79 7544055
Fax : + 91 (0) 79 7541347

Rutuj Plastwel
601, Galav Chmbrs.
Nr. Sardar Patel Statue
Sayajigunj
Vadodara, Gujarat-390005
Tel : + 91 (0) 265 362673
Fax : + 91 (0) 265 363393

Sai Shakti Polymers
2A/2B, Tirupati Indl. Est.
Opp. Rabbani, Somnath Rd.
Daman, Gujarat-396210
Tel : + 91 (0) 236 253270
Fax : + 91 (0) 236 256273

Nero Plast Pvt. Ltd.
307, Sect. 24
Faridabad, Haryana-121005
Tel : + 91 (0) 129 5230051
Fax : + 91 (0) 129 5234788

Super Engineers
82, Indl. Est., Ambala Cantt.
Haryana-133001
Tel : + 91 (0) 171 652156

Advance Extrusion Industries
A-24, Piramal Indl. Est.
S V Rd., Goregaon (W)
Mumbai
Maharashtra-400062
Tel : + 91 (0) 22 8745732

Classic Polymers & Resins
4, Dev Darshan, 424
Mugal Lane, Mahim (W)
Mumbai
Maharashtra-400016
Tel : + 91 (0) 22 24465251
Fax : + 91 (0) 22 24454371
E-mail:
tandonll@hotmail.com

Neeljyot Plastics
13-8, New Empire Indl. Est.
Kondivita Lane
Andheri (E), Mumbai,
Maharashtra-400059
Tel : + 91 (0) 22 28386370
Fax : + 91 (0) 22 28379255
E-mail:
neeljyot@bom5.vsnl.net.in

Romit Resins Pvt. Ltd.
Plot No. 25, Comm. Bldg.
Panvel Co-op. Hsg. Society
Bawan Bunglow, Panvel
Maharashtra-410206
Tel : + 91 (0) 21546-7465272
Fax : + 91 (0) 21546
7455654

Bhulani Plastics
1/1, Perumal Mudali St.
Kondithope
Chennai
Tamil Nadu-600079
Tel : + 91 (0) 44 5265908

Jay K FRP Pvt. Ltd.
B-23, Sect. 7
Noida
Uttar Pradesh-201301
Tel : + 91 (0) 120 4522549
Fax : + 91 (0) 120 4553478
E-mail: jkfrp@vsnl.com

Vibgyor Masterbatches Pvt. Ltd.
594, Urla Indl. Est.
Raipur
Chhattisgarh-493221
Tel : + 91 (0) 771 323355
Fax : + 91 (0) 771 326974
E-mail:
vibgyor@bom6.vsnl.net.in

58

Suppliers of Plant & Machineries

PLASTIC BAG MACHINERY

Hikon H K Industries
3/23, Kirti Ngr. Indl. Area
New Delhi-110015
Tel : + 91 (0) 11 25410553
Fax : + 91 (0) 11 25122481
E-mail: hicon@bol.net.in

Mamata Machinery Pvt. Ltd.
5/1/1A, Phase-I, GIDC
Ahmedabad
Gujarat-382445
Tel : + 91 (0) 79 5832023
Fax : + 91 (0) 79 5832026
E-mail:
mmpl@ad1.vsnl.net.inwww.mamata.com

Jartolia Engg. Works
MCF/B-61
Nr. Bohra Public School
East Chawla Cly.
Ballabhgarh
Haryana-121004
Tel : + 91 (0) 129 5245265

Kalimata Plastic Machinery Manufacturer Pvt. Ltd.
A-5, 3rd Stage, Peenya Indl. Est., Bangalore
Karnataka-560058
Tel : + 91 (0) 80 8394699
Fax : + 91 (0) 80 8392917
E-mai l: kalimata@vsnl.com

Sai Machine Tools Pvt. Ltd.
Plot No. 23-D, Sect. A
Sanwer Rd., Indore
Madhya Pradesh-452015
Tel : + 91 (0) 731 722436
Fax : + 91 (0) 731 721831
E-mail:
saimachine@yahoo.com

Ruchika Pack Industries
J-10, Ansa Indl. Est.
Sakivihar Rd., Sakinaka
Mumbai
Maharashtra-400072
Tel : + 91 (0) 22 28527220
Fax: + 91 (0) 22 28522426
E-mail:
pragatif@bom5.vsnl.net.in

Wave Industries
101A, Rizvi Mahal
Waterfield Rd., Bandra (W)
Mumbai
Maharashtra-400050
Tel : + 91 (0) 22 26435301
Fax : + 91 (0) 22 26454861
E-mail:
wave@bom5.vsnl.net.in

Uniplast & Metal Industries
805-R, Indl. Area-B
Ludhiana, Punjab-141003
Tel : + 91 (0) 161 534433
Fax : + 91 (0) 161 493790

Great Cheran Engg.
482-A, Palghat Rd.
Coimbatore
Tamil Nadu-641008
Tel : + 91 (0) 422 822492
Fax : + 91 (0) 422 823459

PLASTIC COEXTRUSION MACHINERY

Kemtech International Ltd.
A-125, Shivalik
Malviya Ngr. P.O.
New Delhi-110017
Tel : + 91 (0) 11 26682346
Fax : + 91 (0) 11 26684589
E-mail: kemtech@vsnl.com

S S Mechanical Engineers Pvt. Ltd.
WZ-106, Rajouri Garden
Extn. New Delhi-110027
Tel : + 91 (0) 11 25458082
Fax : + 91 (0) 11 25121130
E-mail:
ssmech@ndf.vsnl.net.in

Shaheen Engg. Works
1780, Kalan Mahal
Nr. Pataudi House
Daryaganj
New Delhi-110002
Tel : + 91 (0) 11 23274628

Technico Industrial Corporation Pvt. Ltd.
C-47/7, Chouhan Banger
Gali No. 11, New Seelampur
Delhi-110053
Tel : + 91 (0) 11 22263409
Fax : + 91 (0) 11 23274623

Mamata Machinery Pvt. Ltd.
5/1/1A, Phase-I, GIDC
AhmedabadGujarat-382445
Tel : + 91 (0) 79 5832023
Fax : + 91 (0) 79 5832026
E-mail:
mmpl@ad1.vsnl.net.in

Innsale Teknik
926/A, GIDC, Makarpura
Vadodara, Gujarat-390010
Tel : + 91 (0) 265 2641078
Fax : + 91 (0) 265 2647363
E-mail: intek@india.com

J P Industries
1701, GIDC, Ankleshwar
Gujarat-393002
Tel : + 91 (0) 2646 51083
Fax : + 91 (0) 2646 50196
E-mail:
jpondank@egujarat.net

Konark Plastic Machinery Mfrs.
5, Africawala Est., B/h
Chakudia Mahadev
Opp. Comet House
Rakhial, Ahmedabad
Gujarat-380023
Tel : + 91 (0) 79 2741262
Fax : + 91 (0) 79 2744409
E-mail: sales@konarkplast
icmachinery.com

Mamata Brampton Engg. Pvt. Ltd.
53, Madhuban
Nr. Madalpur Underbridge
Ellisbridge, Ahmedabad
Gujarat-380006
Tel : + 91 (0) 79 440331
Fax : + 91 (0) 79 6421324

Remica Plastic Machinery Manufacturers
2/AB, Sardar Patel Indl. Est.,
Shahwadi, Narol
Ahmedabad
Gujarat-382405
Tel : + 91 (0) 79 5712741
Fax : + 91 (0) 79 5894234
E-mail:
remica@ad1.vsnl.net.in

DGP Windsor India Ltd.
Shah Indl. Est.
'C' Bldg., 1st Flr.
Saki Vihar Rd., Mumbai
Maharashtra-400072
Tel : + 91 (0) 22 28575897
Fax : + 91 (0) 22 28573109
E-mail:
marketing@dgpcorp.sril.in

Boolani Engg. Corp.
Prabhadevi Indl. Est.,
402 V S Marg, Mumbai
Maharashtra-400025
Tel : + 91 (0) 22 24302826
Fax : + 91 (0) 22 24229875
E-mail : plastic@vsnl.com

Machinecraft
5, Nav-Bhavna, 422
V S Marg, Prabhadevi
Mumbai
Maharashtra-400025
Tel : + 91 (0) 22 24227189
Fax : + 91 (0) 22 24221633
E-mail:
mcraft@bom5.vsnl.net.in

Wonderpack Industries Pvt. Ltd.
321, T V Indl. Est.
S K Ahire Marg
Worli,Mumbai
Maharashtra-400025
Tel : + 91 (0) 22 24949580
Fax : + 91 (0) 22 24938796
E-mail:
wonder@bom3.vsnl.net.in

PLASTIC COMPOUNDING MACHINERY

A P Industries
6/13, Indl. Area, Kirti Ngr.
New Delhi-110015
Tel : + 91 (0) 11 25930439
Fax : + 91 (0) 11 25195509
E-mail: ikon@hotmail.com

Shiv Mechanical Works
A-142, Nr. Tool Room
Training Centre
Wazirpur Indl. Area
Delhi-110052
Tel : + 91 (0) 11 27142142

Apex Engineers
Plot No. 1716, Phase-III,
GIDC, Vatva, Ahmedabad
Gujarat-382445
Tel : + 91 (0) 79 5830989
Fax : + 91 (0) 79 5830989

Innsale Teknik
926/A, GIDC, Makarpura
Vadodara, Gujarat-390010
Tel : + 91 (0) 265 641078
Fax : + 91 (0) 265 647363
E-mail: intek@india.com

Spark Engg.
4510, Phase-V
B/h Indo German Tool Room
GIDC Est
Vatva, Gujarat-382445
Tel : + 91 (0) 79 5836243
Fax : + 91 (0) 79 5840191
E-mail: sparkin@icenet.net

Suresh Engg. Works
14B, Kalyan Vishranti Grah
South Tukoganj, Indore
Madhya Pradesh-452001
Te : + 91 (0) 731 529155
Fax : + 91 (0) 731 527872
E-mail:
suresen@bom4.vsnl.net.in

DGP Windsor India Ltd.
Shah Indl. Est.
'C' Bldg., 1st Flr.,
Saki Vihar Rd., Mumbai
Maharashtra-400072
Tel : + 91 (0) 22 8575897
Fax : + 91 (0) 22 8573109
E-mail:
marketing@dgpcorp.sril.in

Pimco Machines Pvt. Ltd.
A/28, Nanddham Est.
Marol Maroshi Rd.
Andheri (E), Mumbai,
Maharashtra-400059
Tel : + 91 (0) 22 28597175
Fax : + 91 (0) 22 28500351
E-mail:
pimco@bom5.vsnl.net.in

SIK Engg. Enterprises
D-24, Indl. Area, Phase-I
SAS Ngr.
Mohali, Punjab-160055
Tel : + 91 (0) 172 675128

PLASTIC COMPOUNDING & MIXING EQUIPMENT

Bry-Air (Asia) Pvt. Ltd.
20, Rajpur Rd, Delhi-110054
Tel : + 91 (0) 11 23912800
Fax : + 91 (0) 11 23915127
E-mail:
enquire@pahwa.comwww.
bryair.com

H K Industries
3/23, Indl. Area, Kirti Ngr.
New Delhi-110015
Tel : + 91 (0) 11 25432993
Fax : + 91 (0) 11 25122481
E-mail: hikon@bol.net.in

Jogindra Engg. Works
70, Rama Rd.
New Delhi-110015
Tel : + 91 (0) 11 25442112
Fax : + 91 (0) 11 25453836
E-mail:
jogindra@ndf.vsnl.net.in

Remica Plastic Machinery Manufacturers
2/AB,Sardar Patel Indl. Est.,
Shahwadi, Narol
Ahmedabad
Gujarat-382405
Tel : + 91 (0) 79 5712741
Fax : + 91 (0) 79 5894234
E-mail:
remica@ad1.vsnl.net.in

Spark Engg.
4510, Phase-V
B/h Indo German Tool Room, GIDC Est.
Vatva, Gujarat-382445
Tel : + 91 (0) 79 5836243
Fax : + 91 (0) 79 5840191
E-mail: sparkin@icenet.net

Suresh Engg. Works
14B, Kalyan Vishranti Grah
South Tukoganj, Indore
Madhya Pradesh-452001
Tel : + 91 (0) 731 529155
Fax : + 91 (0) 731 527872
E-mail:
suresen@bom4.vsnl.net.in

Bainite Machines
C-10, Nand Dham Indl. Est.
Agnishaman Dal Marg,
Marol, Andheri (E), Mumbai
Maharashtra-400059
Tel : + 91 (0) 22 28505910
Fax : + 91 (0) 22 28500465
E-mail:
bainite@bom8.vsnl.net.in

Glow Industries
32, B/h Automatic Co.
Wagle Indl. Est., Thane
Maharashtra-400604
Tel : + 91 (0) 22 25328511
Fax : + 91 (0) 22 25327660
E-mail: info@glowplast.com

Malik Engineers
Unit 1, Shailesh Indl. Est.
No. 1, Navghar
Vasai Rd. (E), Pune,
Maharashtra-401210
Tel : + 91 (0) 20 8839751
Fax : + 91 (0) 20 8830751
E-mail:
malik@malikengg.com

PLASTIC CUTTING CUTTERS & CUTTING TOOLS (MAKING TOOLING)

Paras Engg. Co.
Plot No. C-20/3
MIDC Indl. Area, Taloja
Navi Mumbai
Maharashtra-410208
Tel : + 91 (0) 22 27411212
Fax : + 91 (0) 22 27411211
E-mail:
svshah@satyam.net.in

Millman Tools India
12, DSIDC
Wazirpur Indl. Cmplx.
Delhi-110052
Tel : + 91 (0) 11 27219708

Paras Engg. Co.
Plot No. C-20/3
MIDC Indl. Area
Taloja, Navi Mumbai,
Maharashtra-410208
Tel : + 91 (0) 22 27411212
Fax : + 91 (0) 22 27411211
E-mail:
svshah@satyam.net.in

Noble Polymech Corp.
W-102, Phase-II
MIDC, Dombivili,
Maharashtra-421204
Tel : + 91 (0) 251 2871453
Fax : + 91 (0) 251 2870979
E-mail:
noblepolymech@rediffmail.com

PLASTIC EXTRUDERS

A P Industries
6/13, Indl. Area, Kirti Ngr.
New Delhi-110015
Tel : + 91 (0) 11 25930439
Fax : + 91 (0) 11 25195509
E-mail : ikon@hotmail.com

Dayal Engg. Works
2 C, Gali No. 4
New Rohtak Rd.
Anand Parbat Indl. Area
New Delhi-110005
Tel : + 91 (0) 11 25721481
Fax : + 91 (0) 11 27652184
E-mail:
rlbhalla@mantraonline.com

Dharam Engg. Works
A-142, Wazirpur Indl. Area
New Delhi-110052
Tel : + 91 (0) 11 7418645

H K Industries
3/23, Indl. Area, Kirti Ngr.
New Delhi-110015
Tel : + 91 (0) 11 25432993
Fax : + 91 (0) 11 25122481
E-mail: hikon@bol.net.in

K L Thermoformers Pvt. Ltd.
C-67/2, Phase-II
Okhla indl. Area
New Delhi-110020
Tel : + 91 (0) 11 26821708
Fax : +91 (0) 11 26821708
E-mail :
klthermo@ndb.vsnl.net.in

Aakar Industries
984, GIDC, Opp. Purnima Galvanisers, Makarpura
Vadodara, Gujarat-390010
Tel : + 91 (0) 265 646838
Fax : + 91 (0) 265 641490
E-mail:
ashokind@yahoo.com

Akar Industries
L/4132/1, Phase-IV, GIDC
Mehmdavad High Way
Vatva, Ahmedabad
Gujarat-382445
Tel : + 91 (0) 79 25832859
Fax: + 91 (0) 79 25832543

Apex Engineers
Plot No. 1716, Phase-III,
GIDC, Vatva, Ahmedabad
Gujarat-382445
Tel : + 91 (0) 79 5830989
Fax : + 91 (0) 79 5830989

Ashok Industries
984, GIDC, Opp. Purnima Galvanisers, Makerpura
Vadodara, Gujarat-390010
Tel : + 91 (0) 265 646838
E-mail:
ashokindustries@yahoo.com

Jeet Engg. Works
1041, Jawahar Cly.,
B/h Gurudwara,NIT
Faridabad,
Haryana-121001
Tel : + 91 (0) 129 230604
Fax : + 91 (0) 129 5412596

Kalimata Plastic Machinery Manufacturer Pvt. Ltd.
A-5, 3rd Stage
Peenya Indl. Est., Bangalore
Karnataka-560058
Tel : + 91 (0) 80 8394699
Fax : + 91 (0) 80 8392917
E-mail: kalimata@vsnl.com

Sai Machine Tools Pvt. Ltd.
Plot No. 23-D, Sect. A
Sanwer Rd., Indore
Madhya Pradesh-452015
Tel : + 91 (0) 731 722436
Fax : + 91 (0) 731 721831
E-mail:
saimachine@yahoo.com

Suresh Engg. Works
14B, Kalyan Vishranti Grah
South Tukoganj, Indore
Madhya Pradesh-452001
Tel : + 91 (0) 731 529155
Fax : + 91 (0) 731 527872
E-mail:
suresen@bom4.vsnl.net.in

DGP Windsor India Ltd.
Shah Indl. Est.
'C' Bldg., 1st Flr.
Saki Vihar Rd., Mumbai
Maharashtra-400072
Tel : + 91 (0) 22 8575897
Fax : + 91 (0) 22 8573109
E-mail:
marketing@dgpcorp.sril.in

Allied Industries
K 64, MIDC Area, Jalgaon
Maharashtra-425003
Tel : + 91 (0) 257 210306
Fax : + 91 (0) 257 210094

Bainite Machines
C-10, Nand Dham Indl. Est.
Agnishaman Dal Marg,
Marol, Andheri (E), Mumbai
Maharashtra-400059
Tel : + 91 (0) 22 28505910
Fax : + 91 (0) 22 28500465
E-mail:
bainite@bom8.vsnl.net.in

Boolani Engg. Corp.
Prabhadevi Indl. Est., 402
V S Marg, Mumbai
Maharashtra-400025
Tel : + 91 (0) 22 24302826
Fax : + 91 (0) 22 24229875
E-mail: plastic@vsnl.com

KBM Industries
B-14/15, Virwani Indl. Est.
Western Express Highway
Goregaon (E), Mumbai
Maharashtra-400007
Tel : + 91 (0) 22 28745027
Fax : + 91 (0) 22 28751389
E-mail: kbm@vsnl.com

Mahindra Plastic Industries
Opp. Transport Ngr.
Ganesh Ngr., Indl. Area A
St. No. 2, Link Rd.
Ludhiana, Punjab-141003
Tel : + 91 (0) 161 664337
Fax : + 91 (0) 161 644624

Simco Mechanical Industries
Ganesh Ngr., St. No. 3
Link Rd., Indl. Area-A
Ludhiana, Punjab-141003
Tel : + 91 (0) 161 601487

Inventa Technologies Pvt. Ltd.
4D/1, 3rd Main Rd.
Ambattur Indl. Est., Chennai
Tamil Nadu-600058
Tel : + 91 (0) 44 6259621
Fax : + 91 (0) 44 6257425

Jolite Engg. Works
343, Walltax Rd., Chennai
Tamil Nadu-600079
Tel : + 91 (0) 44 5268672
Fax : + 91 (0) 44 5377909

Simco Mat Machineries
194, T H Rd., Kodungaiyur,
Chennai
Tamil Nadu-600118
Tel : + 91 (0) 44 5583942
Fax : + 91 (0) 44 5587580
E-mail: matloom@usa.net

Impex Engg. Works
C-157, Sect.10, Noida
Uttar Pradesh-201301
Tel : + 91 (0) 120 4526597
Fax : + 91 (0) 120 4534790

KBK Plascon Pvt. Ltd.
24/168, P.O.Box 158
Birhana Rd., Kanpur
Uttar Pradesh-208001
Tel : + 91 (0) 512 369353
Fax : + 91 (0) 512 352058
E-mail: kbk@sancharnet.in

M Plast (I) Ltd.
A-15, Phase-III, Sect. 60
Noida,
Uttar Pradesh-201307
Tel : + 91 (0) 120 4581087
Fax : + 91 (0) 120 4581090
E-mail:
mplast@nda.vsnl.net.in

Neptune Plastic & Metal Industries
7th Flr., 18
R N Mukherjee Rd., Kolkata
West Bengal-700001
Tel : + 91 (0) 33 2481979
Fax : + 91 (0) 33 2485031
E-mail: neplast@vsnl.net

H P Singh & Co.
75, Ganesh Chandra
Avenue, Kolkata
West Bengal-700013
Tel : + 91 (0) 33 2371680
Fax : + 91 (0) 33 2255457
E-mail: hpscocal@vsnl.com

PLASTIC FILM BLOWING MACHINERY

H K Industries
3/23, Indl. Area
Kirti Ngr.
New Delhi-110015
Tel : + 91 (0) 11 25432993
Fax : + 91 (0) 11 25122481
E-mail : hikon@bol.net.in

S K Engg. Works
Opp. Government Higher
Secondory School
Mangolpur Khurd
Delhi-110083
Tel : + 91 (0) 11 27925921
Fax : +91 (0) 11 27923533
E-mail: kuldeep@skengineeringworks.com

SSJS Mechanical Works
6/13, Indl. Area, Kirti Ngr.
New Delhi-110015
Tel : + 91 (0) 11 25417569
Fex : + 91 (0) 11 25195509
E-mail:
goldplast@yahoo.com

Aakar Industries
984, GIDC
Opp. Purnima Galvanisers
Makarpura
Vadodara, Gujarat-390010
Tel : + 91 (0) 265 646838
Fax : + 91 (0) 265 641490
E-mail:
ashokind@yahoo.com

Ahimsa Industries Pvt. Ltd.
C Block, Morpicch Apt.
Nr. Sharda Mandir School
Paldi, Ahmedabad
Gujarat-380007
Tel : + 91 (0) 79 6614888
Fax : + 91 (0) 79 6640483
E-mail:
ahimsa@adl.vsnl.net.in

Ashok Industries
984, GIDC, Opp. Purnima
Galvanisers, Makerpura
Vadodara, Gujarat-390010
Tel : + 91 (0) 265 646838
E-mail:
ashokindustries@yahoo.com

Sai Machine Tools Pvt. Ltd.
Plot No. 23-D, Sect. A
Sanwer Rd., Indore
Madhya Pradesh-452015
Tel : + 91 (0) 731 722436
Fax : + 91 (0) 731 721831
E-mail:
saimachine@yahoo.com

DGP Windsor India Ltd.
Shah Indl. Est.
'C' Bldg., 1st Flr.
Saki Vihar Rd., Mumbai
Maharashtra-400072
Tel : + 91 (0) 22 28575897
Fax : + 91 (0) 22 28573109
E-mail:
marketing@dgpcorp.sril.in

R S Mech Engineers (Regd.)
Ganesh Ngr.
St. No. 3, Link Rd., Opp.
Transport Ngr., Indl. Area-A
Ludhiana, Punjab-141003
Tel : + 91 (0) 161 661143
Fax : + 91 (0) 161 607546
E-mail: info@rsmech.com

Plusmech
62/B/P, Nr. Shakti Peer
J N Mukherjee Rd.
Ghusuri, Howrah
West Bengal-711107
Tel : + 91 (0) 33 6653784
Fax : + 91 (0) 33 6656982
E-mail:
plusmech@searchindians.com

PLACTIC FILM EXTRUDING MACHINERY

DGP Windsor India Ltd.
Shah Indl. Est.
'C' Bldg., 1st Flr.
Saki Vihar Rd., Mumbai
Maharashtra-400072
Tel : + 91 (0) 22 8575897
Fax : + 91 (0) 22 8573109
E-mail:
marketing@dgpcorp.sril.in

Ahimsa Industries Pvt. Ltd.
C Block, Morpicch Apt.
Nr. Sharda Mandir School
Paldi, Ahmedabad
Gujarat-380007
Tel : + 91 (0) 79 6614888
Fax : + 91 (0) 79 6640483
E-mail:
ahimsa@adl.vsnl.net.in

Remica Plastic Machinery Manufacturers
2/AB, Sardar Patel Indl. Est., Shahwadi, Narol
Ahmedabad
Gujarat-382405
Tel : + 91 (0) 79 5712741
Fax : + 91 (0) 79 5894234
E-mail:
remica@ad1.vsnl.net.in

Kalimata Plastic Machinery Manufacturer Pvt. Ltd.
A-5, 3rd Stage
Peenya Indl. Est., Bangalore
Karnataka-560058
Tel : + 91 (0) 80 8394699
Fax : + 91 (0) 80 8392917
E-mail: kalimata@vsnl.com

Sai Machine Tools Pvt. Ltd.
Plot No. 23-D, Sect. A
Sanwer Rd., Indore
Madhya Pradesh-452015
Tel : + 91 (0) 731 722436
Fax : + 91 (0) 731 721831
E-mail:
saimachine@yahoo.com

DGP Windsor India Ltd.
Shah Indl. Est.
'C' Bldg., 1st Flr.
Saki Vihar Rd., Mumbai
Maharashtra-400072
Tel : + 91 (0) 22 8575897
Fax : + 91 (0) 22 8573109
E-mail:
marketing@dgpcorp.sril.in

Boolani Group of Companies
7 & 8, Unique Est.
Off V S Marg, Mumbai
Maharashtra-400025
Tel : + 91 (0) 22 24302826
Fax : +91 (0) 22 4229875
E-mail: plastic@vsnl.com

PLASTIC FILM MACHINERY

G G Industries (I)
5/1-B, Indl. Area, Kirti Ngr.
New Delhi-110015
Tel : + 91 (0) 11 25936280
Fax : + 91 (0) 11 25156951

H K Industries
3/23, Indl. Area, Kirti Ngr.
New Delhi-110015
Tel : + 91 (0) 11 25432993
Fax : + 91 (0) 11 25122481
E-mail: hikon@bol.net.in

R K Engg. Works
Anand Parbat Indl. Area
A-43, Gali No. 6
New Rohtak Rd.
New Delhi-110005
Tel : + 91 (0) 11 25784558
Fax : + 91 (0) 11 25784558

Rajoo Engineers Ltd.
Survey No. 210, Plot No. 1
Indl. Area, Veraval (Shapar)
Rajkot, Gujarat-360002
Tel : + 91 (0) 281 52701
Fax : + 91 (0) 281 52700
E-mail: rel@rajoo.com

Kalimata Plastic Machinery Manufacturer Pvt. Ltd.
A-5, 3rd Stage
Peenya Indl. Est., Bangalore
Karnataka-560058
Tel : + 91 (0) 80 8394699
Fax : + 91 (0) 80 8392917
E-mail: kalimata@vsnl.com

Suresh Engg. Works
14B, Kalyan Vishranti Grah
South Tukoganj, Indore
Madhya Pradesh-452001
Tel : + 91 (0) 731 529155
Fax : + 91 (0) 731 527872
E-mail:
suresen@bom4.vsnl.net.in

R S Mech Engineers (Regd.)
Ganesh Ngr.
St. No. 3, Link Rd.,
Opp. Transport Ngr.
Indl. Area-A
Ludhiana, Punjab-141003
Tel : + 91 (0) 161 661143
Fax : + 91 (0) 161 607546
E-mail : info@rsmech.com

Carmel Engg.
Plot No. 5, Peniel Ngr.
Viraganur Dam, Madurai
Tamil Nadu-625009
Tel : + 91 (0) 452 865667
Fax : + 91 (0) 452 865468

Shaheen Machine Fabric
B-113, Sect. 5, Noida
Uttar Pradesh-201301
Tel : + 91 (0) 120 4555489

Plusmech
62/B/P, Nr. Shakti Peer
J N Mukherjee Rd.
Ghusuri, Howrah
West Bengal-711107
Tel : + 91 (0) 33 6653784
Fax : + 91 (0) 33 6656982
E-mail:
plusmech@searchindians.com

PLASTIC FILM SLITTING MACHINERY

Konark Plastic Machinery Mfrs.
5, Africawala Est., B/h Chakudia Mahadev
Opp. Comet House
Rakhial, Ahmedabad
Gujarat-380023
Tel : + 91 (0) 79 2741262
Fax : + 91 (0) 79 2744409
E-mail: sales@konark plasticmachinery.com

Spark Engg.
4510, Phase-V
B/h Indo German Tool Room, GIDC Est.
Vatva, Gujarat-382445
Tel : + 91 (0) 79 5836243
Fax : + 91 (0) 79 5840191
E-mail: sparkin@icenet.net

Kohli Industries
6/4, Sona Udyog Indl. Est.
Parsi Panchayat Rd.
Andheri, Mumbai,
Maharashtra-400069
Tel : + 91 (0) 22 28362567
Fax : + 91 (0) 22 28390729
E-mail:
kohli@bom2.vsnl.net.in

Marsons Print-Graf Machines Pvt. Ltd.
D/9, Udyog Sadan No. 2
MIDC, Andheri (E), Mumbai
Maharashtra-400093
Tel : + 91 (0) 22 28352976
Fax : + 91 (0) 22 28369359
E-mail:
marsons@bom3.vsnl.net.in

Flex Industries Ltd.
A-107, Sect. IV, Noida
Uttar Pradesh-201301
Tel : + 91 (0) 120 4522558
Fax : + 91 (0) 120 4520877

Moscow Machine Tools
C-293, Mukund Ngr.
Ghaziabad
Uttar Pradesh-201003
Tel : + 91 (0) 120 4731630

T D Printing & Packaging Projects Pvt. Ltd.
Narayanpur, P O Gopalpur
24 Parganas (N)
West Bengal-743518
Tel : + 91 (0) 33 5735080
Fax : + 91 (0) 33 5735080
E-mail: tdp@cal2-vsnl.net.in

Jagritee Engineers (I)
T-29/F-7, Block No.30-31
Nr. West Patel Ngr
Rd. No.20, Baljeet Ngr.
New Delhi-110008
Tel : + 91 (0) 11 25736894

SSJS Mechanical Works
6/13, Indl. Area, Kirti Ngr.
New Delhi-110015
Tel : + 91 (0) 11 25417569
Fax : + 91 (0) 11 25195509
E-mail:
goldplast@yahoo.com

PLASTIC FOAM MACHINERY

DGP Windsor India Ltd.
Shah Indl. Est.
'C' Bldg., 1st Flr.
Saki Vihar Rd., Mumbai
Maharashtra-400072
Tel : + 91 (0) 22 28575897
Fax : + 91 (0) 22 28573109
E-mail:
marketing@dgpcorp.sril.in

A S Enterprises
28/23/2, B/h Shivalya
Village Badli, Delhi-110042
Tel : + 91 (0) 11 27294561
Fax : + 91 (0) 11 27293598
E-mail: info@as-enterprises.com

Delta Rubber & Plastic Products
C1A/1, GIDC Indl.
Township, Odhav
Ahmedabad
Gujarat-382415
Tel : + 91 (0) 79 2872334
Fax : + 91 (0) 79 2870835

Natson Foam Manufacturers Pvt. Ltd.
5, Panchayat Bhavan
Bhadra, Ahmedabad
Gujarat-380001
Tel : + 91 (0) 79 5506484
Fax : + 91 (0) 79 2743803

Truman Engg. Pvt. Ltd.
202, World Trade Center
Sayajigunj
Vadodara, Gujarat-390005
Tel : + 91 (0) 265 361946
Fax : + 91 (0) 265 361690
E-mail: foam.mcs@gnahd.globalnet.ems.vsnl.net.in

DGP Windsor India Ltd.
Shah Indl. Est.,
'C' Bldg., 1st Flr.
Saki Vihar Rd., Mumbai
Maharashtra-400072
Tel : + 91 (0) 22 28575897
Fax : + 91 (0) 22 28573109
E-mail:
marketing@dgpcorp.sril.in

Jayshree Engineers
A/54, Nandjot Indl. Est.
Nr. Safaid Pool
Andheri-Kurla Rd.
Andheri (E), Mumbai,
Maharashtra-400072
Tel : + 91 (0) 22 28515761
Fax : + 91 (0) 22 28590268

Shanbhag & Associates
B-50, Nandbhuvan Indl. Est.
Mahakali Caves Rd.
Andheri (E), Mumbai
Maharashtra-400093
Tel : + 91 (0) 22 28346604
Fax : + 91 (0) 22 28388334
E-mail:
shanbhags@vsnl.com

Modern Foam Udyog
282, Madhopuri Chowk-2
Ludhiana, Punjab-141008
Tel : + 91 (0) 161 704044
Fax : + 91 (0) 161 700566

PLASTIC INJECTION MOULDING MACHINERY

K R Jee Industries
4-145, Fateh Ngr.
Hyderabad
Andhra Pradesh-500018
Tel : + 91 (0) 40 3773584
Fax : + 91 (0) 40 3077028
E-mail:
krghyd@hotmail.com

KRG Machine Tools Pvt. Ltd.
4-145, Fatehnagar
Hyderabad
Andhra Pradesh-500018
Tel : + 91 (0) 40 3773584
Fax : + 91 (0) 40 3077028
E-mail:
krgmt@satyam.net.in

Dynamic Enterprises
30, Madan Park
New Delhi-110026
Tel : + 91 (0) 11 5437698
Fax : + 91 (0) 11 5440765
E-mail:
vkapur7@hotmail.com

A H Hydraulic & Engg. Works
C-177, Phase-I
Naraina Indl. Area
New Delhi-110028
Tel : + 91 (0) 11 5792963
E-mail : ahhydraulicnia @delhi-industry.com

A H Hydro Plast (I)
B-12/A, Manak Vihar Extn.
Tihar Village
New Delhi-110018
Tel : + 91 (0) 11 25792963
Fax : + 91 (0) 11 25798383

British Plastics & Engg. Works
A-89/2, Phase-I
Naraina Indl. Area
New Delhi-110028
Tel : + 91 (0) 11 25793109
Fax : + 91 (0) 11 25798629

Continental Hydraulics (I)
A-57, Group Indl. Area
Wazirpur, Delhi-110052
Tel : + 91 (0) 11 27240390
Fax : + 91 (0) 11 27131595
E-mail: chi@ndf.vsnl.net.in

Friends Hydraulics
B-19, Manak Vihar Extn.
Tihar Village
New Delhi-110018
Tel : + 91 (0) 11 5142456

Hinds Machineries
B-25, 1st Flr.
Manek Vihar Extn.
Subhash Ngr.
New Delhi-110018
TelL : + 91 (0) 11 25409201
Fax : + 91 (0) 11 25497921

Aakar Industries
984, GIDC, Opp. Purnima Galvanisers, Makarpura
Vadodara, Gujarat-390010
Tel : + 91 (0) 265 646838
Fax : + 91 (0) 265 641490
E-mail:
ashokind@yahoo.com

Aaspee Machinery
11, Sukhram Est.,
Margha Farm, N H No. 8,
Opp. Vimal Ghar-Ganti
Rakhial, Ahmedabad,
Gujarat-380023
Tel : + 91 (0) 79 2732315

Amrut Brothers
24, Manorath Est.
Nr. Milan Cinema, Saraspur
Ahmedabad
Gujarat-380018
Tel : + 91 (0) 79 2168163
Fax : + 91 (0) 79 2168163
E-mail : exports@amrut brothers.com

Battenfield India Ltd.
4th Flr., Opp. Sales India
Off AshramRd., Kamdhenu
Ahmedabad
Gujarat-380009
Tel : + 91 (0) 79 448414

Cincinnati Milacron Ltd.
92, Phase-I, GIDC
Vatva, Gujarat-382445
Tel : + 91 (0) 79 5830063
Fax : + 91 (0) 79 5830125
E-mail:
cmplpltd@ad1.vsnl.net.in

Dinsha Industrial Corp.
B/h Aapa Hotel
Nr. Ambica Ngr.,
1st Gate, Odhav
Ahmedabad
Gujarat-382415
Tel : + 91 (0) 79 2890006
Fax : + 91 (0) 79 2891819

Esemplast
132/133, Rajdeep Indl. Est.,
BB Talav, Vatva,
Ahmedabad
Gujarat-382445
Tel : + 91 (0) 79 5891433
Fax : + 91 (0) 79 7556826
E-mail:
swatipolypack@hotmail.com

Hind Hydraulics & Engineers
Plot No. 13, Sect. 24
Faridabad, Haryana-121005
Tel : + 91 (0) 129 5233308
Fax : + 91 (0) 129 5234294
E-mail:
hindhydr@nda.vsnl.net.in

Preswell Industries
152, Sect.-24, Faridabad
Haryana-121005
Tel : + 91 (0) 129 5233665
Fax : + 91 (0) 129 5234788
E-mail:
presswel@vsnl.com

Fanuc India Ltd.
41-A, Electronics City
Hosur Rd., Bangalore
Karnataka-561229
Tel : + 91 (0) 80 8520057
Fax : + 91 (0) 80 8520051
E-mail:
filhq@blr.fanucindia.co.in

Plus-One Machinefabrik
Survey No. 323,
Plot No. 25-26, Udyambag
Belgaum,Karnataka-590008
Tel : + 91 (0) 831 441845
Fax : + 91 (0) 831 441106
E-mail:
plusone@blr.vsnl.net.in

Manek Plastic Pvt. Ltd.
4/19, Diamond Indl. Est.
Village Waliv, Vasai
Madhya Pradesh-401208
Tel : + 91 (0) 250 455458
Fax : + 91 (0) 250 452407
E-mail:
bhavesh@bom3.vsnl.net.in

Triyami Tools
MPLUN, 21, Sect. F
Sanwer Rd., Indore
Madhya Pradesh-452015
Tel : + 91 (0) 731 722762
Fax : + 91 (0) 731 722762

DGP Windsor India Ltd.
Shah Indl. Est.
'C' Bldg., 1st Flr.

Saki Vihar Rd., Mumbai
Maharashtra-400072
Tel : + 91 (0) 22 8575897
Fax : + 91 (0) 22 8573109
E-mail:
marketing@dgpcorp.sril.in

Boolani Engg. Corp.
Prabhadevi Indl. Est., 402
V S Marg, Mumbai
Maharashtra-400025
Tel : + 91 (0) 22 24302826
Fax : + 91 (0) 22 24229875
E-mail : plastic@vsnl.com

Dave Technical Service
Soni Compound, Churiwadi
Goregaon (E), Mumbai
Maharashtra-400063
Tel : + 91 (0) 22 28752038
Fax : + 91 (0) 22 25448855

Delta Machine-Craft
3rd Rd. Mamlatdar Wadi
Malad (W), Mumbai
Maharashtra-400064
Tel : + 91 (0) 22 28822243
Fax : + 91 (0) 22 28822757

Dev Packaging
R.No.34, 1st Flr.,
Chapra Bldg.
Opp. Plaza Cinema
Dadar (W), Mumbai
Maharashtra-400028
Tel : + 91 (0) 22 24379395
Fax : + 91 (0) 22 24379395

Gurpreet Plastic & Engg. Pvt. Ltd.
A/342, Rd. No. 26
Wagle Indl. Est., Mumbai
Maharashtra-400604
Tel : + 91 (0) 22 25822781
Fax : + 91 (0) 22 25322781

Bombay Hydraulic (I)
St. No. 1, Nr. ATI,
New Janta Ngr., Gill Rd.
Ludhiana, Punjab-141003
Tel : + 91 (0) 161 491224
Fax : + 91 (0) 161 491524
E-mail:
bombay@netobjects.net

Bombay Plastic Machinery
3839, New Janta Ngr.
Petrol Pump St., Gill Rd.
Ludhiana, Punjab-141003
Tel : + 91 (0) 161 491185

K D Engg. Works
2263, Nr. Shiv Shakti Mandir
Gurdwara Rd., St. No. 10
Janta Ngr. Ludhiana,
Punjab-141003
Tel : + 91 (0) 161 497424

Hydro Craft
11-B, Vijayalakshmi Layout
1st St., Ganpathy
Coimbatore
Tamil Nadu-641006
Tel : + 91 (0) 422 532704
Fax : + 91 (0) 422 532704
E-mail:
hy@ganeshatengland.com

Modern Plastics Equipments
35, Perumal Kovil Thottam
P N Palayam Rd.,
Nr. Rly. Level Cross
Ganapathy PO, Coimbatore
Tamil Nadu-641006
Tel : + 91 (0) 422 530836

Preetha Heaters
93, Pankaja Mill Rd.
Ramanathapuram.Coimbatore
Tamil Nadu-641045
Tel : + 91 (0) 422 316803

Columbia Machines Co.
1/182, Chiranjiv Vihar
Ghaziabad
Uttar Pradesh-201002
Tel : + 91 (0) 120 4765229

Sandeep Hydraulic Works
E-137, Sect. 7, Noida
Uttar Pradesh-201301
Tel : + 91 (0) 120 4522087

Plascon Machines & Tools
22, Buro Shibtola Rd.
Kolkata
West Bengal-700053
Tel : + 91 (0) 33 4007522

Rupa Engg. Concern Pvt. Ltd.
34/1/3, Buxarah Rd.
Howrah
West Bengal-711306
Tel : + 91 (0) 33 6588454

PLASTIC MOULDING MACHINERY : BLOW MOULDING

Kavacha Engg.
Plot No. D-45
Electronic Cmplx.
Kushaiguda, Hyderabad
Andhra Pradesh-500062
Tel : + 91 (0) 40 7123665
Fax : + 91 (0) 40 7120892

Darshan Mould Maker
Nr. Pooja Dairy, 487/47
Peera Garhi
New Delhi-110087
Tel : + 91 (0) 11 25676148

Friends Hydraulics
B-19, Manak Vihar Extn.
Tihar Village
New Delhi-110018
Tel : + 91 (0) 11 25142456

G G Industries (I)
5/1-B, Indl. Area, Kirti Ngr.
New Delhi-110015
Tel : + 91 (0) 11 5936280
Fax : + 91 (0) 11 25156951

H K Industries
3/23, Indl. Area, Kirti Ngr.
New Delhi-110015
Tel : + 91 (0) 11 25432993
Fax : + 91 (0) 11 25122481
E-mail: hikon@bol.net.in

Aakar Industries
984, GIDC
Opp. Purnima Galvanisers
Makarpura
Vadodara, Gujarat-390010
Tel : + 91 (0) 265 646838
Fax : + 91 (0) 265 641490
E-mail:
ashokind@yahoo.com

Koras Engg. Works
186, Shiv Shakti Est.
Nr. House of Kaydee
Narol-Chandola Rd.
Narol, Ahmedabad
Gujarat-382405
Tel : + 91 (0) 79 5353760
Fax : + 91 (0) 79 5351792

Shyam Plastic Machinery
C-1/4512, Phase-IV, GIDC
Vatva, Ahmedabad
Gujarat-382445
Tel : + 91 (0) 79 5831258
Fax : + 91 (0) 79 5891849
E-mail:
shyam@vd1.vsnl.net.in

Vinitha Industries
90/2, Narayanpura, Nr. IOC
White Fields Rd., Bangalore
Karnataka-560016
Tel : + 91 (0) 80 8510013

Suresh Engg. Works
14B, Kalyan Vishranti Grah
South Tukoganj, Indore
Madhya Pradesh-452001
Tel : + 91 (0) 731 529155
Fax : + 91 (0) 731 527872
E-mail:
suresen@bom4.vsnl.net.in

DGP Windsor India Ltd.
Shah Indl. Est.
'C' Bldg., 1st Flr.
Saki Vihar Rd., Mumbai
Maharashtra-400072
Tel : + 91 (0) 22 28575897
Fax : + 91 (0) 22 28573109
E-mail:
marketing@dgpcorp.sril.in

Accurate Moulds & Dies
United Indl. House
Shanti Ngr., Santacruz (E)
Mumbai
Maharashtra-400055
Tel : + 91 (0) 22 26104101
Fax : + 91 (0) 22 26184491

Boolani Engg. Corp.
Prabhadevi Indl. Est.,
402 V S Marg, Mumbai
Maharashtra-400025
Tel : + 91 (0) 22 24302826
Fax : + 91 (0) 22 24229875
E-mail: plastic@vsnl.com

Dave Technical Service
Soni Compound, Churiwadi
Goregaon (E), Mumbai,
Maharashtra-400063
Tel : + 91 (0) 22 28752038
Fax : + 91 (0) 22 25448855

Delta Machine-Craft
3rd Rd. Mamlatdar Wadi
Malad (W), Mumbai
Maharashtra-400064
Tel : + 91 (0) 22 28822243
Fax : + 91 (0) 22 28822757

Partap Hari Mechanical Works
11410, Nr. Sangeet Cinema
St. No.1, Partap Ngr.
Ludhiana, Punjab-141003
Tel : + 91 (0) 161 530512

Jolite Engg. Works
343, Walltax Rd., Chennai
Tamil Nadu-600079
Tel : + 91 (0) 44 5268672
Fax : + 91 (0) 44 5377909

Modern Plastics Equipments
35, Perumal Kovil Thottam
P N Palayam Rd.
Nr. Rly. Level Cross
Ganapathy PO,Coimbatore
Tamil Nadu-641006
Tel : + 91 (0) 422 530836

Shripet Industries Ltd.
B-162, SIDCO Indl. Est.
Ambattur, Chennai
Tamil Nadu-600098
Tel : + 91 (0) 44 8234351
Fax : + 91 (0) 44 8283691
E-mail:
shripet@md2.vsnl.net.in

Zeenath Industries
123-A-2, Sanganoor Rd.
P.O. Ganapathy, Coimbatore
Tamil Nadu-641006
Tel : + 91 (0) 422 531666
E-mail:
zeenath.ind@sify.com

Allied International
10/19, Hathras Rd., Agra
Uttar Pradesh-282006
Tel : + 91 (0) 562 344138
Fax : + 91 (0) 562 344749

H Mahindera Engineers
D-158, Sect. 10, Noida
Uttar Pradesh-201301
Tel : + 91 (0) 120 4443465

Kwality Engg. Works
48-A, Maktaram Babu St.
Kolkata
West Bengal-700007
Tel : + 91 (0) 33 2391195

MOULDING MACHINERY : COMPRESSION MOULDING

Winstar Hydraulic
1604, GIDC, Phase-I
Naroda, Ahmedabad
Gujarat-382330
Tel : + 91 (0) 79 2820506
Fax : + 91 (0) 79 2800305
E-mail:
winstar@jindalonline.com

Presswel Industries
Plot No. 152, Sect.24
Faridabad, Haryana-121005
Tel : + 91 (0) 129 5233665
Fax : + 91 (0) 129 5234788
E-mail: presswel@vsnl.com

Padgo Hydraulics
Survey No. 69 (Opp. VST)
Whitefield Rd.
Mahadevapura Post
Bangalore
Karnataka-560048
Tel : + 91 (0) 80 8510840
Fax : + 91 (0) 80 8510840
E-mail: ogap@hotmail.com

Quality Engg. & Insulation Products
71-A, Indl. Est.
Govindpura, Bhopal
Madhya Pradesh-462023
Tel : + 91 (0) 755 586665
Fax : + 91 (0) 755 586278
E-mail: qualityengineering.insulation@bhopaltimes.zzn.com

Consolidated Machines
H-137, Ansa Indl. Est.
Saki Vihar Rd., Andheri (E)
Mumbai
Maharashtra-400072
Tel : + 91 (0) 22 28520236
Fax : + 91 (0) 22 28522658
E-mail: jhabvala@vsnl.com

Hindustan Hydraulics Pvt. Ltd.
G T Rd., Suranussi
Jalandhar, Punjab-144027
Tel : + 91 (0) 181 253610
Fax : + 91 (0) 181 250570
E-mail: mms@hindustanhydraulics.com

Larsen & Toubro Limited
Heavy Engg. Division
Plastic Processing Machinery
L & T Chennai House
Post Bag 5247, 10
Club House Rd., Anna Salai
Chennai
Tamil Nadu-600002
Tel : + 91 (0) 44 8460141
Fax : + 91 (0) 44 8460069

Crane-Bel International A Supertech Crane-Bel Group Company
E-7, Kavi Ngr. Indl. Area
Ghaziabad
Uttar Pradesh-201002
Tel : + 91 (0) 120 4702107
Fax : + 91 (0) 120 4700339
E-mail: machinetools@cranebel.com

Max Hydromech Engineers Pvt. Ltd.
Balitikuri, CTI Rd.
Naskarpara, Howrah
West Bengal-711402
Tel : + 91 (0) 33 6531686
Fax : + 91 (0) 33 6531688

Flowmech Engineers Pvt. Ltd.
G-Extn. 1, Kirti Ngr.
New Delhi-110015
Tel : + 91 (0) 11 25435415
Fax : + 91 (0) 11 25191255
E-mail:
flowmech@del3.vsnl.net.in

MOULDING MACHINERY : ROTATIONAL MOULDING

Vinodrai Incorporated
C-28, Additional MIDC Area
Jalna
Madhya Pradesh-431203
Tel : + 91 (0) 2435 31261
Fax : + 91 (0) 2435 30499
E-mail: vinodrai@vsnl.com

Larsen & Toubro Ltd.
Heavy Engineering Divn.
Powai Works
Saki Vihar Rd., Powai
Mumbai
Maharashtra-400072
Tel : + 91 (0) 22 28581401
Fax : + 91 (0) 22 28581594
E-mail:3870-sra@vedak.ltindia.com

Maharashtra Polyplast
15, Sahyog Indl. Est.
Mira-Bhayander Rd.
Mira Rd. (E), Thane
Maharashtra-401104
Tel : + 91 (0) 22 8113994
Fax : + 91 (0) 22 8818093
E-mail:
mplas@bom5.vsnl.net.in

Plasmec Engg. Pvt. Ltd.
Plot A-325, Rd. 21
Wagle Indl. Est., Thane,
Maharashtra-400604
Tel : + 91 (0) 22 5822201
Fax : + 91 (0) 22 5826556
E-mail:
plasmec@bom2.vsnl.net.in

Lotus Machines Pvt. Ltd.
1059, Phase-II, Indl. Area
Chandigarh, Punjab-160002
Tel : + 91 (0) 172 652002
Fax : + 91 (0) 172 43864
E-mail : lotus@cha.i91.net

Larsen & Toubro Limited
Heavy Engg. Division
Plastic Processing Machinery
L & T Chennai House
Post Bag 5247, 10
Club House Rd., Anna Salai
Chennai
Tamil Nadu-600002
Tel : + 91 (0) 44 8460141
Fax : + 91 (0) 44 8460069

M Plast (I) Ltd.
A-15, Phase-III
Sect. 60, Noida
Uttar Pradesh-201307
Tel : + 91 (0) 120 4581087
Fax : + 91 (0) 120 4581090
E-mail:
mplast@nda.vsnl.net.in

N A Corp.
3725, GIDC, Phase-IV
Vatva, Ahmedabad
Gujarat-382445
Tel : + 91 (0) 79 5835374
Fax : + 91 (0) 79 5834787

Reinhardt Roto-Machines Pvt. Ltd.
69, Kunj Soc., Vadodara
Gujarat-390005
Tel : + 91 (0) 265 333719
Fax : + 91 (0) 265 340172
E-mail:
info@reinhardtindia.com

Rotomould (I) Pvt. Ltd.
Vijay Indl. Est., Padra Rd.
Samiala, Vadodara
Gujarat-391410
Tel : + 91 (0) 265 22405
Fax : + 91 (0) 265 22891
E-mail:
rotax@ad1.vsnl.net.in

S N Industries
3725, Phase-IV, GIDC
Vatva, Ahmedabad
Gujarat-382445
Tel : + 91 (0) 79 5835374
Fax : + 91 (0) 79 5834809
E-mail:
nacorp@ad1.vsnl.net.in

Shree Intertrade Pvt. Ltd.
205, Sakar-III, 2nd Flr.
Opp. High Court
Ahmedabad
Gujarat-380014
Tel : + 91 (0) 79 7544102
Fax : + 91 (0) 79 2773721
E-mail : s_oza@vsnl.com

United Industries
Ajanta Saw Mill Compound
Mahavir Ngr., Saijpur Bogha
Naroda Rd., Ahmedabad
Gujarat-382345
Tel : + 91 (0) 79 2820213
Fax : + 91 (0) 79 2821285
E-mail:
unitedin@ad1.vsnl.net.in

PLASTIC MOULDING MACHINERY : STRETCH BLOW MOULDING

Shree Intertrade Pvt. Ltd.
205, Sakar-III, 2nd Flr.
Opp. High Court
Ahmedabad
Gujarat-380014
Tel : + 91 (0) 79 7544102
Fax : + 91 (0) 79 2773721
E-mail: s_oza@vsnl.com

Shyam Plastic Machinery
C-1/4512, Phase-IV, GIDC
Vatva, Ahmedabad
Gujarat-382445
Tel : + 91 (0) 79 5831258
Fax : + 91 (0) 79 5891849
E-mail:
shyam@vd1.vsnl.net.in

Chemix India Pvt. Ltd.
Sanjeevani Apt., E-6, 11th Cross Lane, Prabhat Rd.
Pune, Maharashtra-411004
Tel : + 91 (0) 20 25679001
Fax : + 91 (0) 20 25679000
E-mail:
india@chemixmachinery.com

K & R International
Rawal Mansion,
2nd Hasnabad Lane
Santacruz (W), Mumbai,
Maharashtra-400054
Te; : + 91 (0) 22 26490926
Fax : + 91 (0) 22 26050568
E-mail:
krintl@bom5.vsnl.net.in

Micro Tools
B-9, Aggarwal Indl. Est.,
Chitalsar, Manpada, Thane
Maharashtra-400607
Tel : + 91 (0) 22 25347417
Fax : + 91 (0) 22 25385424
E-mail:
surender@bom5.vsnl.net.in

Print Link
201, Mahesh Indl. Est.
Opp. Silver Park
Mira Bhayander Rd., Thane
Maharashtra-401107
Tel : + 91 (0) 22 28118127
Fax : + 91 (0) 22 28110548
E-mail:
printink@bom5.vsnl.net.in

Larsen & Toubro Limited
Heavy Engg. Division
Plastic Processing
Machinery
L & T Chennai House
Post Bag 5247, 10
Club House Rd.
Anna Salai, Chennai
Tamil Nadu-600002
Tel : + 91 (0) 44 8460141
Fax : + 91 (0) 44 8460069

Nissel ASB Pte. Ltd.
231-233-235, 2nd Flr., Ansal Chmbrs.-II
Bhikaji Cama Place
New Delhi-110066
Tel : + 91 (0) 11 26194031
Fax : + 91 (0) 11 26194129
E-mail:
asbdel@del3.vsnl.net.in

Scolex Packaging
114, Masjid Moth
NDSE-II, New Delhi-110049
Tel : + 91 (0) 11 26250161
Fax : + 91 (0) 11 26250162
E-mail:
sriyug@ndf.vsnl.net.in

Suraj Plastic Industries
81, Reghar Pura,Karol Bagh
New Delhi-110005
Tel : + 91 (0) 11 25719179
Fax : + 91 (0) 11 25710219
E-mail : tej@id.eth.net.

PACKAGING MACHINERY

Orbit Equipments Pvt. Ltd.
H.No. 8-2-82/11
Old Bowenpally
Secunderabad
Andhra Pradesh-500011
Tel : + 91 (0) 40 7750111
Fax : + 91 (0) 40 7751199
E-mail:
orbiteqp@hd2.dot.net.in

Cannon Engg. Industries
7-152/7, G-21, Ravi Cmplx.
Fathenagar, Hyderabad
Andhra Pradesh-500018
Tel : + 91 (0) 40 3774967
Fax : + 91 (0) 40 3779156
E-mail:
info@cannonindia.com

Dianamark
Bible House, 5-2-13/4
Opp. Jabbar Cmplx.
Hyder Basti, Secunderabad
Andhra Pradesh-500003
Tel : + 91 (0) 40 7532548
Fax : + 91 (0) 40 7536451
E-mail:
dianamark@hotmail.com

Eclat Auto Packs Pvt. Ltd.
No. 2-4-82, 301, 3rd Flr.
Misha Gardens
Shamalal Est., Sikh Rd.
Secunderabad
Andhra Pradesh-500009
Tel : + 91 (0) 40 7818896
Fax : + 91 (0) 40 7729132
E-mail:
eclatap@satyam.net.in

La Interpack Pvt. Ltd.
Plot No. 18, E C Extn.
ECIL Post, Kushaiguda
Hyderabad
Andhra Pradesh-500062
Tel : + 91 (0) 40 7120458
Fax : + 91 (0) 40 7141011
E-mail:
interpack@hotmail.com

A-Garg Exim Pvt. Ltd.
42, DLF Indl. Area, Kirti Ngr.
New Delhi-110015
Tel : + 91 (0) 11 25417831
Fax : + 91 (0) 11 25195721
E-mail: pawan@garg.org

Delhi Packaging Pvt. Ltd.
1/3, Ram Mohan
Village Johripur, Shahdara
Delhi-110094
Tel : + 91 (0) 11 22285404

H P Engg. Corp.
S-21-B, Gali No. 12
Anand Parbat Indl. Area
New Delhi-110005
Tel : + 91 (0) 11 25788475
Fax : + 91 (0) 11 25583885

Manoj Plastics
A-99/1, Phase-II
Okhla Indl. Area
New Delhi-110020
Tel : + 91 (0) 11 26839693
Fax : + 91 (0) 11 26913011
E-mail:
mperiwal@del3.vsnl.net.in

Maruti Auto-Mac Engineers
3, Lilabhai Est.
B/h Matru Chhaya
Vidhyalaya, Rajendra Park
Odhav, Gujarat-382415
Tel : + 91 (0) 79 2975760
Fax : + 91 (0) 79 2975760
E-mail:
maruti_123@yahoo.com

Accurate Machines
833, GIDC Indl. Est.
Waghodia, Gujarat-391760
Tel : + 91 (0) 2668 62974
Fax : + 91 (0) 2668 62119
E-mail:
accurate_blister@hotmail.com

Aerotech Engg. Co.
39, Tirupati Indl. Est.
Milan Everest Rd.
Saraspur, Ahmedabad
Gujarat-380018
Tel : + 91 (0) 79 2779832
Fax : + 91 (0) 79 2779832
E-mail:
simit@ad1.vsnl.net.in

Evergreen Engg. Works
Muni Shop 3, 4
Below Asarva Bridge
Ahmedabad
Gujarat-380016
Tel : + 91 (0) 79 2136339
E-mail:
aminpetiwala@hotmai.com

Labh Group of Cos.
309, Chitrarath Cmplx.
Nr. Hotel President, C G Rd.
Navrangpura, Ahmedabad
Gujarat-380009
Tel : + 91 (0) 79 6569261
Fax : + 91 (0) 79 6467821
E-mail:
labhgroup@vsnl.com

Aprotech Engineers Pvt. Ltd.
1573, Sect. 7E
Faridabad, Haryana-121006
Tel : + 91 (0) 129 5242140
Fax : + 91 (0) 129 5243452
E-mail: aprotech@vsnl.com

E C Packaging Pvt. Ltd.
14/7, Mile Stone
Mathura Rd., Faridabad
Haryana-121003
Tel : + 91 (0) 129 5277796
Fax : + 91 (0) 129 5255602
E-mail:
ecppl@del3.vsnl.net.in

Baba Packaging
14, Krishna Palace
Neelam Flyover
Faridabad, Haryana-121007
Tel : + 91 (0) 129 5291107
Fax : + 91 (0) 129 5240741
E-mail:
baba@ndb.vsnl.net.in

Jeevan Champa Corp.
174/6,
Pete Chennappa Indl. Est.
Kamakshipalya, Bangalore
Karnataka-560079
Tel : + 91 (0) 80 3485998
Fax : + 91 (0) 80 3486119
E-mail:
bacchawat@vsnl.com

K K Marketing
Nai Sarak, Lashkar, Gwalior
Madhya Pradesh-474001
Tel : + 91 (0) 751 571323
E-mail: kkm@flashmail.com

Prakash Enterprises
65/5, Jawahar Marg
Nihalpura, Indore
Madhya Pradesh-452004
Tel : + 91 (0) 731 473443
Fax : + 91 (0) 731 473593
E-mail:
prkent@satyam.net.in

Suresh Engg. Works
14B, Kalyan Vishranti Grah
South Tukoganj, Indore
Madhya Pradesh-452001
Tel : + 91 (0) 731 529155
Fax : + 91 (0) 731 527872
E-mail:
suresen@bom4.vsnl.net.in

Nichrome India Ltd.
Safire Park Galleria
2nd Flr., Pune-Mumbai Rd.
Shivajinagar, Wakadewadi
Pune, Maharashtra-411005
Tel : + 91 (0) 20 4011001
Fax : + 91 (0) 20 4011010
E-mail:
corpoff@nichrome.com

Pratham Technologies Pvt. Ltd.
4/2A, Patil Baug, Daulat Ngr.
Mumbai-Bangalore
Highway, Vadgaon (BK)
Pune, Maharashtra-411041
Tel : + 91 (0) 20 4355765
Fax : + 91 (0) 20 4352557
E-mail:
varad@pn2.vsnl.net.in

Alfatech Engineers Pvt. Ltd.
4, Krishna Laxmi Indl. Est.
Vartak Ngr.
Pokhran Rd. No. 1, Thane
Maharashtra-400606
Tel : + 91 (0) 22 5344970
Fax : + 91 (0) 22 5347118
E-mail: diptansu@bol.net.in

Apollo Glass Containers
7, J K Indl. Est.
Off Mahakali Caves Rd.
Andheri (E), Mumbai
Maharashtra-400093
Tel : + 91 (0) 22 28329530
Fax : + 91 (0) 22 28363208

Automatic Devices
105 A, Hind Saurashtra Indl. Est., Marol
Andheri-Kurla Rd.
Andheri (E), Mumbai
Maharashtra-400059
Tel : + 91 (0) 22 28501376
Fax : + 91 (0) 22 28593042
E-mail:
autodevices@vsnl.com

Bubber Machine Tools
6, Nagin Mahal
82, Veer Nariman Rd.
Mumbai
Maharashtra-400020
Tel : + 91 (0) 22 22042774
Fax : + 91 (0) 22 22835926
E-mail:
bubbes@bom3.vsnl.net.in

Dison-Tec
Chandu Studio Compound
Kalina, Santacruz (E)
Mumbai
Maharashtra-400098
Tel : + 91 (0) 22 26116269
Fax : + 91 (0) 22 26191135
E-mail: disontec@vsnl.com

Khosla Machines Pvt. Ltd.
B-17, Phase-II, Indl. Area
Mohali, Punjab-160051
Tel : + 91 (0) 172 670587
Fax : + 91 (0) 172 260146
E-mail:
khosla@khoslamachines.com

Moi Engg. Ltd.
A 7, Phase-I, Indl. Est.
SAS Ngr.
Mohali, Punjab-160051
Tel : + 91 (0) 172 670628
Fax : + 91 (0) 172 670630

Elan Engg. Enterprises
96, SIDCO Indl. Est., Pattarawakkam, Ambattur
Chennai
Tamil Nadu-600098
Tel : + 91 (0) 44 6230535
Fax : + 91 (0) 44 6383383

Genesis Automation Pvt. Ltd.
11 A/B, Soundarajan St.
T Ngr., Chennai
Tamil Nadu-600017
Tel : + 91 (0) 44 4361023
Fax : + 91 (0) 44 4321866
E-mail : genesis1@eth.net

Madras Packaging Machine Co.
418, SIDCO Indl. Est.
Chennai
Tamil Nadu-600098
Tel : + 91 (0) 44 6255061

Select Packaging Machinery Ltd.
159/160, SIDCO Indl. Est.
Ambattur, Chennai
Tamil Nadu-600098
Tel : + 91 (0) 44 6258125

Authentic Designer's
C-112, Sect. 10, Noida
Uttar Pradesh-201301
Tel : + 91 (0) 120 4540451
Fax : + 91 (0) 120 4543233
E-mail:
authdesi@nda.vsnl.net.in

Flex Industries Ltd.
A-107, Sect. IV, Noida
Uttar Pradesh-201301
Tel : + 91 (0) 120 4522558
Fax : + 91 (0) 120 4520877

N S Packaging Pvt. Ltd.
C-69, Sect. 2, Noida
Uttar Pradesh-201301
Tel : + 91 (0) 120 4535119
Fax : + 91 (0) 120 4514973
E-mail:
nsindia@mantraonline.com

PLASTIC PIPE CORRUGATING MACHINERY

KBK Plascon Pvt. Ltd.
24/168, P.O.Box 158
Birhana Rd., Kanpur
Uttar Pradesh-208001
Tel : + 91 (0) 512 369353
Fax : + 91 (0) 512 352058
E-mail: kbk@sancharnet.in

Abhi Plastics & Metal Works
750/A, GIDC Indl. Est.
Makarpura
Vadodara, Gujarat-390010
Tel : + 91 (0) 265 644625
Fax : + 91 (0) 265 651713
E-mail:
udaychoksi@wilnetonline.net

PLASTIC POWDER MIXERS

Jogindra Engg. Works
70, Rama Rd.
New Delhi-110015
Tel : + 91 (0) 11 25442112
Fax : + 91 (0) 11 25453836
E-mail:
jogindra@ndf.vsnl.net.in

Gems Engg. Works
7/B, Gujarat Laghu Udyog Vikas Mandal
Dudheshwar Rd., Dhobighat
Ahmedabad
Gujarat-380004
Tel : + 91 (0) 79 5622594
Fax : + 91 (0) 79 6423061

Mecon Engg.
Opp. IIMB
Bannerghatta Rd.,
Bangalore
Karnataka-560070
Tel : + 91 (0) 80 6631217
Fax : + 91 (0) 80 6646125

Pharmaceutical Machinery Manufacturing Works
47/B, Laxmibai Ngr., Indore
Madhya Pradesh-452006
Tel : + 91 (0) 731 410963
Fax : + 91 (0) 731 410071
E-mail:
pharmamach@satyam.net.in

Adam Fabriwerk Pvt. Ltd.
203, Rajguru Apts.
New Nagardas Rd.
Andheri (E), Mumbai
Maharashtra-400069
Tel : + 91 (0) 22 28380548
Fax : + 91 (0) 22 28390195
E-mail: adamfab@vsnl.com

PLASTIC SHEETS & SHEETING MACHINERY

Moscow Machine Tools
C-293, Mukund Ngr.
Ghaziabad
Uttar Pradesh-201003
Tel : + 91 (0) 120 4731630

DGP Windsor India Ltd.
Shah Indl. Est.
'C' Bldg., 1st Flr.
Saki Vihar Rd., Mumbai
Maharashtra-400072
Tel : + 91 (0) 22 28575897
Fax : + 91 (0) 22 28573109
E-mail:
marketing@dgpcorp.sril.in

Super Engg. Works (Regd.)
CB-87/2, Ring Rd.
Naraina, New Delhi-110028
Tel : + 91 (0) 11 25698281
Fax : + 91 (0) 11 25692117

J P Industries
1701, GIDC, Ankleshwar
Gujarat-393002
Tel : + 91 (0) 2646 51083
Fax : + 91 (0) 2646 50196
E-mail:
jpondank@egujarat.net

Konark Plastic Machinery Mfrs.
5, Africawala Est.
B/h Chakudia Mahadev
Opp. Comet House
Rakhial, Ahmedabad
Gujarat-380023
Tel : + 91 (0) 79 2741262
Fax : + 91 (0) 79 2744409
E-mail: sales@konark plasticmachinery.com

Rajoo Engineers Ltd.
Survey No. 210, Plot No. 1
Indl. Area, Veraval (Shapar)
Rajkot, Gujarat-360002
Tel : + 91 (0) 281 52701
Fax : + 91 (0) 281 52700
E-mail : rel@rajoo.com

Spark Engg.
4510, Phase-V
B/h Indo German Tool Room
GIDC Est.
Vatva, Gujarat-382445
Tel : + 91 (0) 79 5836243
Fax : + 91 (0) 79 5840191
E-mail: sparkin@icenet.net

Kalimata Plastic Machinery Manufacturer Pvt. Ltd.
A-5, 3rd Stage
Peenya Indl. Est., Bangalore
Karnataka-560058
Tel : + 91 (0) 80 8394699
Fax : + 91 (0) 80 8392917
E-mail: kalimata@vsnl.com

DGP Windsor India Ltd.
Shah Indl. Est.
'C' Bldg., 1st Flr.
Saki Vihar Rd., Mumbai
Maharashtra-400072
Tel : + 91 (0) 22 28575897
Fax : + 91 (0) 22 28573109
E-mail:
marketing@dgpcorp.sril.in

Europack Machines (I) Pvt. Ltd.
Akash Business Centre
CST Rd.,Kurla (W), Mumbai
Maharashtra-400070
Tel : + 91 (0) 22 26504919
Fax : + 91 (0) 22 26505368
E-mail:
europack@vsnl.com

Yemee Tooling
209, SIDCO Indl. Est.
Chennai
Tamil Nadu-600098
Tel : + 91 (0) 44 6252396
Fax : + 91 (0) 44 6252396
E-mail: yemee@yahoo.com

PLASTIC THERMOFORMING MACHINERY

DGP Windsor India Ltd.
Shah Indl. Est.
'C' Bldg., 1st Flr.
Saki Vihar Rd., Mumbai
Maharashtra-400072
Tel : + 91 (0) 22 28575897
Fax : + 91 (0) 22 28573109
E-mail:
marketing@dgpcorp.sril.in

K L Thermoformers Pvt. Ltd.
C-67/2, Phase-II
Okhla Indl. Area
New Delhi-110020
Tel : + 91 (0) 11 26821708
Fax : + 91 (0) 11 26821708
E-mail:
klthermo@ndb.vsnl.net.in

Saraswati Business Pvt. Ltd.
A-15, Saraswati Vihar
Pitampura, Delhi-110034
Tel : + 91 (0) 11 27913726
Fax : + 91 (0) 11 27910291
E-mail:
sales@zedpack.com

Suraj Plastic Industries
81, Reghar Pura,Karol Bagh
New Delhi-110005
Tel : + 91 (0) 11 25719179
Fax : + 91 (0) 11 25710219
E-mail : tej@id.eth.net.

DGP Windsor India Ltd.
Shah Indl. Est.
'C' Bldg., 1st Flr.
Saki Vihar Rd., Mumbai
Maharashtra-400072
Tel : + 91 (0) 22 8575897
Fax : + 91 (0) 22 8573109
E-mail:
marketing@dgpcorp.sril.in

Europack Machines (I) Pvt. Ltd.
Akash Business Centre
CST Rd.,Kurla (W), Mumbai
Maharashtra-400070
Tel : + 91 (0) 22 26504919
Fax : + 91 (0) 22 26505368
E-mail:europack@vsnl.com

Machinecraft
5, Nav-Bhavna, 422
V S Marg, Prabhadevi
Mumbai
Maharashtra-400025
Tel : + 91 (0) 22 24227189
Fax : + 91 (0) 22 24221633
E-mail:
mcraft@bom5.vsnl.net.in

Pakona Engineers (I) Pvt. Ltd.
22-D, Wadia Charities Bldg.
Office No. 110
S A Brelvi Rd., Fort, Mumbai
Maharashtra-400023
Tel : + 91 (0) 22 22854138
Fax : + 91 (0) 22 22876171
E-mail:
rkothari@bom3.vsnl.net.in

Wonderpack Industries Pvt. Ltd.
321, T V Indl. Est.
S K Ahire Marg
Worli, Mumbai
Maharashtra-400025
Tel : +91 (0) 22 4949580
Fax : +91 (0) 22 4938796
E-mail:
wonder@bom3.vsnl.net.in

Century Machine Craaft
161/10, Pollachi Main Rd.
LIC Cly., Coimbatore
Tamil Nadu-641021
Tel : + 91 (0) 422 873730

Kanchana Pack Machins
No. 213, New Tiny Sect.
Indl. Est., Ambattur,Chennai
Tamil Nadu-600058
Tel : + 91 (0) 44 6256005

Mona Industries
57, Dr. Radhakrishnan Ngr.
Opp. Vaishnava College
Poonamallee High Rd.
Arumbakkam, Chennai
Tamil Nadu-600106
Tel : + 91 (0) 44 6282919
Fax : + 91 (0) 44 6213371

Plastopack Machineries (I) Pvt. Ltd.
B-15, Mugappair Indl. Est.
(W), Chennai
Tamil Nadu-600058
Tel : + 91 (0) 44 6246283

Universal Polypack
2 & 3, Old ESI Rd.
Ramapuram, Ambattur
Chennai,
Tamil Nadu-600053
Tel : + 91 (0) 44 6359707
Fax : + 91 (0) 44 6358050

Vikaash Packaging
No. 120, 1st Flr.
Mugappair Rd., Padi
Chennai
Tamil Nadu-600050
Tel : + 91 (0) 44 6244189
Fax : + 91 (0) 44 6521703
E-mail: rvs@eth.net

Micron International
6/1, New Rd., Kolkata
West Bengal-700027
Tel : + 91 (0) 33 4398301
Fax : + 91 (0) 33 4220712
E-mail: bks@vsnl.com

MLEW Engg. Pvt. Ltd.
Formerly: Maa Lakshmi Engg. Works
24/63, Nabalia Para Rd.
Behala Chowrasta, Kolkata
West Bengal-700008
Tel : + 91 (0) 33 4477888
Fax : + 91 (0) 33 4478504
E-mail:mlew@cal.vsnl.net.in

CALANDERING MACHINERY PLASTICS

Nantech Plastic Industries Pvt. Ltd.
1, Jyoti Sadan, 28th Rd.
Bandra (W), Mumbai
Maharashtra-400050
Tel : + 91 (0) 22 26439143
Fax : + 91 (0) 22 26427139

Kemtech International Ltd.
A-125, Shivalik
Malviya Ngr. P.O.
New Delhi-110017
Tel : + 91 (0) 11 26682346
Fax : + 91 (0) 11 26684589
E-mail: kemtech@vsnl.com

DRYERS : PLASTICS

Bry-Air (Asia) Pvt. Ltd.
20, Rajpur Rd.
Delhi-110054
Tel : + 91 (0) 11 23912800
Fax : + 91 (0) 11 23915127
E-mail:
enquire@pahwa.com

Artic Aircon Pvt. Ltd.
Plot No. 120/5
IDA, Phase-II, Cherlapally
Hyderabad
Andhra Pradesh-500051
Tel : + 91 (0) 40 7807583
Fax : + 91 (0) 40 7806518

NSW India Ltd.
Plot No. 43-44, Sect. 34
EHTP
Gurgaon, Haryana-122001
Tel : + 91 (0) 124 6371106
Fax : + 91 (0) 124 6372859
E-mail:
pnarang@del2.vsnl.net.in

Grovers Pvt. Ltd.
3F-4, Shankardham
Sundervan Cmplx.
off Lokhandwala Cmplx. Rd.
Andheri (W), Mumbai
Maharashtra-400053
Tel : + 91 (0) 22 26314574
Fax : + 91 (0) 22 26313014
E-mail:
vivek@groversequip.com

Mechem Engg. Works
Plot No.J-80, MIDC
Bhosari
Pune, Maharashtra-411026
Tel : + 91 (0) 20 27120903
Fax : + 91 (0) 20 2780239

Larsen & Toubro Limited
Heavy Engg. Division
Plastic Processing
Machinery
L & T Chennai House
Post Bag 5247, 10
Club House Rd., Anna Salai
Chennai
Tamil Nadu-600002
Tel : + 91 (0) 44 8460141
Fax : + 91 (0) 44 8460069

Aerodry Projects Pvt. Ltd.
F-69, Sect. 8, Noida
Uttar Pradesh-201301
Tel : + 91 (0) 120 4442291
Fax : + 91 (0) 120 4551244
E-mail: earodry@vsnl.com

TESTERS : PLASTICS

Prolific Engineers
D-91, Sect. 2, Noida
Uttar Pradesh-201301
Tel : + 91 (0) 120 4524251
Fax : + 91 (0) 120 4522648
E-mail:
gkedia@ndf.vsnl.net.in

Elmech Pneumatic Industries Pvt. Ltd.
DDA Sheds, 103 Type-A
Phase-II, Okhla Indl. Area
New Delhi-110020
Tel : + 91 (0) 11 26841320
Fax : + 91 (0) 11 26841369
E-mail:
elemech@ndf.vsnl.net.in

Nutan Scientific Instruments
438-B, St. No. 8
Durga Puri Extn., Shahdara
Delhi-110093
Tel : + 91 (0) 11 22284766
Fax : + 91 (0) 11 22119239

Precision Standard Testing Equipment Corp.
C-117,FF Cmplx., Phase-III
Okhla Indl. Area
New Delhi-110020
Tel : + 91 (0) 11 26915846
Fax : + 91 (0) 11 26834850
E-mail: presto@vsnl.com

Scientific Testing (I)
2/5, Phase-II,
DSIDC Cmplx., Nand Nagri
Delhi-110093
Tel : + 91 (0) 11 22111777
Fax : + 91 (0) 11 22292176
E-mail:
scientifictesting@usa.net

Topps Enterprises
A 13, First Flr., Meera Bagh
Delhi-110033
Tel : + 91 (0) 11 25252576
Fax : + 91 (0) 11 27133458
E-mail : neerash@usa.net

Deepak Poly-Plast Pvt. Ltd.
155, Rajdeep Indl. Est.
B/h Saurashtra Paints
Nr. Vatva Village, Tolnaka
Vatva,Ahmedabad
Gujarat-382440
Tel : + 91 (0) 79 5833206
Fax : + 91 (0) 79 5833206
E-mail:
deepak@wilnetonline.net

Kamal Metal Industries
Subhash Indl. Est., (202)
Ramol Rd., Ahmedabad
Gujarat-380026
Tel : + 91 (0) 79 5855880
Fax : + 91 (0) 79 5855921
E-mail:
kmigroup@yahoo.com

Shanta Engg.
10, Anusaya, Opp. Mangala
High School, Kopri, Thane
Maharashtra-400623
Tel : + 91 (0) 22 23820485
Fax : + 91 (0) 22 23808745

Prolific Engineers
D-9, Sect. 2, Noida
Uttar Pradesh-201301
Tel : + 91 (0) 120 4524251
Fax : + 91 (0) 120 4522648
E-mail:
gkedia@ndf.vsnl.net.in

Universal Engg. Corp.
Sabri Mills, Ambala Rd.
Saharanpur
Uttar Pradesh-247001
Tel : + 91 (0) 132 648427
Fax : + 91 (0) 132 640062
E-mail:
info@universalenggcorp.org

Precision Balance (I)
6, Wood St., Kolkata
West Bengal-700016
Tel : + 91 (0) 33 2403476
Fax : + 91 (0) 33 2400168

PRINTING MACHINERY : PLASTICS

Deepak Poly-Plast Pvt. Ltd.
155, Rajdeep Indl. Est.,B/h
Saurashtra Paints
Nr. Vatva Village, Tolnaka
Vatva, Ahmedabad
Gujarat-382440
Tel : + 91 (0) 79 5833206
Fax : + 91 (0) 79 5833206
E-mail:
deepak@wilnetonline.net

Remica Plastic Machinery Manufacturers
2/AB, Sardar Patel Indl. Est., Shahwadi, Narol
Ahmedabad
Gujarat-382405
Tel : + 91 (0) 79 5712741
Fax : + 91 (0) 79 5894234
E-mail:
remica@ad1.vsnl.net.in

Boolani Engg. Corp.
Prabhadevi Indl. Est., 402
V S Marg, Mumbai
Maharashtra-400025
Tel : + 91 (0) 22 24302826
Fax : + 91 (0) 22 24229875
E-mail: plastic@vsnl.com

Marsons Print-Graf Machines Pvt. Ltd.
D/9, Udyog Sadan No. 2
MIDC, Andheri (E), Mumbai
Maharashtra-400093
Tel : + 91 (0) 22 28352976
Fax : + 91 (0) 22 28369359
E-mail:
marsons@bom3.vsnl.net.in

Moscow Machine Tools
C-293, Mukund Ngr.
Ghaziabad
Uttar Pradesh-201003
Tel : + 91 (0) 120 4731630

Shaheen Machine Fabric
B-113, Sect. 5, Noida
Uttar Pradesh-201301
Tel : + 91 (0) 120 4555489

HEATERS : PLASTICS PROCESSING

Electro Heat Engineers
A-18A, Phase-I
Naraina Indl. Area
New Delhi-110028
Tel : + 91 (0) 11 25795752
Fax : + 91 (0) 11 25792375
E-mail:
electroheat@vsnl.net

Heatking Industries
C/2, Mahalaxmi Tower
Karnavati Hospital Bldg.,
Opp. Town Hall
Ellisbridge, Ahmedabad
Gujarat-380006
Tel : + 91 (0) 79 6576247
Fax :+ 91 (0) 79 6576686

Bharat Heaters
304, Parvati Indl. Est.
New Sun Mill Compd.
Lower Parel, Mumbai
Maharashtra-400013
Tel : + 91 (0) 22 4926285
Fax : + 91 (0) 22 4964077
E-mail: bhheat@vsnl.com

Simplicon
D-140, Bonanza Indl. Est.
Ashok Chakravati Rd.
Kandivali (E), Mumbai
Maharashtra-400101
Tel : + 91 (0) 22 8875300
Fax : + 91 (0) 22 8873469
E-mail:
simpli@bom5.vsnl.net.in/
simplicon@vsnl.com

Elmec Heaters & Controllers
TS No. 103-A
SIDCO Indl. Est.
Ekkaduthangal, Chennai
Tamil Nadu-600097
Tel : + 91 (0) 44 2326713
Fax : + 91 (0) 44 2323554
E-mail:
elmecheaters@eth.net

Subhot Enterprises
A-45, Nand Gram
Meerut Rd., Ghaziabad
Uttar Pradesh-201301
Tel : + 91 (0) 120 4733866
E-mail: shubot@indya.com

PROCESSING OVENS : PLASTICS

AMI Industries
8, Surve Indl. Est.
1st Sonawala Cross Rd.
Goregaon (E), Mumbai
Maharashtra-400063
Tel : + 91 (0) 22 28727120
Fax : + 91 (0) 22 28734753
E-mail:
oven@bom5.vsnl.net.in

Bharat Engg. Industries
Chitalsar Manpada
Ghodbunder Rd., Thane
Maharashtra-400607
Tel : + 91 (0) 22 25346098
Fax : + 91 (0) 22 25346098

Thermex Industrial & Laboratory Instrument Co.
113, Satyam Indl. Est.
Govandi Stn. Rd.
Deonar, Mumbai
Maharashtra-400088
Tel : + 91 (0) 22 25512070
Fax : + 91 (0) 22 25584519

Gambaks Instruments Co.
5 Brindavan Ngr.
Door No.14, Venkateswara Ngr. Main Rd.
Valasaravakkam, Chennai
Tamil Nadu-600087
Tel : + 91 (0) 44 4869541
Fax : + 91 (0) 44 4867044
E-mail:
gambaks@md3.vsnl.net.in

Kwality Engg. Works
48-A, Maktaram Babu St. Kolkata
West Bengal-700007
Tel : + 91 (0) 33 2391195

The Wesman Engg. Company Pvt. Ltd.
"Wesman Center", 8
Mayfair Rd., Kolkata
West Bengal-700019
Tel : + 91 (0) 33 2405320
Fax : + 91 (0) 33 2478050
E-mail:
mailbox@wesman.com

NSW India Ltd.
Plot No. 43-44,
Sect. 34, EHTP
Gurgaon, Haryana-122001
Tel : + 91 (0) 124 6371106
Fax : + 91 (0) 124 6372859
E-mail:
pnarang@del2.vsnl.net.in

ELDING MACHINERY : PLASTICS

Strayfield Heating Pvt. Ltd.
B-17, 1st Cross, 1st Stage
Peenya Indl. Est., Bangalore
Karnataka-560058
Tel : + 91 (0) 80 8392571
Fax : + 91 (0) 80 8396040
E-mail:
stray@bgl.vsnl.net.in

Boolani Engg. Corp.
Prabhadevi Indl. Est., 402
V S Marg, Mumbai
Maharashtra-400025
Tel : + 91 (0) 22 24302826
Fax : + 91 (0) 22 24229875
E-mail: plastic@vsnl.com

New Vimco Plastics
B-131, Ghatkopar Indl. Est.
Mumbai
Maharashtra-400086
Tel : + 91 (0) 22 25170040
Fax : + 91 (0) 22 25007183
E-mail:
vimko@bom5.vsnl.net.in

Rajdeep Enterprises
4th & 2nd Flr., 10, Clive Rd.
Kolkata
West Bengal-700001
Tel : + 91 (0) 33 2424725
Fax : + 91 (0) 33 2433639

Uday Bharathi Engg. Pvt. Ltd.
12-13-372, UBE House
St. No. 2, Tarnaka
Secunderabad
Andhra Pradesh-500017
Tel : + 91 (0) 40 7016031

59

Suppliers of Dies & Moulds

PLASTIC BLOW MOULDS

Alekya Dies & Moulds
26B, S V Co-op. Indl. Est.
Balanagar, Hyderabad,
Andhra Pradesh-500037
Tel : + 91 (0) 40 3770286

Indo-Danish Tool Room
M-4 (Part), Phase-VI
Tata Kandra Rd., Gamharia
Jamshedpur, Bihar-832108
Tel : + 91 (0) 657 408061
Fax : + 91 (0) 657 407723
E-mail: idtr@dte.vsnl.net.in

Dhanjal Engg. Works
1774/131, Shanti Ngr.
Tri Ngr., Delhi-110035
Tel : + 91 (0) 11 27190311

Kamet Plastics Pvt. Ltd.
F-40, Part-I, South Extn.
New Delhi-110049
Tel : + 91 (0) 11 24618130
Fax : + 91 (0) 11 24640325
E-mail:
abc@ajaybahlco.com

Ajanta Industries
Plot No. 2602,GIDC, Phase-IV, Nr. Mahavir Rolling Mill
Ramol Chokdi, Vatva
Ahmedabad
Gujarat-382445
Tel : + 91 (0) 79 5890713

Mukesh Industries
19, Lalita Indl. Est.,
B/h Dena Bank
Nr. Jagannath Est.
Rakhial, Ahmedabad
Gujarat-382023
Tel : + 91 (0) 79 2741604
Fax : + 91 (0) 79 5830572

Orcan Engg. Products Pvt. Ltd.
Plot No. 51, Indl. Area, NIT
Faridabad, Haryana-121001
Tel : + 91 (0) 129 232394
Fax : + 91 (0) 129 230687
E-mail:
orcan@giasdl01.vsnl.net.in

Edizi Gauge & Tools
C-4, 1st Main,
Kalappa Block, R C Puram
Bangalore
Karnataka-560021
Tel : + 91 (0) 80 3383025
Fax : + 91 (0) 80 3200602
E-mail:
edizi@bg1.vsnl.net.in

M-Tech Industries
M-Tech House
Diamond Indl. Est., Walive
Vasai
Madhya Pradesh-401208
Tel : + 91 (0) 250 452545
Fax : + 91 (0) 250 454631
E-mail:
mtech@bom3.vsnl.net.in

Triyami Tools
MPLUN, 21, Sect. F
Sanwer Rd., Indore
Madhya Pradesh-452015
Tel : + 91 (0) 731 722762
Fax : + 91 (0) 731 722762

A B Tools
5, Saikripa Soc.
RWC 43-1/3, Ganesh Ngr.
Kandivli (W), Mumbai
Maharashtra-400067
Tel : + 91 (0) 22 28641967
Fax : + 91 (0) 22 28053704

Bindu Die Works
Shop No.4
Ramchandra Lane
Kanchapada, No.1
Malad (W), Mumbai
Maharashtra-400064
Tel : + 91 (0) 22 8813827

Cam - Tek
D-11G, Malad Indl. Unit
Ramchandra Lane
Kacha Pada
Malad (W), Mumbai
Maharashtra-400064
Tel : + 91 (0) 22 28814245
Fax: + 91 (0) 22 28806506

Creative Tools
67,
Bombay Talkies Compds.
Malad (W), Mumbai
Maharashtra-400064
Tel : + 91 (0) 22 8812652

Daniel & Sons
1-3, Vaibhav Indl. Est.
Andheri (E), Mumbai
Maharashtra-400093
Tel : + 91 (0) 22 8351554
Fax : + 91 (0) 22 8364272

J B Dies
633/15, PH Rd., Aminjikari
Chennai
Tamil Nadu-600029
Tel : + 91 (0) 44 6283681

Venu Engg. Services
TS-90, Guindy Indl. Est.
Ekaduthangal, Chennai
Tamil Nadu-600097
Tel : + 91 (0) 44 2328167
Fax : + 91 (0) 44 2332091
E-mail:
venuengg@md3.vsnl.net.in

Anja Moulds
C-447, Sect.10, Noida
Uttar Pradesh-201301
Tel : + 91 (0) 120 4525964

Jiwan Die Makers
D-122, Sect. 10, Noida
Uttar Pradesh-201301
Tel : + 91 (0) 120 4556041
Fax : + 91 (0) 120 4520803
E-mail : jiwan@id.eth.net

Rupali Plastic Pvt. Ltd.
34/1/3, Buxarah Rd.
P.O. Buxarah, Howrah
West Bengal-711306
Tel : + 91 (0) 33 6588454
Fax : + 91 (0) 33 682186

PLASTIC EXTRUSION DIES

Paras Engg. Co.
Plot No. C-20/3
MIDC Indl. Area
Taloja, Navi Mumbai
Maharashtra-410208
Tel : + 91 (0) 22 27411212
Fax : + 91 (0) 22 27411211
E-mail:
svshah@satyam.net.in

Ratna Tool & Engg. Pvt. Ltd.
Plot No. 8
Phase-IV (Extn.), IDA
Jeedimetla, Hyderabad
Andhra Pradesh-500055
Tel : + 91 (0) 40 3096150
Fax : + 91 (0) 40 3098031

Indo-Danish Tool Room
M-4 (Part), Phase-VI
Tata Kandra Rd.
Gamharia, Jamshedpur
Bihar-832108
Tel : + 91 (0) 657 408061
Fax : + 91 (0) 657 407723
E-mail: idtr@dte.vsnl.net.in

Kemtech International Ltd.
A-125, Shivalik
Malviya Ngr. P.O.
New Delhi-110017
Tel : + 91 (0) 11 26682346
Fax : + 91 (0) 11 26684589
E-mail: kemtech@vsnl.com

Saroj Rubber Industries
14, Indl. Area, Tilak Ngr.
New Delhi-110018
Tel : + 91 (0) 11 25447994
Fax : + 91 (0) 11 25461509

Ajanta Industries
Plot No. 2602
GIDC, Phase-IV
Nr. Mahavir Rolling Mill
Ramol Chokdi, Vatva
Ahmedabad
Gujarat-382445
Tel : + 91 (0) 79 5890713

Paras Engg. Co.
Plot No. C-20/3
MIDC Indl. Area
Taloja, Navi Mumbai,
Maharashtra-410208
Tel : + 91 (0) 22 27411212
Fax : + 91 (0) 22 27411211
E-mail:
svshah@satyam.net.in

Nantech Plastic Industries Pvt. Ltd.
1, Jyoti Sadan, 28th Rd.
Bandra (W), Mumbai
Maharashtra-400050
Tel : + 91 (0) 22 26439143
Fax : + 91 (0) 22 26427139

RRR Industries
A/109, Ansa Indl. Est.
Saki Vihar Rd., Mumbai
Maharashtra-400072
Tel : + 91 (0) 22 28521974
Fax : + 91 (0) 22 28593611

Sri Devi Engg. Works
46, Kambar St.,
TMP Ngr., Padi, Chennai
Tamil Nadu-600050
Tel : + 91 (0) 44 6259708

PLASTIC INJECTION MOULDS

Sun Glisten Tools Pvt. Ltd.
2-109, Old Airport Rd.,
Sobhana Cly., Balanagar
Hyderabad
Andhra Pradesh-500042
Tel : + 91 (0) 40 3777716
Fax : + 91 (0) 40 3777716
E-mail:
vkrreddy@satyam.net.in

Delite Engineers Pvt. Ltd.
935/1 & 2, GIDC Indl. Est.
Vaghodia, Gujarat-391760
Tel : + 91 (0) 2668 62158
Fax : + 91 (0) 2668 62750
E-mail:
deliteengg@hotmail.com

Sun Glisten Tools Pvt. Ltd.
2-109, Old Airport Rd.,
Sobhana Cly., Balanagar
Hyderabad
Andhra Pradesh-500042
Tel : + 91 (0) 40 3777716
Fax : + 91 (0) 40 3777716
E-mail:
vkrreddy@satyam.net.in

Akhila Polymers
5-36/1/21
Kukatpally Indl. ESt.
Prashanti Ngr., Hyderabad
Andhra Pradesh-500037
Tel : + 91 (0) 40 3076969
Fax : + 91 (0) 40 3075397

Bhagyalaxmi Industries
51,
Electronic Cmplx. (Extn.)
Kushaiguda, Hyderabad
Andhra Pradesh-500062
Tel : + 91 (0) 40 7122671
Fax : + 91 (0) 40 7125084
E-mail:
bhagyala@hd2.vsnl.net.in

Maxwell Tools
20-B, Type 3, Indl. Est.
Kukatpally, Hyderabad
Andhra Pradesh-500037
Tel : + 91 (0) 40 3079009

Moldtroniks
7-4-219
Geethanagar, Ferozguda
Balanagar, Hyderabad
Andhra Pradesh-500011
Tel : + 91 (0) 40 3774445
Fax : + 91 (0) 40 3774446
E-mail: m-troniks@usa.net

Indo-Danish Tool Room
M-4 (Part), Phase-VI
Tata Kandra Rd., Gamharia
Jamshedpur, Bihar-832108
Tel : + 91 (0) 657 408061
Fax : + 91 (0) 657 407723
E-mail: idtr@dte.vsnl.net.in

Arrow Plast Pvt. Ltd.
Opp. Jahangir Puri, 64
Rajasthan Udyog Ngr.
Delhi-110033
Tel : + 91 (0) 11 27234787

Bell Polymers
H-3, DSIDC Cmplx.
Rohtak Rd., Nangloi
New Delhi-110041
Tel : + 91 (0) 11 25475440
Fax : + 91 (0) 11 25474124
E-mail: bellpoly@vsnl.com

Delite Engineers Pvt. Ltd.
935/1 & 2, GIDC Indl. Est.
Vaghodia, Gujarat-391760
Tel : + 91 (0) 2668 62158
Fax : + 91 (0) 2668 62750
E-mail:
deliteengg@hotmail.com

Alps Enterprise
"Jay" Nandi Park
Nr. Jyotinagar, Kalawad Rd.
Rajkot, Gujarat-360005
Tel : + 91 (0) 281 78362
Fax : + 91 (0) 281 573949
E-mail:
iffcorjit@rajkotonline.com

Amrut Brothers
24, Manorath Est.
Nr. Milan Cinema
Saraspur, Ahmedabad
Gujarat-380018
Tel : + 91 (0) 79 2168163
Fax : + 91 (0) 79 2168163
E-mail:
exports@amrutbrothers.com

Aar Aar Plastics
18/1, Mathura Rd.
Faridabad,
Haryana-121001
Tel : + 91 (0) 129 5289000
Fax : + 91 (0) 129 5286666

Motherson Tools
Badkal Cmplx., Faridabad
Haryana-121001
Tel : + 91 (0) 129 5410621
Fax : + 91 (0) 129 5410621
E-mail:
motherson@ndf.vsnl.net.in

Omni Matrix Pvt. Ltd.
B-9, Indl. Est., 6th Block
Rajaji Ngr., Bangalore
Karnataka-560044
Tel : + 91 (0) 80 3200311
Fax : + 91 (0) 80 3386876

Spark Engineers
N-4, Phase-III
SIDCO Indl. Est.
Hosur, Karnataka-635126
Tel : + 91 (0) 4344 77736

TV Plastics
75/1, Opp. Bank of Baroda
Dr. Raj Rd., Prakash Ngr.
Bangalore
Karnataka-560021
Tel : + 91 (0) 80 3355523
Fax : + 91 (0) 80 3355523
E-mail:
tvplast@bgl.vsnl.net.in

M-Tech Industries
M-Tech House
Diamond Indl. Est.
Walive, Vasai
Madhya Pradesh-401208
Tel : + 91 (0) 250 452545
Fax : + 91 (0) 250 454631
E-mail:
mtech@bom3.vsnl.net.in

Accurate Dies & Moulds
Plot No. 3
Chitabhai Pael Rd.
Kandivali (E), Mumbai
Maharashtra-400101
Tel : + 91 (0) 22 2691721

Bindu Die Works
Shop No.4
Ramchandra Lane
Kanchapada, No.1
Malad (W), Mumbai
Maharashtra-400064
Tel : + 91 (0) 22 8813827

Bombay Dies
A/9, Vaibhav Indl. Est.
Nr. MTNI Exch. Powai
Saki Vihar Rd., Mumbai
Maharashtra-400072
Tel : + 91 (0) 22 8570648
E-mail:
bombaydies@yahoo.com

Central Tool Room & Training Centre
B-36, Post Patia
Chandra Indl. Area
Bhubaneshwar
Orissa-751024
Tel : + 91 (0) 674 320210
Fax : + 91 (0) 674 320291
E-mail: cttc@satyam.net.in

60

PET Machinery & Raw Material Suppliers

P.K.Industries
D-26, D.D.A. Shed, Okhla Indl. Area,
Phase-II,New Delhi-110 020 (India)
Ph: 26388488, 28611319,
28611151,
28613320, 24317154, 24316418
Fax: 91-11-26186324, 28611151
(For Mfrs: Pet/Hd Bottles, Jars,
Plastic Caps, Preforms, Injection
Moulded Products, Pet Stretch
Blow Moulding Machine & Moulds,
Traders: Pet Resin)

M/s Plama Gmbh
Bergischestr., 15, D-42781 Haan,
Ph: 49.21 29/94 16-0, Fax: 94 16 99
E-mail: infa@plama.de,
PlamaGmbH@aol.com.
Website: www.plama.de
(For Pet Machiners,
Extrusion lines etc.)

Sig Corpoplast Gmbh+Co. Kg.
Post fach 73 03 40, D-22/23
Hamburg
Ph: +49(40) 67907-0,
Fax: +49(40) 67907-270
www.sigplastics.com
(For Pet Bottles Technology &
Machines)

Abexmatic Hydraulics Pvt Ltd.
487/41, Peera Garhi,
New Delhi - 110 087
E-mail:
mr_sk_sharma@mantraonline.com
Ph: 25277908,25275975,
Fax: 25289581
(For Mfrs: Pet Bottles/Jar Making,
Stretch Blowing M/c,
Preform Injection Moulding
Machine)

N E C Engineering Industries (R)
A-115, Vikas Marg, Shakarpur,
New Delhi - 92
Ph: 22410774
(For PVC Cable/Pipe, Polyhene Tubing, Pet Bott, Jar Making, Injection Moulding other Plastic M/c)

Krupp Corpoplast Maschinenbau GmbH
P.O.Box 73 03 40, D-22123
Hamburg
Ph: +49(40) 6 79 07-0,
Fax: +49(40) 6 79 07-270
E-mail: corpo@kch.hh.uunet.de
http:// www.krupp-corpoplast.com
(Machines for producing Pet containers in a single stage process)

Darshan Mould Maker
487/47, Peera Garhi,
Near Pooja Dairy,
New Delhi - 87 (India)
Ph: 25676148,
Fax: 91-11-25684926
(Semi-Auto Pet Preform Blow Moulding Machine & Pet-Mould)

Admit OY
Malminraitti 17-F1-00700 Helsinki
Ph: +358 9 3859 312,
Fax: +358 9 3451,
E-mail: admit@admit.fi
(All Kinds of Second hand Plastic machines including Pet Bottling Plant)

Jomar Europe
Ph: 44-(0) 2392-269661,
Fax: 44-(0) 2392-269671
E-mail: jomareurop@aol.com
Website: www.jomarcorp.com
(For Complete Plant Supplier for Pet Bottling Plant andMoulds)

Sidel Far East Ltd.
Hong-Kong.,
Ph: +852 27 35 68 22/24/49
Fax: +852 27 35 67 97
E-mail: mail@sidelfe.com.hk
Website: www.sidel.com
(For Complete Plant Supplier for Pet Bottling Plant andMoulds)

Sidel Singapore
Ph: +65 981 574 42
Fax: +65 475 46 10
E-mail: sgpsidel@mbox.singnet.com.sg
Website: www.sidel.com
(For Complete Plant Supplier for Pet Bottling Plant andMoulds)

Sidel Malaysia
Ph: +603 512 04 01
Fax: +603 512 04 11
E-mail: sidelma@pojaring.my
Website: www.sidel.com
(For Complete Plant Supplier for Pet Bottling Plant andMoulds)

Krones (Beijing)
Representative Office
Ph: +86-10-65 15 97
Fax: 65 15 65 99
E-mail: kroneskb@eastnet.com.cn
(Krones Contiform, a stretch blow-moulding machine for thetwo-stage process offers you the advantages of an innovative new design)

Krones Asia Limited
Hongkong
Ph: + 852-27 21 26 18
Fax: 27 23 25 98
E-mail: info@krones.com.hk
(Krones Contiform, a stretch blow-moulding machine for the two-stage process offers you the advantages of an innovative new design)

Krones AG
Ph: + 49(0) 94 01/70-3800
Fax: 70-36 08
E-mail: appel.otto@krones.de
www.krones.be
(Krones Contiform, a stretch blow-moulding machine for the two-stage process, offers you the advantages of an innovative new design)

Soni Polyplast Pvt Ltd.
1143/2, Old Madhupura
O/s Delhi Gate
Ahmedabad - 380 004 (India)
Ph: 2159149, 2165983
Fax: (079) 2130033
E-mail: soni@wilnetonline.net
Website: www.sonipet.com
(Mtr. of: Pet Preforms, Bottles & jars
Stretch Blow Molding Machines for Pet Bottles & Jars)

Netionalpet
Plot No. D-24,
Govt. Industrial Estate
Kandivali (W)
Mumbai - 67
Ph: 869 228, 869 4980
Fax: 869 9682
E-mail:
npet@bom5.vsnl.net.in
Website; www.npetmachi8nes.com
(Manufacture & Exporter of:
Pet Stretch Blow Moulding Machines & Plastic Blow Moulding Machines)

AGR International, Inc.
Bulter, PA USA
Ph: 724/482-2163
Fax: 724/482-2767
Website: www.agrinti.com
(Equipment for the Plastic Container Industry)

Polytech Manufacturers & Engineers
Gala No. A-5, to A-8
Agarwal Industrial Estate,
Chitalsar, Manpada
Thane - 400 607,

Ph: 5971315,
Fax: 5892317
E-mail:
rewponse@horapolytech.com
Website: www.horapolytech.com
(Manufacturers & Exporters of Pet Blow Moulding Machines and Moulds)

AMPEE Shrijk-Pac
Gala No. 11, Bharat Ind. Compound,Behind Autl Marble, Near Hindustan Circle
Charkop, Kandivali (W),
Mumbai - 400 067
Ph: 8628024/8062873
Fax: 8073722
E-mail: ampee@vsnl.com
(Pet Bottle Machine)

Rana Sons Pvt Ltd.
128-A, Government Industrial Estate,Charkop,
Kandivalil (W)
Mumbai - 400 067
Ph:868 3897,868 3408,
868 4181, 868 4709
Fax: +91-22-868 2244
E-mail: ranasons@vsnl.com
Website: www.ranasons.com
(Pet-Preform Injection Moulding Machines)

Rana & Sons Engineering Pvt. Ltd.
Plot No. 114-C ,Government Industrial Estate,
Charkop, Kandivali (W)
Mumbai - 400 067
Ph: 868 4661, 868 2890, 868 6147
(Pet-Preform Injection Moulding Machines)

Plasticos
15, Devki Villa,Goraswadi
Malad-West
Mumbai- 400 064
Ph: +81-22-8619550
Fax: +91-22-8086565
E-mail:
plasticos@mantraonline.com
utsav_m@yahoo.com
(Pet Stretch Blow Moulding Machines Single Stage & Two Stage, Injection Moulding Machines for Pet Preforms, Moulds & Dies.)

117. MANUFACTURE OF TIN CONTAINERS
118. MANUFACTURE OF STORAGE TANKS, PRESSURE VESSELS, HEAT EXCHANGERS
119. MARK II HAND PUMPS
120. MARUTI WORKSHOP CUM - SERVICE STATION
121. MECHANICAL JACKS
122. METAL CUTTING DIE DESIGN
123. METAL CUTTING OF AND GRINDING WHEELS (ABBRASIVE CUTTING WHEELS)
124. METAL HOOKS & CLIPS
125. METAL SEPARATION (COPPER, TIN, LEAD) FROM SPENT WASH ACID
126. METALLIC RING JOINTS
127. METALLIC GASKET (SPIRAL WOUND)
128. MICROVEE & ABSOLUTE FILTER
129. MICROWAVE OVEN
130. MILD STEEL INGOTS
131. MINI STEEL PLANT
132. MODERN VEHICLE WORKSHOP
133. MOPED
134. M.S.HINGES
135. M.S.INGOT AND HR. STEEL STRUCTURALS
136. M.S.INGOT BY INDUCTION FURNACES
137. M.S.PIPES
138. M.S. WELDING ELECTRODE
139. MUFFLERS & SILENCERS FOR THREE WHEELERS
140. NAIL CUTTER WITH FILER & MANICURE
141. NICHROME WIRE
142. NICKEL LINED SCREENS
143. NON-FERROUS ALLOY ROLLING
144. NON-FERROUS FORGING
145. NON-FERROUS FOUNDRY
146. NON PRESSURE
147. INCANDESCENT LAMP
148. NUMBER COMBINATION LOCKS FOR LUGGAGES
149. NUTS & BOLTS
150. PAPER COATED ALUMINIUM AND COPPER WIRE
151. PETROMAX CONTAINER
152. PHOTO ETCHING OF STAINLESS STEEL PLATES
153. PIPE GALVANIZING PLANT
154. PISTON RING-AUTOMOBILE
155. PLANT PROTECTION EQUIPMENTS
156. PLATINUM LABORATORY APPARATUS
157. PRESSURE COOKER & ALUMINIUM UTENSILS
158. PRESSURE COOKER (ALUMINIUM)
159. PRESSURE DIE CASTING
160. PRINTED ALUMINIUM COLLAPSIBLE TUBES
161. PRINTED TIN CONTAINERS
162. PRINTING PRESS (CYLINDER MACHINE)
163. PUMPS FOR CHEMICAL INDUSTRY (SPECIAL)
164. RAILWAY SLEEPERS (M.S.)
165. RAZOR TWIN BLADE
166. R.C.C SPUN PIPES
167. RECONDITIONING OF M.S. DRUMS/BARRELS
168. RE-ROLLING COPPER AND BRASS SHEET AND RODS
169. RE-ROLLING MILLS
170. RESIN COATED SAND
171. RESIN CORED SOFT SOLDER WIRES
172. ROLLING MILL (BY INDUCTION FURNACE) & MANUFACTURE OF BARS, ANGLES, SQUARES, TUBES AND OTHERS
173. ROLLER BEARING & FORGING
174. ROLLING OF STAINLESS STEEL PATTA
175. RUBBER INSULATED PLIERS (HAND TOOLS)
176. RUBBING COMPOUND FOR AUTOMOBILES
177. SCIENTIFIC LABORATORY EQUIPMENTS
178. SCOOTER ASSEMBLING
179. SECONDARY LEAD EXTRAC-TION BY SCRAP BATTERY PLATES,PIPES & SHEET
180. SEAMLESS M.S. TUBES & PIPES
181. SELF TAPPING STEEL SCREW
182. SEWING NEEDLES
183. S.G. IRON & ALLOY STEEL
184. SHEET METAL PRODUCTS, (FERROUS/NON-FERROUS)
185. SHIP/MARINE CONTAINER
186. SHOCK ABSORBERS
187. SHOE EYELETS
188. SHOT AND GRITS BY AUTOMIZATION PROCESS
189. SHOVELS
190. SILICO MANGANESE ALLOYS
191. SILENCERS (MUFFLERS) EXHAUST & TAIL PIPE FOR ALL TYPES OF VEHICLES
192. SINTERED BEARING
193. SINTERED BUSHES
194. SINTERED METAL PRODUCTS
195. SOFT AND HARD FERRITES
196. SPANNERS
197. SPARK PLUGS
198. STEEL PLANT (ELECTRIC ARC FURNACE BASED- EAF)
199. SPHERIODAL GRAPHITE CAST IRON
200. SPRAY DRYER
201. STAINLESS STEEL HINGES
202. STAINLESS STEEL SHEET ROLLING TO PRODUCE STAINLESS STEEL UTENSILS
203. STAINLESS STEEL UTENSILS
204. STAPLE PINS,PAPER PIN, GEM CLIPS ETC.
205. STEEL CASTINGS
206. STEEL CHAIN
207. STEEL FOUNDRY
208. STEEL FURNITURES AND ELECTRICAL APPLIANCES
209. STEEL PLANT (MINI)
210. STEEL RODS AND COILS FROM SCRAPS
211. STEEL ROLLING MILL
212. STEEL STRIPS (COLD ROLLED) SILICON WITH GRAIN RIENTED FOR ELECTRIC USE
213. STEEL TRANSMISSION LINE TOWERS & ROLLING MILL TO PRODUCE STEEL SECTION
214. STEEL FURNITURES AND ELECTRICAL APPLIANCES
215. STEEL WIRE DRAWING AND GALVANIZING
216. STEEL WOOL
217. SUBMERGED ARC WELDED PIPES
218. SUBMERSIBLE PUMP MANUFACTURING
219. SUPER ENAMELLED COPPER WIRE
220. THREE WHEELERS
221. TIE-ROD ENDS
222. TIN CONTAINERS
223. TOOLROOM AND SHEET METAL PRODUCTS
224. TRACTOR TRAILERS
225. TRANSMISSION POWER FITTING
226. TUBULAR POLES
227. SUPER ENAMELLED COPPER WIRES
228. TUBULAR POLES FOR ELECTRICAL TRANSMISSION (BY FABRICATION PROCESS)
229. TUBULAR POLES OF M.S. & HIGH TENSILE STEEL
230. VACUUM CLEANERS
231. VACUUM FLASK (STAINLESS STEEL)
232. VALVES FOR REFRIGERA TION AND AIR-CONDITION
233. VEHICLE WELDING & PAINTING
234. VENETION BLIND
235. WASHING MACHINES (AUTOMATIC & COMPUTERISED)
236. WATER CONTROLLER (AUTOMATIC)
237. WATCH STRAPS/CHAINS/ BRACELETS/BELT BRASS & STAINLESS STEEL
238. WATER COOLERS
239. WELDED WIRE MESH
240. WELDING ELECTRODES
241. WICK STOVES
242. WIND MILL WINDOW FRAME (FERROUS & NON-FERROUS)
243. WRIST WATCH

359. DI ETHYL OXALATE
360. DI METHYL ORTHOPHTHALATE
361. DI-METHYL PHTHALATE
362. DICLOFENAC GEL
363. DIOCTYL PHTHALATE (DOP)
364. DI PHENYL GLYCERINE
365. DI PHENYL OXIDE
366. DINITRO-CHLORO BENZENE
367. DISTILLED WATER
368. DODECYL BENZENE SULPHONATE
369. DUSTLESS CHALK
370. EDTA & ITS SALTS
371. ELECTROLESS NICKEL PLATING ON PLASTICS
372. ENDOSULFAN
373. EPOXY RESIN BASED COMPOUND
374. ETHYL ACETATE
375. EHTYL ETHER
376. ETHYL ALCOHOL (POTABLE LIQUOR)
377. ETHYL HEXANOL
378. EXTRACTION OF ESSENTIAL OILS BY SUGAR CRITICAL FLUID (CARBON DIOXIDE) METHOD FROM FLOWERS, HERBAL & SPICES
379. FERRIC ALUM
380. FERRO CHROME LIGNO SULPHONATE
381. FERRO MANGANESE
382. FERRO SILICONE
383. FERRO VANADIUM FROM VANADIUM SLUDGE
384. FERROUS SILICATE
385 FERROUS SULPHATE
386. FERTILIZER FROM ANIMAL BLOOD & LEATHER WASTE
387. FLUORESCENT TUBE LIGHT POWDER
388. FOAMED PVC COMPOUNDING & ITS PRODUCTS
389. FORMALDEHYDE
390. FRACTIONAL DISTILLATION OF D.M.O (DEMENTHOLIZED OIL)
391. FRACTIONAL DISTILLATION OF ESSENTIAL OIL & MEDICINAL PLANT EXTRACT
392. FRICTION DUST (LIQUID & POWDER) FROM CNSL
393. FRUIT FLAVOURS
394. FURFURAL FROM RICE HUSK
395. GARLIC ACID
396. GASKET SHELLAC COMPOUND
397. GEAR OIL
398. GIBBERELLIC ACID
399. GLASS PUTTY
400. GLYCERINE
401. GOSSYPOL (POLY PHENOL) FROM COTTON SEED OIL
402. GUAR GUM POWDER
403. HAIR FIXER (HAIR GEL TYPE)
404. H - ACID
405. HENNA PASTE MAKING
406. HEPTAL DEHYDE
407. HIGH CARBON FERRO CHROME
408. HYDRATED CALCIUM SILICATE BRICK
409. HYDRATED LIME FROM SEA SHELL
410. HYDROCHLORIC ACID
411. HYDRO FLUORIC ACID
412. HYDROGEN PEROXIDE (BY AUTO-OXIDATION PROCESS)
413. ICE PACKS (SOLUTIONS TYPE, WHITE GEL TYPE, VIOLET SEMI SOLID POLYMER TYPE)
414. IMPROVING DROP POINT PARAFFIN WAX FROM 45-50°C TO 75-80°C
415. INDUSTRIAL ALCOHOL
416. INTEGERATED COMPLEX OF EASTER & ALLIED PRODUCTS (D.O.P, D.B.P, ETHYL ACETATE WIRE ENAMEL & CABLE JELLY)
417. IMFL (WHISKY) & COUNTRY LIQUOR
418. IRON OXIDE FOR MAKING FERITTE
419. IRON SULPHIDE
420. JUTE BATCHING OIL
421. KESH KALA TEL (HAIR DYE LOTION) (VASMOL 33, BLACK NITE TYPE)
422. L-LYSINE MONOHYDROCHLORIDE
423. LACTIC ACID FROM WHITE SUGAR BY FERMENTATION PROCESS
424. LDPE GRANULES FROM VIRGIN (LDPE RESIN)
425. LEAD EXTRACTION FROM BATTERY SCRAP
426. LEAD OXIDE (A) LEAD MONOXIDE
(B) LEAD TETRA OXIDE
(C) GREYLEAD OXIDE
427. LIQUID GLUCOSE & ITS BY PRODUCTS
428. LIQUID OXYGEN BOTTLING PLANT
429. LIQUID SHOE POLISH
430. LIQUID FLOOR POLISH
431. LUBE OIL VISCOSITY IMPROVED FOR P.P.G/P.E.G.
432. LUBRICANTS ASHLESS 100% COMBUSTION
433. MAGNESIUM CARBONATE AND MAGNESIUM BICARMONATE
434. MAGNESIUM HYDROXIDE POWDER
435. MAGNESIUM SILICATE
436. MAGNESIUM SULPHATE
437. MALACHITE GREEN
438. MALEIC ANHYDRIDE
439. MANGANESE SULPHATE
440. MANUFACTURING OF CARBON MONO-OXIDE WATER GAS
441. MENTHOL BOLD CRYSTALS FROM FLAKES
442. MENTHOL CRYSTAL & MENTHA OIL
443. MERCURIC OXIDE
444. METAL PRE-TREATMENT CHEMICALS
445. METHANE GAS BY SODIUM ACETATE & SODA LIME
446. METHYL ACETYL RICINOLATE
447. METOL
448. METOL FROM HYDROQUINONE & METHYLAMINE
449. MICANITE
450. MICRO NUTRIENT MIXTURE
451. MINERAL WATER
452. MINERAL WATER AND PET BOTTILNG PLANT
453. MINERAL WATER IN BOTTLES, GLASS AND POUCHES
454. MINI CEMENT PLANT (BY ROTARY KILN PROCESS)
455. MIXED FERTILIZER
456. MOSQUITO & FLIES REPELLENT AGARBATTI (INCENSE STICKS)
457. MONO CHLORO ACETIC ACID
458. MONOCROTOPHOS (TECHNICAL)
459. MOSQUITO COIL
460. MOSQUITO COIL & MAT
461. MOSQUITO MAT
462. MOTHER TINCTURE & BIO CHEMIC MEDICINES
463. NAPHTHALENE & PHENYL (INTEGRATED UNIT)
464. NATURAL MINERAL WATER BY REVERSE OSMOSIS PROCESS
465. NICKEL PLATING BRIGHTNER (PRIMARY OR CARRIER BRIGHTNER & SECONDARY BRIGHTNER)
466. NICKEL SULPHATE
467. NICOTINE FROM TOBACCO WASTE
468. NICOTINE SULPHATE FROM TOBACCO WASTE
469. NITRO BENZENE
470. NITRO CELLULOSE SANDING SEALER/LACQUER
471. NITRO MUSK
472. NITROGEN & OXYGEN GAS PLANT
473. NON-IONIC SURFACTANT (WETTING AGENT)
474. NO-CARB PASTE
475. OCTANOL
476. ORTHO NITRO PHENOL
477. OXALIC ACID FROM MOLASSES
478. OXALIC ACID FROMRICE HUSK
479. OXALIC ACID FROM TREE BARK
470. OXALIC ACID FROM WASTE VEGETABLES
471. OXYGEN GAS PLANT
472. OXYGEN GAS PLANT (AIR SEPERATION METHOD)
473. PARA-AMINO BENZOIC ACID
474. PARA-AMINO PHENOL
475. PARA TOLUENE SULPHONIC ACID
476. PECTIN FROM RAW PAPAYA
477. PERFUME (LEMON & OTHERS)

CRUDE NAPHTHA
570. TRIMETHYL AMMONIUM CHLORIDE
571. TRIPHENYL PHOSPHITE (T.P.P)
572. ULTRAMARINE BLUE (LIQUID)
573. UREA FORMALDEHYDE & MELAMINE FORMALDEHYDE POWDER
574. UNDECYLINIC ACID
575. VINYL ACETATE MONOMER
576. VITAMIN C
577. VITAMIN E
578. WASTE WATER TREATMENT PLANT FOR INDUSTRIAL SECTOR IN INDIA (ONLY MARKER SURVEY)
579. WIRE DRAWING LUBRICANT
580. WIRE ENAMEL
581. XANTHATES
582. YELLOW DEXTRIN
583. ZINC CHLORIDE
584. ZINC OXIDE
585. ZINC PHOSPHATING BY COLD PROCESS
586. ZINC SILICATE
587. ZINC STEARATE
588. ZINC SULPHATE
589. ZINC SULPHATE MONOHYDRATE
590. ACID BLACK
591. AURAMINE'O'
592. AZO DYES STUFF
593. DYE & DYE INTERMEDIATE
594. DYE INTERMEDIATES
595. MALACHITE GREEN
596. METHYLENE BLUE
597. PHTHALOCYANINE BLUE
598. PHTHALOCYANINE BLUE & GREEN
599. REACTIVE DYES
600. SULPHUR BLACK DYE
601. VAT DYES
602. WATER CHILLING PLANT
603. WADDING OIL (100%) FOR WADDING OF COTTON HOSIERY CLOTH IN THE DYEING PROCESS
604. WHITE OIL
605. WAX FLOOR POLISH

ELECTRICAL, ELECTONICS, COMPUTERS AND INFOTECH/IT PROJECTS

606. AIR CONDITIONING
607. ALUMINIUM ALLOY CONDUCTOR
608. ALUMINIUM CABLE
609. ALUMINIUM ELECTROYTIC CAPACITORS
610. AUDIO CASSETTE ASSEMBLING & RECORDING
611. AUDIO CASSETTES DUPLICATING RECORDING
612. AUDIO CASSETTES & AUDIO STUDIO
613. AUDIO CASSETTES PLANE & RECORDED
614. AUDIO MAGNETIC HEADS
615. AUDIO MAGNETIC TAPE
616. AUDIO/VIDEO CASSETTES
617. AUTO BULB/LAMPS
618. AUTOMATIC VOLTAGE STABILIZER
619. BATTERY PLATES
620. BACK OFFICE (Rs. 5000/-)
621. B/W TV & COMPUTER MONITOR PICTURE TUBE
622. BREAD BOARDS
623. CALL CENTRE
624. CAMERA (35 MM)
625. CAPACITORS
626. CARBON ELECTRODE USED FOR BATTERY CELL
627. CARBON POTETIOMETERS
628. CEILING FAN
629. CERAMIC INSULATOR
630. CHILDREN INFOTECH TRAINING INSTITUTE (Rs. 5000/-)
631. CHOKE AND PATTI
632. CHOKE AND STARTER
633. CHOKE USED FOR FLUORESCENT LAMPS
634. COLOUR TELEVISION
635. COLOUR AND BLACK & WHITE TELEVISION
636. COMPACT DISC
637. COMPACT DISC PLAYER (AUDIO/VIDEO)
638. COMPUTER EDUCATION INSTITUTE
639. COMPUTER ASSEMBLY
640. COMPUTER HARDWARE
641. COMPUTER KEYBOARD
642. COMPUTER PERIPHERALS
643. COMPUTER PRINTERS
644. COMPUTER RIBBON
645. COMPUTER RIBBON REINKING OR REFILLING
646. COMPUTER STATIONERY
647. COMPUTER STATIONERY &

IMPORTED HARDWARE PARTS
648. COMPUTER TERMINALS
649. COMPUTERISED WASHING MACHINE (AUTOMATIC)
650. COMPUTER SOFTWARE
651. CONDENSER FOR MOTOR USING MPP FILM
652. CONTENT DEVELOPMENT CENTRE (EOU) (Rs. 5000/-)
653. CONTROL PANEL BOARD
654. COOLING COIL FOR AIR CONDITIONERS
655. COPPER STRIP COIL FROM SCRAP
656. CORDLESS TELEPHONES
657. CYBER CAFE
658. CYBERKIOSK (Rs. 5000/-)
659. DATA PROCESSING CENTRE (Rs. 5000/-)
660. D.C. MICRO MOTORS
661. D.G.SETS
662. DISH ANTENNA AND CABLE T.V. NETWORK EQUIPMENT
663. DISTRIBUTION TRANSFORMERS & REPAIRS
664. DOMESTIC ELECTRICAL APPLIANCES- ROOM COOLER, WASHING MACHINE, WATER HEATER, ELECTRIC ROOM HEATER
665. E-SCHOOL
666. E-COMMERCE/BUSINESS
667. ELECTRIC ENERGY METER
668. ELECTRIC FANS
669. ELECTRIC HORN FOR AUTOMOBILE
670. ELECTRIC LAMP/GLS (INCANDESCENT LAMP)
671. ELECTRIC MIXER
672. ELECTRIC MOTORS UP TO 10 HP. REWINDING OF ALL TYPES OF MOTORS WATER PUMPS
673. ELECTRIC MOTOR WINDING (FOR FAN, MIXIES, ETC.)
674. ELECTRIC STEAM IRON
675. ELECTRICAL APPLIANCES
676. ELECTRICAL FIXTURES
677. ELECTRICAL STAMPING
678. ELECTROLYTIC CAPACITORS
679. ELECTROMAGNETIC RELAY
680. ELECTRONIC BALAST/CHOK
681. ELECTRICAL CHOKE
682. ELECTRONIC DIGITAL WATCHES
683. ELECTRONIC DIGITAL WEIGHING MACHINE
684. ELECTRONIC FIRE ALARM
685. ELECTRONIC GAS STOVE LIGHTERS
686. ELECTRONIC PRESSURE INDICATORS, ELECTRICALS, ELECTRONIC LIQUID LEVEL INDICATORS, ELECTRONIC TEMPERATURE INDICATOR, DIGITAL TACHOMETER
687. ELECTRONIC TELEPHONE INSTRUMENTS
688. ELECTRONIC TOYS
689. ELECTRONIC WATCHES & CLOCKS
690. FAX MACHINES
691. F.H.P MOTORS
692. FLOPPY DISKETTES
693. FLUORESCENT LAMP STARTER
694. FLUORESCENT TUBULAR

LAMPS WITH INTRODUCTION TO MERCURY VAPOUR LAMP
695. FRANCHISEE COMPUTER EDUCATION CENTRE (Rs. 5000)
696. GAS DETECTOR (L.P.G)
697. GENERATOR SET & PUMP SETS
698. GENERATOR (BATTERY OPERATED)
699. GIS SERVICE CENTRE (GEOGRAPHICAL INFORMATION SYSTEMS)
700. HARDWARE FITTING FOR TRANSMISSION LINE (OVERHEAD LINE MATERIAL
701. HEADERS FOR TRANSISTOR ICS SEMI CONDUCTOR
702. H.T & L.T INSULATORS
703. H.T & M.V INDUSTRIAL CUBICAL SWITCH BOARD
704. INFORMATION MOVING DISPLAY (L.E.D TYPE)
705. INSURANCE CLAIM PROCESSING CENTRE (EOU) (Rs. 5000/-)
706. INTEGRATED CIRCUITS
707. INTERNET BASED STOCK TRADING (Rs. 5000/-)
708. INTERNET SERVICE PROVIDER (I.S.P.)
709. JELLY FILLED TELEPHONE CABLES
710. LAP TOP COMPUTERS
711. LEAD ACID BATTERIES
712. LEAD ACID BATTERY PLATES AND ASSEMBLING OF BATTERY
713. LEGAL TRANSCRIPTION & SECRETARIAL SERVICES CENTER (EOU)(Rs. 5000/-)
714. LIGHT EMITTING DIODES (L.E.D)
715. LINEAR ICS TRAINER KIT
716. LOUD SPEAKER
717. L.T TRANSFORMER REPAIRING
718. MEDICAL TRANSCRIPTION CENTRE
719. METAL FILM RESISTORS
720. METALLISED POLYPROPYLENE, POLYESTER FILM CAPACITOR
721. MICA BASE ELECTRONIC COMPONENTS
722. MICA PAPER WASTE PAPER FROM MICA WASTE
723. MICRO PROCESSORS TRAINER KITS BASED ON MICRO PROCESSORS
724. MINI COMPUTER (PERSONAL COMPUTER)
725. MINIATURE CIRCUIT BREAKER (M.C.B)
726. MINIATURE WATCH BATTERIES (BUTTON CELL)
727. MIXER/GRINDER (MIXI)
728. MONO CHROME COMPUTER MONITOR
729. MOTOR START ELECTROLYTIC CAPACITOR
730. MULTI LAYER P.C.B
731. MULTIPLE RELAY FOR LOW VOLTAGE
732. NEON INDICATOR
733. NEON SIGN MANUFACTURE
734. OPTICAL FIBRE CABLES
735. ON LINE SHOPPING MALL (Rs. 5000/-)
736. OPTO MECHANICAL & ELECTRICAL EQUIPMENTS
737. PHOTO COLOUR LAB
738. PICTURE TUBE (B/W)
739. PLAIN PAPER COPIER
740. PLASTIC FILM CAPACITORS
741. POLYESTER CAPACITORS
742. PORTABLE GENERATOR SET
743. PORTAL
744. PORTABLE TELEVISION(TV)
745. POWER CAPACITORS
746. POWER INVERTERS
747. POWER PLANT
748. POWER TRANSFORMERS UP TO 600 KVA
749. PRINTED CIRCUIT BOARD
750. PVC WIRES & CABLES
751. RE-CONDITIONING OF PICTURE TUBE
752. RESIN CAST CT & PT (1 KV)
753. SEMI CONDUCTOR DEVICE
754. SEMI CONDUCTORS FOR TRANSISTORS & DIODES
755. SETTING UP OF A VIDEO STUDIO
756. SMOKE DETECTORS
757. SOLAR CELLS
758. SOLAR MODULES
759. SOLAR PHOTO VOLTAIC SYSTEM
760. SOLDER FLUXES
761. SOLAR WATER HEATING PANELS
762. STEEL FURNITURE & ELECTRICAL APPLIANCES
763. STEREO AMPLIFIERS
764. STEREO CASSETTE RECORDERS/PLAYERS
765. STREET LIGHT FITTINGS SURGE SUPPRESSOR
766. TANTALUM CAPACITORS
767. TEFLON COATED ELECTRIC CABLE
768. TELEMEDICINE (DISTANCE HEALTH CARE) (Rs. 5000/-)
769. TELEPHONE CORD/CABLE
770. TELEPHONE (PUSH BUTTON TYPE)
771. TELEPHONE (PUSH BUTTON & CORDLESS)
772. TELEVISION (CTV & B/W)
773. TELEVISION (3-D)
774. TELEVISION DEFLECTION COMPONENTS
775. TELEVISION SIGNAL BOOSTERS
776. TELEVISION TUNERS
777. TRACTION BATTERIES
778. TRAINING INSTITUTE OF MEDICAL TRANSCRIPTION
779. TRANSFORMER FOR B/W TV
780. TRANSFORMER FOR VOLTAGE STABILIZER & E.H.T
781. TRANSMISSION POWER LINE FITTING
782. TRANSMISSION TOWER FITTING
783. TV AUDIO EQUIPMENT CABINETS & THEIR ASSEMBLING UNIT
784. UN-INTERRUPTED POWER SUPPLY (U.P.S)
785. VARIABLE FREQUENCY
786. VARIABLE VOLTAGE A.C. DRIVE
787. VIDEO CASSETTES (COMPLETE MANUFACTURING & ASSEMBLING)
788. VIDEO CASSETTES RECORDER (V.C.R)
789. VIDEO FILM STUDIO
790. VOLTAGE REGULATOR FOR AUTOMOBILES
791. VOLTAGE STABILIZERS
792. VOLTAGE STABLIZER & T.V. GAIN BOOSTER
793. WAX AND CHEMICAL COATED, BRAIDED TINSEL WIRE
794. WEBSITE DESIGN & E-MAIL REGISTERING
795. WELDING ELECTRODES
796. WIND ENERGY POWER PROJECT (10 MW)
796A WIRES (METAL)

FOOD, AGRO FOOD, PROCESSED FOOD, AGRO PLANTATION , CULTIVATION, FARMING, DAIRY/MILK, TOBACCO/PAN MASALA, BREWERY & DISTILLERY, EDIBLE OILS, EOU FOOD PRODUCTS AND ALLIED PRODUCTS

797. ALCOHOLIC BEVERAGES & VENEGAR FROM COCONUT WATER
798. ALCOHOL DRINKS FROM ETHYL ALCOHOL BY MIXING OF VARIOUS FLAVOURS
799. ANTI SCALE COMPOUND FOR ADDING INTO SUGAR JUICE BOILING
800. APPLE JUICE CONCENTRATED & DEHYDRATED FRUIT & VEGETABLES
801. ARTIFICIAL FISH MEAL FOR POULTRY FEED
802. AUTOMATIC BISCUIT PLANT
803. BABY CEREAL FOOD AND MILK POWDER
804. BACTERIA FOR CANE JUICE
805. BAKER'S YEAST
806. BAKERY INDUSTRY
807. BANANA PUREE
808. BEER & WINE
809. BEER PLANT (BREWERY)
810. BIDI
811. BIDI & CIGARETTE
812. BISCUIT PLANT

813. BREAD (AUTOMATIC PLANT)
814. BLACK PEPPER (SPICES)
815. BREAD AND BISCUITS
816. BREEDING FARM
817. BROILER CHICKEN
819. BUTTON MUSHROOM CULTIVATION & PROCESSING
820. CANNING OF RASAGULLAS IN METAL CANS
821. CAFFEIN FROM TEA WASTE
822. CANNING OF FRUITS & VEGETABLES
823. CASEIN AND BY-PRODUCTS
824. CASHEW FRUIT JUICE FROM CASHEW FRUIT APPLE
825. CASHEWNUT KERNEL EXTRACTION FROM CASHEWNUT FRUIT
826. CASHEWNUT SHELL LIQUID & KERNEL PROCESSING
827. CASHEW FENI
828. CATECHEU (BY CHEMICAL PROCESS)
829. CATTLE FEED FROM TAPIOCA
830. CHEWING & BUBBLE GUM
831. CHICKEN/SHEEP MEAT PROCESSING
832. CHOCOLATE (MILK)
833. CIGARETTE AND BEEDIES
834. COCOA BUTTER FROM COCOA MASS
835. COCONUT PRODUCTS & BY PRODUCTS PROCESS COMPLEX
836. COLD/SOFT DRINKS
837. COLLECTION OF MILK AND MILK MAKING POWDER
838. COLLECTION OF MILK AND PACKING IN POLYTHENE POUCH (1/2 KG.1 KG. & 2 KG.)
839. CONDENSED MILK (SWEETNED)
840. CONFECTIONERY INDUSTRY (TOFFEE & CANDY, SEMI-AUTOMATIC PLANT)
841. COUNTRY LIQUOR FROM MOLASSES
842. CIGARETTE
843. DAIRY FARM AND DAIRY (MILK) PRODUCTS (PASTEURISED MILK, BUTTER, GHEE, PANEER)
844. DAIRY FARM TO PRODUCE MILK & PACKING IN POUCHES (50%) & CAN(50%)
845. DAIRY FOR MILK PROCESSING
846. DAIRY FARM (BUFALO)
847. DAL (PULSE) MILL UNIT
848. DEHYDRATION OF CARROT & GARLIC
849. DEHYDRATION & CANNING OF FRUITS & VEGETABLES
850. DEHYDRATION OF FIGS
851. DEHYDRATION OF FRUITS AND VEGETABLES
852. DEHYDRATED ONIONS AND ONION POWDER
853. DRY ICE BY BREAKING OF AIR
854. DRYING OF RED CHILLIES, HALDI, DHANIA, AND GREEN PEAS
855. EGG POWDER (40,000 EGGS PROCESSING PER DAY)
856. EXPORT OF PROCESSED FOODS AND MARINE PRODUCTS
857. FISH CANNING & POUCHING
859. FISH FARMING (PRAWN & OTHER MARINE PRODUCTS)
860. FISH MEAL
861. FLOUR MILL AND MUSTARD OIL
862. FOOD COLOUR & ORASTED GROUNDNUT GRAM PEAS, ETC IN POUCHES
863. FROG LEGS PROCESSING
864. FROZEN MEATS PROCESSING
865. FOOD FLAVOURS (WHISKY) VODKA, GRAPE, BUTTER SCOTCH)
866. FOOD PRODUCTS COMPLEX (DEHYDRATED ONIONS, GARLIC POWDER & FLAKES, CATTLE FEED, TOMATO POWDER, TOMATO PRODUCTS, CANNED FRUITS & VEGETABLES, TOMATO PURE, GROUN NUT OIL, REFIND OIL, DEHYDRATED GRAPES, BANANA POWDER & WAFFERS)
867. FRUIT JUICE, JAM, JELLIES & ALLIED PRODUCTS
868. FRUIT JUICE, PICKLES PROCESSING AND CANNING
869. FRUIT JUICE MAKING & PACKING IN PLASTIC CONTAINER/POUCHES
870. FRUIT PROCESSING (JAM & JELLIES)
871. FRUIT PULP & JUICE CONCENTRATES
872. FRUIT & VEGETABLE DRYING (FREEZE DRYING METHOD)
873. GOAT & SHEEP FARMING
874. GRAM DALL/PULSE MILL
875. GRAPE DEHYDRATION
876. HARD BOILED CANDY (TOFFEE & CANDY)
877. HERBAL CIGARETTES
878. HONEY PROCESSING & PACKAGING
879. ICE CREAM OF DIFFERENT FLAVOURS
880. ICE CREAM STABILIZER
881. ICE MAKING PLANT
882. INDIAN MADE FOREIGN LIQUOR (I.M.F.L)
883. INSTANT FOOD (IDLI MIX, DOSA MIX, GULAB JAMUN MIX)
884. INSTANT FOOD (INSTANT FOOD & FAST FOOD PARLOUR)
885. INSTANT NOODLES
886. INSTANT TEA
887. INSTANT TEA FROM BLACK TEA
888. INTEGERATED STARCH BAKING POWDER/YEAST INDUSTRY
889. IODIZED SALT
890. IODIZED SALT (ORDINARY MOISTURE-LESS/FREE FLOWING IN PLASTIC BAGS AND CONTAINERS)
891. JAM, JELLIES, FRUIT JUICE & ALLIED PRODUCTS
892. KATHA AND CUTCH
893. KHANDSARI SUGAR
894. KHANDSARI SUGAR & IMFL
895. LACTIC ACID FROM WHITE SUGAR BY FERMENTATION PROCESS
896. LACTOSE & BY PRODUCTS PROCESSING FROM MILK
897. LIQUID GLUCOSE AND ITS BYE PRODUCTS
898. MACRONI AND VERMICILLI
899. MALT EXTRACTION FROM BARLEY
900. MANGO PROCESSING (MANGO PULP, JUICE & SLICES)
901. MAYUR BRAND TYPE CHEWING TOBACCO
902. MINERAL WATER
903. MILK PRESERVATION & MARKETING TO WHOLE SELLERS (INPOUCH PACKING BY UHT TECHNOLOGY)
904. MILK PROCESSING AND PACKAGING OF MILK PRODUCTS
905. MILK PRODUCTS (CASEIN, LACTOSE, GHEE & WHEY POWDER)
906. MILK TOFFEE
907. MINI FLOUR MILL
908. MINI SUGAR PLANT
909. MISRI (PEARL SUGAR CANDIES)
910. MODERN RICE MILL
911. MURABBA
912. MUSTARD OIL EXTRACTION & REFINING
913. MUTTON TALLOW
914. NAMKEEN INDUSTRY (BHUJIA, CHANA CHUR ETC.)
915. NAMKEEN & SWEETS
916. NON-BASMATI RICE FROM PADDY
917. OLEORESIN, ESSENTIAL OIL, DYES & POWDER OF SPICES
918. OLEORESIN EXTRACTION FROM DIPTERO-CARPUT TURMINATUS AND PINUS KHASYANA
919. OLEORESIN EXTRACTION FROM CHILLI
920. PAN MASALA AND POUCH

Apart from the above mentioned reports EIRI is also having other most lucrative projects (as many as 30,000). You just name it and we have that report.

MAKING
921. PAN MASALA, TOBACCO, ZARDA & KIMAM
922. PANEER FROM MILK
923. PAPPAD PLANT
924. PAPAIN FROM PAPAYA (PAPAYA LATEX)
925. PECTIN FROM MANGO PEEL PECTIN FROM APPLE POMACE
926. PHYTO TEA (HERBAL TEA)
927. PICKLES AND SAUCES
928. PICKLES MURABBA ETC. (VEG. & NON. VEG.PICKLES)
929. PIGGERY MEAT PROCESS
930. PINE-APPLE JUICE PREPARATION & PACKAGING
931. POTATO CHIPS/WAFFERS
932. POTATO POWDER
933. POUCH FILLING & PACKAGING OF EDIBLE OIL & GHEE
934. POULTRY FEED
935. PROCESSED FOODS & SPICES (EOU)
936. PROCESSED READYMADE FOOD
937. PROCESSING OF FRUITS & VEGETABLES
938. RABBIT FARMING
939. RASGULLAS MAKING & CANNING IN METAL CANS
940. READY TO EAT PROCESSED COOKED FOOD
941. READY TO EAT SNACK FOOD (CRAX, ROLL & BALL TYPE)
942. RICE & CORN FLAKES
943. ROASTED/SALTED/ MASALA,CASHEW NUTS, ALMONDS & PEANUTS
944. ROLLER FLOUR MILL
945. SALT LICKS FOR CATTLE
946. SAUSAGES FOOD CASING
947. SOFT DRINKS
948. SOFT DRINKS ESSENCES
949. SOFT DRINKS (NON CARBONATED) MANGO, LICCHI, PINEAPPLE FLAVOURS FROOTI TYPE IN TETRAPACK)
950. SOFTY ICE CREAM CONES (FULLY AUTOMATIC)
951. SOFT/COLD DRINKS (COLA, ORANGE, LEMON ETC. FLAVOURS)
952. SOYABEAN PRODUCTS
953. SOYA MILK & PANEER
954. STARCH & ALLIED PROPDUCT FROM BROKEN RICE
955. STRAWBERRY CULTIVATION & PROCESSING
956. SUGARCANE JUICE PRESERVATION
957. SUGAR CUBES FROM CANE SUGAR
988. SUGAR PLANT
989. SWEET AROMA BETEL NUT
990. SYNTHETIC TALLOW
991. TAMARIND JUICE POWDER
992. TEA & COFFEE PROCESSING & PACKAGING
993. TOFFEES, GOLIES, CANDY (HARD BOILED)
994. TOMATO PRODUCTS
994. TRADING BUSINESS OF SPICES & PAN MASALA
995. TUITY FRUITY
996. VODKA FROM POTATOES
997. WINE, BRANDY, WHISKY & CHAMPAGNE
997. WINE FROM DATES
998. YEAST FROM MOLASSES
999. ZARDA, KIMAM NO. 60,90,120,160,240,300 & 400 (TOBACCO)
1000. ZARDA-ZAFRANI (BABACHHAP TYPE)

GUMS & ADHESIVE

1001. ACRYLIC ADHESIVE
1002. ADHESIVE (FEVICOL TYPE)
1003. ADHESIVE BASED ON POLYURETHANE
1004. ADHESIVE FOR BAND AID (JOHNSON & JOHNSON TYPE)
1005. ADHESIVE INDUSTRIES (LAMINATED, STICKER,DDL & OTHER TYPES)
1006. ADHESIVE FOR GASKET (LIQUID/PASTE)
1007. GUAR GUM
1008. GUM BOTTLE (PVC)
1009. GUM FOR PASTING LABELS
1010. OFFICE PASTE
1011. RUBBER ADHESIVE
1012. SURGICAL ADHESIVE PLASTER

LEATHER & LEATHER PRODUCTS

1013. HANDMADE LEATHER
1014. LEATHER AUXILLARIES & CHEMICALS
1015. LEATHER DYES
1016. LEATHER WASHERS
1017. LEATHER BOARD FROM LEATHER WASTE
1018. LEATHER FOR UPHOLSTRY (SOFA)
1019. LEATHER GARMENTS
1020. LEATHER GOODS
1021. LEATHER SHOES
1022. LEATHER SHOE & CHAPPAL
1023. LEATHER SUITCASES, BRIEFCASES & TRAVELLING BAGS
1024. LEATHER GOODS AND GARMENTS
1025. LEATHER GARMENTS, SHOE & CHAPPAL
1026. LEATHER TANNING
1027. LEATHER TANNING & GARMENTS (EOU)
1028. SHEEP SKIN PICKLING PLANT
1029. SHOE UPPER
1030. SPORT SHOES (PLASTIC)

MISCELLANEOUS PRODUCTS

1031. AGARBATTI (INSENCE STICK)
1032. AGARBATTI (Mosquito Repellent)
1033. AGARBATI BAMBOO STICK
1034. AGARBATTI SYNTHETIC PERFUMERY COMPOUND
1035. AIR FRESHNER(ODONIL TYPE)
1036. AIR TAXI
1037. AMUSEMENT PARK
1038. ANODIC ALUMINIUM LABEL
1039. AQUACULTURE PRAWN FARMING (100% EOU)
1040. AQUA CULTURE SHRIMP FARMING (100% EOU)
1041. ARTIFICIAL FLOWERS
1042. ARTIFICIAL JEWELLERY
1043. ASBESTOS YARN
1044. ASH TRAYS FOR MARUTI VEHICLE
1045. AIR BUBBLE PACKAGING
1046. ASPHALTIC ROOFING SHEET (METAL COMPONENTS)
1047. AUTOMATIC BOOK BINDING
1048. ALKYD RESIN
1049. APPLE JUICE CONCENTRATE
1050. BALL POINT PEN FEFILLS (JOTTER TYPE)
1051. BANK BRANCH BUILDING
1052. BANQUET HALL
1053. BIO-COAL BRIQUETTES FROM AGRICULTURAL CELLULOSE WASTE
1054. BOOT CREAM/POLISH
1055. BUFFING & POLISHING COMPOUND
1056. BRASS BADGES BY ETCHING
1057. BRIQUETTED FUEL FROM AGRO WASTE
1058. BRIQUETTING OF LIGNITE COAL

Price Rs. 4200/- for each "Detailed Project Report" Payable in advance through Draft/Cash/ M.O. in favour of *"ENGINEERS INDIA RESEARCH INSTITUTE"*. 4449, Nai Sarak (D), Main Road Delhi - 110 006 *OR Ask by V.P.P.* ● Ph : 23918117, 2391 6431, 2392 0361, 2396 0797 ●Fax : 91-11- 2391 6431 ●E-Mail : eirisidi@bol.net.in ● WebSite : www.startindustry.com

1059. BUFFALO HORN TIP, HOOF
1060. BANQUET HALL
1061. BUTTON
1062. CALCINED PETROLEUM (C.P) COKE
1063. CANVAS SHOES
1064. CANVAS SHOES, JUNGLE BOOTS
1065. CARBON BRUSH, BRUSH HOLDER & SLIP RING
1066. CEMENT SHEETS WITH COIR FIBRE & OTHER SEGMENTS
1067. CERAMIC TILES (GLAZED) BY DOUBLE FIRING/HEATING
1068. CHILDREN RECREATION CENTRE
1069. COAL BRIQUETTES
1070. COLD STORAGE & ICE
1071. COLD STORAGE FOR FRUITS AND VEGETABLES
1072. COMPRESSOR (HERMETIC) FOR AIR CONDITIONER
1073. COSTUME JEWELLERY/ IMITATION JEWELLERY
1074. DECORATIVE LAMINATED SHEET (SUNMICA)
1075. DIAMOND CUTTING & EXPORTS
1076. DRINKING STRAW FROM PROPYLENE
1077. ENGINEERING COLLEGE
1078. ENTERTAINMENT CLUB
1079. FASHION TECHNOLOGY INSTITUTE
1080. FAST FOOD PARLOUR
1081. FAST FOOD (INSTANT FOOD & FAST FOOD PARLOUR)
1082. FIRE EXTINGUISHERS (SODA ACID TYPE)
1083. FISH NET
1084. FLORICULTURE (CUT FLOWER ROSE) WITH GREEN HOUSE
1085. FLOOR COVERING SHEET
1086. FILM STUDIO (VIDEO)
1087. FLUSH DOOR, CHIP BOARD, WOOD WOOL & OTHER INSULATING BOARDS
1088. GAS DETECTORS OF L.P.G
1089. GEMS MANUFACTURING
1090. GLASS BOTTLE BY SCRAP
1092. GOAT & SHEEP FARMING
1093. GOLD ELECTROPLATING
1094. GOLD JEWELLERY (E.O.U)
1095. GOLD PLATED SILVER JEWELLERY & CUTLERY
1096. GRANITE SLAB AND TILES
1097. GREEN HOUSE
1098. HARD CHROMIUM PLATING
1099. HEALTH CLUB AND BEAUTY PARLOUR CUM HAIR SALOON WITH SONA BATH
1100. HEALTH CLUB CUM BEAUTY PARLOUR TRAININGINSTITUTE
1101. HORN TIP,HOOVE BUTTON
1102. HOSPITAL
1103. HOSPITAL (100 BEDS)
1104. HOSPITAL (200 BEDS)
1105. ICE MAKING PLANT
1106. IMITATION AND COSTUME
1107. JEWELLERY (NECKLACE, EARRINGS EAR TOP ETC.)
1108. INITMATE SCENT CHEMICALS FROM ALL TYPES OF FLAVOUR
1109. INVESTMENT CASTING
1110. JUTE, COIR, GLASS ROPE/ SUTLI
1111. JUTE TWINE
1112. L.P.G BOTTLING PLANT
1113. L.P.G REGULATOR (DOMESTIC PURPOSE)
1114. LAMINATED PARTICLE BOARD & HARD BOARD
1115. LAMINATED SAFETY AND TOUGHENED GLASS
1116. LEASING & HIRE PURCHASE
1117. LICHEN (CHARILA)
1118. MANILA ROPES
1119. MEDICAL COLLEGE
1120. MATCH UNIT FROM WAXED PAPER
1121. MEDIUM DENSITY FIBRE BOARD
1122. MELAMINE CROCKERY
1123. MINERAL WATER
1124. MINI CEMENT PLANT
1125. MIRROR SILVER, GOLDEN, PINK, BLACK & SMOKES
1126. MODERN ADVERTISING AGENCY WITH DTP & FILM STUDIO
1127. MOTEL/SMALL HOTEL
1128. MULTI COLOUR PRINTING
1129. MULTI STOREY COMMERCIAL COMPLEX ALONGWITH RESIDENTIAL AND DELUX FLATS FOR FOREIGN TOURISTS & REVOLVING RESTAURENT AT THE TOP
1130. MULTIPLE LAMINATION INDUSTRY
1131. MUSHROOM GROWING AND PROCESSING (BY DEEP FREEZING METHOD)
1132. NEWS PAPER PRINTING
1133. NICKEL LINED INDUSTRIAL SCREEN
1134. OFFSET COLOUR PRINTING PRESS (SIX COLOUR)
1135. OFFSET PRINTING PRESS
1136. P.C.C ELECTRIC POLES
1137. PHOTOGRAPHIC DEVELOPER & FIXER
1138. PVC EXTRUSION PROFILE (DOOR & WINDOWS)
1139. POP-CORN
1140. PHOTO ETCHING OF S.S.
1141. PRE STRESSED CEMENT CONCRETE PIPES
1142. PILFER PROOF CAPS
1143. PILFER PROOF CAPS AND CROWN CAP
1144. POUCH MAKING & GRAVURE PRINTING (ROTO PRINTING)
1145. POULTRY & FISH FARMING (INTEGERATED UNIT)
1146. PRINTING OF TIN SHEETS
1147. READYMADE GARMENTS
1148. RESTAURANT
1149. ROSE PLANTATION AND ROSE OIL EXTRACTION
1150. ROTOGRAVURE PRINTING
1151. SAFETY BELTS
1152. SAFETY MATCHES
1153. SHOE LACES
1154. SILK COCOON CULTIVATION (GROWING OF SILK COCOON WARM)
1155. SILK SCREEN PRINTING FORMULATIONS FOR PLASTIC, PAPER & CLOTH
1156. SPIKENARD (JATAMANSI)
1157. STENCIL COATING SOLUTION
1158. SUGAR CANDY (MISRI)
1159. SUGAR CANE PLANTATION
1160. SUGAR CANE JUICE PRESERVATION
1161. SURAT ZARI
1162. SYNTHETIC SHOES & SOLES
1163. TEA PACKAGING INDUSTRY
1164. TENNIS BALLS
1165. THREE STAR HOTEL
1166. TRAVELLING AGENCY
1167. TRAYS, TROLLEYS FOR HOSPITAL WITH SCRATCHLESS COATING
1168. WAX EXTRACTS (TANNING POWDER)
1169. WIRE ROPE SLINGS
1170. WOOD WOOL SLAB
1171. WOODEN CANE FURNITURE WITH EXPORT POTENTIAL
1172. WOODEN FURNITURE
1173. WOODEN PANEL INCLUDING KILN SEASONING
1174. WOODEN FURNITURE
1175. WATCH CASE BUFFING
1176. WATCH DIAL
1177. WRIST WATCHES
1178. WATCHES (ELECTRONIC)
1179. ZEDOARY (KACHUR)

EDIBLE OILS, ESSENTIAL OILS LURICATIING OILS, GREASES, VEGETABLE OILS, WAXES, CAMPHOR, PERFUMES & PERFUMERY COMPOUNDS AND REFINED OILS ETC.

1180. AROMATIC PERFUMERY COMPOUND
1181. AEROSOL
1182. AGARBATTI PERFUMERY COMPOUND
1183. BEES WAX MANUFACTURE
1184. CAMPHOR
1185. CARDANOL FROM CASHEW NUT SHELL LIQUID
1186. CASTOR OIL
1187. CASTOR OIL DERIVATIVE OLEORESINS
1188. CHILLI OIL
1189. CITRONELLA OILS
1190. CLOVE OIL
1191. CONCENTRATE OF ROSE JASMINE & LILY ETC.
1192. COLOURED FLAME CANDLE

Price Rs. 4200/- for each "Detailed Project Report" Payable in advance through Draft/Cash/ M.O. in favour of *"ENGINEERS INDIA RESEARCH INSTITUTE"*. 4449, Nai Sarak (D), Main Road Delhi - 110 006 *OR Ask by V.P.P.* ● Ph : 23918117, 2391 6431, 2392 0361, 2396 0797 ●Fax : 91-11- 2391 6431 ●E-Mail : eirisidi@bol.net.in ● WebSite : www.startindustry.com

1193. CANDLES (SEMI-AUTOMATIC)
1194. CORN OIL (MAIZE OIL)
1195. DEHYDRATED CASTOR OIL
1196. EUGENOL FROM CINNAMON LEAF OIL
1197. EXTRACTION OF ESSENTIAL OIL (CARDAMON, JEERA, AJOWAN, GINGER OILS ETC. & PACKAGING OF GROUND SPICES)
1198. EXTRACTION OF JASMINE ESSENCE
1199. EXTRACTION OF ESSENTIAL OILS BY SUPER CRITICAL FLUID METHOD FROM FLOWERS, HERBS & SPICES
1200. EUCALYPTUS OIL
1201. EXTRACTION OF OIL FROM OIL SEED EXPANDEREXTRUSION TECHNOLOGY)
1202. FAT LIQUOR SULPHATED OIL
1203. FLAVOURS FOR FOOD
1204. GARLIC OIL & POWDER
1205. GINGER OIL, SANDALWOOD OIL AND NAGARMOTHA OIL
1206. GINGER OIL
1207. GINGER OIL & GINGER DUST
1208. INTEGERATED WAX COMPLEX
1209. IONONE FROM LEMON GRASS OIL
1210. JASMINE & LILLY FLOWER OIL
1211. LEMON GRASS OIL
1212. LIQUID PARAFFIN
1213. LUBE OIL & GREASE
1214. LUBRICATING OIL
1215. MENTHOL CRYSTALS
1216. MENTHOL OIL & CRYSTAL
1217. MICRO CRYSTALLINE WAX
1218. MUSTARD OIL (EDIBLE OIL)
1219. OIL FROM ARTEMISIA HERBS
1220. PALM OIL CRUSHING UNIT
1221. PAN MASALA
1222. PARAFFIN WAX
1223. PARAFFIN WAX FROM SLACK WAX
1224. REFINED OIL-SUN FLOWER OIL, GROUNDNUT OIL, STAFF FLOWER OIL & COTTON SEED OIL
1225. REFINED VEGETABLE OIL
1226. RECLAMATION OF USED ENGINE OIL
1227. RICE BRAN OIL (R.B.O)
1228. ROSE OIL EXTRACTION
1229. SMOKE LESS CANDLE
1230. SPICE OIL & OLEORESINS
1231. SOLVENT EXTRACTION PLANT (OIL CAKE BASED)
1232. SYNTHETIC ALMOND OIL
1233. SYNTHETIC TALLOW
1234. SYNTHETIC GHEE
1235. VEGETABLE OIL EXTRACTION & REFINING
1236. WADDING OIL (100%) FOR WADDING OF COTTON HOSIERY CLOTH IN DYEING PROCESS
1237. WAX EMULSION FOR TEXTILE
1238. WAX FLOOR POLISH

PAINT, ENAMEL, SOLVENTS, THINNERS, INKS & VARNISH

1239. ACRYLIC EMULSION PAINTS
1240. ALUMINIUM PAINT
1241. AUTOMOBILE PAINTS
1242. BALL POINT PEN REFILL INK
1243. BITUMINIOUS ROAD EMULSION
1244. BITUMEN
1245. BITUMINIOUS FELTS FOR WATER & DAMP PROOFING
1246. BITUMINIOUS ROAD EMULSION RAPID MEDIUM & SLOW SETTING
1247. BUFFING & POLISHING
1248. CEMENT PAINT FOR WHITE & GREY CEMENT

1249. DISPERSANT
1250. DRY DISTEMPER
1251. DRY DISTEMPER & CEMENT PAINT
1252. DUPLICATING INK BLACK FOR GESTNER DUPLICATOR
1255. EMULSION PAINTS (WATER BASED)
1256. HAMMERTONE PAINT
1257. INSULATING VARNISH & WIRE ENAMEL
1258. IRON OXIDE PIGMENTS
1259. INSULATING VARNISH (POLY VINYL BUTYRAL BASED, FFC GRADE)
1260. LIME COLOUR (CEMENT COLOUR)
1261. SYNTHETIC RED OXIDE FOR FLOORINGS
1262. SOLVENT & THINNERS
1263. MARKING INKS (WATER PROOF)
1264. METAL NAPHTHANATE (AS DRIER FOR PAINTS)
1265. N.C.PUTTY
1266. OFFSET PRINTING INK
1267. OIL BOUND DISTEMPER PAINT
1268. PAINT BRUSHES
1269. PAINT REMOVERS
1270. PAINT INDUSTRY
1271. PAINT & VARNISH
1272. PICTURE VARNISH
1273. POWDER COATING PAINT
1274. PRINTING INKS (OFFSET, FLEXO & ROTO GRAVURE)
1275. PRIMER PAINT & ENAMEL PAINT
1276. PUTTY & WATER PROOFING PAINT
1277. PRINTING INKS (FLEXO-GRAPHIC INK)
1278. PUTTY (METAL CASEMENT)
1279. RED OXIDE PRIMER (ANTI CORROSIVE)
1280. REFRECTORY PAINT (GRAPHITE BASED)
1281. SCREEN PRINTING INKS
1282. SILK SCREEN PRINTING INK FORMULATION FOR PLASTIC, PAPER, CLOTH
1283. STAMP & PAD INK
1284. STOVING PAINT
1285. SPIRIT SOLUBLE MALEIC RESIN
1286. TEXTURE PAINT
1287. THINNERS AND ITS ALLIED PRODUCTS
1288. TONER INK
1289. VARNISH THINNER (SOLVENT)
1290. VACUUM METALLIZING LACQUERS
1291. WOOD PRIMER

PHARMACEUTICAL, DRUGS, AYURVEDIC/HERBAL COSMETICS & MEDICINES, HOMOEOPATHIC MEDICINES, DISPOSABLE SYRINGE, DENTAL COLLEGE & FINE CHEMICALS ETC.

1292. AROMATIC PILLS
1293. ASPIRIN
1294. AYURVEDIC PAIN BALM OINTMENTS
1295. AYURVEDIC CHURAN AND TABLETS
1296. AYURVEDIC TABLETS (HAJMOLA TYPE)
1297. AYURVEDIC/HERBAL PHARMACY
1298. AYURVEDIC SHERBATS
1299. AYURVEDIC PRODUCTS
1300. BULK DRUGS (E.O.U)
1301. BLOOD BAGS
1302. CALCIUM GLUCONATE
1303. CAPSULE, TABLET & INJECTION WITH MODERN INSTRUMENTS
1304. CASHEW FENI
1305. CHLOROQUINONE PHOSPHATE (BULK DRUGS)
1306. CLINICAL THERMOMETER
1307. DENTAL CLINIC

1308. DENTAL COLLEGE
1309. DENTAL GRADE EUGENOL
1310. DEXTROSE MONOHYDRATE, LIQUID GLUCOSE
1311. DEHYDRATED ONION & ONION POWDER
1312. DEXTROSE POWDER (ANHYDROUS FROM STARCH)
1314. DEXTROSE SALINE SOLUTION
1315. DISTILLERY (I.M.F.L)
1316. DISPOSABLE NEEDLES FOR SYRINGES
1317. DISPRIN
1318. DISTILLED WATER
1319. EMPTY HARD GELATINE CAPSULES
1320. FILLING & PACKING OF CAPSULES
1321. GLUCOSE - D - POWDER
1322. GLYCERINE
1323. HERBAL COSMETICS
1324. HERBAL SHAMPOO
1325. HERBAL HAIR OILS (AYURVEDIC)
1326. HOMOE & BIO-MEDICINES WITH MOTHER TINCTURE
1327. HOMOEPATHIC MEDICINES
1328. HYPODERMIC NEEDLES
1329. I.V. FLUIDS
1330. IBUPROFEN
1331. INFUSION & TRANSFUSION SETS (I.V. SET)
1332. INJECTABLE FOR PHARMACEUTICALS
1333. INJECTION AMPOULES PACKAGING BOX
1334. INTEGERATED SURGICAL COTTON
1335. ICE MAKING PLANT
1336. ICE & COLD STORAGE
1337. LACTOSE & BY PRODUCTS PROCESSING FROM MILK
1338. LICHEN (JATAMANSI CHARILA)
1339. LIQUID GLUCOSE AND ITS BY-PRODUCTS
1340. L-LYSINE MONOHYDRO CHLORIDE
1341. LIQUID GLUCOSE FROM POTATOES
1342. MEDICAL COLLEGE
1343. NICOTINE FROM TOBACCO WASTE
1344. OINTMENT-AYURVEDIC (YELLOW & WHITE)
1345. PHARMACEUTICAL AND FOOD GRADE GELATINE
1346. PHARMACEUTICAL INDUSTRY (TABLETS, CAPSULES, LIQUID, GEL, OINTMENT POWDER INJECTABLE)
1347. PHARMACEUTICAL UNIT (EOU) WITH FORMULA TIONS, INJECTABLES, ETC. PYRIDINE & DERIVATIVES
1348. SALT (IODIZED SALT)
1349. SALINE & INJECTION WATER
1350. SALINE WATER & DEXTROSE SOLUTION (I.V.FLUID IN PLASTIC BOTTLES)
1351. SORBITOL
1352. STARCH (MAIZE)
1353. SURGICAL ADHESIVE PLASTER
1354. SURGICAL BANDAGES
1355. SURGICAL GLOVES
1357. SURGICAL COTTON
1358. SURGICAL COTTON AND BANDAGE
1359. SYNTHETIC CAMPHOR POWDER
1360. TABLETS & CAPSULES
1361. TISSUE CULTURE
1362. TINCTURE FROM RECTIFIED SPIRIT
1363. TRIMETHOPIME
1364. VETERENARY MEDICINES (ONLY FORMULATIONS)
1365. VITAMIN 'C', SORBITOL' ANHYDROUS DEXTROSE, STARCH

PULP, PAPER, STRAW/GREY BOARD, KRAFT PAPER, PACKAGING, PAPER CARRY BAGE, PAPER FROM AGRO WASTE & STATIONERY ETC.

1366. AMMONIA PAPER
1367. AUTOMATIC BOOK BINDING
1368. ADHESIVE (FEVICOL TYPE)
1369. ALL PIN & GEM CLIPS
1370. CARBON PAPER
1371. CARD BOARD
1372. CARBON LESS PAPER
1373. CELLPHANE PAPER
1374. COMPUTER FORMS & SECURITY PRINTING PRESS
1375. CORRUGATED BOARD & BOX (PRINTED & LAMINATED)
1376. CORRUGATED BOARD AND BOXES FROM FROM CARD BOARDS
1377. CORRUGATED CARTONS FROM PLAIN PAPERS
1378. CORRUGATRED PACKING & MATERIAL (BULB & TUBES PACKING)
1379. DESK TOP PUBLISHING
1380. DEFOAMING AGENT FOR PAPER PLANT
1381. DRINKING STRAW PAPER
1382. D.T.P CUM OFFSET PRESS
1383. EGG TRAYS
1384. EXERCISE NOTE BOOK, REGISTER AND PAD
1385. FLEXOGRAPHIC INK
1386. GREETING CARD BY OFFSET PRESS
1387. HAND MADE PAPER FILTER PAPER
1388. HARD BOARD
1389. INJECTION AMPOULES PACKAGING BOXES
1390. INSULATIING PAPER
1391. KRAFT PAPER
1392. KRAFT PAPER FROM BAGASSE
1393. LAMINATED PACKAGING PAPER WITH PRINTING
1394. LAMINATION & COATING ON PAPER
1395. M.G. PAPER FROM WASTE PAPER
1396. MILL PAPER FROM WASTE PAPER
1397. MILL BOARD FROM RICE & WHEAT STRAWS
1398. MILL BOARD FROM WASTE PAPER
1399. MINI PAPER PLANT FROM SISAL
1400. MINI PAPER PLANT
1401. MULTI WALL PAPER SACKS
1402. NEWS PAPER FOR CHILDREN
1403. NEWS PRINT PAPER FROM RICE STRAW BAGASSE
1404. NEWS PAPER CHILDRENS
1405. NEWS PRINT PAPER
1406. OFFSET AND TREADLE TYPE PRINTING PRESS
1407. MILL BOARD BASED ON RICE STRAW
1408. PAPER AND BOARD FROM STRAW
1409. PAPER & PAPER PRODUCTS
1410. PAPER ENVELOPES
1411. PAPER CARRY BAGS
1412. PAPER BOARD CARTON
1413. PAPER CONES FOR LOUD SPEAKERS
1414. PAPER FROM AKRA
1415. PAPER FROM BAGASSE WITH CORRUGATED BOARD & BOXES
1416. PAPER FROM BAMBOO
1417. PAPER GLASSES FOR BEVERAGES
1418. PAPER FROM RICE HUSK & WHEAT HUSK
1419. PAPER FROM TREE BARK, EUCALYPRUS WOOD
1420. PAPER PRODUCTS
1421. PAPER PLANT (WHITE WRITING & NEWS PAPER FOR PULP & WASTE PAPER)
1422. PAPER PLATES, PAPER GLASS
1423. PAPER CONES & TUBES
1425. PAPER PLANT WITH DTP & PRINTING & PUBLISHING UNIT
1426. PAPER BASED PHENOLIC SHEET
1427. PAPER CUP FOR ICE CREAM
1428. PAPER TUBES SPIRAL WINDING COMPOSIT CONTAINER
1429. PAPER LABLE FOR BEER BOTTLES
1430. PARTICLE BOARD & BLACK BOARD WITH SANDING & LAMINATION OF PARTICLE BOARD
1431. PARTICLE BOARD FROM RICE HUSK
1432. POUCH FILLING & MAKING FOR TOMATO SAUCE
1433. POUCH MAKING &

GRAVURE PRINTING
1434. PROCESSING OF PAPER FOR FEEDING IN COMPUTER
1435. PULP FROM BAMBOO & WOOD
1436. PAPER FILES
1437. PLAYING CARDS
1438. ROSIN SIZING AGENT (FOR PAPER PLANT)
1439. SAND PAPER
1440. SANITRY NAPKINS
1441. SILICON COATED PAPER
1442. STENCIL PAPER
1443. STRAW BOARD AND GREY BOARD
1444. STRAW BOARD & MILL BOARD
1445. STRAW BOARD AND PAPER BOARD
1446. TISSUE PAPER FACIAL
1447. TISSUE MOIST TOILETERY CLEANSING TISSUE AND RELATED PRODUCTS
1448. TISSUE PAPER ROLLS
1449. TETRA PACK FOR MILK PACKAGING, GHEE & OTHER LIQUIDS
1450. TOILET PAPER ROLLS
1451. TOILET PAPER & NAPKINS
1452. WAX COATED PRINTED PAPER
1453. WET FACE FRESHNER TISSUE
1454. WHITE WRITING & PRINTING PAPER
1455. WRITING & PRINTING PAPER (PAPER MILLS)

PLASTIC, B.O.P.P, ACRYLIC, DISPOSABLE PLASTIC PRODUCTS, PET PRODUCTS, P.V.C, H.D.P.E, P.P, L.D.P.E., P.U, A.B.S, THERMOFOARMING, MASTER BATCHES, & POLYMER AND RUBBER PRODUCTS, TYRE, TUBE, ADHESIVE, SHEET, COIR & MANY OTHERS

1456. ABS GRANULES FROM ABS SCRAPS FROM OLD T.V. CABINETS, WHITE GOODS ETC.
1457. ACRYLIC BEADS
1458. ACRYLIC COPOLYMER EMULSION
1459. ACRYLIC LATEX
1460. ACRYLIC SHEET
1461. ACRYLIC SHEET & MOULDED PRODUCTS
1462. ACRYLIC TEETH
1463. AUTO TUBES
1464. AUTO FLAPS FOR TRUCKS & BUSES
1465. AUTO TYRES & TUBES
1466. BABY BOTTLES (PLASTIC) WITH WHITESILICON RUBBER NIPPLES
1467. B.O.P.P. FILM
1468. B.O.P.P. PRESSURE SENSITIVE SELF ADHESIVE TAPE
1469. BABY NIPPLE (SILICON)
1470. BABY NIPPLE (BIG SIZE)
1471. BALLOON PLASTIC ADVERTISING
1472. BLISTER FILM PVC
1473. BLISTER PACKAGING & POUCH PAKAGING
1474. BLOW MOULDING PLASTIC CONTAINER
1475. COATING ON METALIZED POLYESTER FILM/METALISED PAPER/ ALIMINIUM FOIL
1476. COATING ON PLASTIC (ELECTROLYSIS) & GLASS
1477. COIR FOAM (RUBBERISED)
1478. COLOUR COATING ON PLASTICS
1479. COLOUR MASTER BATCHES FOR VARIOUS PLASTICS
1480. CYCLE TYRES AND TUBES
1481. DISPOSABLE PLASTIC CUPS GLASSES, ETC.
1482. DISPOSABLE PLASTIC SYRINGES & NEEDLES
1483. DISPOSABLE PLASTIC SYRINGES
1484. DOUGH MOULDING COMPOUND (D.M.C)
1485. EPOXY RESIN
1486. EXPANDED POLYESTRENE MOULDING (THERMOCOLE)
1487. F.R.P AUTO,SCOOTER ROOFS & CEILINGS
1488. F.R.P PRODUCTS (HELMET, WASHBASIN SHEETS, ROOFING SHEETS)
1489. FIBRE REINFORCED PLASTIC (HIGH PRESSURE MOULDING WITH SMC BMC AND DMC)
1490. FIELD RUBBER CONVERTED TO THE 60% LATEX RUBBER
1491. FLEXIBLE P.U. FOAM
1492. FORMALDEHYDE CROCKERY & OTHER ITEMS
1493. FORMALDEHYDE RESIN (UREA, PHENOL,MELEMINE)
1494. GASKET SHEET
1495. GUM BOTTLE (PVC)
1496. GLASS BEADS
1497. HDPE COATED PAPER SACK
1498. H.D.P.E. BAGS
1499. H.D.P.E. CONTAINERS (BLOW MOULDING)
1500. H.D.P.E. CONTAINER, POLY JARS BY INJECTION MOULDING (FOOD GRADE)
1501. H.D.P.E. JERRY CANS
1502. HDPE MANUFACTURING FROM ETHYLALCOHOL
1503. H.D.P.E PIPE AND FITTINGS
1504. H.D.P.E. PIPES
1505. H.D.P.E PRINTED BAGS
1506. H.D.P.E TWINES AND ROPES
1507. H.D.P.E. & L.D.P.E PIPES AND FITTINGS
1508. H.D.P.E/PP BOX STRAPPING
1509. H.D.P.E/PP WOVEN SACKS USING PLAIN LOOMS
1510. HOLOGRAM STICKERS-3D
1511. H.M BAG PLANT WITH PRINTING UNIT
1512. HAWAI CHAPPALS (RUBBER)
1513. I.V PLASTIC BOTTLE
1514. ICE CREAM CUP (PLASTIC)
1515. INJECTION MOULDED AUTO COMPONENTS
1516. INJECTION & BLOW MOULDED PLASTIC PRODUCTS
1517. INJECTION MOULDED PLASTIC PRODUCTS
1518. INTEGERATED COMPLEX ESTER'S & ALLIED PRODUCTS (D.O.P,D.B.P, & ETHYL ACETATE, BUYTL ACETATE, WIRE ENAMELS, JELLY CABLE COMPOUND)
1519. L.D.P.E. (LOW DENSITY POLY ETHYLENE) GRANULES FROM VIRGIN (L.D.P.E. RESIN)
1520. INTEGERATED SURGICAL RUBBER GOODS INDUSTRY
1521. INJECTION MOULDED PLASTIC BALLS
1522. L.D.P.E FROM ETHYL ALCOHOL
1523. LDPE MOULDED PRODUCTS
1524. LAMINATION OF COEXTRUSION MULTILAYER FILM IN ROLL FORM
1525. LATEX RUBBER
1526. LATEX RUBBER CONDOM
1527. MASTER BATCHES (COLOURED, P.V.C, L.D.P.E, H.D.P.E, ETC.)
1528. MELAMINE FORMALHYDE RESIN
1529. MOULDED LUGGAGE
1530. MULTI-LAYER (3 LAYER BAGS)
1531. MULTI-LAYER (3 LAYER) FILM WITH LAMINATION & PRINTING
1532. OIL SEAL
1533. PET BOTTLE/CONTAINERS
1534. PET BOTTLES FROM PRE FORM
1535. PET BOTTLE & MINERAL WATER
1536. PET PRE-FORM FROM PET RESIN
1537. PET PRE-FORM CUM PET BOTTLES
1538. PET PRE-FORM PET BOTTLES CUM MINERAL WATERS
1539. POLY CARBONATE RESIN
1540. PTFE COMPONENTS
1541. PU/PVC SOLE FOR SPORT SHOE BY IMPORTED M/C.
1542. PVC BATTERY SEPARATOR
1543. P.V.C COMPOUNDS (FRESH)
1544. P.V.C COMPOUNDS (SCRAP)
1545. P.V.C ELECTRICAL INSULATING TAPE
1546. P.V.C. EXTRUSION PROFILES
1547. P.V.C FITTINGS
1548. P.V.C FLEXIBLE FUSIBLE POWDER HEAT FUSIBLE POWDER
1549. P.V.C GRANULES (FOR

INSULATION & SHEETS GRADES)
1550. P.V.C GRANULES FROM PVC SCRAPS (WITH POLLUTION CONTROL)
1551. P.V.C HOSES
1552. P.V.C LEATHER CLOTH
1553. P.V.C FLEXIBLE PIPES
1554. P.V.C PIPES AND FITTINGS
1555. POLYTHENE BAGS (PRINTED)
1556. PVC PLASTICS FILM SHEET SOFT/RIGID
1557. PVC RESIN AND COMPOUND
1558. PVC RULAR
1559. PVC STABLIZERS (SINGLE PACK SYSTEM)
1560. PVC WIRE AND CABLES
1561. PAPER BASED PHENOLIC SHEET FOR ELECTRICAL
1562. PHENOL FORMALDEHYDE RESIN
1563. PHENOLIC RESIN
1564. PLASTIC BEADS FROM PLASTIC SCRAPS
1565. PLASTIC BUTTONS
1566. PLASTIC CANS
1567. PLASTIC COLLAPSIBLE TUBE
1568. PLASTIC CORRUGATED SHEET & BOXES
1569. PLASTIC FILM AND SHEETS WITH PRINTING FLEXO & ROTO/LDPE/HDPE/PP/HM/PVC
1570. PLASTIC FILTER MASTER BATCH & OTHER MASTER BATCHES FOR VARIOUS PLASTICS
1571. PLASTIC JERRY CANS
1572. PLASTIC GRANULES OR POWDER FROM PLASTIC SCRAP
1573. PLASTIC INJECTION MOULDED T.V. CABINETS
1574. PLASTIC ITEMS MANUFAC TURE FROM POWDER MELAMINE
1575. PLASTIC GOODS
1576. PLASTIC PIPES & TARPAULINES
1577. PLASTIC SHEET FROM SCRAP
1578. PLASTIC PLANT (BLOW MOULDING & INJECTION MOULDING)
1579. PLASTIC PRODUCTS (GOLD, SILVER, NICKEL)
1580. PLASTIC TOYS
1581. POLYESTER BEADING
1582. POLYESTER FILM
1583. POLYTHENE BAGS & AUTOMATIC PRINTING
1584. POLYTHENE PRINTED BAGS
1585. POLYURETHANE FOAM AND ITS PRODUCTS
1586. PROPYLENE FILM (PRINTED) & BAG MANUFACTURING
1587. PLASTIC MATS
1588. RAINBOW COLOUR ON PVC FILM & SHEET
1589. RED MUD PVC PIPES AND FITTINGS
1590. RE-RUBBERISED OF SOLID TYPE
1591. RESIN COATED SAND REXINE
1592. REXINE CLOTH & ALLIED PRODUCTS
1593. RUBBER ADHESIVE
1594. RUBBER AUTO PARTS
1595. RUBBER BELTING
1596. RUBBER MOULDING UNIT INCLUDING LINING RUBBER SHEETING
1597. RUBBER RECLAIMING
1598. RUBBER ROLLERS FOR TEXTILE MILLS & PAPER INDUSTRIES
1599. RUBBER & PLASTIC SHEETS, MATS & FLAPS
1600. RUBBER SHEET AND ALLIED HOSPITAL RUBBER GOODS
1601. RUBBERIZED PVC GASKET
1602. RUBBERISED COIR
1603. RUBBER COMPOUND FOR AUTOMOBILES
1604. SAFETY BELTS
1605. SILVER AND GOLD PLATING ON PVC AND NYLON-6
1606. SILICONE RUBBER NIPPLES/ TEATS
1607. SPECTACLE FRAMES (PLASTIC)
1608. SPUNGE RUBBER
1609. SURGICAL EXAMINATION GLOVES
1610. SYNTHETIC PEARL COATING ON POLYSTYRENE BEADS
1611. SYNTHETIC RUBBER ADHESIVE
1612. TEFLON MANUFACTURING
1613. TEFLON TAPE
1614. TEFLON TAPES & CABLES
1615. THERMOCOLE SHEET AND MOULDED PRODUCTS EXPANDED POLYESTERENE EXTRUSION PROFILES
1616. THERMOFORMED PACKAGING (BLISTER PACKAGING & POUCH PACKAGING)
1617. THERMOPLASTIC POLYURETHANE
1618. THERMOFORMED CUPS, PLATES & GLASS WITH HIPS SHEET
1619. THERMOCOLE
1620. THERMOCOLE BASED DISPOSABLE GLASS, CUPS & PLATES
1621. TOOTH BRUSHES
1622. TOY BALLOON, DECORA TIVE & INDUSTRIAL BALLOONS
1623. TREAD RUBBER
1624. TYRE RETREADING (HOT)
1625. TYRE RETREADING BY COLD PROCESS
1626. TYRE TUBES & FLAPS
1627. TYRE & TUBES
1628. UNSATURATED POLYESTER FOR REXINE
1629. V-BELT AND FAN BELT
1630. VINYL ASBESTOS AND PVC WALL PAPER
1631. VITON (FLUORO ELASTOMER)

SOAP, COSMETICS & PERFUMS

1632. ACID SLURRY, SYNTHETIC DETERGENT POWDER
1632. ACID SLURRY
1633. AGARBATTI SYNTHETIC, PERFUMERY COMPOUND
1634. AFTER SHAVE LOTION
1635. ANTISEPTIC CREAM
1636. BETA IONONE
1637. BLEACHING POWDER
1638. BLUE DETERGENT POWDER
1639. CLEANING POWDER (VIMTYPE)
1640. COLD CREAM
1641. COLOURED FLAME & PERFUMED CANDLES (RED, BLUE, GREEN FLAME)
1642. COSMETIC INDUSTRY (MODERN)
1643. COSMETIC INDUSTRY (SHAMPOO, SPRAY PERFUME, TALCUM POWDER
1644. DETERGENT POWDER (ARIEL TYPE)
1645. DETERGENT POWDER (NIRMA TYPE) FULLY AUTOMATIC PLANT
1646. DETERGENT WASHING POWDER
1647. FISH OIL SOAP
1648. GLYCERINE TRANSPARENT SOAP
1649. HAIR REMOVING CREAM
1650. HERBAL COSMETICS
1651. HERBAL SHAMPO & CREAM
1652. HERBAL/AYURVEDIC COSMETICS
1653. INCENSE POWDER, INCENSE STICKS & INCENSE CAKE
1654. OPTICAL WHITENERS
1655. ROSE OIL EXTRACTION
1656. SHAMPOOS (COCONUT OIL BASED COLD PROCESS)
1657. SHAVING CREAM
1658. SINDUR (KUMKUM)
1659. SOAP COATED PAPER
1660. SPRAY DRIED DETERGENT POWDER
1661. STAIN REMOVER
1662. TALCUM POWDER (FACE & TOILET POWDER)
1663. TOILET AND HERBAL SOAP
1664. TOOTH PASTE & POWDER
1665. WASHING DETERGENT POWDER AND WASHING SOAP
1666. WASHING POWDER LIQUID DETERGENTS, LOTION & SHAMPOO

TEXTILE INDUSTRIES, READYMADE GARMENTS, COTTON, DYEING, BLEACHING, CLOTH, HOSIERY, POWER LOOM, HAND LOOM, WOOLLEN, SILK, SOCKS, SURGICAL COTTON & MANY OTHERS

1667. ANGORA RABBIT WOOL
1668. BUCKRAM
1669. CANVAS SHOES, JUNGLE BOOT, BOOT RUBBER KNEES & BOOT COMBAT
1670. CARPET FROM COTTON WASTE
1671. CERAMIC THREAD GUIDE
1672. COTTON BUDS/SWABS
1673. COTTON FROM WASTE YARN
1674. COTTON ROLLS
1675. COTTON SPIDERS FOR LOUD SPEAKERS
1676. DENIM CLOTH
1677. DENIM CLOTH (INTEGERATED UNIT WITH BLEACHING, DYEING AND PRINTING)
1678. DISPERSENT FOR TEXTILE
1679. DYEING & BLEACHING
1680. DYEING OF HANK YARN
1681. EMULSIFIER FOR WOOL BATCHING OIL
1682. EMBROIDERY ON FABRICS
1683. GARMENT DYEING, WASHING & STITCHING (JEANS, JACKETS, SKIRTS & SHIRTS)
1684. GOVES KNITTING
1685. GUNNY BAGS
1687. HDPE WOVEN SACKS
1688. HDPE TARPAULINS USING PLAIN LOOM WITH LAMINATION
1689. HDPE/PP WOVEN SACKS USING CIRCULAR LOOMS
1690. HOSIERY CLOTH (COTTON) PROCESSING (BLEACHING, DYEING, FINISHING OF CLOTH)
1691. HOSIERY INDUSTRY
1692. HOSIERY MERCERISING
1693. HOSIERY PRODUCTS LIKE VEST, BRIEF, T-SHIRTS & SOCKS
1694. JACQUARD FABRICS
1695. JUTE COIR, GRASS ROPE/ SUTLI MAKING
1696. JUTE FELT
1697. JUTE TWINES
1698. KNITTED FABRICS
1699. LAMINATED JUTE BAGS
1700. LAMINATION OF HDPE WOVEN CLOTH (JUTE,COTTON, PAPER)
1701. NYLON YARN CRIMPING, DOUBLING AND BLEACHING
1702. PIGMENT BINDER FOR TEXTILE PRINTING
1704. POLYESTER RESIN FOR WIRE ENAMEL
1705. POLYESTER RESIN
1706. POLYESTER YARN FROM WASTE POLYESTER ZIP FASTENERS
1707. POWER LOOM
1708. READYMADE GARMENTS & HOSIERY
1709. READYMADE GARMENTS MERCHANDISE
1710. READYMADE GARMENTS & COVERS
1711. READYMADE GARMENTS & EMBROIDERY OF GOWNS, SHIRTS, BLOUSES, T-SHIRTS ETC. (ONLY LADIES)
1712. READYMADE SALWAR SUIT
1713. RECOVERY OF NYLON FROM NYLON WASTE
1714. ROTARY PRINTING AND DYEING ON COTTON, SYNTHETIC TEXTILE
1715. SANITARY NAPKINS
1716. SCREEN PRINTING ON COTTON CLOTH
1717. SEWING THREAD REELS & BALLS MAKING INDUSTRIES
1718. SCREEN PRINTING ON COTTON, POLYESTER & ACRYLIC
1719. SHAWLS (WOOLLEN)
1720. SHOE LACES
1721. SILK FABRICS ON HANDLOOM
1722. SOCKS KNITTING
1723. SPINNING, DOUBLING DYEING MERCERISING & BLEACHING OF COTTON YARN
1724. SPINNING & CARDING OF WOOL INTO YARNS
1725. STARCH BOOK BINDING CLOTH
1726. SURAT JARI
1727. SURGICAL COTTON & BANDAGE
1728. SYNTHETIC TEXTILE INDUSTRY(SUITING, SHIRTING, SAREES) TERRY CLOTH
1729. T-SHIRTS
1730. TOWELS, BED SHEET COVERS
1731. TERRY TOWEL
1732. TERRY FABRICS WEAVING UNIT
1733. TEXTILE AUXILLIARIES & CHEMICALS
1734. TEXTILE BLEACHING, DYEING & FINISHING & PRINTING OF COTTON FABRICS
1735. TEXTILE (HOSIERY)
1736. TEXTILE MILL
1737. TEXTILE DYEING & PRINTING
1738. TEXTILE PRINTING (JOB WORK)
1739. TEXTILE PIGMENT PRINTING BINDER
1740. TOWEL (TERRY)
1741. VELVET CLOTH BY FLOCKING PROCESS
1742. VISCOSE STAPLE FIBRE
1743. WADDING OIL (100%) FOR WADDING OF COTTON HOSIERY CLOTH IN THE DYEING PROCESS
1744. WEAVING OF DASUTI CLOTH WITH PRINTING, DYEING, EMBROIDERY & FINISHING
1745. WASHING OF JEANS & OTHER GARMENTS
1746. WORSTED WOOLLEN YARN CLOTH
1747. ZARI GLITTER SALMA SITARA OF PLASTIC FILM

INFOTECH/IT, HOSPITALITY, HOSPITAL, COLLEGE, SCHOOL, MEDICAL, ENTERTAINMENT CLUB, WARE HOUSING & REAL ESTATE, PROJECTS

1748. AMUSEMENT PARK
1749. AMUSEMENT PARK CUM WATER PARK
1750. BANQUET HALL
1751. CALL CENTER (DOMESTIC)
1752. CALL CENTER (INTERNATIONAL)
1753. CHILDREN RECREATION CENTRE
1754. COLD STORAGE
1755. COMMUNITY HALL
1756. COMPUTER EDUCATION INSTITUTE
1757. COMPUTER SOFTWARE
1758. COLLEGE
1759. CYBER CAFE
1760. DENTAL CLINIC
1761. DENTAL COLLEGE
1762. DIAGONOSTIC CENTRE
1763. E-COMMERCE/BUSINESS
1764. E-SCHOOL (Rs. 5000/-)
1765. ENGINEERING COLLEGE
1766. ENTERTAINMENT CLUB
1767. ENTERTAINMENT CLUB, HOLIDAY RESORT, 4 STAR HOTEL, AMUSEMENT PARK CUM WATER PARK, MUSHROOM & ITS PRODUCTS, FISH FARMING, LAKE FOR BOATING, DEER PARK
1768. FASHION TECHNOLOGY INSTITUTE
1769. FAST FOOD PARLOUR
1770. FIVE STAR HOTEL
1771. FOOD PARLOUR
1772. FRANCHISE TRAINING PROGRAMME FOR IIT & ENGINEERING ENTRANCE EXAMS.
1773. GOLF COURSE
1774. HEALTH CLUB, BEAUTY PARLOUR
1775. HEALTH CLUB AND FITNESS CENTER
1776. HEALTH RESORTS
1777. HOLIDAY RESORTS
1778. HOLIDAY RESORT CUM

Price Rs. 4200/- for each "Detailed Project Report" Payable in advance through Draft/Cash/ M.O. in favour of *"ENGINEERS INDIA RESEARCH INSTITUTE"*. 4449, Nai Sarak (D), Main Road Delhi - 110 006 *OR Ask by V.P.P.* ● Ph : 23918117, 2391 6431, 2392 0361, 2396 0797 ●Fax : 91-11- 2391 6431 ●E-Mail : eirisidi@bol.net.in ● WebSite : www.startindustry.com

ENTERTAINMENT CLUB WITH 4 STAR HOTEL
1779. HOSPITALS
1780. ICE CREAM PARLOUR
1781. INTERNET SERVICE PROVIDER (I.S.P.)
1782. MEDICAL COLLEGE
1783. MEDICAL COLLEGE, HOSPITAL & RESEARCH INSTITUTE
1784. MEDICAL TRANSCRIPTION CENTRE
1785. MENTAL RETARDATION HOSPITAL & CEREBRAL PALSY
1786. MOTEL/SMALL HOTEL
1787. MULTISTOREY COMMERCIAL COMPLEX
1788. MULTISTOREY RESIDENTIAL COMPLEX
1789. NURSERY SCHOOL
1790. NATURE CARE CENTRE
1791. NURSING HOME
1792. ONLINE SHOPPING MALL (RS. 5000/- REPORT)
1793. PORTAL
1794. REHABILITATION CENTRE FOR AGED & NEEDY PERSONS
1795. RESIDENTIAL CUM COMMERCIAL COMPLEX
1796. RESTAURANT
1797. RESTAURANT WITH PUB
1798. SCHOOL (PRIMARY)
1799. SCHOOL (HIGHER SECONDARY)
1800. THREE STAR HOTEL
1801. TOURIST CLUB
1802. TRAINING INSTITUTE FOR MEDICAL TRANSCRIPTION
1803. VIDEO FILM STUDIO
1804. WARE HOUSE
1805. WEBSITE DESIGN & E-MAIL REGISTERING

AGRO BASED INDUSTRIES

1806. COAL BRIQUETTES FROM AGROWASTE
1807. FURFURALFROM RICEHULL
1808. MUSHROOM CULTIVATION & PROCESSING (BUTTON)
1809. MUSHROOM GROWING & PROCESSING WITH AIR CONDITIONING
1810. MUSHROOM CULTIVATION & PROCESSING UNIT DEHYDRATION & PACKAGING OF OYSTER & PADDY STRAW MUSHROOMS
1811. ORGANIC MANURE
1812. PAPAYA CULTIVATION
1813. PAPAYA & TOMATO CULTIVATION
1814. PROCESSING & UTILISATION OF COCONUT
1815. PROCESSING OF SHEEP HAIR TO PRODUCE WOOL

BAKERY, CONFECTIONERY & FOOD PRODUCTS

1816. AGROLACTOR SOYA MILK
1817. APPLE FRUIT JUICE WITH CANNING BOTTLING
1818. AYURVEDIC SHARBAT
1819. BAKERY UNIT (PASTRIES, BREAD, BUNS, CAKE, TOFFEE ETC.)
1820. BAKING POWDER
1821. BANANA & ITS BY PRODUCTS
1822. BANANA POWDER
1823. BANANA WAFERS
1824. BANANA CULTIVATION
1825. BEER INDUSTRY
1826. DEHULLING OF JAUN FOR BEER
1827. BEER & WINE
1828. BEER, ALCOHOL, IMFL
1829. BESEN PLANT
1830. BISCUIT PLANT
1831. BREAD & BISCUIT PLANT
1832. BOTTLING PLANT COUNTRY LIQUOR FROM RECTIFIED SPIRIT
1833. BRANDY
1834. BREAD RUSKS
1835. CANNED FRUITS & VEGETABLES
1836. CANNING & PRESERVATION OF MEAT
1837. CANNING & PRESERVATION OF VEGETABLES
1838. CANNING OF MANGO PULP & MANGO SLICES
1839. CARBONATED BEVERAGS
1840. CASHEW FENI
1841. CASHEW NUT (DRIED & FRIED)
1842. CATTLE BREEDING
1843. CATTLE BREEDING & DAIRY FARM TO PRODUCE MILK
1844. CATTLE FEED FROM TAPIOCA
1845. CHEWING GINGER & AMLOKI
1846. CHEWING GUM
1847. CHILLI SAUCE
1848. CHILLI POWDER
1849. CHOCOLATE
1850. CIDER PLANT
1851. COCOA POWDER
1852. COCOA BUTTER & COCOA POWDER
1853. COCONUT SHELL POWDER
1854. COCONUT WATER
1855. COCONUT SWEET (WATERY)
1856. COCONUT MILK POWDER (DEHYDRATED)
1857. COCONUT PRODUCTS & BY PRODUCTS (INTEGRATED PLANT)
1858. COLD DRINK
1859. CURRY POWDER
1860. DAIRY FOR MILK PROCESSING (GHEE, BUTTER & PANEER)
1861. DAIRY PRODUCTS
1862. DAIRY PRODUCTS MILK PACKAGING IN POUCH (GHEE, BUTTER, ETC.
1863. DAIRY FARM TO PRDUCE MILK WITH PACKAGING (COW)
1864. DAIRY FARM TO PRDUCE MILK WITH PACKAGING (BUFALLOE)
1865. DAIRY FARM & MILK PRODUCTS
1866. DAL MOTH, CHANACHUR & BHUJIYA
1867. DEHYDRATION OF FRUITS & VEGETABLE
1868. DESICCATED COCONUT POWDER FROM COCONUTS
1869. DEHYDRATION & CANNING OF FRUITS & VEGETABLES
1870. DRY FRUIT ROASTING & PACKAGING
1871. DRYING OF RED CHILLIES, HALDI, DHANIYA, PEAS & GROUND NUT
1872. EGG POWDER
1873. FISH CANNING IN TIN & POUCHES
1874. FISH DEHYRATION (DRYING OF FISH)
1875. FISH MEAL
1876. FISH PROCESSING (BEAST FREEZING PROCESSES)
1877. FLAVOURS FOR FOOD INDUSTRIES
1878. FLOUR MILL (ROLLER)
1879. FROZEN MEAT
1880. FOOD DEHYDRATION (FRUITS & VEGETABLES)
1881. FRIED & ROASTED GROUND NUT, GRAMS, PEAR ETC.
1882. FRUIT JUICE MAKING & PACKAGING IN PLASTIC CONTAINER
1883. FRUIT JUICE IN TETRA PACK (DRINKS)
1884. FRUIT JUICE, SQUASHES, SAUCE & KETCHUP, JAM, JELLY, VINEGAR ETC.
1885. GARLIC FLAKES
1886. GARLIC POWDER
1887. GHEE & BUTTER
1888. GINGER (PULVERISED)
1889. GINGER GLAZING & PRESERVATION
1890. GINGER STORAGE
1891. GINGER PROCESSING
1892. GINGER OIL & GINGER DUST
1893. GINGER POWDER (DRY) & OLEORESIN
1894. GRAPE DEHYDRATION
1895. GRAPE CULTIVATION
1896. GRAPE JUICE
1897. HONEY PROCESSING & PACKAGING
1898. ICE CREAM & ICE CANDY
1899. ICE CUBE
1900. INVERT SUGAR
1901. IDLI MIX, DOSA MIX SAMBHAR MIX, VADA MIX, GULAB JAMUN MIX
1902. INSTANT COFFEE & INSTANT TEA

1903. INSTANT NOODLES
1904. INSTANT SOUPS
1905. IODIZED SALT FROM CRUDE SALT
1906. JAM CHUTNEY PICKLES & SQUASHES
1907. KATHA MANUFACTURING
1908. LECITHIN (SOYA BASED)
1909. LEMON & ITS PRODUCTS
1910. MACARONI MANUFACTURING
1911. MACARONI, SPAGHETTI, VERMICELLI & NOODLES
1912. MAIZE & ITS BY PRODUCTS MALTING PLANT
1913. MANGO PAPPAD (AAM PAPPAD)
1914. MANGO POWDER RIPE
1915. MANGO POWDER
1916. MANGO PROCESSING & CANNING (MANGO PULP)
1917. MEAT PROCESSING (CHICKEN MUTTON)
1918. MEAT PROCESSING (BUFFALO)
1919. MENTHOL BOLD FROM MENTHOL FLAKES
1020. MILK POWDER
1921. MILK POWDER & GHEE
1922. MILK POWDER, GHEE & SPICES
1923. MILK PRESERVATION & MARKETING TO WHOLE SELLERS
1924. MILK PRESERVATION & MARKETING TO WHOLE SELLERS (IN POUCHES)
1925. MILK TOFFEE MANUFACTURES
1926. MINERAL WATER
1927. MINERAL WATER IN POUCHES
1928. MINI FLOUR MILL ATTA MAIDA, SUJI & WHEAT BRAN
1929. MITHAI/HALWAI (SWEET & NAMKEEN)
1930. MUTTON PROCESSING
1931. PAN MASALA (MEETHA, SADA, ZARDA) MAKING & PACKING
1932. PAN MASALA AND POUCH MAKING
1933. PANEER (CHEESE)
1934. PAPAD & BARIYAN
1935. PAPAD PLANT
1936. PEPSICOLA IN POLYTUBES
1937. PETHA PACKAGING
1938. PICKLES
1939. PIGGERY/MEAT/CHICKEN PROCESSING
1940. PINE APPLE JUICE CANNING
1941. POTATO & ONION POWDER
1942. POTATO & ONION FLAKES
1943. POTATO CHIPS
1944. POTATO GRANULES
1945. POUCH FILLING FOR SAUNF SUPARI ILAICHI ETC.
1946. PRESERVATION OF RAWS MANGO JUICE
1947. PROCESSED CHEESE & MARINE PDTS.
1948. PULP FROM TARMARIND
1949. READYMATE PROCESSED FOOD
1950. RICE & CORN FLAKES
1951. RICE BASMATI (TRADING)
1952. RICE POLISHING & PACKAGING IN POUCH
1953. ROASTED/SALTED/MASALA/ CASHEW NUTS ALMONDS & PEA NUT
1954. ROLLER FLOUR MILL

INFOTECH/IT PROJECTS

1955. MEDICAL TRANSCRIPTION
1956. E-COMMERCE
1957. CYBERCAFE
1958. INTERNET SERVICE PROVIDER (ISP)
1959. COMPUTER EDUCATION CENTRE
1960. PORTAL (WEBSITE DESIGN)
1961. CALL CENTRE

TERMS AND CONDITIONS

FOR INDIA

1. **Price Rs. 4200/- (Rs. Four Thousand Two Hundred Only) for Each *Market Survey Cum Detailed Techno Economic Feasibility Report*. Payable in advance through Draft/M.O./Cash in favour of 'ENGINEERS INDIA RESEARCH INSTITUTE', Delhi. Delivery by Regd.post within 2 Days. (Postage Free)**

2. **Reputed Firms/Companies may place their orders by V.P.P. for full amount in India Only.**

FOR OVERSEAS

1. **Price US $ 250/- (US Dollars Two Hundred Fifty Only) for Each *Market Survey Cum Detailed Techno Economic Feasibility Report.***

2. **Payable fully in advance through Draft in favour of 'ENGINEERS INDIA RESEARCH INSTITUTE', Delhi (Payable in India) Delivery by Regd. Air Mail Post within 2 Days.**

ENGINEERS INDIA RESEARCH INSTITUTE

4449, Nai Sarak (D), Main Road, Delhi - 110 006 (India)
Ph:. 91-11-23918117, 23916431, 23920361, 23960797
Fax: 91-11-23916431 E-Mail : eirisidi@bol.net.in
Website:www.startindustry.com
Also at : 4/27, Roop Nagar, Near Roop Nagar No. 1 School, Delhi - 110 007 (India) Ph:. 2396 0797, 2392 0361